CROSSING EMPIRES

AMERICAN ENCOUNTERS / GLOBAL INTERACTIONS
A series edited by Gilbert M. Joseph and Penny von Eschen

This series aims to stimulate critical perspectives and fresh interpretive frameworks for scholarship on the history of the imposing global presence of the United States. Its primary concerns include the deployment and contestation of power, the construction and deconstruction of cultural and political borders, the fluid meaning of intercultural encounters, and the complex interplay between the global and the local. American Encounters seeks to strengthen dialogue and collaboration between historians of U.S. international relations and area studies specialists.

The series encourages scholarship based on multiarchive historical research. At the same time, it supports a recognition of the representational character of all stories about the past and promotes critical inquiry into issues of subjectivity and narrative. In the process, American Encounters strives to understand the context in which meanings related to nations, cultures, and political economy are continually produced, challenged, and reshaped.

CROSSING EMPIRES

TAKING U.S. HISTORY INTO

TRANSIMPERIAL TERRAIN

Edited by Kristin L. Hoganson and Jay Sexton

Duke University Press   *Durham and London*   2020

© 2020 DUKE UNIVERSITY PRESS
All rights reserved.

Printed in the United States of America on acid-free paper ∞.

Designed by Courtney Leigh Baker
Typeset in Whitman and Helvetica LT Std by Westchester
Publishing Services

Library of Congress Cataloging-in-Publication Data
Names: Hoganson, Kristin L., editor. | Sexton, Jay, [date] editor.
Title: Crossing empires : taking U.S. history into transimperial
terrain / edited by Kristin Hoganson and Jay Sexton.
Other titles: American encounters/global interactions.
Description: Durham : Duke University Press, 2020. | Series:
American encounters / global interactions | Includes
bibliographical references and index.
Identifiers: LCCN 2019015472 (print) |
LCCN 2019017689 (ebook)
ISBN 9781478006039 (hardcover : alk. paper)
ISBN 9781478006947 (pbk. : alk. paper)
Subjects: LCSH: Transnationalism. | Cosmopolitanism—
United States. | Transnationalism—Political aspects—
United States. | International relations.
Classification: LCC JZ1320 .C76 2020 (print) |
LCC JZ1320 (ebook) | DDC 327.73—dc23
LC record available at https://lccn.loc.gov/2019015472
LC ebook record available at https://lccn.loc.gov/2019017689

Cover art: *Fracked World*. © Rebecca Riley. Courtesy of the
artist.

Contents

Preface

This book began as a conference held at Oxford's Rothermere American Institute. A group of scholars assembled to explore the various imperial terrains through which people, ideas, and things circulated, as well as to unpack the layered experiences of empire found in particular communities and places. "The central challenge posed by this conference," the call for papers asserted, "is to make the imperial visible in ways that early work in transnational history has not." The project has gone through many twists and expansive turns since then, but its core objective of uncovering and making sense of transimperial phenomena, connections, and relations has remained.

As is always the case, this book is the product of the particular moment in which it was written. The transnational, global, and imperial turns of recent historical writing inform the essays that follow. As the introduction argues, this scholarship has revealed the limits of national history, while opening up new doors to the power relationships central to the study of empire. In the bigger picture, the unexpected developments of recent years also left their mark on this volume. The conference was a held a month before the Brexit referendum; the essays were drafted during the 2016 U.S. presidential campaign and its aftershocks. These events were more than expressions of resurgent nationalism. They were also the unanticipated products of the imperial entanglements that have given modern globalization its distinctive form: immigration; economic inequality; ethnic, racial, gender, and cultural tensions; and the persistence of geopolitical rivalries. In this age of conflict over the terms of global integration, it behooves us to look anew at imperial crossings, conflicts, and inheritances.

In the course of producing this volume, we have incurred many intellectual debts. We came to this topic not only through our own research but also through the findings of our students, among them David Greenstein, Matt Harshman, Mike Hughes, Koji Ito, Mandy Izadi, Tariq Khan, Josh Levy, Seb Page, Mark Petersen, Karen Phoenix, Andy Siebert, David Sim, Yuki Takauchi, and Megan White. The pages that follow bear the imprint of the many interventions and comments made by those who participated in the conference, including Nathan Cardon, John Darwin, Brian DeLay, Augusto Espiritu, Nick Guyatt, Paul Kramer, Diana Paton, Tamson Pietsch, and Karine Walther. Skye Montgomery, Koji Ito, and Ed Green provided essential organizational support as well as insights drawn from their scholarly expertise. Big thanks are also owed to the anonymous peer reviewers of the manuscript and to Duke University Press editor Miriam Angress, who has been a pleasure to work with.

We gratefully acknowledge the institutional support that made the conference possible. Without the backing of the Vere Harmsworth Professorship and the Rothermere American Institute this project would never have happened. We are likewise beholden to the great enablers at the Rothermere Institute: Nigel Bowles, Huw David, Jane Rawson, and Jo Steventon. Further support came from The Queen's College, Corpus Christi College, St. Anne's College, the University of Illinois, and the Kinder Institute on Constitutional Democracy at the University of Missouri.

INTRODUCTION

Kristin L. Hoganson and Jay Sexton

This book originated in a desire to call out empire, which has all too often slunk out of view as nation-centered histories have opened up to the world. The nationalist fervor of recent years has only underscored the value of both the *trans* and the *imperial* approaches brought together in this volume. In such times, it is worth recalling that no polity has ever gone it alone, whether rising or declining in might, and that only-us nationalism has a long history of entwinement with imperialist impulses. Times of unraveling likewise make us take heed of the raveling, reminding us that global connections have never been inevitable, that our own global moment is the contingent product of high-stakes struggles over power. The fabric of our times has been knit together over millennia, unevenly, with plenty of dropped stitches and new threads. Some of the strands may have torn over time, but we are still enmeshed in the residual filaments of the past.

One such filament, heralded with great acclaim in its day, was the first transatlantic cable. Laid from Ireland to Newfoundland in 1858, this cable enabled electrical impulses to be sent via a copper wire from one shore of the Atlantic to the other. Policymakers at the time saw this and subsequent cables as strategically valuable technologies and as conduits for diplomatic dispatches. Recognizing the usefulness of cables for state purposes, officials helped negotiate cable arrangements and offered subsidies to cable firms.[1] Cable communications affected *international* relations by reducing the likelihood of major battles being fought after the declaration of peace and reducing the autonomy granted by foreign offices to their diplomats. They also accelerated the pace of diplomacy, at times heightening the pressure on policymakers to act hastily in response to inflamed public passions and hair-trigger military dynamics.[2]

Yet even as transatlantic cables affected *international* relations—that is, official relations between nation-states—most of the signals they transmitted carried market updates, syndicate news, and other nonstate messages. The potential for profit, not just state interest, motivated private-sector investment in cables. The greatest champion of the transatlantic telegraph was not a president or a prime minister but the Anglo-American financier Cyrus Field, the mastermind of the Atlantic Telegraph Company. Field recognized that monetary value could be extracted from the accelerated flow of information. By the 1860s, steam technology had reduced the time lag of news across the Atlantic by several weeks, to less than ten days.[3] The telegraph, however, transported information across the Atlantic in hours and for short messages, mere minutes. This new communications technology kept readers up to date on important developments in business, politics, even weather, thus bringing a range of markets on either side of the Atlantic into closer sync, felting global capital more densely.[4]

Given that the first transatlantic cable did not so much connect nation-states as it connected a variety of nonstate actors and interests across national boundaries, enabling quicker U.S.-British connections via Canada, the resulting histories might seem to merit the label *transnational*. Though its roots can be traced back decades, indeed generations, in histories of migration, diaspora, movement politics, and the Atlantic World, the term *transnational* took off in U.S. history writing in 2002, with the publication of *Rethinking American History in a Global Age*, edited by Thomas Bender. This anthology aimed to make sense of an increasingly interconnected world by breaking history out of the national containers that had come to structure understandings of the past. In his contribution to *Rethinking American History*, Akira Iriye distinguished between the terms *international* and *transnational*: "Whereas 'international' implies a relationship among nations, 'transnational' suggests various types of interactions across national boundaries. Extraterritorial movements of individuals, goods, capital, and even ideas would seem to be less international than transnational phenomena."[5] Following this definition, the transatlantic cable appears to have resulted from *transnational* corporate relationships and facilitated *transnational* communications.

But even the term *transnational* does not fully capture the relationships stitched into being by the first transatlantic cables. Given that the cable bound the receivers in Valentia Harbor, Ireland, to those in Trinity Bay, Newfoundland, the crews of the cable-laying ships to the people in the coastal towns where they docked, the markets in London to those in New York, we could regard the resulting relationships as more site-specific than the term *transnational* suggests. The word *translocal* can capture the smaller-scale nature of some of the links forged by the cable, but it still doesn't capture the entire array of the relationships brought into being when the cable-laying ship reached shore. For that, the more capacious term *transborder* might be more apt. We might even drop the *trans* prefix in favor of different conceptual vocabularies: communications revolution, capitalism, entanglements, globalization, Atlantic World, and the like. But all of these terms continue to obscure some of the most important political formations spliced together by these cables: the powerful empires of the day.

The transatlantic cable was a product of Victorian imperialism. The copper wires that formed the core of the cable were wrapped in an insulating layer of gutta percha. This substance—a rubber-like gum from the gutta percha tree—came from tropical rainforests in Siam; the British colonies of Malaya and Sarawak; the Dutch colonies of Java, Sumatra, and Borneo; French Indochina and the Spanish (and subsequently U.S.) colony of the Philippines. The final layer of wrapping, before the tar and pitch outer coating, consisted of jute yarn. Like gutta percha, jute came from the tropics, where it was grown mostly by colonial subjects in Bengal.[6] The rapid growth of global telegraphy in the late nineteenth century in turn intensified imperial control and resource extraction in these regions.[7]

Not only were the transatlantic cables literally wrapped in the stuff of empire, but they also traveled imperial routes. It is worth reiterating that the early transatlantic cable did not directly connect the United States and England. Rather it connected the British colonies of Ireland and Newfoundland. The newly laid cables fed into larger webs of empire, unspooling on the eastern side of the Atlantic to the southern tip of Africa or through the Red Sea to Aden, before going on to Singapore and Hong Kong.[8] One of the catalysts for the boom in British telegraphy was the major imperial crisis of the mid-Victorian era, the "Great Rebellion" of 1857 in India. Imperial officials, urged on by metropolitan telegraph boosters, vowed never again to be kept weeks away from news of colonial uprisings.[9] As the foregoing suggests, the new telegraph wires of the era were predominantly the products of British power and enterprise.

It was through the global circuits of its former colonial master that the United States came into telegraphic contact with Europe and its colonies. On the American side of the Atlantic, the cables fed into the expanding telegraph network that was helping the United States extend its power across the continent and onward in the hemisphere. The transatlantic cables thus joined different imperial geographies and forms. But no bond is permanent. The first transatlantic cable snapped shortly after being laid in 1858, widening once again the distance between North America and the world during one of the great global crises of the nineteenth century, the American Civil War. The ensuing irregularity of Atlantic communications contributed to the destabilization of political relations and markets during the conflict. When transatlantic telegraphic exchange resumed in 1866, much had changed: the world's mightiest slaveholding empire had morphed into an industrializing behemoth whose imperial capabilities were evident in its breakneck colonization of the North American West and rapidly expanding influence in the Caribbean and Pacific.

TELEGRAPH CABLES WERE NOT the only things entangled in empire in the Victorian era, for empires played a fundamental role in the making of the modern world. Writing on the years since 1405, the British historian John Darwin has argued that "the default position so far as politics went was imperial power."[10] The seeming rise of the sovereign nation-state by the seventeenth century hid the ongoing significance of imperial states in the modern world. Prior to the great age of decolonization in the aftermath of World War II, most of the world's people were incorporated into formal empires. Some of these—such as the Qing, Habsburg, Ottoman, Russian, German, and U.S. empires—were primarily land based, with a central state exercising control over Indigenous people or smaller nations. Even some polities without central state bureaucracies created land-based empires, as seen in the example of the Comanche empire.[11] Other empires—such as the Portuguese, Spanish, Dutch, French, British, Danish, Belgian, Japanese, and Italian—were especially notable for overseas colonies, stretching from New Zealand to Greenland. Some imperial formations, such as the American republics that emerged from European rule in the nineteenth century, have long been labeled as nations and yet existed in the gray zone where nations shade into empires, with central states exercising colonial forms of power over the Indigenous peoples within their borders and often pursuing expansionist policies at the expense of neighboring states.[12] In the global era of empire building that stretched from the fifteenth to the twentieth centuries, some colonial subjects even had colonial subjects. Not only did settler colonists exercise power over Indigenous people, but Europeanized elites in places like the Philippines also exercised power over animist "tribes."[13]

Historians generally define *empire* as a political unit that encompasses an extensive sweep of territory containing various peoples or polities. Empires are known for according varying degrees of autonomy and different rights, dependent on geography and population group. They are typically characterized by vast disparities in power, sustained by the use or threat of force, as well as through asymmetric structures of economic and ecological exchange. Empires might extend their power through *settler colonialism*—meaning an influx of newcomers who dominate, displace, or kill Indigenous peoples, typically upending ecological systems as well.[14] They might be characterized more by *territorial annexation* without substantial demographic change or with substantial intergroup mixing. They might rely heavily on *indirect rule*, that is, the exercise of power without sovereign claims, through collaborators, economic dominance, or military intimidation. They might mix all of the above. The term *imperial formations* can serve as an umbrella for this wide range of definitions, in the process drawing attention to the making and unmaking of empires as an "active and contingent process."[15]

Until recently, scholarship on imperial formations treated them much as historians treated nation-states prior to calls for transnational scholarship—that is, as well bounded. This particularly has been the case in the U.S. historiography, which has had to deal with a persistent case of empire denial. To navigate this peculiar terrain, historians of the United States have written brief after brief debunking the deniers. One of the leading surveys of U.S. foreign relations through 1865, for example, opens with a ten-point list as to why the United States should be classified as an empire.[16] The persistent struggle to "prove" the existence of U.S. empire to audiences fixed on nationalist narratives has had the unintended effect of cordoning off U.S. imperial formations from those established by other imperial powers. Historians have brought other empires into the U.S. picture mostly to add comparative angles to their unclosseting efforts.[17]

To the extent that historians have understood various empires as bumping up against each other, clashing, or even collaborating, they long have emphasized official *interimperial* relations, though often labeling these relations *international*. They have, for example, paid ample attention to imperial rivalries, wars, and transfers of colonies from one empire to another. They have also studied interimperial collaborations such as the Berlin Conference that carved up Africa and the multi-imperial force that landed troops in China in 1900 to quell the Boxer Uprising.[18] Yet these latter relationships have been so overshadowed by the former that the historian Richard Drayton has come up with the term *masked condominia* to describe the largely hidden partnerships between empires.[19]

Among these partnerships are those that thickened the network of nineteenth-century telegraph cables, described in a recent account as a product of "interimperial collaboration."[20] Traceable to the early twentieth-century writings of J. A. Hobson, *interimperialism* is a useful concept for the interactions between imperial formations.[21] Yet in our historiographical age, the term connotes official dealings of governments and armed forces in much the same way that *international* is taken to mean a focus on state-to-state relations. The term *interimperial* thus hides the types of nonstate relations brought to mind by the prefix *trans*, thereby perpetuating conceptions of empires as official units that interact with each other only as such.[22]

THIS VOLUME SEEKS TO bring sharper definition and meaning to an emerging historiography that is seeking to break free from the stand-alone paradigm to probe the connections between empires. Despite the particular dynamics driving inward-looking histories of U.S. imperial formations, there are counterdynamics that provide the background to this volume. As national histories have opened up so as to encompass border crossings of various kinds, it has become increasingly difficult to contain the imperial. In keeping with the turn toward more transnational scholarship, histories of empire have begun venturing into *transimperial* terrain. In some cases they have done so explicitly, using the term that appears in the subtitle of this volume. In a history of Pacific Rim settler colonies, Penelope Edmonds identifies the construction of Anglo-Saxon exceptionalism as a transimperial process across British dominions and the United States.[23] Paul Kramer has characterized U.S. colonial officials' adoption of the structures and practices of Spanish colonialism in the Philippines as "historias transimperiales."[24] Jesse Cromwell has written on the "trans-imperial lives" of mobile people; Volker Barth and Roland Cvetkovski have alluded to "transimperial networks of contact and debate"; Richard Drayton has analyzed "the trans-imperial campaign" to save natural resources; and Julian Go has used the term "trans-imperial" in reference to Irish nationalism's influence on Puerto Rican anticolonialism.[25] The term *transimperial*—sometimes hyphenated, sometimes not—has popped up in other contexts too, ranging from the connections between the Venetian and Ottoman empires to the character of the "Greater Caribbean world."[26]

The scholarship that inspired this volume traces its genealogy back to the transnational turn and its predecessors and also to the boom in global, imperial, and postcolonial history. Much of this work has been produced by scholars outside of the United States. Studies of the "British world," for example, have foregrounded the connections between imperial center and specific colonies, as well as the *intra-imperial* or *transcolonial* networks that linked various British colonies to one another, whether as parts of entire webs, as the former term suggests, or as the linked peripheries brought to mind by the latter.[27] Studies of "imperial careering," institutional networks, and labor mobility have been particularly successful at uncovering these dimensions of the British Empire.[28] British imperial scholars also have called for more "connected histories of empire" that extend beyond the British world to consider the synergies and frictions between different empires.[29] Such a connected imperial history can find inspiration in global histories of empire and more regionally specific studies of oceanic "worlds," such as those of the Atlantic, Indian, and Pacific.[30] This rapidly growing body of transimperial research runs the gamut of lines of inquiry. "Migrant workers, missionaries, social reformers, highly educated professionals, and humble pilgrims, as well as money, commodities, technologies, and even diseases, moved among imperial systems," Tony Ballantyne and Antoinette Burton point out in an influential study that traces the development of what they label "imperial globality."[31]

This emerging transimperial scholarship signals a more geographically capacious and politically aware approach that offers much to historians of U.S. empire. It invites further investigation into border-crossing relationships in which imperial formations figure prominently and in which the main dynamic is not the affirmation of boundaries through official state-to-state relations but the blurring of them through mobility, connectivity, exchange, and adaptation. Far from being just interesting sideshows, such transimperial processes are key to our understanding of the origins, development, and erosion of imperialism in modern history. Awareness of the bridges between empires and the traffic they have carried also brings into focus the countervailing construction of barriers and walls. Approaching the past with connectivity in mind can help us place interimperial rivalries and conflicts in the larger context of coexistence. Rather than appearing the norm, wars stand out as times of conspicuous disruption that have severed some connections across empires, even as they have forged new ones, not least of which were the anti-imperial movements that swept across the globe during and after the world wars of the twentieth century.

Much of the emerging scholarship on transimperial connections has focused on the high age of empire in the late nineteenth and early twentieth centuries. These are the years that even the most vociferous deniers of U.S. imperialism grudgingly cede as an aberration, due to military interventions, occupations, annexations, and financial control in places such as Hawai'i, Cuba, Puerto Rico, the Philippines, Guam, Panama, Haiti, the Dominican Republic, Mexico, Nicaragua, the Virgin Islands, and numerous so-called guano islands (some of which are now administered as refuges by the U.S. Fish and Wildlife Service). These years marked the consolidation of U.S. control over Indigenous peoples within its newly fixed North American borders. They were also the heyday of a European-dominated global imperial order, spanning the time from the so-called scramble for Africa to the rise of national self-determination as a fundamental liberal principle, the invigoration of anticolonial nationalist movements amid the crisis of World War I, and the seeming promise of communist alternatives to colonial rule following the Bolshevik Revolution.[32] Histories of this thoroughly imperial—yet highly contested—span of time are beginning to reveal hidden dimensions of the American past: those of an imperial formation in an imperial world.[33]

Our efforts to track down the mobility of organisms, goods, and capital and the systems that made such mobility possible first drew our attention to imperial crossings. As the example of the transatlantic cable suggests, the United States and its expanding empire became increasingly integrated into the imperial structures and systems of the European powers. But this is just the tip of the iceberg. From the nineteenth century into the twentieth, American companies traded and invested in European colonies, seeking, for example, rubber, oil, bauxite, and tin, as well as export markets in Southeast Asia. Corporate agents linked their own interests to European colonial power (especially in the face of Japanese assertiveness in East Asia and the Pacific), even while professing anticolonial commitments.[34] Transimperial ties can be found in histories of consumption as well as production. The sugar, teas, bananas, tropical hardwoods, Oriental rugs, and cashmere shawls so relished by U.S. consumers were among a wide array of products that arrived through imperial routes.[35] Many of the animals that populated U.S. zoos in the late nineteenth century likewise came from imperial snares.[36] In ports around the world, U.S. steamships voraciously consumed foreign coals, particularly those mined in Britain and its imperial possessions.[37] One of the editors of this volume started thinking about the value of an anthology following research on bioprospecting, salt pork, and curry. The other editor came to this topic through his research on the transimperial passageways of the Pacific Mail Steamship Company.

Some other early glimmerings that the word *transnational* was distorting the past emerged from mappings of human mobility. American slave traders, like their European partners and rivals, coursed in and out of imperial outposts in their nefarious dealings.[38] The migration from the U.S. eastern seaboard to California in the mid-nineteenth century is traditionally presented as a national story. Yet more migrants traveled to the goldfields via Central America than in the overland covered wagons of American folklore. Such transit routes, especially the world's first transcontinental railroad in Panama (completed in 1855), facilitated the exchange of people, goods, and services across a number of empires.[39]

Numerous accounts reveal the inadequacy of strictly national frameworks for understanding labor migrants and other mobile people.[40] These include histories of the British colonial subjects from Barbados and Jamaica who worked on the Panama Railroad and, later, the Panama Canal.[41] Histories of human mobility across the Pacific have also tracked the ways in which imperial circuits threading through South Asia, Japan, China, the Philippines, Hawai'i, Australia, New Zealand, and South Africa became enmeshed with settler colonialism in places such as British Columbia, Washington, and Oregon.[42] Borderlands accounts of Native Americans who moved back and forth between U.S., Mexican, and Canadian jurisdiction further trouble the assumption that cross-border mobility can be contained within histories of nation-states.[43] Missionary histories also cross imperial domains, for most of the missionaries who set forth from the United States for "heathen" lands in the long nineteenth century (stretching through World War I) landed in European colonies, where they depended on European power for security and access.[44] Stories of individuals likewise reveal imperial crossings, as seen in writings on Mary Leiter Curzon, the Chicago-born heiress who became vicereine of India; Santukno Hiramura, an Ainu woman who found some common ground with a native Patagonian woman at the 1904 St. Louis Fair; and the Filipino nationalist José Rizal, who named his anti-Spanish movement "los indios bravos" after the Native Americans he had seen performing in a Wild West show.[45]

Once we started thinking about transimperial connections, still more examples started jumping out in our readings on colonial governance. British imperialists looked to the United States as a potential model for imperial federation, and twentieth-century German and Japanese expansionists also referenced the United States.[46] Anti-Asian immigration policies were not just a matter of national, much less transnational politics—they played out across the British, U.S., Japanese and other empires.[47] Ideas about coolie labor circulated among the sugar planters of the British West Indies, the Spanish colony of Cuba, and Louisiana, with consequences for U.S. migration policies, naturalization law, and racial politics.[48] Colonial state builders in the U.S.-occupied Philippines and other island territories looked to European colonies for ideas.[49] And European colonial administrators looked back. The German colonial government in Togo, for example, brought in cotton-growing experts from Tuskegee Institute in Alabama to enhance the productivity of their African labor force, and hence the profits of German planters.[50]

These kinds of affinities and connections also appear in histories of anti-colonial resistance. Pan-Africanist politics connected black intellectuals and activists in the Caribbean, Central and North America, Europe, and Africa.[51]

Anticolonial and antiracist movements crossed the Pacific as well.[52] Mobilizing more on the grounds of colored cosmopolitanism than diasporic affinities, African American activists joined South Asian nationalists in professing common commitments to antiracism and decolonization.[53] Pan-Asianist advocates positioned themselves in opposition to an entire network of interlaced powers.[54] People subject to changing or overlapping colonial rulers can also be seen as acting transimperially. The Trinidadians who used the U.S. presence during World War II to advance anticolonial struggles against the British may have positioned themselves *interimperially* (meaning between empires), but they also navigated two layered empires so as to advance their own interests.[55]

With our antennae attuned, we picked up more evidence of transimperialism in histories of imperial transfer and succession, including the U.S. acquisition of one-time Spanish holdings and the growing U.S. footprint in one-time European colonies during the Cold War.[56] Allusions to U.S. nationals and imperial subjects as peripheral or bit players in other empires began to register as further evidence of transimperial pasts. Our forays outside of our main field in U.S. history persistently reminded us that there are plenty of transimperial histories—whether written or yet to be told—in which the United States only hovers off stage, if it is present at all.[57]

Recent scholarship on the history of capitalism has played a particularly significant role in busting open nationalist frameworks so as to better reveal the workings of power. The new literature on the U.S. South in the nineteenth century has illuminated the many ways in which the economic vitality of slavery rested upon the transimperial processes that enabled Indian removal and field clearing, international commodity market development, transoceanic transportation, industrial capitalist production, and global consumption of southern staple crops, particularly cotton.[58] The southern slave empire was less a distinctly American phenomenon than it was the product of the expansion of Victorian capitalism, which produced a wave of "second slavery" in the New World, as well as coercive labor regimes within the colonial world more generally.[59] Recent work on the various forms of political economy that underwrote nineteenth-century capitalist development also have highlighted connections to imperialism. Take the case of debates over protectionism versus free trade. These were framed in relation to national development but also, crucially, with imperial market rivalries in mind.[60] New infrastructures of empire owed much to emerging imperial states, which lavished subsidies upon steam transport companies arms-race-style.[61]

Historians also are returning to an older literature probing the links between imperialism and capital flows that can be traced back to J. A. Hobson's writings around 1900. This literature positions the late nineteenth-century United States as both an upstart, imperialist exporter of capital and, paradoxically, a satellite within the orbit of the powerful financial empire based in London.[62] Recognizing the ways that traders, investors, resource extractors, managers, workers, and corporations navigated multiple imperial formations can help us grasp the larger politics of economic connections. This recognition has particular significance for understandings of the U.S. role in Latin America and the Caribbean. Although the world systems writings that took off in the 1960s analyzed the role of the "developed world" in forging Latin American dependency, more specific studies focused on either U.S. or European penetration of the Latin American periphery. As a result of this either-or bilateral approach, the foreign relations historians who have focused on U.S. financial and military power have argued for U.S. hegemony, even in the years leading up to World War I, when European rivals still exercised considerable clout. Approaching the history of this region with transimperialism in mind can thus do more than power up relations previously described as transnational—it can better explain the workings and extent of U.S. power in the historical stomping grounds of European empires.[63]

The more we thought about the range of scholarship outlined above, as well as the propensity of scholars to stamp it all with the transnational label, for lack of a better term, the more we became convinced that historians need to be more explicit about the political formations and power dynamics that shaped the border-crossing histories they tell. They need to stop using *transnational* as a default term and call out empire when it appears. Assuming all border-crossing histories to be transnational in nature writes the contemporary prominence of the nation-state anachronistically into the past, collapsing power relationships into national frames. Even terms such as *translocal* and *transborder* can hide important structures of power. Opening up beyond *transcolonial*, the term *transimperial* also encompasses imperial centers, geographies of indirect governance, and nonsovereign forms of power. The words we choose do analytical work—hence our efforts to define so many. Misleading terminology keeps us from understanding the politics of transimperial pasts.

The essays in this volume do not ignore national formations. They recognize that empires and nations are tangled up in all kinds of messy ways that sometimes defy clear distinctions. But they all start from the assumption that making imperial formations visible can help us to recognize the many asymmetric power relations that have crisscrossed over time and space. The point is larger than just labeling empires as such when relevant, however. It is to follow the admonition to ask what empire does.[64] How can recognizing imperial formations enhance our understandings of particular circuits, connections, and paths? How can it sharpen our analyses of power? Our appraisals of globalization and the makings of the modern world? These are some of the questions that drive this volume.

THE ESSAYS THAT FOLLOW probe these questions. Rather than attempt to provide an overarching narrative of transimperialism as it has related to U.S. history, the chapters in this volume paint a more pointillist picture, showcasing cutting-edge research on the topic. The contributors are joined together by their interests in globalizing U.S. history, in understanding empire, and in historicizing the global. But they come from a variety of subdisciplines, including the histories of business, diplomacy, the environment, gender, Indigenous peoples, labor, material culture, medicine, migration, politics, and race and ethnicity. Their work scrambles the old historiographic divides between traditional diplomatic history and newer work deeply inflected by social, cultural, transnational, and postcolonial approaches. Of particular note, it helps us avoid the seeming inevitability suggested by impersonal broad-brushstroke histories and advance the "histories from below" perspectives that have figured so prominently in postcolonial studies. Though attuned to structural considerations, these essays foreground agency and individual experience in ways that remind us of the possibilities for social and political change as well as of the ways that the most intimate and small-scale matters have been formed by vast fields of power and vice versa. If microhistories contain the global, the reverse is also true: the power lines and force fields of the global can be truly grasped only through their fine-grained constituent parts. We welcome this volume's commingling of approaches, geographies, concerns, and scales because of the resulting insights into the power relations that have forged the modern world.

Part I opens with essays by John Soluri and Stephen Tuffnell that reveal how the pursuit of profit unsettled imperial boundaries, as well as accelerated the exploitation of labor and resources. Part II, comprising essays by Michel Gobat, Julian Go, and Anne L. Foster, examines political ideas, practices, and institutions that straddled imperial borders. This subject is further developed in the essays by Nicole M. Phelps, Marc-William Palen, and Oliver Charbonneau in part III, which assess the structures of governance that sought to order transimperial relations and commerce. The essays of part IV, written by Ikuko Asaka, Julie Greene, and Genevieve Clutario, zoom in on the migrants, laborers, and colonial subjects whose experiences were conditioned by transimperial interactions and successions. The final section, part V, comprising essays by Moon-Ho

Jung and Margaret D. Jacobs, considers how resistance to imperial power has gathered momentum through transimperial crossings.

Taken together, these essays de-exceptionalize the study of U.S. imperialism by weaving the strands of empire involving the United States and U.S. actors into world history. This makes it harder to deny the history of U.S. imperialism, for to do so would mean to rend the fabric of global history; it also illuminates the workings of empire and the processes of imperial formation. Historians researching across present-day boundaries have always faced plenty of hurdles (financial, linguistic, and otherwise). Only a collective effort can begin to bring the larger landscape of transimperial histories into view, and these essays do that well. They relegate the term *transnational* to specific relations with specific (mostly European) states, at least prior to decolonization. For border crossings elsewhere, they bring state power out of the shadows and give it form. They are sensitive to moving borders, to changes in sovereignty in particular places, to bird's-eye and ground-level views. They navigate the fuzzy lines between inter- and trans-; between colonial, national, and imperial. Joining with global historians who have rejected the premise that change only radiated outward from imperial centers, they map its multidirectionality.[65] Recognizing the divisions and hierarchies within imperial formations as well as across them, they track lateral and vertical vectors in multiple fields.

Just as important, this attention to imperial formations helps illuminate the borders and barriers that inhibited movement and connection, that channeled transiness in particular directions.[66] These essays, in other words, are alert to the ways that cross-border interactions and processes served the interests of imperial regimes, as well as undermined them, often in unexpected ways. Along with helping us to understand the specific routes and limited-access lanes traveled by people, ideas, and things, these essays draw attention to the overlaid experiences of empire found in particular communities and places. Together they provide a better accounting of the imperial roots of the world system we inhabit today. Their sensitivity to the limits of U.S. power, as well as to moments of rupture and reconfiguration, makes them especially timely.

In unearthing these previously hidden imperial histories, this volume seeks to do more than simply slot the United States into Europe-centered frameworks of global history and empire. Indeed this volume has emerged from postcolonial critiques of core and periphery models.[67] Integrating America's entangled imperial past into global history matters not simply because it de-exceptionalizes the United States but also because it provides new possibilities for understanding the origins of what we now call *globalization*. When viewed through a transimperial prism, globalization looks different than when seen as an outgrowth of individual colonial regimes. The formal trappings of colonialism—the color-coded maps and metropole-periphery binaries—recede in importance, giving ground to a more Jackson Pollock–like world of mobile labor, cross-border political negotiation, and multifaceted exchanges, that, however random they may seem at first glance, still reveal patterns and power.

Although this volume focuses on the years before the United States could call itself a superpower—the years in which it had to carefully navigate between other empires as it laid the groundwork for its future might—the sensitivity to power found in these essays can help us understand the origins of the post-1945 sphere presided over by the United States. For what were the international institutions constructed by the United States after 1945 other than transimperial configurations of governance, economy, and defense? Even in the supposed American century, the border-straddling infrastructures that knit the transatlantic alliance and larger anticommunist bloc together advanced more global cross-border phenomena. The economic liberalism and material exchanges of this era did more than consolidate wealth, especially across the so-called Global North. As mass migrations and ecological transformations dramatically reveal, they also linked North to South, East to West, aligned to nonaligned, urban to rural, rich to poor, in thoroughly encompassing ways, still shot through by power as before. Even after the great wave of decolonization in the second half of the twentieth century and the rise of new non-Western configurations, transimperial girders from the prewar past continued to structure the modern world. The current fracturing of the post–World War II order is exposing transimperial trusses among the I-beams of self-interested states. The more that postwar structures teeter, the more apparent it becomes that the United States has never been as hegemonic as both celebrants and critics of the Pax Americana have maintained.

Although the essays in this volume provide the backstory to the age of U.S.-led globalization, they pick up the story midsentence. Historians of the eighteenth century have long written transimperial histories, even if not using that term. This volume extends their approaches to the post-1815 period, but much more could be done in this respect. Other future lines of inquiry might venture into historical terrain in which the United States does not figure largely, if at all, and to imperial formations beyond the scope of this launch-stage volume. A short collection such as this could not possibly do justice to every topic, and we must confess to egregious gaps. We look forward to more transimperial histories centering on groups such as women and Indigenous people; topics such as slavery, black radicalism, science, and agriculture; nonhuman animals and organisms; reinterpretations of global institutions such as the United Nations and World Bank; and places such as borderlands, enclaves, and military bases. We believe that studies of the Anthropocene must keep an eye on the transimperial ledger sheets of benefits, costs, and culpability. Truly there is much work to be done. But to see the possibilities that might follow from putting empire into greater conversation with transiness, these essays are a great place to start.

NOTES

1. For the complex interactions between states and the development of telegraphy, see Peter J. Hugill, *Global Communications since 1844: Geopolitics and Technology* (Baltimore: Johns Hopkins University Press, 1999); Richard R. John, *Network Nation: Inventing American Telecommunications* (Cambridge, MA: Belknap Press of Harvard University Press, 2010).

2. David Paull Nickles, *Under the Wire: How the Telegraph Changed Diplomacy* (Cambridge, MA: Harvard University Press, 2003); Daniel R. Headrick, *The Invisible Weapon: Telecommunications and International Politics, 1851–1945* (New York: Oxford University Press, 1991), 14–46; John A. Britton, *Cables, Crises, and the Press: The Geopolitics of the New International Information System in the Americas, 1866–1903* (Albuquerque: University of New Mexico Press, 2014).

3. The uneven compression of time and space is considered in Richard D. Knowles, "Transport Shaping Space: Differential Collapse in Time-Space," *Journal of Transport Geography*, 14 (2006): 407–25.

4. Dwayne R. Winseck and Robert M. Pike, *Communication and Empire: Media, Markets, and Globalization, 1860–1930* (Durham, NC: Duke University Press, 2007), xvii.

5. Akira Iriye, "Internationalizing International History," in *Rethinking American History in a Global Age*, edited by Thomas Bender (Berkeley: University of California Press, 2002), 51. An earlier usage of this term can be found in Linda Basch, Nina Glick Schiller, and Cristina Szanton Blanc, *Nations Unbound: Transnational Projects, Postcolonial Predicaments, and Deterritorialized Nation-States* (Langhorne, PA: Gordon and Breach, 1994). For some examples of scholarship that provided transnational analyses prior to *Rethinking American History*, see Frank Thistlethwaite, *The Anglo-American Connection in the Early Nineteenth Century* (Philadelphia: University of Pennsylvania Press, 1959); Ian Tyrrell, *Woman's World, Woman's Empire: The Woman's Christian Temperance Union in International Perspective, 1880–1930* (Chapel Hill: University of North Carolina Press, 1991); Paul Gilroy, *The Black Atlantic: Modernity and Double Consciousness* (Cambridge, MA: Harvard University Press, 1995); Leila J. Rupp, *Worlds of Women: The Making of an International Women's Movement* (Princeton, NJ: Princeton University Press, 1997); Daniel T. Rodgers, *Atlantic Crossings: Social Politics in a Progressive Age* (Cambridge, MA: Belknap Press of Harvard University Press, 1998). For assessments of transnational approaches that critique U.S.-centrism and highlight the need for more attentiveness to power, see Louis A. Pérez Jr., "We Are the World: Internationalizing the National, Nationalizing the International," *Journal of American History* 89 (September 2002): 558–66; Laura Briggs, Gladys McCormick, and J. T. Way, "Transnationalism: A Category of Analysis," *American Quarterly* 60 (September 2008): 625–48.

6. Steven C. Topik and Allen Wells, "Commodity Chains in a Global Economy," in *A World Connecting, 1870–1945*, edited by Emily S. Rosenberg (Cambridge, MA: Belknap Press of Harvard University Press, 2012), 740; Tariq Omar Ali, *A Local History of Global Capital: Jute and Peasant Life in the Bengal Delta* (Princeton, NJ: Princeton University Press, 2018).

7. John Tully, "A Victorian Ecological Disaster: Imperialism, the Telegraph, and Gutta-Percha," *Journal of World History* 20 (December 2009): 567.

8. Headrick, *The Invisible Weapon*, 46; Martin Redfern, "Wiring Up the 'Victorian Internet,'" *BBC News*, November 29, 2005, http://news.bbc.co.uk/2/hi/science/nature /4475394.stm.

9. Daniel R. Headrick, *The Tentacles of Progress: Technology Transfer in the Age of Imperialism, 1850–1940* (New York: Oxford University Press, 1988), 99.

10. John Darwin, *After Tamerlane: The Global History of Empire since 1405* (New York: Bloomsbury, 2007), 491. Chris Bayly makes a similar point in a recent roundtable conversation: "Before 1850, large parts of the globe were not dominated by nations so much as by empires, city-states, diasporas, etc. . . . To designate 'global history' as 'transnational history' would not be very useful before 1914, if then." He goes on to say that global and transnational historians have "continued to grapple with the problem of modeling the element of power into the concept of circulation," C. A. Bayly, Sven Beckert, Matthew Connelly, Isabel Hofmeyr, Wendy Kozol, and Patricia Seed, "AHR Conversation: On Transnational History," *American Historical Review* 111 (December 2006): 1442, 1452.

11. Pekka Hämäläinen, *The Comanche Empire* (New Haven, CT: Yale University Press, 2008). See also Anne F. Hyde, *Empires, Nations, and Families: A New History of the North American West, 1800–1860* (Lincoln: University of Nebraska Press, 2011).

12. Krishan Kumar, "Empires and Nations: Convergence or Divergence?," in *Sociology and Empire: The Imperial Entanglements of a Discipline*, edited by George Steinmetz (Durham, NC: Duke University Press, 2013), 279–99.

13. Paul A. Kramer, *The Blood of Government: Race, Empire, the United States, and the Philippines* (Chapel Hill: University of North Carolina Press, 2006), 380.

14. Margaret D. Jacobs, *White Mother to a Dark Race: Settler Colonialism, Maternalism, and the Removal of Indigenous Children in the American West and Australia, 1880–1940* (Lincoln: University of Nebraska Press, 2009); James Belich, *Replenishing the Earth: The Settler Revolution and the Rise of the Anglo-World, 1783–1939* (Oxford: Oxford University Press, 2009).

15. Ann Laura Stoler and Carole McGranahan, "Introduction: Refiguring Imperial Terrains," in *Imperial Formations*, edited by Ann Laura Stoler, Carole McGranahan, and Peter C. Perdue (Santa Fe, NM: School for Advanced Research Press, 2007), 8.

16. William Earl Weeks, *The New Cambridge History of American Foreign Relations*, vol. 1: *Dimensions of the Early American Empire, 1754–1865* (New York: Cambridge University Press, 2013). We use the "duck" test developed by historian Ian Tyrrell: "If it walks like an empire, if it quacks like an empire, then it probably is, no matter what professions to the contrary." Ian Tyrrell, "Empire of Denial: American Empire, Past, Present and Future," October 8, 2008, https://iantyrrell.wordpress.com/empire-of-denial-american -empire-past-present-and-future/.

17. Charles S. Maier, *Among Empires: American Ascendancy and Its Predecessors* (Cambridge, MA: Harvard University Press, 2006); Kimberly Kagan, ed., *The Imperial Moment* (Cambridge, MA: Harvard University Press, 2010).

18. For a survey of U.S. foreign relations that touches briefly on interimperial relations, see Walter LaFeber, *The Cambridge History of American Foreign Relations*, vol. 2: *The American Search for Opportunity, 1865–1913* (Cambridge, U.K.: Cambridge University Press, 1993), rivalries over Samoa, 91; intervention in China, 173. On U.S. and Spanish conflicts in Cuba (and the importance of Cuban nationalists to this history), see Louis A. Pérez Jr., *The War of 1898: The United States and Cuba in History and Historiography* (Chapel Hill: University of North Carolina Press, 1998); John Lawrence Tone, *War and Genocide in Cuba, 1895–1898* (Chapel Hill: University of North Carolina Press, 2006); Nancy Mitchell, *The Danger of Dreams: German and American Imperialism in Latin America* (Chapel Hill: University of North Carolina Press, 1999). On World War I as a war of empires, see Robert Gerwarth and Erez Manela, eds., *Empires at War: 1911–1923* (Oxford: Oxford University Press, 2014).

19. Richard Drayton, *The Masks of Empire: The World History underneath Modern Empires and Nations, c. 1500 to the Present* (London: Palgrave, 2017).

20. Dwayne R. Winseck and Robert M. Pike, *Communication and Empire: Media, Markets, and Globalization, 1860–1930* (Durham, NC: Duke University Press, 2007), xvii.

21. For Hobson, see the conclusion of Steve Tuffnell's essay in this volume.

22. After his initial call for transnational histories, Thomas Bender wrote an essay, "An Empire among Empires," that briefly touched on imperial crossings. But this essay dwelt more on categorization (what might it mean to label the United States an empire?) than transiness, and as one chapter in a larger work titled *A Nation among Nations*, this essay did not dislodge the nation as the main unit for border-crossing histories. Thomas Bender, "An Empire among Empires," in *A Nation among Nations: America's Place in World History* (New York: Hill and Wang, 2006), 182–245.

23. Penelope Edmonds, "'I Followed England round the World': The Rise of Trans-Imperial Anglo-Saxon Exceptionalism and the Spatial Narratives of Nineteenth-Century British Settler Colonies of the Pacific Rim," in *Re-Orienting Whiteness*, edited by K. Ellinghaus, J. Carey, and L. Boucher (New York: Palgrave Macmillan, 2009).

24. Paul Kramer, "Historias Transimperiales: Raices Espanoles del Estado Colonial EEUU en Filipinas," in *Filipina: Un Pais Entre Dos Imperios*, edited by María Elizalde (Barcelona: Bellaterra, 2011).

25. Jesse Cromwell, "More than Slaves and Sugar: Recent Historiography of the Trans-imperial Caribbean and Its Sinew Populations," *History Compass*, December 2014, 778; Volker Barth and Roland Cvetkovski, eds., "Encounters of Empire: Methodological Approaches," in *Imperial Co-operation and Transfer, 1870–1930: Empires and Encounters* (New York: Bloomsbury, 2015), 22; Richard Drayton, *Nature's Government: Science, Imperial Britain, and the "Improvement" of the World* (New Haven, CT: Yale University Press, 2000), 238; Julian Go, "Anti-Imperialism in the U.S. Territories after 1898," in *Empire's Twin: U.S. Anti-Imperialism from the Founding Era to the Age of Terror*, edited by Ian Tyrrell and Jay Sexton (Ithaca, NY: Cornell University Press, 2015), chapter 4.

26. E. Natalie Rothman, *Brokering Empire: Trans-Imperial Subjects between Venice and Istanbul* (Ithaca, NY: Cornell University Press, 2012); Ernesto Bassi, *An Aqueous Territory: Sailor Geographies and New Granada's Transimperial Greater Caribbean World* (Durham, NC: Duke University Press, 2016). See also Gotha Research Centre and Erfurt University Conference, Trans-Imperial Cooperation and Transfers in the Age of Colonial Globalization: Towards a Triangular History of Colonialism?, March 23–24, 2018, http://www .forum-global-condition.de/veranstaltung/trans-imperial-cooperation-and-transfers -in-the-age-of-colonial-globalization/; Nathan Cardon and Simon Jackson, "Everyday Empires: Trans-Imperial Circulations in a Multi-disciplinary Perspective—Origins, Inspirations, Ways Forward," *Past and Present*, May 5, 2017, http://pastandpresent.org .uk/everyday-empries-trans-imperial-circulations-multi-disciplinary-perspective-origins -inspirations-ways-forward/.

27. For an introduction, see Carl Bridge and Kent Fedorowich eds., *The British World: Diaspora, Culture and Identity* (London: Routledge, 2003).

28. Durba Ghosh and Dane Kennedy, eds., *Decentring Empire: Britain, India, and the Transcolonial World* (Hyderabad, India: Orient Longman, 2006); David M. Pomfret, *Youth and Empire: Trans-colonial Childhoods in British and French Asia* (Stanford, CA: Stanford University Press, 2016). For other examples of works that develop the term *transcolonial*, see Julia Martínez and Claire Lowrie, "Transcolonial Influences of Everyday American Imperialism: The Politics of Chinese Domestic Servants in the Philippines," *Pacific Historical Review* 81 (November 2012): 511–36; Sara E. Johnson, *The Fear of French Negroes: Transcolonial Collaboration in the Revolutionary Americas* (Berkeley: University of California Press, 2012). On imperial careering, institutions, and labor mobility, see David Lambert and Alan Lester, eds., *Colonial Lives across the British Empire: Imperial Careering in the Long Nineteenth Century* (Cambridge, U.K.: Cambridge University Press, 2006); Tamson Pietsch, *Empire of Scholars: Universities, Networks and the British Academic World, 1850–1939* (Manchester, U.K.: Manchester University Press, 2013); Lara Putnam, "The Making and Unmaking of the Circum-Caribbean Migratory Sphere: Mobility, Sex across Boundaries, and Collective Destinies, 1840–1940," in *Migrants and Migration in Modern North America: Cross-Border Lives, Labor Markets, and Politics*, edited by Dirk Hoerder and Nora Faires (Durham, NC: Duke University Press, 2011), 99–126.

29. Simon J. Potter and Jonathan Saha, "Global History, Imperial History and Connected Histories of Empire," *Journal of Colonialism and Colonial History* 16, no. 1 (Spring 2015).

30. For an influential global history of empire, see Darwin, *After Tamerlane*. For representative works on the various oceanic worlds, see Bernard Bailyn, *Atlantic History: Concept and Contours* (Cambridge, MA: Harvard University Press, 2005); K. N. Chaudhuri, "The Unity and Disunity of Indian Ocean History from the Rise of Islam to 1750: The Outline of a Theory and Historical Discourse," *Journal of World History* 4 (1994): 1–21; Sugata Bose, *A Hundred Horizons: The Indian Ocean in the Age of Global Empire* (Cambridge, MA: Harvard University Press), 2006; Thomas R. Metcalf, *Imperial Connections: India in the Indian Ocean Arena, 1860–1920* (Berkeley: University of California Press, 2008); David Armitage and Alison Bashford, eds., *Pacific Histories: Ocean, Land, People* (London: Palgrave Macmillan, 2014).

31. Tony Ballantyne and Antoinette Burton, "Empires and the Reach of the Global," in *A World Connecting: 1870–1945*, edited by Emily Rosenberg (Cambridge, MA: Belknap Press of Harvard University Press, 2012), 295.

32. Erez Manela, *The Wilsonian Moment: Self-Determination and the International Origins of Anticolonial Nationalism* (New York: Oxford University Press, 2007).

33. Transnational histories that are attuned to empire include Bender, *A Nation among Nations*; Ian Tyrrell, *Transnational Nation: United States History in Global Perspective since 1789* (New York: Palgrave Macmillan, 2007).

34. Anne L. Foster, *Projections of Power: The United States and Europe in Colonial Southeast Asia, 1919–1941* (Durham, NC: Duke University Press, 2010). On capital, see, for example, Peter James Hudson, "On the History and Historiography of Banking in the Caribbean," *Small Axe* 18 (March 2014): 22–37.

35. Kristin L. Hoganson, *Consumers' Imperium: The Global Production of American Domesticity, 1865–1920* (Chapel Hill: University of North Carolina Press, 2007).

36. Daniel E. Bender, *The Animal Game: Searching for Wildness at the American Zoo* (Cambridge, MA: Harvard University Press, 2016).

37. Peter A. Shulman, *Coal and Empire: The Birth of Energy Security in Industrial America* (Baltimore: Johns Hopkins University Press, 2015).

38. Stephanie E. Smallwood, *Saltwater Slavery: A Middle Passage from Africa to American Diaspora* (Cambridge, MA: Harvard University Press, 2007); Greg Grandin, *The Empire of Necessity: Slavery, Freedom, and Deception in the New World* (New York: Metropolitan Books, 2014).

39. John Haskell Kemble, *The Panama Route, 1848–1869* (Berkeley: University of California Press, 1943); Aims McGuinness, *Path of Empire: Panama and the California Gold Rush* (Ithaca, NY: Cornell University Press, 2008).

40. Daniel E. Bender and Jana K. Lipman, eds., *Making the Empire Work: Labor and United States Imperialism* (New York: New York University Press, 2015).

41. Julie Greene, *The Canal Builders: Making America's Empire at the Panama Canal* (New York: Penguin Press, 2009); Lara Putnam, *Radical Moves: Caribbean Migrants and the Politics of Race in the Jazz Age* (Chapel Hill: University of North Carolina Press, 2013).

42. Nayan Shah, *Stranger Intimacy: Contesting Race, Sexuality, and the Law in the North American West* (Berkeley: University of California Press, 2011); Kornel Chang, *Pacific Connections: The Making of the U.S.-Canadian Borderlands* (Berkeley: University of California Press, 2012); Elizabeth Sinn, *Pacific Crossing: California Gold, Chinese Migration, and the Making of Hong Kong* (Hong Kong: Hong Kong University Press, 2013); Seema Sohi, *Echoes of Mutiny: Race, Surveillance and Indian Anticolonialism in North America* (New York: Oxford University Press, 2014); Paul A. Kramer, "Imperial Openings: Civilization, Exemption, and the Geopolitics of Mobility in the History of Chinese Exclusion, 1868–1910," *Journal of the Gilded Age and Progressive Era* 14 (July 2015): 317–47.

43. Shelley Bowen Hatfield, *Chasing Shadows: Indians along the United States–Mexico Border 1876–1911* (Albuquerque: University of New Mexico Press, 1998); Beth LaDow, *The Medicine Line: Life and Death on a North American Borderland* (New York: Routledge, 2001); Sheila McManus, *The Line Which Separates: Race, Gender, and the Making of the Alberta-Montana Borderlands* (Lincoln: University of Nebraska Press, 2005); Eric W.

Meeks, *Border Citizens: The Making of Indians, Mexicans, and Anglos in Arizona* (Austin: University of Texas Press, 2007); Kristin L. Hoganson, "Struggles for Place and Space: Kickapoo Traces from the Midwest to Mexico," in *Transnational Indians in the North American West*, edited by Clarissa Confer, Andrae Marak, and Laura Tuennerman (College Station: Texas A&M University Press, 2015), 210–25; Michael Hogue, *Métis and the Medicine Line: Creating a Border and Dividing a People* (Chapel Hill: University of North Carolina Press, 2015).

44. For works considering this point, see Ian Tyrrell, *Reforming the World: The Creation of America's Moral Empire* (Princeton, NJ: Princeton University Press, 2010); Emily Conroy-Krutz, *Christian Imperialism: Converting the World in the Early American Republic* (Ithaca, NY: Cornell University Press, 2015); Barbara Reeves-Ellington, Kathryn Kish Sklar, and Connie A. Shemo, eds., *Competing Kingdoms: Women, Mission, Nation, and the American Protestant Empire, 1812–1960* (Durham, NC: Duke University Press, 2010); Karen Phoenix, "A Social Gospel for India," *Journal of the History of the Gilded Age and Progressive Era* 13 (April 2014): 200–222.

45. Dana Cooper, *Informal Ambassadors: American Women, Transatlantic Marriages, and Anglo-American Relations, 1865–1945* (Kent, OH: Kent State University Press, 2014), 104; Danika Medak-Saltzman, "Transnational Indigenous Exchange: Rethinking Global Interactions of Indigenous Peoples at the 1904 St. Louis Exposition," *American Quarterly* 62 (September 2010): 591–615; Joy S. Kasson, *Buffalo Bill's Wild West: Celebrity, Memory, and Popular History* (New York: Hill and Wang, 2000), 161–219; Sharon Delmendo, *The Star-Entangled Banner: One Hundred Years of America in the Philippines* (New Brunswick, NJ: Rutgers University Press, 2004), 27–30. On world's fair and circus performers, see also Robert W. Rydell, *All the World's a Fair: Visions of Empire at American International Expositions, 1876–1916* (Chicago: University of Chicago Press, 1984); Janet M. Davis, *The Circus Age: Culture and Society under the American Big Top* (Chapel Hill: University of North Carolina Press, 2002), 216.

46. Duncan Bell, *The Idea of Greater Britain: Empire and the Future of World Order, 1860–1900* (Cambridge, U.K.: Cambridge University Press, 2009), 231–59; Paul A. Kramer, "Empires, Exceptions and Anglo-Saxons: Race and Rule between the British and United States Empires, 1880–1910," *Journal of American History* 88 (March 2002): 1315–53; Julian Go, *Patterns of Empire: The British and American Empires, 1688 to the Present* (New York: Cambridge University Press, 2011), 3; Jens-Uwe Guettel, *German Expansionism, Imperial Liberalism, and the United States, 1776–1945* (New York: Cambridge University Press, 2012).

47. Although they speak of transnational collaborations to protect white privilege, Marilyn Lake and Henry Reynolds write about settler colonies—Australia, South Africa, the United States, and Canada—embedded in larger imperial systems. Marilyn Lake and Henry Reynolds, *Drawing the Global Colour Line: White Men's Countries and the International Challenge of Racial Equality* (New York: Cambridge University Press, 2008).

48. Moon-Ho Jung, *Coolies and Cane: Race, Labor, and Sugar in the Age of Emancipation* (Baltimore: Johns Hopkins University Press, 2006); Stacey L. Smith, *Freedom's Frontier: California and the Struggle over Unfree Labor, Emancipation, and Reconstruction* (Chapel Hill: University of North Carolina Press, 2013).

49. Julian Go and Anne L. Foster, eds., *The American Colonial State in the Philippines: Global Perspectives* (Durham, NC: Duke University Press, 2003); Kramer, "Historias Transimperiales"; Karine V. Walther, *Sacred Interests: The United States and the Islamic World, 1821–1921* (Chapel Hill: University of North Carolina Press, 2015), esp. 157–240.

50. Andrew Zimmerman, *Alabama in Africa: Booker T. Washington, the German Empire, and the Globalization of the New South* (Princeton, NJ: Princeton University Press, 2010).

51. Van Gosse, "'As a Nation the English Are Our Friends': The Emergence of African American Politics in the British Atlantic World, 1772–1861," *American Historical Review* 113, no. 4 (October 2008): 1003–28; Adam Ewing, *The Age of Garvey: How a Jamaican Activist Created a Mass Movement and Changed Global Black Politics* (Princeton, NJ: Princeton University Press, 2014); Frank Andre Guridy, *Forging Diaspora: Afro-Cubans and African Americans in a World of Empire and Jim Crow* (Chapel Hill: University of North Carolina Press, 2010); Michelle Ann Stephens, *Black Empire: The Masculine Global Imaginary of Caribbean Intellectuals in the United States, 1914–1962* (Durham, NC: Duke University Press, 2005); David Luis-Brown, *Waves of Decolonization: Discourses of Race and Hemispheric Citizenship in Cuba, Mexico, and the United States* (Durham, NC: Duke University Press, 2008).

52. Moon-Ho Jung, ed., *The Rising Tide of Color: Race, State Violence, and Radical Movements across the Pacific* (Seattle: University of Washington Press, 2014).

53. Nico Slate, *Colored Cosmopolitanism: The Shared Struggle for Freedom in the United States and India* (Cambridge, MA: Harvard University Press, 2012); Penny M. Von Eschen, *Race against Empire: Black Americans and Anticolonialism, 1937–1957* (Ithaca, NY: Cornell University Press, 1997).

54. Eri Hotta, *Pan-Asianism and Japan's War, 1931–1945* (New York: Palgrave Macmillan, 2007); Torsten Weber, *Embracing "Asia" in China and Japan: Asianism Discourse and the Contest for Hegemony, 1912–1933* (New York: Palgrave Macmillan, 2018).

55. Harvey R. Neptune, *Caliban and the Yankees: Trinidad and the United States Occupation* (Chapel Hill: University of North Carolina Press, 2007). This usage of *interimperial* extends Eiichiro Azuma's term *inter-National*, which he applies to the Japanese immigrants to the United States who found themselves wedged between the categories of Japan and the United States. Eiichiro Azuma, *Between Two Empires: Race, History, and Transnationalism in Japanese America* (New York: Oxford University Press, 2005), 6.

56. Eileen Findlay, *Imposing Decency: The Politics of Sexuality and Race in Puerto Rico, 1870–1920* (Durham, NC: Duke University Press, 1999); Louis A. Pérez, *Cuba: Between Reform and Revolution* (New York: Oxford University Press, 1988); Julian Go, *Patterns of Empire: The British and American Empires, 1688 to Present* (New York: Cambridge University Press, 2011), 237; Nick Cullather, "Damming Afghanistan: Modernization in a Buffer State," *Journal of American History* 89 (September 2002): 512–37.

57. See, for example, Adam Hochschild, *King Leopold's Ghost: A Story of Greed, Terror, and Heroism in Colonial Africa* (Boston: Houghton Mifflin, 1998); Rebecca E. Karl, *Staging the World: Chinese Nationalism at the Turn of the Twentieth Century* (Durham, NC: Duke University Press, 2002); Duncan Bell, *Empire and the Future of World Order, 1860–1900* (Princeton, NJ: Princeton University Press, 2007).

58. Sven Beckert, *Empire of Cotton: A Global History* (New York: Knopf, 2014); Sven Beckert and Seth Rockman, eds., *Slavery's Capitalism: A New History of American Economic Development* (Philadelphia: University of Pennsylvania Press, 2016); Edward Baptist, *The Half Has Never Been Told: Slavery and the Making of American Capitalism* (New York: Basic Books, 2014); Walter Johnson, *River of Dark Dreams: Slavery and Empire in the Cotton Kingdom* (Cambridge, MA: Harvard University Press, 2013).

59. Dale Tomich and Michael Zeuske, "Introduction: The Second Slavery. Mass Slavery, World-Economy, and Comparative Microhistories," *Review (Fernand Braudel Center)* 31, no. 2 (2008): 91–100.

60. Marc-William Palen, *The "Conspiracy" of Free Trade: The Anglo-American Struggle over Empire and Economic Globalisation, 1846–1896* (Cambridge, U.K.: Cambridge University Press, 2016).

61. For explorations of the importance of subsidies to global steam companies, see William Wray, *Mitsubishi and the N.Y.K., 1870–1914: Business Strategy in the Japanese Shipping Industry* (Cambridge, MA: Harvard University Press, 1984); Freda Harcourt, *Flagships of Imperialism: The P&O Company and the Politics of Empire from Its Origins to 1867* (Manchester, U.K.: Manchester University Press, 2006).

62. Gary B. Magee and Andrew S. Thompson, *Empire and Globalisation: Networks of People, Goods and Capital in the British World, c. 1850–1914* (Cambridge, U.K.: Cambridge University Press, 2010); A. G. Hopkins, "The United States, 1783–1861: Britain's Honorary Dominion?," *Britain and the World* 4, no. 2 (2011): 232–46; J. A. Hobson, *Imperialism: A Study* (New York: James Pott, 1902).

63. Gilbert M. Joseph, "Close Encounters: Toward a New Cultural History of U.S.–Latin American Relations," in *Close Encounters of Empire: Writing the Cultural History of U.S.–Latin American Relations*, edited by Gilbert M. Joseph, Catherine C. Legrand, and Ricardo D. Salvatore (Durham, NC: Duke University Press, 1998), 3–46.

64. Paul A. Kramer, "Power and Connection: Imperial Histories of the United States in the World," *American Historical Review* 116 (December 2011): 1348–49.

65. Ballantyne and Burton, *Empires and the Reach of the Global*, 286, 300–301.

66. Sukanya Banerjee, "Who, or What, Is Victorian? Ecology, Indigo, and the Transimperial," *Victorian Studies* 58 (Winter 2016): 213–23.

67. For a review of the British imperial turn that critiques Eurocentrism, applauds postcolonial approaches, and skates over the U.S. role in global history, see Durba Ghosh, "AHR Forum: Another Set of Imperial Turns?," *American Historical Review* 117 (June 2012): 772–93.

PART I. IN PURSUIT OF PROFIT

1. FUR SEALING AND UNSETTLED SOVEREIGNTIES

John Soluri

Now this is the Law of the Muscovite, that he proves with shot and steel,
When ye come by his isles in the Smoky Sea ye must not take the seal,
Where the gray sea goes nakedly between the weed-hung shelves,
And the little blue fox he is bred for his skin and the seal they breed for themselves. . . .
But since our women must walk gay and money buys their gear,
The sealing-boats they filch that way at hazard year by year.
English they be and Japanee that hang on the Brown Bear's flank,
And some be Scot, but the worst of the lot, and the boldest thieves, be Yank!
—Rudyard Kipling, "The Rhyme of the Three Sealers," 1893

In 1796 the ship *Neptune* departed from New Haven, Connecticut, bound for the South Atlantic to hunt fur seals. Upon reaching the Falkland/Malvinas Islands, the *Neptune* met the *Juno*, a New York–based ship. The captains of the two vessels, David Greene and Paul Bunker, joined forces to search for seals along the coast of Patagonia. They encountered a small Spanish garrison at a place called Puerto Deseado. The garrison's commander detained Greene and Bunker under the suspicion that they were British subjects. The two captains fled when the Spanish soldiers were attending an evening mass:

> They [Green and Bunker] started and were soon hold of their whaleboat, which had been hauled up. The movement was so quick that it was not

known whether an alarm had been given, and after they were afloat (and it was too dark to be fired at) there was little danger but that they could row two feet to one of any boat rowed by the Spaniards. They muffled their oars and got alongside the sloop about midnight, jumped on deck and got possession of the arms, the soldiers being asleep. They then made the soldiers get into their own boat and, knocking out the flints, returned to them their muskets—and treated them to a drink of grog. The soldiers were told to tell their commander that he did not know how to keep Yankees.[1]

This tale of Yankee exceptionalism, related in the journal of Eben Townsend, supercargo on the *Neptune*, reveals how U.S. fur sealers disregarded geopolitical borders in the pursuit of prey, crossing into South Atlantic waters claimed by the Spanish Empire.[2]

Some thirty years later the border-crossing ways of U.S. fur sealers continued to provoke conflicts in the South Atlantic. In 1831 Louis Vernet, acting as governor of the Malvinas and Tierra del Fuego under the authority of the newly constituted Argentine Confederation, arrested Gilbert Davison, captain of the *Harriet*, a vessel based in Stonington, Connecticut, engaged in sealing. Vernet confiscated the *Harriet*'s sealskins and sent the vessel to Buenos Aires, where he sought to have the Argentine courts rule on the legitimacy of the seizure. He allowed three other U.S. sealers to continue hunting with the proviso that their sealskins would be held in trust until the Argentine courts issued a ruling.[3] Vernet based his daring actions on an 1829 Argentine decree that granted him a monopoly on sealing activities in Patagonia.

However, when Captain Davison reached Buenos Aires, he gave a deposition before U.S. Consul George Slacum in which he described Vernet as "pretending" to act as governor. Davison detailed the seizure of U.S. vessels and alleged that Vernet was not interfering with British sealers.[4] Viewing the matter to be an urgent question of the "free use of unappropriated fisheries," Consul Slacum took the issue before Argentine foreign minister Tómas Manuel Anchorena. The Argentine official considered the seizure a private matter to be settled in local courts. Slacum responded by giving an ultimatum: if Argentina did not agree to cease interfering with U.S. sealing vessels, he would order a naval frigate, the USS *Lexington*, to proceed to the Malvinas/Falklands. Anchorena in turn promised to lodge a formal protest if the *Lexington* entered the Malvinas.

A resolute Slacum dispatched the *Lexington* under the command of Silas Duncan. Upon reaching the Malvinas, Commander Duncan compelled some forty residents of Port Louis—described by Duncan as a "band of pirates"—to leave the island. Duncan later declared that he had acted in order to protect "citizens and commerce of the United States engaged in the fisheries in question."[5] U.S. president Andrew Jackson conveyed his approval of Duncan's actions and the "firmness of his measures."[6] However, in Buenos Aires the press reported that U.S. marines had destroyed weaponry and confiscated the contents of Vernet's storehouse. In 1832 the United States and Argentina severed relations over the incident. The British Empire took advantage of the dispute to expel the small Argentine garrison in Port Louis in 1833; the following year, the HMS *Challenger* landed Henry Smith, who, bearing the title of naval governor, initiated the long-term British occupation of the "Falklands."[7]

Meanwhile, in the United States, the Suffolk Insurance Company denied claims filed by the owners of the U.S. vessels impounded by Vernet, contending that the ships' crews had been engaged in illegal activities when they were captured. The ship owners sued the insurance company, initiating a legal dispute that reached the U.S. Supreme Court in 1839. The Court ruled in favor of the ship owners, noting in its decision that the executive authority of the U.S. government "has insisted . . . that the Falkland Islands do not constitute any part of the dominions within the sovereignty of the government of Buenos Ayres."[8] The case reveals the shifting and pragmatic relationship between private enterprise and the state: New England–based fur sealers must have appreciated the U.S. government's willingness to project its power in support of their right to an "unappropriated fishery" in the distant South Atlantic, but a New England insurance firm might be prepared to recognize the sovereign rights of a foreign power (be it the Argentine Confederation or the British Empire) when it served its financial interest.

These two stories of U.S. fur sealers in the South Atlantic reveal important changes in territorial sovereignty that took place in the early nineteenth century. In 1796 the "Yankee" sealers Greene and Bunker traversed land and waters nominally claimed and lightly defended by the Spanish Empire. However, when Davison and Vernet clashed in 1831, U.S. fur sealers in the South Atlantic encountered an altered geopolitical world in which a new state, the Confederation of Argentina, struggled to assert its sovereignty in the face of challenges from Britain, Spain, and the United States, in addition to multiple indigenous societies. That the British Empire gained control of the Falklands largely reflected its unsurpassed naval power in the 1830s.

The two stories also reveal a noteworthy continuity: the presence of capitalistic fur sealers transgressing territorial boundaries. The nineteenth-century fur seal trade forged unlikely ties among places like Stonington, Connecticut; the Malvinas/Falkland Islands; Punta Arenas, Chile; the Pribilof Islands;

and Victoria, Canada; in addition to more familiar centers of commerce like London, New York, and Canton (Guangzhou).[9] This sprawling, dynamic network cut across and connected empires, indigenous societies, and postcolonial states in South America. It also linked ecosystems and distinct populations of marine mammals inhabiting subpolar regions in the northern and southern hemispheres. Commercial hunting devastated populations of fur seals while unsettling territorial sovereignties. Rising concerns about the overhunting of fur seals led to one of the first multilateral, conservation treaties, the Convention between the United States and Other Powers Providing for the Preservation and Protection of Fur Seals (1911), that initiated a century of interstate diplomacy related to ocean resources in which indigenous peoples would find their territories increasingly subsumed by expanding states.[10]

Tracing the movements of commercial fur sealers in the nineteenth and early twentieth centuries reveals the limits of transnational frameworks and the value of "powering up" environmental histories to consider transimperial connections while also "touching ground" in specific localities where power was exercised, contested, and deflected. In this essay, I "power up" in two, complementary ways. First, I adopt a transoceanic framework in order to show connections between commercial fur sealing in North Pacific and South Pacific/South Atlantic seas. I build on scholarship that explores the intersection of empires and ecological phenomena by emphasizing, along with a growing number of scholars, that oceans are not only passageways but also contested resource bases.[11] Second, I increase the resolution of my narrative lens in order to glimpse—if seldom fully capture—the entanglements of fur seal ecologies, capitalist enterprises, and contested territorial sovereignties in two important hunting grounds: the Pribilof Islands in the Bering Sea, and Tierra del Fuego, the southernmost point of South America.

After briefly describing some key aspects of fur seal ecology and lifecycles, I examine the transimperial politics of fur sealing in the North Pacific, where first the Russian Empire and then the United States negotiated with indigenous Unangan (Aleuts) as well as the British and Japanese empires for control over the northern fur seals that formed massive colonies on the Pribilof Islands. I then shift to Tierra del Fuego to reveal some of the transoceanic reverberations of the U.S. acquisition of Alaska's sealing grounds, including the revival of fur sealing in the southern hemisphere. In contrast to Alaska, the presence of U.S. fur sealers in Tierra del Fuego did not contribute to U.S. territorial acquisition, but it unsettled the sovereignties of the indigenous Yámana and Kawéskar. In the third part of the essay I consider how state-led initiatives to conserve fur seals in both Alaska and Tierra del Fuego simultaneously reinforced the power of colonizing states over indigenous societies while revealing how the movements of fur seals and hunters unsettled claims to sovereignty. I conclude with some remarks on the value of writing environmental histories that transgress political boundaries.

Taking Seals: Alaska

The movements of fur sealers largely reflected the circulations and life cycles of their prey. Dozens of species of seals—what taxonomists call otarids—inhabit the earth's oceans and littoral zones. Those designated "fur seals" possess inner and outer coats of fur. In the modern world, commercial markets in China, Europe, Russia, and the United States coveted the soft, dense, inner layer of fur that served as a raw material for making garments. The most prized fur seal pelts generally came from high-latitude regions, where seals grew particularly dense layers of fur. If imperial projects in the tropics took advantage of intense solar radiation to produce plantation crops like sugar or rubber, commercial marine hunters sought out the opposite: regions where marine mammals adapted to the absence of heat by producing layers of fat or extremely dense undercoats of hair.

Fur seals spend a great portion of their lives in open water, ranging over enormous distances. These periods of often solitary travel are punctuated by seasonal congregations on land to shed fur, to mate, and for females to give birth and nurse offspring. Commercial hunters generally tried to time their operations to coincide with the nearly simultaneous birthing, mating, and nursing seasons when fur seals tended to form large colonies for several weeks. Although indigenous and commercial hunters harpooned or shot fur seals in open water (pelagic hunting), the mass killings that enabled some sealers to reap fortunes while driving local seal populations to near extinction exploited fur seals' own sense of territoriality: large colonies often formed on the same island littorals from one year to the next.[12]

Hunters exploited fur seals' territoriality and transformed birthplaces into killing zones. In general, sealers killed as many animals as possible due in part to the fact that crewmembers on sealing vessels, like their counterparts on whaling ships, received a share of the take. This wage form, along with the deprivations endured on long voyages, no doubt left sealers with little incentive to conserve fur seals for an uncertain future.[13] In most cases this practice led to a rapid and sharp drop in fur seal populations in given localities, compelling sealers to search for new "fishing" grounds. As a result, nineteenth-century U.S.-based sealing vessels traversed the littoral zones of the Americas and beyond, unsettling sovereignties and ecologies from the South Atlantic to the North Pacific.

When Yankee mariners began hunting fur seals in the North Pacific, they entered a region already altered by Russian hunters who, authorized by the imperial government in St. Petersburg, sought out sea otters for trade with China. Over the course of the 1700s, Russian hunters severely depleted sea otter populations while exploiting Unangan labor; brutal treatment and introduced diseases reduced the Unangan population from an estimated twelve thousand to approximately two thousand.[14] In 1786 Gavriil Pribylov, an employee of a Russian company trading in sea otter pelts, visited an island (Saint George) with massive colonies of northern fur seals (*Calorhinus ursinus*). The following year Russian mariners found another large fur seal colony on an adjacent island (Saint Paul). This sparked a frenzy of hunting activity on the two islands (later renamed Pribilof), led by various Russian companies that rapidly depleted colonies of fur seals whose total population reached at least one million.[15]

Concerned about indiscriminate hunting, indigenous resistance, and an increased presence of British and U.S. traders, Tsar Paul I chartered the Russian American Company (RAC), Russia's first joint-stock company, in 1799.[16] The RAC enjoyed a monopoly over trade in "Russian America" and ownership of the region's marine mammals. In the early nineteenth century, the company transplanted a Unangan village to the Pribilof Islands, where indigenous workers killed and processed fur seals under harsh living conditions. The RAC paid Unangan workers wages that were distributed via a community fund managed by indigenous leaders, a bending to Unangan customs by the RAC that the anthropologist Dorothy Jones has suggested was likely a pragmatic decision necessary to maintain a reliable labor force.[17] Nevertheless company charters issued in the mid-nineteenth century stripped Unangan of their sovereignty by declaring them to be Russian subjects obligated to abide by imperial law.[18]

As early as 1805 RAC officials instituted conservation measures for fur seals.[19] By the late 1820s the RAC's Alaskan administrators prohibited killing female seals and encouraged hunters to take young males, operating on the assumption that the "bachelor seals" were not crucial to the species' ability to reproduce itself. These measures appear to have enabled the northern fur seal to make a partial recovery in the mid-nineteenth century. According to historian Briton Cooper Busch, the population of northern fur seals reached its precommercial hunting level in the 1860s.[20]

Following the California Gold Rush, Russian control of the North Pacific fur trade came under a rising threat from British and U.S. interests. The U.S. government raised the prospect of purchasing Alaska as early as 1854. The onset of the Civil War disrupted U.S. efforts to purchase Alaska until 1867, when the Russian Empire, seeking to consolidate its power elsewhere, sold the enormous territory to the United States for $7 million.[21] The transfer of imperial sovereignty triggered a flurry of activity among investors, ships' captains, and others based in San Francisco and Victoria. In 1868 the Alaska Commercial Company (ACC) formed and immediately began staking claims over key sealing beaches on the Pribilof Islands. A killing frenzy ensued: hunters slaughtered more than 250,000 fur seals before a U.S. Revenue officer arrived on the scene. The U.S. government banned all sealing in 1869 except that carried out by Unangan for autoconsumption.[22]

In 1870 the U.S. Congress created regulations for the hunting of fur seals in Alaska. The act authorized the U.S. Treasury to grant hunting privileges to "responsible parties" and charged the department with ensuring the preservation of the fur seal trade and the "comfort, maintenance, and education of the natives thereof."[23] That same year, the Treasury Department awarded a twenty-year lease to the ACC to hunt as many as 100,000 fur seals per year. During the life of the lease, the ACC's employees killed more than two million fur seals, generating $6 million in government revenue and nearly $17 million for company shareholders.[24] The ACC's reach extended beyond the newly acquired U.S. territory; working through a Russian intermediary, the company also gained twenty-year monopoly rights to hunt fur seals on the Russian-controlled Commander Islands and Robben Island.[25]

The ACC shipped the vast majority of the fur seal skins that it obtained from the North Pacific to San Francisco, where they were repacked for overland shipment to New York.[26] From New York, the skins traveled to London, where the Curtis Lampson Company auctioned them, along with myriad other furs sourced from all over the world. The labor-intensive process of turning sealskins into a supple, dyed material suitable for garment manufacture employed thousands of people in late nineteenth-century London. Buyers in the United States, particularly New York City, then re-imported most of the dyed seal furs to produce luxury outerwear. This circuitous pathway of turning a life form into a luxury good—not unlike contemporary tuna-to-sushi transformations—further illustrates the complex relationships between colonialism, territoriality, and commodification.[27]

The ACC's takeover of Alaska's sealing grounds did not initially lead to dramatic changes in the lives of Unangan workers; they continued to perform many of the same tasks they had done under Russian authority, including herding, killing, and skinning fur seals in return for piece-wage rates comparable to what their Russian employers had paid before selling the islands.[28]

Unangan earnings were comparable to those of manual laborers in the continental United States.[29] However, U.S. Treasury agents stationed on the islands frequently undermined the authority of Unangan community leaders and compelled Unangan residents to perform unpaid labor. This situation worsened during the second concessionary period (1890–1910), when the depletion of fur seals reduced the piece-wages earned by Unangan workers. U.S. Treasury agents, now faced with the prospect of running deficits in Alaska, increasingly adopted colonial mentalities and practices, marked by a discursive shift that transformed Unangan people from "employees" to "wards" of the state. When the federal government ended the Pribilof concession in 1910, Unangan residing on the islands lost their only source of income.[30] The presence of U.S. commercial sealers and state agents, like that of the Russian Empire before them, led to the loss of Unangan political sovereignty.[31]

The late nineteenth-century impoverishment of the Unangan inhabiting the Pribilof Islands resulted largely from dwindling fur seal populations linked to an increase in open-sea (pelagic) hunting of fur seals in the Bering Sea by Canadian, Japanese, and Russian sealers. In fact, less than half of the documented sealing vessels operating in the North Pacific held a U.S. registry; approximately one-third came from the British Dominion of Canada, including fifty constructed in Atlantic ports such as Nova Scotia.[32] Between 1870 and 1910 vessels operating from British Columbia and Nova Scotia took more than one million seals from the waters surrounding the Pribilof Islands. However, many contemporary observers regarded pelagic hunting to be extremely wasteful on account of the inconvenient reality that fur seal carcasses lacked buoyancy and quickly sank beyond the reach of boat crews. Consequently the number of fur seals killed in open waters far surpassed the quantity of skins that entered commercial markets.[33]

In the late 1880s the U.S. government seized several U.S. and Canadian vessels (bearing British flags) engaged in pelagic hunting, raising immediate protests from Canadian authorities. In 1893 a tribunal convened in Paris affirmed the Russian transfer of Alaska to the United States but denied the U.S. claim that the Bering Sea was "territorial water." The Paris tribunal imposed a summertime ban (May through July) on pelagic hunting within sixty miles of the Pribilof Islands for a period of five years.[34] The negotiations over pelagic hunting were entangled with conflicting imperial interests: British authorities (who handled Canada's foreign affairs) had to balance the demands of resident Canadians to share in the wealth of the Alaska trade with U.S. claims that pelagic hunting threatened the stability of an industry whose raw material fed London's economy. The 1893 agreement put an end to controversial seizures and confiscations, but it did not resolve the question of pelagic hunting. U.S. officials could not effectively patrol the waters around the Pribilof Islands; moreover, Japanese sealers—not party to the Paris agreements—intensified their hunting in the region. Entering the twentieth century, most government officials supported a complete ban on pelagic hunting but struggled to find a political compromise. In the meantime, social tensions heightened; in 1905 hunters employed by Canadian sealing companies went on strike in order to renegotiate their piece-wage scales in the face of a shrinking seal population.[35]

The transimperial contests that took place over sealing in the North Pacific had ripple effects as far away as Tierra del Fuego. The reorientation of the flow of fur seal skins from Asian markets to London following the U.S. takeover of the Pribilof Islands stimulated demand for fur seals from other regions, including South America. Access to the principal London auction house enabled the formation of a local fur sealing fleet based in Punta Arenas, a Chilean port on the Straits of Magellan. In addition, vessels from the United States also hunted fur seals in and around Tierra del Fuego; Canadian-based sealers also plied the region's waters, particularly after the U.S. began interfering with vessels engaged in pelagic hunting in the North Pacific. Although the United States made no territorial claims in the region, the heightened presence of fur sealers in Tierra del Fuego provoked changes not unlike those that took place in the late nineteenth-century North Pacific, including the depletion of fur seals and challenges to the sovereignty of the Yámana and Kawéskar, the indigenous "canoe people" who inhabited the region's labyrinthine waterways.[36]

Pursuing Seals: Tierra del Fuego

In 1868 (one year after the U.S. purchased Alaska) the Chilean government declared Punta Arenas, a penal colony populated primarily by prisoners and soldiers, to be a duty-free port. The government also contracted the Pacific Navigation Company to provide regular steamer service linking Punta Arenas to Valparaíso and London. Around this time, an Argentine named Luís Piedra Buena and a young Portuguese sailor named José Nogueira arrived in Punta Arenas and began hunting South American fur seals (*Arctocephalus australis*) in the region's channels and islets. Over the next twenty years, Nogueira purchased several vessels and became Punta Arenas's first and most important shipper.[37] The fur seal trade provided the foundation for his business. Chilean officials registered exports of more than twenty-five thousand sealskins between 1877 and 1880, a figure that did not include additional thousands taken by foreign sealers.[38] In the early 1880s Chilean authorities reported that sealing "contributed mightily" to the development of business, including the establishment of five import houses in Punta Arenas that purchased skins and furs and provisioned visiting ships. At its peak the local sealing fleet consisted of twenty-eight vessels and six hundred seasonal workers.[39]

Fur sealers based in the United States first hunted South American fur seals in the vicinity of Tierra del Fuego in the late eighteenth century, when maritime hunters oriented their activities toward Canton (Guangzhou), where traders eagerly exchanged Chinese manufactured goods for the pelts of sea otters and fur seals.[40] However, by the early nineteenth century fur sealers had found prime hunting grounds elsewhere, including the South Shetland Islands (650 kilometers south of Cape Horn) and on the Juan Fernández Islands in the Southeastern Pacific, where they reportedly took at least a million sealskins.[41] In fact, when the Argentine government attempted to establish its sovereignty over the Malvinas/Falkland Islands in the early 1830s, fur sealing in the region was in sharp decline.

Fur seal hunters from the United States had returned to Tierra del Fuego by 1874, when two U.S. schooners spent time resupplying in Punta Arenas, to the delight of Chile's territorial governor, who noted that the vessels purchased goods from local businesses.[42] The Stonington-based *Thomas Hunt* journeyed to Cape Horn in 1874 and 1878, taking thousands of fur seals.[43] Between 1878 and 1881 Captain James Buddington took eighty-six thousand sealskins from "Cape Horn rookeries," a haul that netted him an enormous profit, with which he purchased a large home in Stonington.[44] Fellow New Englander George Comer's trip to Tierra del Fuego and Patagonia during the same period yielded far fewer sealskins (four thousand) yet was a financial success.[45]

The salted skins of South American fur seals ended up in the same London warehouses as the skins taken from fur seals in the North Pacific. Late nineteenth-century traders at Lampson Company auctions generally viewed "Cape Horn" skins as inferior to those from Alaska, but quality assessments and auction prices varied from season to season. In addition, a segmented market existed in which some buyers sought out high-quality skins for "dressing and dyeing," while other buyers purchased "inferior" quality skins at discount prices for what trade journals referred to as "washing and drying."[46] All told, between 1870 and 1900 the skins of some 300,000 South American fur seals passed through London auction houses before reaching end-markets in Europe, Russia, and the United States.[47] The (briefly) connected economies of places like Punta Arenas, Stonington, and London demonstrate how transnational frameworks can obscure not only the significance of transimperial interactions but also translocal connections that operate in relation to, but are not fully subsumed by, territorial states.

Commercial fur seal hunters plying the myriad channels of the Fuegian archipelago frequently encountered the canoes and/or shoreline settlements of Yámana and Kawéskar. Sealers and Yámana also met one another when visiting the Anglican mission situated near the Argentine settlement of Ushuaia on the Beagle Channel. For example, in 1879 an English missionary, Thomas Bridges, reported that a Yámana man named Eemyoosa had "lived and worked happily for some months" with a sealing crew.[48] Eemyoosa's relative Meenataga also found satisfactory work with a sealing crew. The following year the mission's staff appealed to their superiors for guidance as to whether to allow "Christian natives" to work for the sealers "frequenting the neighborhood." They noted that sealing crews increasingly sought Yámana men who were skilled in "chasing the seal" and "civilized by the Gospel."[49] Sealing captains continued to enlist indigenous help in the early 1880s, but unlike the larger, geographically fixed sealing operations on the Pribilof Islands, commercial sealing in Tierra del Fuego never relied primarily on indigenous laborers.[50]

Sporadic violence marked late nineteenth-century encounters between sealers and Yámana communities. In 1876 the crew of the *Charles Shearer* landed at Tierra del Fuego with the intention of trading. When they approached a group of Yámana dwellings, the crew came under attack. In the ensuing violence, two sealers and four Yámanas perished.[51] Three years later a Norwegian sealer named John Stole reported that his crew had repulsed an indigenous attack on their vessel, killing eight men and capturing a woman, whom they turned over to the missionary Thomas Bridges—a decision highly suggestive, among other things, of the region's uncertain sovereignties.[52] In another incident reported by the British naval surgeon Richard Coppinger, seven canoes launched a nocturnal attack on the schooner *Annita*, killing five sealers before retreating.[53] Sealers' narratives usually portrayed indigenous men as acting violently without reason. However, Captain J. Willis, pilot of the South American Missionary Society's vessel, attributed the violence to the sealing crews: "We know that these natives are continually being killed or shot at by lawless sealers, also their wives and daughters taken by force, so that it is no wonder that they kill white men whenever they have the opportunity."[54] In 1882–83 the members of a French scientific expedition to Cape Horn reported that a dispute provoked by the rape of indigenous women (probably Yámana) had ended in the killing of fifteen indigenous men by a sealing crew.[55]

The violence provoked by fur sealers did not single-handedly destroy Tierra del Fuego's indigenous societies. In a dynamic repeated throughout the Americas for centuries, nonindigenous interlopers (including fur sealers, missionaries, and traders) introduced communicable diseases that took the lives of hundreds of indigenous people. For example, in 1882 Thomas Bridges sought out the doctor accompanying the French scientific expedition cited above to diagnose the cause of a fever that was killing the mission's indigenous residents. Describing his visit to the mission located near the settlement of Ushuaia, the doctor observed that most of the Yámana "fled from Ushuaia because there diseases, be it tuberculosis or another introduced disease, claim more victims than in any other part [of Tierra del Fuego]."[56] Two years later smallpox killed more than five hundred Yámana—approximately one half of the population recorded by the missionaries.[57] In 1887 Bridges, noting that "various epidemics" killed many "native-settled families," lamented, "We have to almost commence again."[58] Bridges's expression of paternalistic despair conveyed the colonial mind-set and changing ecologies that together unsettled indigenous sovereignties in Tierra del Fuego.

Somewhat paradoxically, interloping commercial sealers in Tierra del Fuego served to strengthen the colonizing projects of the Chilean state by generating valuable commodities that ruling elites in Santiago claimed to be "national patrimony." At nearly the same time that the United States sought to prevent Canadian and Japanese vessels from hunting fur seals in open seas, the Chilean government—along with the governments of neighboring Argentina and the British-controlled Falkland Islands, sought to restrict foreign vessels from sealing in their respective territories. However, the wide-ranging movements of fur seals, not unlike migratory birds, compelled territorial states to recognize the limits of their ability to enforce their sovereignty at all times and places. Fur seal conservation, like fur seal hunting, was simultaneously a translocal, transnational, and transimperial affair.

Conserving Fur Seals, Claiming Sovereignty

In 1881 Francisco Sampaio, the Punta Arenas–based governor of the Chilean territory of Magallanes, alerted his superior in distant Santiago that foreign sealers threatened to put an end to "the only industry that nourishes this colony." He urged the government to issue a temporary ban on fur seal hunting in order to avoid "the complete extinction of such a valuable product for the future of Punta Arenas."[59] Two years later a three-person Chilean commission produced a lengthy report on fur seal hunting that explicitly linked nationalism and conservation. Acknowledging the presence of both Punta Arenas–based and foreign sealers, the commission argued, "Given that hunting occurs in places considered to be territorial waters [mar territorial], the vessels of foreign origin . . . are in violation of the Civil Code that guarantees the rights of Chilean citizens and resident foreigners to carry out this industry."[60] The commission confessed that they lacked precise data on the number of fur seals killed by foreign crews but offered the example of the "American schooner" *Florence* that had reportedly taken thirteen thousand fur seal skins.[61]

The report then described the measures taken by the U.S. government to regulate fur sealing on the Pribilof Islands, including a ban on foreign vessels. It praised the regulations put in place by "the Great Republic" in order to guarantee "a monopoly on sealing for its own citizens and flag of the nation," while simultaneously preventing the extinction of the species.[62] Noting that enforcing such regulations would be costly, the report's authors suggested that the Chilean government follow the United States in granting a private concession: "This is undoubtedly a correct measure given that there is no one better to guard against violations than the self-interested concessionaire."[63] The report concluded with a set of proposed regulations for Chile; the first article restricted fur seal hunting to vessels "flying the national flag."

The 1883 report did not stray far from the economic and political liberalism ascendant in Chile at the time.[64] On the one hand, its authors expressed concerns about the presence of U.S. sealing vessels violating Chilean sovereignty and the rights of Chilean citizens to valuable, that is, marketable, resources. On the other hand, the authors praised the United States for its regulatory scheme in Alaska and urged the Chilean government to use it as a model. This points to the ambivalence with which at least some Chilean authorities viewed the distant United States, whose presence in Cape Horn was largely limited to maritime traffic and sealers. For Chilean authorities eager to strengthen their country's territorial claims, the expansionist United States—"the Great Republic"—could serve as a model precisely because the Chilean state, like its powerful, distant neighbor, pursued territorial expansion via the colonization of indigenous lands.[65]

For observers in the United States, the history of sealing in the southern hemisphere served as a cautionary tale, not a model for emulation. Official government reports, newspaper editorials, and trade magazines almost always portrayed the "southern sealing grounds" as overexploited due to the absence of regulation.[66] For example, describing the experience of the San Francisco–based sealing schooner *John Hancock* in Cape Horn, a trade journal reported that "Chilian" sealers were already in the area: "As soon as a seal, no matter if it were a pup, showed his head above water, he was killed. It was found that the same condition of things existed all about the coast and the neighboring islands. The Chilian hunters have exterminated the seals entirely in the South."[67] As shown earlier, the situation in Alaska was hardly better; pelagic hunting thwarted U.S. attempts to regulate fur sealing.

The central government in Chile did not act to protect fur seals until 1892, when newly elected president Jorge Montt decreed a one-year ban on fur seal hunting in Chilean territory. One year later the Chilean Congress, with minimal debate, extended the ban to four years.[68] That same year the governor of Magallanes reported that two "American schooners" were hunting fur seals in Chilean territory. The Chilean government responded by authorizing a naval cutter, the *Cóndor*, to patrol "national waters" for foreign sealers.[69] The efforts of the *Cóndor* notwithstanding, the ban came under criticism from some observers in Chile for "favoring foreigners who, due to the lack of vigilance along our coasts, have been able to dedicate themselves to the industry without any risk of any kind."[70]

The 1893 ban coincided with the Paris Tribunal that resulted in a temporary agreement between the United States and the British Empire concerning pelagic fur sealing in the waters around the Pribilof Islands. Although tensions remained in the Bering Sea due to the entry of sealers from Japan and Canada, the number of vessels engaged in pelagic hunting in Alaskan waters decreased sharply in the years following the Paris Tribunal.[71] Canadian companies began sending sealers to the southern hemisphere. In 1901 the schooner *Edward Roy* brought 1,600 fur seal skins from the "Cape Horn" region to Halifax.[72] The following year the Victoria Sealing Company sent two of their best schooners and experienced masters to the Falkland Islands.[73]

Canadian sealers, primarily from Nova Scotia, engaged in pelagic hunting in the South Atlantic, including the Falklands, where the government had banned unlicensed hunting in 1899. Although Governor Allardyce of the Falkland Islands confessed to "a certain feeling of satisfaction" that the illegal hunting did not benefit "foreigners" (i.e., Chileans), Canadian sealing activities brought few economic benefits to the region.[74] When the Falkland Islands government imposed a tariff on the transshipment of furs through Port Stanley in 1903, fur sealers responded by boosting exports during the grace period (1903–4) and subsequently bypassing Port Stanley in favor of Punta Arenas and Montevideo, Uruguay. For example, the Canadian vessel *E. B. Marvin* transshipped 1,148 skins from Punta Arenas and 1,014 from its homeport of Halifax to London in 1905–6. In 1907 the *E. B. Marvin* transshipped a mere 640 from Port Stanley. That year, amid growing local protest over lost business, the Falkland Islands government lifted the tariff, but by that point most of the sealing fleet had left.[75]

In 1911 the North Pacific Fur Seal Convention banned pelagic seal hunting in the North Pacific Ocean. Signed by a president (United States), a king (Great Britain), an emperor (Japan), and a tsar (Russia), the accord was one of the first multilateral agreements signed by territorial states to protect wildlife. Ten years later (1921) the Falkland Islands government banned fur sealing throughout its jurisdiction. In Chile a ban on hunting and trading fur seals took effect in 1929; neighboring Argentina imposed a similar ban in 1937.[76] Commercial fur seal hunting in the southern hemisphere had all but ceased. Fur seal hunting would continue in Alaska under the direct control of the U.S. government, which continued to contract Unangan labor into the 1970s.[77]

Transgressive Environmental Histories

By tracking their wide-ranging movements during a "long" nineteenth century, this essay reveals several ways that fur sealers transgressed geopolitical boundaries. A sealing ship leaving New England for China in the early nineteenth century might routinely pass through territories claimed by indigenous societies, South American republics, and European empires; fur sealing, like whaling ventures, linked Atlantic and Pacific worlds. Investors in the United States financed fur sealing expeditions largely on the expectation of market demands in two different empires: first, Qing China and, later, Victorian Britain. Following the Civil War, fur seals caught in the U.S. territory of Alaska often ended up in retail stores in New York City, but they continued to pass through London auction houses and workshops until the onset of the Great War. In the late nineteenth century, Chilean, Canadian, and U.S. fur sealers operated in Tierra del Fuego, where they undermined the sovereignties of indigenous societies. Throughout the nineteenth century, then, the fur seal trade was simultaneously translocal, transnational, and transimperial in its organization and historical significance.

Following fur sealers demonstrates that U.S. power stretched across oceans well before 1898. Refocusing on maritime actors and movements challenges both chauvinistic and critical accounts of "westward" expansion by demonstrating that projections of U.S. power during the first half of the nineteenth century took multiple forms and trajectories, entangling maritime Americans in the multidimensional imperial politics of the nineteenth century. Yankee whalers and fur sealers reached California, Alaska, and Tierra del Fuego before their gold-seeking compatriots. Fur sealers clashed with indigenous people on littorals and islands long before U.S. soldiers fought Filipino nationalists. If the scale of violence was far less than what would take place in the Philippines, the long-term outcomes of sealer-indigenous contact were every bit as significant: in many cases, fur sealers were at the forefront of processes that would result in the destruction of indigenous societies.

Histories of fur sealing also point to the limits of power based on territorial sovereignty. In the northern Pacific, a growing U.S. commercial presence, including whalers and sealers, helped to compel the Russian Empire to sell Alaska to the U.S. government. The United States subsequently created a lucrative fur seal business run by a private concessionaire that in turn depended on British markets and industries in order to transform animal tissue into an item of high-end exchange. At the same time, Canadian and Japanese fur sealers challenged U.S. territorial sovereignty via their open-sea hunting practices. Sealing activities in the North Pacific sent waves as far as Cape Horn, where fur sealing briefly reemerged in the late nineteenth century fueled by the same London markets that purchased Alaskan furs. Fur sealing in Cape Horn served to strengthen the central authority of the Chilean state by giving an economic boost to its southernmost territorial claim, but the presence of U.S. and later Canadian sealers served as a frequent reminder to Chilean authorities of the limits of their power. The crosscutting effects of long-distance trade on sovereignty, then, are not unique to early twenty-first-century "globalization."

The trajectory of the fur seal trade transgresses familiar historical periodizations. Fur trades and whaling are familiar topics for colonial North America and the antebellum United States. However, by extending the story of the commercial fur trade into the early twentieth century, we gain an appreciation for the seldom acknowledged role that the products of commercial hunting played in processes of industrialization. A staggering variety and volume of animal pelts, skins, and feathers reached London auction houses in the second half of the nineteenth century. Fur seal skins were prized for the manufacture of luxury garments, but marine mammals supplied a much more diverse range of products, including illuminants, lubricants, detergents, and furnishings.[78] In other words, industrialization in the North Atlantic world did not replace hunting economies but rather increased their scale and scope in the late nineteenth century as guns, clubs, and wind-powered sailing vessels became integrated with telegraphs, railroads, and steamships that spanned and connected empires.

Finally, fur sealers not only prompted and challenged claims to political sovereignty; they also unsettled ecosystems by killing millions of fur seals, carnivorous marine mammals whose populations shaped the marine environments they inhabited. Although it is difficult to determine the potentially cascading ecological effects of the mass killing of a high-level predator like fur seals, the transoceanic history of fur sealing is highly suggestive of the power of capitalistic markets to deplete resources even without the benefit of fossil fuel–powered technologies. Scientists do not presently categorize either northern or southern fur seals as endangered, yet current population levels for the two species do not approach population estimates for the early nineteenth century.[79]

If the long-term effects of fur sealing on marine biodiversity remain unclear, the impacts on indigenous societies are less debatable: commercial fur sealing played a major role in destroying the sovereignty of indigenous groups caught up in tides of change that swept over much of the nineteenth-century world and spawned a contemporary era of unprecedented socioenvironmental transformations marked by transgressions that are again destabilizing territorial sovereignty. Environmental histories of the modern world, therefore, should not be limited to transnational frameworks but should also "power up" to consider transimperial interactions while simultaneously touching ground (or water!) in the particular places where contests over sovereignty and resources have played out.

NOTES

1. Eben Townsend's journal was published in 1888 by the New Haven Historical Society; quoted in Edouard A. Stackpole, *The Sea-Hunters: The New England Whalemen during Two Centuries, 1635–1835* (Philadelphia: J. B. Lippincott, 1953), 209–10.

2. For another example of U.S. sealers tangling with imperial powers, see Greg Grandin, *The Empire of Necessity: Slavery, Freedom, and Deception in the New World* (New York: Picador, 2014). Note that the *Neptune* described here is not the same vessel as the British slave ship at the center of Grandin's book.

3. Anthony B. Dickinson, "Early Nineteenth-Century Sealing on the Falkland Islands: Attempts to Develop a Regulated Industry, 1820–1834," *Northern Mariner/Le Marin du nord* 4 (1994): 39–49.

4. Alexander G. Monroe, "Commander Silas Duncan and the Falkland Islands Affair," *Log of Mystic Seaport* 25 (1973): 76–77.

5. Quoted in Dickinson, "Early Nineteenth-Century Sealing on the Falkland Islands," 43.

6. U.S. Secretary of the Navy Levi Woodbury, quoted in Monroe, "Commander Silas Duncan and the Falkland Islands Affair," 83.

7. Dickinson, "Early Nineteenth-Century Sealing on the Falkland Islands," 46.

8. *Charles L. Williams v. The Suffolk Insurance Company* (1839), in *Reports of Cases Argued and Adjudged in the Supreme Court of the United States*, vol. 38 (New York: Banks Law Publishing, 1903).

9. For Stonington's role in early nineteenth-century sealing, see Richard M. Jones, "Sealing and Stonington: A Short-Lived Bonanza," *Log of Mystic Seaport* 28 (1977): 119–26.

10. Mark Cioc, *The Game of Conservation: International Treaties to Protect the World's Migratory Animals* (Athens: Ohio University Press, 2009); Camilo Quintera Toro, *Birds of Empire, Birds of Nation: A History of Science, Economy and Conservation in United States–Colombia Relations* (Bogotá: Universidad de los Andes, 2012); Kurkpatrick Dorsey, *The*

Dawn of Conservation Diplomacy: U.S.-Canadian Wildlife Protection Treaties in the Progressive Era (Seattle: University of Washington Press, 1998).

11. Helen M. Rozwadowski, "The Promise of Ocean History for Environmental History," *Journal of American History* 100 (2013): 136–39; Karen Wigen, "AHR Forum: Oceans of History: Introduction," *American Historical Review* 111 (2006): 717–21. For examples of scholarship, see Greg Cushman, *Guano and the Opening of the Pacific World* (New York: Cambridge University Press, 2013); David Igler, *The Great Ocean: Pacific Worlds from Captain Cook to the Gold Rush* (Oxford: Oxford University Press, 2013); Lance E. Davis, Robert E. Gallman, and Karin Gleiter, *In Pursuit of Leviathan: Technology, Institutions, Productivity, and Profits in American Whaling, 1816–1906* (Chicago: University of Chicago Press, 1997).

12. For accessible introductions to biological approaches to fur seals, see National Audubon Society, *Guide to Marine Mammals of the World* (New York: Knopf, 2002); William F. Perrin, Bernd Würsig, and J. G. M. Thewissen, eds., *Encyclopedia of Marine Mammals* (New York: Academic Press, 2002); Ronald W. Nowak, *Walker's Marine Mammals of the World* (Baltimore: Johns Hopkins University Press, 2003).

13. The tensions that could arise from seeking to maximize profits in a dangerous environment lay at the heart of James Fenimore Cooper's novel *The Sea Lions or, the Lost Sealers* (1860), http://www.gutenberg.org/files/10545/10545-h/10545-h.htm.

14. Ryan Tucker Jones, *Empire of Extinction: Russians and the North Pacific's Strange Beasts of the Sea, 1741–1867* (New York: Oxford University Press, 2014), 84.

15. Jones, *Empire of Extinction*, 94–96.

16. Jones, *Empire of Extinction*, 17.

17. Dorothy Miriam Jones, *A Century of Servitude: Pribilof Aleuts under U.S. Rule* (Lanham, MD: University Press of America, 1980), http://arcticcircle.uconn.edu /HistoryCulture/Aleut/Jones/jonesindex.html.

18. D. M. Jones, *A Century of Servitude*.

19. R. T. Jones, *Empire of Extinction*, 196.

20. Briton Cooper Busch, *The War against the Seals: A History of the North American Seal Fishery* (Montreal: McGill-Queens University Press, 1985), 100; R. T. Jones, *Empire of Extinction*, 204–7; D. M. Jones, *A Century of Servitude*, chapter 1.

21. John R. Bockstoce, *Furs and Frontiers in the Far North* (New Haven, CT: Yale University Press, 2009), 260–95.

22. Busch, *The War against the Seals*, 107–10.

23. U.S. Congress, "An Act to Prevent the Extermination of Fur-Bearing Animals in Alaska," July 1, 1870, https://www.loc.gov/law/help/statutes-at-large/41st-congress/session -2/c41s2ch189.pdf.

24. Busch, *The War against the Seals*, 109–11.

25. Busch, *The War against the Seals*, 114.

26. Busch, *The War against the Seals*, 113.

27. Scholars have devoted little attention to the industrial-era fur trade, but see C. H. Stevenson, "Utilization of Skins of Aquatic Animals," in *Report of Commissioner of Fish and Fisheries for Year Ending 30 June 1902* (Washington, DC, 1904), 283–352. On twenty-first-century tuna, see Theodore C. Bestor, "How Sushi Went Global," *Foreign Policy* 121 (2000): 54–63.

28. D. M. Jones, *A Century of Servitude*.

29. R. T. Jones, *Empire of Extinction*, 95.

30. D. M. Jones, *A Century of Servitude*, chapters 3 and 4.

31. Busch, *The War against the Seals*, 115–18; Bockstoce, *Furs and Frontiers in the Far North*, 296–323.

32. A. B. Dickinson, "Southern Hemisphere Fur Sealing from Atlantic Canada," *American Neptune* 49 (1989): 278–90; Busch, *The War against the Seals*, 129–38.

33. Busch, *The War against the Seals*, 144–45.

34. Busch, *The War against the Seals*, 145–50.

35. "Vancouver Letter," *Fur Trade Review* 32 (1905): 105.

36. There is a large body of anthropological research on Tierra del Fuego's indigenous societies. See Luis Abel Orquera, "The Late-Nineteenth-Century Crisis in the Survival of the Magellan-Fuegian Littoral Natives," in *Archaeological and Anthropological Perspectives on the Native Peoples of Pampa, Patagonia, and Tierra del Fuego to the Nineteenth Century*, edited by Claudia Briones and José Luís Lanata (Westport, CT: Greenwood Press, 2002), 146; Luis Abel Orquera and Ernesto Luis Piana, *La Vida Material y Social de Los Yámana* (Buenos Aires: Editorial de la Universidad de Buenos Aires, 1999).

37. Mateo Martinic, "Actividad Lobera y Ballenera en Litorales y Aguas de Magallanes y Antartica, 1866–1916," *Revista de Estudios del Pacífico* 7 (1973): 7–26.

38. H. A. Alfredo de Rodt and Oscar Viel, "Informe pasado al Sr. Ministro de Relaciones Esteriores sobre la caza de lobos marinos," May 17, 1883, Chile, Ministerio de Relaciones Exteriores, Archivo General Histórico, Fondo Histórico (hereafter "Chile, RREE"], vol. 107; Joaquín Gomez to Minister of Foreign Relations, November 6, 1880, Chile RREE, vol. 72B.

39. Mariano Guerrero Bascuñan, *Memoria que el delegado del Supremo Gobierno en el territorio de Magallanes, don Mariano Guerrero Bascuñan, presenta al señor Ministro de Colonización* (Santiago de Chile: Imprenta y Librería Ercilla, 1897), 407.

40. Marcelo Mayorga Z., "Antecedentes históricos referidos a la caza de Lobos Marinos y su interacción con el medio geográfico y humano en el extremo Austral Americano: El caso del lobero escocés William Low," *Magallania* 44 (2016): 37–64; Mateo Martinic B., "Navegantes norteamericanos en aguas de Magallanes durante primer mitad del siglo XIX," *Anales del Instituto de la Patagonia*, Serie Ciencias Sociales, 17 (1987): 11–17; A. G. E. Jones, "The British Southern Whale and Seal Fisheries," *Great Circle* 3 (1981): 20–29.

41. On the South Shetlands, see Jorge Berguño, "Las Shetland del Sur: El ciclo lobero," *Boletín Antártico Chileno* 12 (1993): 5–13. On the Juan Fernández Islands, see Busch, *The War against the Seals*, 10–19.

42. Oscar Viel to Ministro de Relaciones Exteriores, May 1, 1874, Punta Arenas, Chile RREE, vol. 49A.

43. Logbook of Schooner *Thomas Hunt* (Stonington), entries for October 13, 1874; September 6, 1878; September 16–18, 1878, Log 841, New Bedford Whaling Museum, New Bedford, Rhode Island.

44. Buddington's haul netted him $30,000; see Barnard L. Colby, *For Oil and Buggy Whips: Whaling Captains of New London County* (Mystic, CT: Mystic Seaport Museum, 1990), 166.

45. Comer's account was an affidavit cited by J. A. Allen, "Fur-Seal Hunting in the Southern Hemisphere." In United States, *Fur Seal Arbitration* v. II (Washington: Government Printing Office, 1895): 397.

46. See, for example, *Fur Trade Review* 31 (1904): 278.

47. Stevenson, *Utilization of the Skins of Aquatic Animals*; A. Howard Clark, "The Antarctic Fur-Seal and Sea-Elephant Industry," in *The Fisheries and Fishery Industries of the United States*, edited by George Brown Goode (Washington, DC: GPO, 1884–87), 402. Also see Federico Albert, "Los Lobos Marinos de Chile," *Revista Chilena de Historia Natural* 5 (1901): 33–41; Bartolomé Bossi, *Exploración de la Tierra del Fuego* (Montevideo: La España, 1882), 53.

48. Thomas Bridges, "Southern Mission. Tierra del Fuego," *South American Missionary Magazine*, October 1, 1879, 221.

49. "General Intelligence," *South American Missionary Magazine*, December 1, 1880, 265.

50. "The Southern Mission. Tierra del Fuego. Ooshooia,"*South American Missionary Magazine*, February 1, 1884, 32; Rubén Stehberg, *Arqueología Histórica Antártica: Aborígenes Sudamericanos en Los Mares Subantárticos en el Siglo XIX* (Santiago, Chile: DIBAM, 2003).

51. "The Perils of Patagonia," *Whalemen's Shipping List and Merchants' Transcript* 34 (April 11, 1876), p. 2.

52. R. W. Coppinger, *Cruise of the Alert: Four Years in Patagonian, Polynesian and Mascarene Waters* (London: W. Swan Sonnenschein, 1883), 112–13.

53. Coppinger, *Cruise of the Alert*, 55.

54. "The Allen Gardner Mission Yawl," *South American Missionary Magazine*, March 1, 1883, 63.

55. L. Martial, "Trabajos de la Comisión Científica Francesa del Cabo de Hornos en 1882–83," translated by Chilean Office of Hydrography, *Anuario Hidrográfico de la Marina de Chile* 14 (1889): 369.

56. Dr. Hyades, "Un Año en el Cabo de Hornos," translated by Ramón Serrano M., *Anuario Hidrográfico de Chile* 11 (1886): 488.

57. Martial, "Trabajos de la Comisión Científica Francesa," 478–79.

58. Thomas Bridges, "The Southern Mission: Tierra del Fuego," *South American Missionary Magazine*, February 1, 1884; "Tierra del Fuego: Past, Present, and Future," *South American Missionary Magazine*, January 1, 1887, 7–8.

59. Francisco Sampaio to Ministro de Relaciones Exteriores, October 27, 1880, Chile RREE, vol. 72B; Sampaio to J. M. Balmaceda, October 24, 1881, Chile RREE, vol. 72A.

60. Rodt, Howland, and Viel, "Informe pasado al Sr Ministro de RREE sobre la pesca de lobos marinos," 2.

61. Rodt, Howland, and Viel, "Informe pasado al Sr Ministro de RREE sobre la pesca de lobos marinos," 5.

62. Rodt, Howland, and Viel, "Informe pasado al Sr Ministro de RREE sobre la pesca de lobos marinos," 7.

63. Rodt, Howland, and Viel, "Informe pasado al Sr Ministro de RREE sobre la pesca de lobos marinos," 10.

64. Patrick Barr-Mele, *Reforming Chile: Cultural Politics, Nationalism, and the Rise of the Middle Class* (Chapel Hill: University of North Carolina, 2001); Rafael Zarita, "Ecos de Europa: La Representación Parlamentaria en el Chile Liberal del Siglo XIX," *Journal of Iberian and Latin American Research* 20 (2014): 98–110, https://doi.org/10.1080/13260219.2014.888944.

65. Thomas Miller Klubock, *La Frontera: Forests and Ecological Conflict in Chile's Frontier Territory* (Durham, NC: Duke University Press, 2014); Florencia Mallon, *Courage Tastes of Blood: The Mapuche Community of Nicolás Ailío and the Chilean State, 1906–2001* (Durham, NC: Duke University Press, 2005).

66. See, for example, Charles H. Townsend, "Fur Seals and the Seal Fisheries," *Bulletin of the Bureau of Fisheries* 28 (1910): 315–22; "Destruction of the Seal," *Rocky Mountain News* (Denver CO), February 16, 1891, 2, infotrac.galegroup.com.

67. *Fur Trade Review* 19 (May 1892): 207.

68. Chile, Cámara de Diputados, *Boletín de las Sesiones Ordinarias en 1893* (Santiago, Chile: Imprenta Nacional, 1893), 372.

69. Decreto No. 1303 del Ministerio de Industria y Obras Públicas, Santiago, September 12, 1893, Chile, Archivo Nacional, Fondo: Gobernación de Magallanes, vol. 3; Tomás King to Ministry of the Navy, August 20, 1894, oficio 409, Chile, Archivo Nacional, Ministerio de Marina, vol. 602.

70. Guerrero Bascuñan, *Memoria*, 408; Albert, "Los Lobos Marinos de Chile," 41.

71. Stories of violence among sealers circulated far and wide; Rudyard Kipling's inspiration for "The Rhyme of the Three Sealers" came from tales that he heard while visiting Japan.

72. *Fur Trade Review* 28 (1900–1901): 295, 346.

73. *Fur Trade Review* 30 (1902–3): 34.

74. Dickinson, "Southern Hemisphere Fur Sealing from Atlantic Canada," 283.

75. Dickinson, "Southern Hemisphere Fur Sealing from Atlantic Canada," 287.

76. Juan Carlos Godoy, *Fauna Silvestre*, vol. 1 (Buenos Aires: Consejo Federal de Inversiones, 1963); J. Agustín Iriarte and Fabian M. Jaksic, "The Fur Trade in Chile: An Overview of Seventy-Five Years of Export Data (1910–1984)," *Biological Conservation* 38 (1986): 244–45.

77. For a synopsis of Pribilof Island fur sealing under U.S. government control, see Busch, *The War against the Seals*, 223–41.

78. Samuel George Archibald, *Some Account of the Seal Fishery of Newfoundland and the Mode of Preparing Seal Oil* (Edinburgh: Murray and Gibb, 1852), https://hdl.handle.net/2027/aeu.ark:/13960/t8nc6jm4k.

79. T. Gelatt, R. Ream, and D. Johnson, "Northern Fur Seal: *Callorhinus ursinus*," IUCN Red List of Threatened Species 2015: e.T3590A45224953, https://www.iucnredlist.org/species/3590/45224953.

2. CROSSING THE RIFT: AMERICAN STEEL AND COLONIAL LABOR IN BRITAIN'S EAST AFRICA PROTECTORATE

Stephen Tuffnell

Beginning in the late 1860s, U.S. engineering firms won lucrative contracts to erect bridges, viaducts, and railways around the globe.[1] The Phoenix Bridge Company, the leading bridge fabrication and erection firm in North America by the 1890s, built steel bridges and viaducts in Guatemala, Nicaragua, Peru, Costa Rica, Cuba, Mexico, Brazil, Canada, Russia, China, and Japan between 1869 and 1885.[2] These far-flung projects set in motion the movement of goods, people, and expertise across the world. For each project, gangs of American engineers traveled overseas to supervise the erection of Phoenix's prefabricated designs and to manage the imported and local labor put at their disposal. These engineers shared their experience around the world in new forums of international cooperation, such as conferences and technical journals, and incorporated it into a global, professional identity.[3] Joining a much larger network of American travelers, businessmen, expatriates, conservationists, and missionaries laboring in the Americas, Asia, and Africa, the U.S. engineering diaspora connected the United States to empires across the world.[4]

This species of transimperial connection and exchange was particularly noticeable in the British imperial world and is key to the writing of a new history of American empire. Through a series of transimperial projects, U.S. capitalist and industrial expansion became enmeshed in the proliferating networks of communication, investment, commerce, and migration that characterized British imperialism.[5] From settler colonies to protectorates and condominiums, American contractors helped Britain consolidate its grip on imperial power, building strategically vital railway bridges for its armed forces and accelerating the integration of interior regions with major ports and centers of extraction. In 1899 one of Phoenix's major rivals, the Pennsylvania Steel Company, underbid British competitors to build the Gokteik viaduct in Upper Burma for £100,000, connecting important mineral fields near the town of Lashio with Mandalay, the chief city of Upper Burma under British rule.[6] The Burma Railway Company also placed large orders with Pennsylvania Steel and with the Maryland Steel Company for locomotives, rails, and ties.[7] In the same year, British armed forces in the Sudan contracted the Pencoyd Iron Works of Philadelphia to build the Atbara Bridge over the confluence of the Atbara and Blue Nile rivers. At a cost of £6,500 and a construction time of six weeks, the bridge enabled the supply and organization of British and Egyptian troops then advancing against the Mahdist State near Khartoum, 177 miles to the southwest.[8] In Britain's white settler dominions, American firms built bridges and viaducts along the Intercolonial Railway and Grand Trunk Railways in Canada; the Nairne Viaducts in Adelaide, South Australia; and the Nowra and Hawkesbury River Bridges in New South Wales, Australia.[9] "Money is being poured out like water in order to secure the market for British manufacturers," complained one British observer, "and lo! The American steps in and carries off the contracts for building these bridges without having incurred a penny of expense or an atom of responsibility in opening up the country."[10]

American corporations—many of which had risen to greatness by developing and exploiting recently incorporated areas of the U.S. West—played major roles in advancing the British empire of industrial extraction.[11] Ten miles east of Cape Town, Cecil Rhodes's British South Africa Company (BSAC) employed the Californian William Russell Quinan to design and build the Cape Explosive Works to supply dynamite for the Rand's gold mines; similarly American mining engineers were employed in large numbers by the BSAC, De Beers Consolidated Mines, and Bewick, Moering & Co. to transform the mineral industries of southern Africa, Rhodesia, and Australia.[12] North of the Atbara Bridge in the Anglo-Egyptian Sudan, the American financier Leigh Hunt directed the Sudan Plantations Syndicate, an experimental farming project funded by Wernher, Beit & Co. that employed Tuskegee graduates to cultivate cotton, tomatoes, and alfalfa.[13] "Whether or not we are to have a political imperialism," wrote one American observer of these collaborations, "we already have an industrial imperialism."[14]

Taking these projects as its starting point, this chapter proposes a framework of global connectivity defined by transimperial interaction as one solution to navigating the tensions between imperial and global history.[15] Empires were organized in multiple ways through degrees of entanglement with global migration patterns, commodity chains and capital flows, and the communications infrastructure and nonstate institutions that made this exchange possible. Nonstate actors may have noted official boundaries, but they were not contained by them: they moved regularly between empires to supervise industrial subcontracting, participate in colonial wars, and gather and spread knowledge. These overlaid patterns of consumption and production, exchange and collaboration are central to the transimperial character of global connectivity.

Taking center stage here are the networks of globe-crossing American engineers and experts who transferred ideas, expertise, and technology between empires and who disseminated news of the lucrative industrial opportunities offered by the British Empire to audiences at home. "Out in the broad world at large," wrote one American commentator, imperial Britons and Americans "understand each other, join hands, and work shoulder to shoulder . . . in a silent alliance."[16] Migrations of this sort linked U.S. corporations both psychologically and materially with a world fundamentally reshaped by British and European imperialism. Although it was commonplace for empires to outsource some industrial tasks, send observers to learn from other empires, and exchange personnel for particular projects, for many Britons this form of American expansion was a deeply parasitic phenomenon.[17]

Recognizing the work done by U.S. corporations in European colonies places the dynamic, transimperial flow of strategies of rule between and across empires at the center of analysis, while also drawing attention to the nonstate actors and institutions involved in these exchanges and to the exercise of power.[18] Historians seeking to globalize the U.S. past require a sharper, more precise analytical vocabulary to discuss global connectivity in the nineteenth century. Labeling all connections "transnational" attenuates our analysis by distorting the nature of global connectivity; the term *transimperial* makes visible the powerful imperial formations that figured prominently in the border-crossing relationships of a world of empires. This term owes clear debts to earlier transnational scholarship, but I am not proposing a contextual thickening of key moments in the development of the U.S. Empire-State, as envisaged by earlier theorists of transnationalism.[19] Instead I see transimperial contacts as the vantage point for perceiving the interwoven relationships between national, imperial, and global scales of analysis. This conceptual framing offers one solution for historians seeking to avoid the restrictions of metropole-periphery binaries and the potentially flattening terminology of globalization.[20]

Historians of transimperial connections can draw on the new methodological breadth of research focusing on the practice, and politics, of imperial comparison.[21] This scholarship captures one of the central dynamics of imperial power: its control over the collection and subsequent organization of knowledge in hierarchical terms. On the one hand, shared or comparable concepts of race, science, and civilization lent credibility to the idea that empires faced universal problems to which interchangeable solutions could be applied. These assumptions underpinned the creation of horizontal circuits of imperial experts dedicated to observing the administrative structures, labor policies, and medical and sanitary reforms of other empires.[22] On the other hand, in the realm of interimperial competition, imperial comparisons legitimized claims to exceptional status among other empires.[23] In the context of U.S. imperial historiography, the direct comparisons between the U.S. and British empires made by imperialists in the United States have long been recognized, as has the utility of the politics of imperial comparison in justifying the transition from Spanish to U.S. rule in the Philippines, Cuba, and Puerto Rico.[24]

The central achievement of scholarship examining the politics of imperial comparison is its posing of familiar questions about U.S. imperialism from a wider angle. Yet this approach does little to "re-engineer" the questions themselves.[25] For this reason, the geographic center of this chapter moves to Eastern Africa—a part of the world unacknowledged in the traditional historiography of U.S. imperialism and a region widely understood as being peripheral to U.S. geopolitical interests in the age of European "high imperialism."[26] Stepping outside the traditional geographic and historiographical boundaries of U.S. imperialism, this chapter examines the Uganda Protectorate's subcontracting of the American Bridge Company (ABC) to erect twenty-seven railway viaducts on the Uganda Railway. The centerpiece of Britain's project to develop the economy of East Africa, this railway offers an opportunity to view the interwoven imperial networks that characterized Anglo-American transimperial connections. By focusing on a region of the world where American power was not the primary transformative force, historians can begin to reframe the questions we ask of the nature and geography of U.S. imperialism.

Through the ABC, U.S. engineers became substantively involved in British efforts to assert power by seizing land and coercing labor in East Africa. The intent here is not to annex the Uganda Protectorate as an outpost of the American Empire but to emphasize the centrality of transimperial collaboration to the processes of turn-of-the-twentieth-century imperialism—and in turn to highlight the delimiting nature of national-imperial frameworks on U.S. imperial historiography. In the Uganda Protectorate, U.S. capitalist expansion, the regional dynamics of Indian subimperialism in the Indian Ocean world, and the global circulations of goods, experts, and labor management strategies all converged at the railhead.[27]

Building the Ugandan Railway

On April 12, 1894, the Imperial British East Africa Company transferred its territorial rights to the Kingdom of Buganda to the British government, and the Uganda Protectorate was formally declared. The Salisbury government moved quickly to develop the colony's infrastructure so as to advance commerce in the region. The key to this was a proposed railway linking the coast with the interior. Political, economic, and strategic priorities were entwined in the rationale of the proposed 582-mile Uganda Railway, from Mombasa to Lake Victoria. To its promoters, a railway from the shores of the Indian Ocean to the shores of Lake Victoria was "the obvious method of attacking all of East Africa" and overcoming the limits of a harsh physical environment for travel and commerce.[28]

Imperial strategists also envisaged the line as a key element of British imperial defense of the Nile Valley. In their calculations, the railway would secure control of the Nile's headwaters and forestall French attempts to claim eastern Sudan, thereby easing anxiety over the security of Egypt and India. Not far south of the line lay the border with German East Africa, a territory roughly the size of contemporary Tanzania, Rwanda, and Burundi combined. While the border had been stabilized by Lord Salisbury and Leo von Caprivi in the Heligoland-Zanzibar Treaty of 1890, the German East Africa Company remained Britain's preeminent commercial rival in the region. "The Germans are pushing on their line from Tanga," warned London's *Fortnightly Review*, "with the ostensible aim of reaching the Victoria Lake, it is surely high time we defend our own interests."[29] Among the most vocal supporters of the line were lobbyists from the British and Foreign Anti-Slavery Society who believed it would also be the most effective means of suppressing the inland slave trade.[30]

Connectivity was therefore central to the railway's objectives. For many missionaries, merchants, and imperial commentators, Africa was defined by disconnection. They believed that railway technology would fundamentally reconfigure East Africa's place in the world, unlocking the continent's agricultural potential by providing access to the interior, where vast cotton, rubber, coffee, sugar, sansevieria (for ropes), wheat, groundnut, chili, and simsim plantations could be cultivated. Upon completion, the line reduced freight rates to 48 shillings per ton, compared to £100 to £300 per ton when head-loaded.[31] To radical-minded MPs such as Henry Labouchere, who dubbed the project a "lunatic line," and Fabian intellectuals during the late Victorian period, the line dangerously imperiled the Treasury's financial integrity and was a waste of tax-payers' money.[32] British imperial historians have similarly concluded that the overbudget and overschedule line "did little, and at great cost" to advance its stated objectives.[33]

The Uganda Railway presented a series of formidable engineering chal-lenges. To connect the Indian Ocean and Lake Victoria, the tracks had to cross large parts of the Great Rift Valley. Bordered by steep escarpments to the east and west, the valley's floor is broken by volcanos, lakes, and the Taru Desert—an area of waterless scrub that stretched deep inland from around the fiftieth mile of track. The first supply of fresh water the line would reach beyond the Taru was the Tsavo River, 132 miles from Mombasa. Where the brush was thin, the British engineers found the track laying easy and could lay 5,200 feet of line in a single day. But once the town of Nakuru, west of Nairobi, had been cleared, the route led sharply up the western side of the Rift Valley onto the Mau Escarp-ment. Beyond this the terrain fell rapidly, through a difficult country of small valleys and riverbeds.

British engineers built temporary switchbacks to climb the steepest gradi-ents and erected wooden viaducts over some ravines, but in 1901 the consulting engineer Alexander M. Rendel had the Foreign Office advertise in London for steel viaducts to bridge the steep slopes. Historians of empire and technology have shown that consulting engineers like Rendel belonged to informal profes-sional networks through which they exchanged information, advertised con-tracts, and promoted, planned, and designed imperial projects.[34] The networks that crisscrossed professional society in imperial London also extended farther afield. The London correspondents of American professional periodicals, such as the *Engineering Record*, *Dun's Review*, and *Iron Age*, advertised colonial proj-ects to American firms. This was the most likely avenue through which the eventual contractor, the ABC, heard of the contract. In all, ten British and three American firms submitted proposals to the crown agent. ABC outbid its closest rivals, the Pennsylvania Steel Company and the Phoenix Bridge Company, on both time and cost, securing the contract with the lowest bid of £135,000 and a construction time of thirty-two weeks.[35]

ABC's bid was ambitious, as the project required the transportation of seven thousand tons of steel and a thirty-ton traveling crane from New York to Mom-basa.[36] Eight of the twenty-seven viaducts were on the approach to the Mau Summit, a fault scarp standing ten thousand feet above sea level. A further nineteen descended the Mau escarpment to the railway's terminus on the shores of Lake Victoria.[37] As a measure of the terrain's treacherous character, the viaducts were to be built 8,300 feet above sea level, along just seventy-two

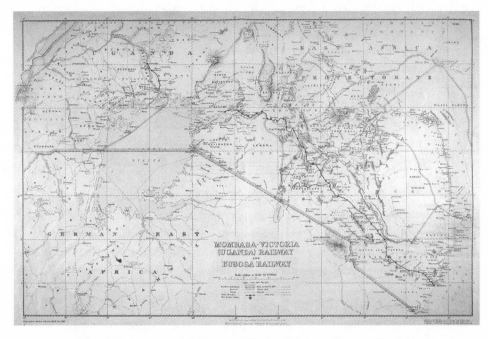

FIGURE 2.1. The engineers of the American Bridge Company constructed viaducts along the part of the line beginning at the Mau Summit just below the equator at 36° longitude. The border with German East Africa runs from the mouth of the Umba to a point east of Lake Victoria at 1°s. At a point roughly halfway between the Indian Ocean and Lake Victoria, George Whitehouse chose Nairobi as the logical location to place a rail depot and maintenance workshops—helped by its access to fresh water. Mombasa-Victoria (Uganda) Railway and Busoga Railway (1916). Used by permission of British Library, London. © British Library Board. All rights reserved/Bridgeman Images.

miles of track. The highest was 102 feet tall, 560 feet long, and had nineteen spans; the longest was 881 feet and twenty-nine spans (figure 2.1).[38]

Each viaduct was built "knocked down" in Manayunk, northwestern Philadelphia, at the mills of the Pencoyd Iron Works, before being shipped via steamer to Mombasa in the winter of 1901–2. To make sense of this huge flat-pack, the parts for each viaduct were painted a different color, which were then matched and bolted together. Accompanying the prefabricated bridges was an erection gang of twenty-one Pennsylvania laborers that included sixteen skilled fabricators; a foreman (N. P. Jarrett of Selinsgrove, Pennsylvania); a timekeeper (Charles N. Gemberling of Philadelphia); Edward Taylor, a restauranteur from Selinsgrove who served as head cook; a clerk; and as superintendent a twenty-four-year-old engineer named Archibald Byron Lueder, a Cornell graduate from Wilkes-Barre, Pennsylvania—all at twice their usual wages.[39]

On arrival in December 1901, the group traveled from Mombasa to Nairobi, and from there to a base camp at the foot of the Mau Escarpment, where construction would begin. Within three days, the steel traveling crane with seventy-foot booms was swung out over the first ravine to lift the great girders and bents into place. The first viaduct was assembled in less than a week.[40] After the initial success, work slowed. The thirty-ton traveler inched along the railway on just four sixteen-inch wheels, and the locomotives moving the steel bents derailed several times on route to the construction site.[41] Each time the team moved to a new viaduct, camp was broken down by an army of porters, who then transported it on foot to the next erection site. The American engineers, meanwhile, advanced via train. They were obliged to live in tents while they waited for the porters to arrive, which left them exposed to the extreme nighttime cold of such high altitudes, leading in turn to frequent illness.[42] "At this rate 1 year is required to complete contract," the deputy chief engineer, R. Anderson, telegrammed home to London. "Advise putting pressure on Americans."[43]

If the speed of the American work was one concern, the quality was even more pressing. Although the American press declared that "American men, American methods, and American machinery" had "achieved [a] notable victory" over "our British cousins," the reality was more prosaic.[44] The work of the American engineers came under close scrutiny from the project's chief engineer, Sir George Whitehouse, who found many aspects of it deficient. "What riveting has been done was very unsatisfactory," he noted in one report, which found that only one-quarter of the rivet holes had been filled. "This, in viaducts which are over 80 & 90 feet high, is, I consider, dangerous," Whitehouse noted drily to his superiors in London.[45] On viaduct BB (figure 2.2), a five-hundred-foot-long bridge of nineteen spans, Anderson noted that some rivets were loose and could be "shoved . . . out with his finger."[46] With the contract behind schedule, Whitehouse and Anderson pressed the Railway Committee to refuse payment to the Americans.[47] Nevertheless the Americans were paid, and on March 3, 1903, after just over a year's work, the line was opened to the lake terminus.

In one sense, this outpost of the American engineering diaspora was emblematic of surging U.S. commercial expansion. Like mission stations, the railhead was an island of American commerce.[48] American-made industrial equipment such as compressors, pneumatic riveting hammers, and hoisting engines, in addition to American-produced canned goods, seeds, and vegetables, were all imported into the colony.[49] Half a million feet of southern pine lumber was

AMERICAN BRIDGES ON THE UGANDA RAILWAY.
(For Description, see Page 249.)

Fig. 2. Viaduct B B of Nineteen Spans.

FIGURE 2.2. American-built viaduct BB along the Mau Escarpment, the longest of the viaducts installed by the ABC in Uganda. Source: Frederick W. Emett, "American Bridges on the Uganda Railway," *Engineering*, August 21, 1903, 249.

used to floor the bridges.[50] Thirty-six locomotives from Baldwin's Philadelphia workshops sped along its rails, while all of the rolling stock was equipped with American-engineered Westinghouse brakes. According to one observer, the entire project "indicates that the expansion of the British Empire and the opening of new markets tend to promote American industrial interests."[51]

In East Africa senior officials in the Protectorate government encouraged the settlement of non-British personnel, especially Indians, to settle and develop the colony.[52] American expansion occurred in the web of interregional networks that made up the Indian subimperial system spanning the port cities of the Indian Ocean rim from Zanzibar to Singapore, from Durban to Basra and Penang. As Britain extended control into the interior of East Africa, it further drew on and advanced this system. Sir Harry Johnston, the special commissioner sent to rationalize colonial administration in the Protectorate, mixed imperial security concerns with a strategy for racial uplift among both Indian migrants and black Africans. Control over East Africa and the Nile's headwaters, Johnston stressed to the Salisbury government in 1901, "is necessitated by our regard for the political future of India." He advised that "Indian trade, enterprise, and emigration require a suitable outlet," noting that "East Africa is, and should be, from that point of view an America of the Hindu."[53] The line, then, amounted to "the driving of a wedge of India two miles broad right across East Africa."[54]

Against this backdrop of encouraging nonwhite settlement in the region, European imperialists began to view tropical climates as unsuited to European exertion. In the view of Uganda's rulers, white settlers would inhabit parts of the British East Africa Protectorate, but not the interior along the line of the railway. As Sir James Hayes Sadler, the commissioner following Johnston, explained, "I do not consider that Uganda will ever be a white man's country in the sense that South Africa is and other parts of East Africa will prove to be. The climate is not conducive to European colonization."[55] Indian migrants, British officials hoped, would cultivate the interior and initiate a process of racial improvement among the indigenous populations of East Africa by, Johnston imagined, "carrying the Indian Penal Code, the Indian postal system, Indian coinage, Indian clothing, right across these wastes . . . tenanted hitherto by native savages or wild beasts."[56]

To that end, an enormous labor force of Indian Sikhs and Muslims was imported from the Punjab into Mombasa when construction on the line commenced in 1896. Between 1896 and 1902 a total of 31,983 Indian laborers were engaged for service by the railway, overseen by just 107 European technicians.[57] Locally engaged African laborers, driven into the labor market by hut taxes imposed in 1900, varying in number from 1,500 to 2,500, were also employed on the line for such tasks as clearing brush and leveling ground before the arrival of the Indian workers laying the track (figure 2.3)—though in total Africans made up less than 20 percent of the mostly Indian labor force.[58]

Indian recruitment ended in 1901 as track laying reached completion, but the Protectorate's Asian community proved invaluable in the lower rungs of the colonial administration, in local commerce, and on the railway as technical and service staff. As a result, the ABC inherited a number of migrant laborers. Lueder and the ABC used gangs of Indian workers as riveters on wages of between 12 and 45 rupees ($4 to $15) a month with food; alongside these squads the ABC used several hundred black Africans as menial workers (figure 2.4).

The same labor circuits also converged on the Pennsylvania Steel Company's project in the Shan Hills of Burma. There the migration of Tamil and Telegu unskilled laborers from South India swelled rapidly as the colony became one of the world's largest rice producers. Rice fields, paddy-processing industries, timber yards, mineral oil refineries, and the railways were the chief sources of employment for these free and unfree migrants.[59] By 1901 Indian migrants constituted some 5.4 percent of the Burmese population and were concentrated largely in Lower Burma.[60] The Burma Railways Company contracted Indian laborers to work on the Gokteik viaduct, where they were overseen by thirty-

FIGURE 2.3. African and Indian laborers leveling the ground before the arrival of track. These workers battled not only dense, tangled roots and shallow stream courses, but also the bites of chiggers and the tsetse fly, which spread "sleeping sickness" (African trypanosomiasis), a parasitic disease that results in fevers, headaches, and joint pains before causing neurological problems whose symptoms include confusion and trouble sleeping. Used by permission of A. W. Read Collection, Weston Library, The Bodleian Libraries, The University of Oxford.

five Americans from Pennsylvania Steel. Close to five hundred Indian riveters pieced together more than 230,000 individual pieces of steelwork at $17 per month.[61] John C. Turk, in Burma as the chief engineer for Pennsylvania Steel, animalized the Indian workers as having "the same respect for their European overseers that sheep have for a collie." The American workman, he concluded, was equal to "at least four natives."[62]

Having been pulled into this web of Indian labor migration, the ABC's engineers in Uganda posed as cosmopolitan race experts to imperial Britons and U.S. audiences alike.[63] "I had much to learn about handling, organizing, and providing for this exceedingly raw and barbarous material," Lueder reported on his return to the United States.[64] Much to his frustration, and overlooking that the majority of laborers on the railway were contracted, he found that "the

FIGURE 2.4. When construction began in 1896, the Uganda Railway required enormous amounts of labor: 6,000 Indians, including 4,800 Punjabi Muslims, and 17,400 male and female Swahili-speakers, comprising 14,600 free persons, 2,650 slaves, and 150 prisoners. By 1921 Asian migrants to East Africa amounted to 54,400. Used by permission of A. W. Read Collection, Weston Library, The Bodleian Libraries, The University of Oxford.

coolie had a way of organizing himself as an individual striker and refusing to work."[65] Lueder wrote approvingly that it had been necessary "to go back to old slave days" and to "act as police, judge, and executioner yourself."[66] The punishment for striking—and the U.S.-managed side of the project was beset by strikes—was twenty-five lashes with a rhinoceros hide cane.[67]

Yet the American engineers were not as adept as they portrayed themselves to U.S. audiences in technical journals and middle-class magazines such as *World's Work*. In March 1902 the chief engineer for the whole project, Sir George Whitehouse, wrote to the Railway Committee that "the Company have had considerable difficulty in working the Indian labour" and found that "practically all the Indian rivetters had struck work."[68] The Americans, Whitehouse wrote home again in June, "had no experienced supervision on their staff to look after the men that they engaged locally," and "many months were lost" as a result.[69]

Coercive power over labor was systemic to both industrial management at home and to imperial capitalist expansion overseas. As American engineers adapted labor regimes between industrial contexts, they paid special attention to the management of nonwhite workers and developed a professional identity that centered on a self-proclaimed ability to manage native labor worldwide. Establishing ratios of productivity and profitability and designating competency at skilled and unskilled tasks between white and nonwhite workers were hallmarks of the identity of the transnational American engineer. The corporations employing elite engineers were tied to a variety of forms of unfree labor—be it the control of nonwhite laborers in the American West, the segregation of African Americans, or the coercion of laborers in the Philippines and colonial contexts outside the United States.[70] From these experiences, and others besides, elite engineers staked claims to possessing unique knowledge of nonwhite capacity.[71] ABC engineers were preoccupied with recruiting, managing, and disciplining laborers, and Lueder measured the efficiency of Indian riveters at a ratio of "one American [to] five of the African or coolies."[72] Americans found like-minded military and civilian engineers on British industrial-imperial projects who were similarly committed to the fiction that the "Anglo-Saxon race" embodied the practices of wise management. It wasn't simply the case that empires provided an outlet for these activities, but key characteristics of professionalism were defined, and their prestige enhanced, through empire itself.[73]

Amalgamation and Empire

Focusing on the Ugandan Railway in this way also highlights new dimensions to the complex interconnections between empire-building and the expansion of American industrial capitalism. As Julie Greene has written, "U.S. imperialism and capitalism were profoundly intertwined," but the empire did not simply supply the needs of U.S. corporations.[74] In the search for opportunity overseas, U.S. corporate capitalism found expansionist opportunities in collaborations with European empires and, in turn, sustained a global system of shared colonial labor management. In the case of ABC, two innovations are of particular note. First, in 1899, in the midst of the spree of trust creation known as the "great merger movement," American Bridge became an industrywide holding company when J. P. Morgan consolidated twenty-nine of the largest steel fabricators and constructors in the United States into one corporate structure. The new amalgamation accounted for 90 percent of the bridge tonnage erected in the United States.[75] This was growth by acquisition, not innovation. In 1901 ABC's absorption into the newly formed U.S. Steel Corporation, encompassing 138 companies, strengthened this trend.[76] This marked a radical change in the competitive structure of American industry, prompting increased efficiency and technological innovation, that in turn incentivized economies of speed (in the case of steel, it was cheaper to convert molten pig iron into steel and roll and shape it while still hot, than it was to reheat it), meaning these new giants were able to break into foreign markets, and undersell foreign competitors, even at the expense of short-run losses.[77]

Additional changes in the U.S. economy prepared the ground for the overseas expansion of U.S. steel. At the turn of the twentieth century, steel was used with increasing frequency in the construction industries, which boosted the production of large, standardized structural shapes to cater to the enormous volume of bridge building in the United States. Philadelphia's Pencoyd Iron Works was one of the few firms rolling such shapes, and in 1899 it was one of the firms absorbed into ABC. Falling international freight rates, combined with low-priced natural resources, an abundance of unskilled labor, and expertise acquired managing the massive economies of scale required for imposing corporate will over the natural environment of the American West were the keys to ABC's success.[78] Stated simply: mass-produced structural steel work enabled U.S. firms to reduce the manufacture of bridges to such simple terms that export prices—even to Britain's East African colonies—were not significantly higher than those of bridges erected in the United States.[79]

Both Britons and Americans conceived of the mobility at the center of this story as "invasion."[80] Of the British literature examining the so-called American invasion, the shrewdest observers pointed out that it was U.S. corporations, not simply products, that dominated in almost every new industry. "The result of the formation of the trust has been to enable the Americans to produce at lower cost than ever before," wrote the Scots Canadian journalist Frederick McKenzie in his widely read and widely quoted work, *The American Invaders*. "American bridge competition is typical of the whole," he wrote, having "reduced the work to an exact science," with the result that "American bridges . . . are cheaper, simpler, better designed, and can be much more rapidly constructed."[81]

The language of invasion was in some ways an effort to extract a national story from the international entanglement at the center of capitalism's expansion. Yet the success of the American contract was as much attributable to the great engineers' lockout between 1897 and 1898—a thirty-week strike, involving some twenty-five thousand engineers who slowed down the work of 702 firms, paralyzing Britain's heavy machine business—as the quick march of commercial invasion.[82] But, combined with the technical innovations prompted by corporate consolidations, it does reveal the capacity of American industry to fulfill global demands with great speed. A backlog in production kept British firms occupied, leading to long delivery times, and provided the opportunity for ABC to enter the marketplace. For the same reason, thirty-six of the seventy locomotives deployed on the Ugandan Railway were supplied by the Baldwin Locomotive Works between 1899 and 1900.[83] Despite vigorous debate in the British press and among British colonial officials, the U.S. engines were deemed "better suited for rough work during construction."[84] Transimperial connections, then, were as much about the relations between metropolitan economies as about peripheral entanglements. Similarly, the national was not undermined by transimperial connections but heightened by them, as the language of invasion reveals.

Conclusion

Britain's grip on imperial power was consolidated by the co-optation and contracting of U.S. industrial capacity and technological innovation. As the British sociologist Benjamin Kidd argued at the Royal Colonial Institute, it was "undoubtedly a fact, from the nature of our trade and the character of our fiscal system, that we even offer peculiar facilities" to the expansion of American firms. This left Britain "peculiarly open," Kidd continued, to "being drawn deeply into the organization of trade and production now proceeding outwards from the United States."[85] American firms exploited the overseas opportunities offered by the British Empire's globe-spanning commercial infrastructure—without any of the expense of building and maintaining it. As one American observer surmised, "The United States can co-operate only with Great Britain in its material interests beyond its border. . . . The expansion of England and its opening out of the world's ports to commerce is *ipso facto* the expansion of American commerce without the cost of blood and substance to the United States."[86]

But the United States was less an upstart than it was an accomplice. By managing lucrative industrial contracts in the British imperial world, expansionist American corporations coproduced projects of imperial rule, and their employees posed as the partners of British imperialists in the process of colonization. By the turn of the twentieth century, U.S. capitalism was enmeshed in transimperial patterns of migration, trade, capital, and industry central to the operation of imperial power around the world.[87] American corporations were both beneficiaries of the globalizing effects of transimperial connection and expert assemblers of the infrastructure that enabled traffic of various kinds to move easily across imperial boundaries. It was through these deeplaid transimperial relationships that the modern world system emerged.

1. "American Contracting in Brazil," *Engineering News* 9 (1882): 241; "American Bridges in Mexico," *Engineering Record*, August 31, 1901, 196–97.

2. This list was compiled from the *Album of Designs of the Phoenix Bridge Company* (Philadelphia: J. B. Lippincott, 1885), 7–10; "American Bridges in Japan," *Engineering Record*, December 23, 1899, 700.

3. Ian Tyrrell, *Crisis of the Wasteful Nation: Empire and Conservation in Theodore Roosevelt's America* (Chicago: University of Chicago Press, 2015), 26.

4. See, for example, Ian Tyrrell, "Woman, Missions, and Empire: New Approaches to American Cultural Expansion," in *Competing Kingdoms: Women, Mission, Nation, and the American Protestant Empire, 1812–1960*, edited by Barbara Reeves-Ellington et al. (Durham, NC: Duke University Press, 2010), 61; Ian Tyrrell, *Reforming the World: The Creation of America's Moral Empire* (Princeton, NJ: Princeton University Press, 2010), 80, 236–37; Emily Conroy-Krutz, *Christian Imperialism: Converting the World in the Early American Republic* (Ithaca, NY: Cornell University Press, 2015).

5. Gary Magee and Andrew Thompson, *Empire and Globalisation: Networks of People, Goods and Capital in the British World, c. 1850–1914* (Cambridge, U.K.: Cambridge University Press, 2010); John Darwin, *The Empire Project: The Rise and Fall of the British World-System, 1830–1970* (Cambridge, U.K.: Cambridge University Press, 2009).

6. *From Steelton to Mandalay* (Steelton, PA: Pennsylvania Steel Company, 1902); Paul Kramer, "Empires, Exceptions, and Anglo-Saxons: Race and Rule between the British and United States Empires, 1880–1910," *Journal of American History* 88 (2002): 1327–30.

7. Stuart Sweeney, *Financing India's Imperial Railways, 1875–1914* (London: Pickering and Chatto, 2011), 28.

8. "Opening of the Atbara Bridge," *Illustrated London News*, September 2, 1899, 310. For the role of the Atbara Bridge in Kitchener's campaign against the Mahdist state, see M. W. Daly, *Empire on the Nile: The Anglo-Egyptian Sudan, 1898–1934* (Cambridge, U.K.: Cambridge University Press, 1986), 202. Also operating across imperial boundaries, an Italian firm sank the concrete piers in the powerful stream and eddying swells where the rivers met.

9. "American Bridges in English Colonies," *Engineering News*, November 28, 1885, 345; Walter Cook, "Erection of the Nairne Viaducts, near Adelaide, South Australia," *Minutes of the Proceedings of the Institution of Civil Engineers*, 1903, 185–87; "American Bridge Building in the Antipodes," *Engineering News*, January 14, 1882, 15.

10. William T. Stead, *The Americanization of the World, or, the Trend of the Twentieth Century* (London: Horace Markley, 1902), 362.

11. John Darwin, *Unfinished Empire: The Global Expansion of Britain* (London: Penguin, 2012), 178–88; Martin Thomas and Andrew Thompson, "Empire and Globalisation: from 'High Imperialism' to Decolonisation," *International History Review* 36 (2014): 145.

12. Stephen Tuffnell, "Engineering Inter-Imperialism: American Miners and the Transformation of Global Mining," *Journal of Global History* 10 (2015): 53–76; Jessica Teisch, *Engineering Nature: Water, Development and the Global Spread of American Environmental Expertise* (Chapel Hill: University of North Carolina Press, 2011).

13. This was also true of the German Empire: Andrew Zimmerman, *Alabama in Africa: Booker T. Washington, the German Empire, and the Globalization of the New South* (Princeton, NJ: Princeton University Press, 2010).

14. Arthur Judson Brown, "The Opened World," *American Monthly Review of Reviews*, October 1904, 461.

15. For landmark studies in these discussions, see Simon Potter and Jonathan Saha, "Global History, Imperial History and Connected Histories of Empire," *Journal of Colonialism and Colonial History* 16 (2015), doi:10.1353/cch.2015.0009; Thomas and Thompson, "Empire and Globalisation," 142–70; Gareth Curless, Stacey Hynd, Temilola Alanamu, and Katherine Roscoe, "Networks in Imperial History," *Journal of World History* 26 (2015): 705–32.

16. William Elliot Griffis, "America in the Far East II: The Anglo-Saxon in the Tropics," *Outlook*, December 1898, 907.

17. Tuffnell, "Engineering Inter-Imperialism," 58–62; Stead, *Americanization of the World*, 361.

18. Julian Go, "Introduction: Global Perspectives on the U.S. Colonial State in the Philippines," in *The American Colonial State in the Philippines: Global Perspectives*, edited by Julian Go and Anne L. Foster (Durham, NC: Duke University Press, 2003), 21.

19. Thomas Bender, *Nation among Nations: America's Place in World History* (New York: Hill and Wang, 2006).

20. Potter and Saha, "Connected Histories of Empire"; Lynn Hunt, *Writing History in the Global Era* (New York: Norton, 2014).

21. Alex Middleton, "French Algeria in British Imperial Thought, 1830–70," *Journal of Colonialism and Colonial History* 16 (2015), doi:10.1353/cch.2015.0012.

22. See the chapter by Anne L. Foster in this volume; Laura Briggs, *Reproducing Empire: Race, Sex, Science, and U.S. Imperialism in Puerto Rico* (Berkeley: University of California Press, 2002), 33–38; Warwick Anderson, *Colonial Pathologies: American Tropical Medicine, Race, and Hygiene in the Philippines* (Durham, NC: Duke University Press, 2006), 99; Natalie J. Ring, *The Problem South: Region, Empire, and the New Liberal State, 1880–1930* (Athens: University of Georgia Press, 2012), 209–11.

23. Ann Laura Stoler, "Considerations on Imperial Comparisons," in *Empire Speaks Out: Languages of Rationalization and Self-Description in the Russian Empire*, edited by Ilya Gerasimov et al. (Boston: Brill, 2009), 44–45; Volker Barth and Roland Cvetkovski, "Encounters of Empires: Methodological Approaches," in *Imperial Co-operation and Transfer, 1870–1930: Empires and Encounters*, edited by Volker Barth and Roland Cvetkovski (London: Bloomsbury Academic, 2015), 9.

24. Josep M. Fradera, "Reading Imperial Transitions: Spanish Contraction, British Expansion, and American Irruption," in *Colonial Crucible: Empire in the Making of the Modern American State*, edited by Alfred W. McCoy and Francisco A. Scarano (Madison: University of Wisconsin Press, 2009), 34–63; Andrew Priest, "Thinking about Empire: The Administration of Ulysses S. Grant, Spanish Colonialism and the Ten Years' War with Cuba," *Journal of American Studies* 48 (2014): 541–58; Andrew Priest, "Imperial Exchange: American Views of the British Empire during the Civil War and Reconstruction," *Journal of Colonialism and Colonial History* 16 (2015), doi:10.1353/cch.2015.0015.

25. Paul Kramer, "Power and Connection: Imperial Histories of the United States in the World," *American Historical Review* 116 (2011): 1365n50.

26. David M. Pletcher, *The Diplomacy of Trade and Investment: American Economic Expansion in the Hemisphere, 1865–1900* (Columbia: University of Missouri Press, 1998); Emily S. Rosenberg, *Financial Missionaries to the World: The Politics and Culture of Dollar Diplomacy, 1900–1930* (Cambridge, MA: Harvard University Press, 1999); Cyrus Veeser, *A World Safe for Capitalism: Dollar Diplomacy and America's Rise to Global Power* (New York: Columbia University Press, 2002). As Paul Kramer has argued elsewhere, the category of informal empire has delimited the geography and conception of state power in U.S. imperial historiography ("Power and Connection," 1374–75).

27. Potter and Saha, "Connected Histories of Empire."

28. H. G. Prout, "The Economic Conquest of Africa," *Engineering Magazine*, February 1900, 668.

29. George S. Mackenzie, "Uganda and the East African Protectorates," *Fortnightly Review*, December 1894, 884; "Securing Uganda," *Chamber of Commerce Journal*, June 1895, 97–98.

30. "The Uganda Protectorate," *Chamber of Commerce Journal*, April 1894, 4–5; Richard Huzzey, *Freedom Burning: Anti-Slavery and Empire in Victorian Britain* (Ithaca, NY: Cornell University Press, 2012), 195–96.

31. Jan S. Hogendron, "Economic Initiative and African Cash Farming," in *Colonialism in Africa, 1870–1960*, 5 vols., edited by L. H. Gann and Peter Duigan (Cambridge, U.K.: Cambridge University Press, 1969–74), 4:313.

32. L. H. Gann and Peter Duigan, *The Rulers of British Africa, 1870–1914* (Stanford, CA: Stanford University Press, 1978), 29, 279.

33. Thomas Metcalf, *Imperial Connections: India in the Indian Ocean Arena, 1860–1920* (Berkeley: University of California Press, 2007), 203.

34. Casper Andersen, *British Engineers and Africa, 1875–1914* (London: Pickering and Chatto), 57–86.

35. *Africa No.1, Return of the Names of the British and American Firms who tendered for the supply of certain bridges for the Uganda Railway and the Amounts of the Various Tenders* (London: HM Stationary Office, 1901).

36. Marc Linder, *Projecting Capitalism: A History of the Internationalization of the Construction Industry* (Westport, CT: Greenwood Press, 1994), 99.

37. Henry Gunston, "The Planning and Construction of the Uganda Railway," *Transactions of the Newcomen Society* 74 (2004): 64.

38. Gunston, "The Planning and Construction of the Uganda Railway," 47; *Africa No. 11. Final Report of the Uganda Railway Committee* (London: HM Stationary Office, 1904), 18.

39. "American Bridge Building in Equatorial Africa," *Engineering Record*, September 3, 1904, 310–11.

40. "The Uganda Exploit," *Boston Evening Transcript*, July 3, 1903; "Erection of the Uganda Railway Viaducts," *Engineering Record*, August 2, 1902, 105.

41. George Whitehouse to Uganda Railway Committee (hereafter URC), September 16, 1902, CO537/78, National Archives, Kew, London (hereafter NA).

42. George Whitehouse to Uganda Railway Committee.

43. R. Anderson to Whitehouse, April 10, 1902, CO537/77, NA.

44. Joseph M. Rogers, "The American Invasion of Uganda," *American Monthly Review of Reviews*, July 1903, 44.

45. Whitehouse to URC, March 17, 1902, CO537/77, NA.

46. Whitehouse to URC, June 28, 1902; Anderson to Whitehouse, June 14, 1902, CO537/78, NA.

47. Whitehouse to URC, June 11, 1902, CO587/78, NA.

48. *Dun's Review*, January 4, 1902, 34; *Dun's Review*, January 11, 1902, 15.

49. Rogers, "American Invasion of Uganda," 49.

50. A. B. Lueder, "Building American Bridges in Mid-Africa," *World's Work*, June 1903, 3661.

51. "Foreign Industrial News," *Modern Machinery*, January 1, 1901, 12; Rogers, "American Invasion of Uganda," 44.

52. Metcalf, *Imperial Connections*, 166–87.

53. *Report by Her Majesty's Special Commissioner on the Protectorate of Uganda* (London: HM Stationary Office, 1901), 7.

54. Quoted in Roland Oliver, *Sir Harry Johnston and the Scramble for Africa* (London: Chatto and Windus, 1957), 293.

55. *General Report on the Uganda Protectorate for the Year Ending March 31, 1904* (London: HM Stationary Office, 1904), 28.

56. Quoted in Oliver, *Harry Johnston*, 293.

57. Metcalf, *Imperial Connections*, 200.

58. Metcalf, *Imperial Connections*, 200; Colin Newbury, "Historical Aspects of Manpower and Migration," in Gann and Duigan, *Colonialism in Africa*, 4:525.

59. Amarjit Kaur, "Indian Labour, Labour Standards, and Workers' Health in Burma and Malaya," *Modern Asian Studies* 40 (2006): 430.

60. Kaur, "Indian Labour, Labour Standards, and Workers' Health in Burma and Malaya," 431.

61. *From Steelton to Mandalay*.

62. J. C. Turk, "Building an American Bridge in Burma," *World's Work*, September 1901, 1165.

63. David Roediger and Elizabeth D. Esch, *The Production of Difference: Race and the Management of Labor in U.S. History* (New York: Oxford University Press, 2012).

64. "The Uganda Exploit."

65. Lueder, "Building American Bridges in Mid-Africa," 3664.

66. A. B. Lueder, "Experience in the Erection of American Viaducts on the Uganda Railway," *Engineering News*, April 14, 1904, 346.

67. Lueder, "Building American Bridges in Mid-Africa," 3664.

68. Whitehouse to URC, March 17, 1902, CO537/77, NA.

69. Whitehouse to URC, June 11, 1902, and September 16, 1902, CO537/78, NA.

70. Michael Adas, *Dominance by Design: Technological Imperatives and America's Civilizing Mission* (Cambridge, MA: Belknap Press of Harvard University Press, 2006), 129–82; Roediger and Esch, *Production of Difference*, 11; Tuffnell, "Engineering Inter-Imperialism," 62–67; Marilyn Lake and Henry Reynolds, *Drawing the Global Colour Line: White Men's Countries and the International Challenge of Racial Equality* (Cambridge, U.K.: Cambridge University Press, 2008).

71. See also Roediger and Esch, *The Production of Difference*, 98–135.

72. "The Uganda Exploit."

73. Magee and Thompson, *Empire and Globalisation*, 137.

74. Julie Greene, "The Wages of Empire: Capitalism, Expansion, and Working-Class Formation," in *Making the Empire Work: Labor and United States Imperialism*, edited by Daniel Bender et al. (New York: New York University Press, 2015), 35–58, 38.

75. Linder, *Projecting Capitalism*, 98.

76. Walter LaFeber, *The New Cambridge History of American Foreign Relations*, vol. 2: *The Search for Opportunity, 1865–1913* (Cambridge, U.K.: Cambridge University Press, 2013), 176.

77. Naomi R. Lamoreaux, *Great Merger Movement in American Business* (Cambridge, U.K.: Cambridge University Press, 1985), 32–33; William H. Becker, *The Dynamic of Business-Government Relations: Industry and Exports, 1893–1921* (Chicago: University of Chicago Press, 1982), 1.

78. Historians have yet to fully examine the connection between the extension of corporate control over the American West and subsequent expansion overseas. Mining historians have mapped some of the transnational relationships essential to the capitalist transformation of the West; see, for example, David Igler, "The Industrial Far West: Region and Nation in the Late Nineteenth Century," *Pacific Historical Review* 69, no.2 (2000): 159–92; Samuel Truett, *Fugitive Landscapes: The Forgotten History of the U.S.-Mexico Borderlands* (New Haven, CT: Yale University Press, 2006).

79. Linder, *Projecting Capitalism*, 99; "Presidential Address before the Institution of Civil Engineers," *Engineering News*, November 30, 1899, 355.

80. Sebastian Conrad, *Globalisation and the Nation in Imperial Germany* (Cambridge, U.K.: Cambridge University Press, 2010), 395.

81. Frederick A. McKenzie, *The American Invaders* (London: Grant Richards, 1902), 70, 75–76. See also the extensive analysis of Andrew Williamson in *British Trade and Foreign Competition* (London, 1894), 226–41.

82. Frederick W. Emett, "Physical and Economic Features of the Uganda Railway," *Engineering Magazine*, June 1901, 559; McKenzie, *American Invaders*, 74; B. P. Cronin, *Technology Industrial Conflict, and the Development of Technical Education in 19th-Century England* (Aldershot, U.K.: Ashgate, 2001), 134, 145; "The British Defense of American Engineering," *Engineering Record*, June 15, 1901, 565–66.

83. Gunston, "Planning and Construction," 57; *Africa No. 11. Final Report of the Uganda Railway Committee*, 24. At the same time, forty-five were bought by the colonial government in East India (*Iron Age*, April 20, 1899, 13).

84. *Africa No. 11. Final Report of the Uganda Railway Committee*, 24.

85. Benjamin Kidd, "The State in Relation to Trade," *Proceedings of the Royal Colonial Institute: Vol. 34, 1902–1903* (London: Royal Colonial Institute, 1903), 260.

86. Charles Waldstein, *The Expansion of Western Ideals and the World's Peace* (New York: Bodley Head, 1899), 185–86.

87. Paul Kramer, "Embedding Capital: Political-Economic History, the United States, and the World," *Journal of the Gilded Age and Progressive Era* 15 (2016): 331–62.

PART II. TRANSIMPERIAL POLITICS

3. "OUR INDIAN EMPIRE": THE TRANSIMPERIAL ORIGINS OF U.S. LIBERAL IMPERIALISM

Michel Gobat

This essay explores the transimperial origins of U.S. liberal imperialism—meaning the efforts of a foreign power to impose a liberal order on a subjugated society—by focusing on the empire that William Walker and his band of about twelve thousand colonists sought to build in Central America during the 1850s.[1] The origins of U.S. liberal imperialism are typically associated with the immediate post-1898 era, when the United States created overseas colonies and protectorates under a banner of civilization, democracy, open trade, and progress.[2] As a result, the global rise of liberal imperialism in the mid-nineteenth century is usually dissociated from Manifest Destiny expansion of the antebellum era and instead linked with the "civilizing mission" of European powers in Africa and Asia.[3] Yet the Walker episode reveals that Manifest Destiny entailed expansion by sea that was shaped by European efforts to merge liberalism with imperialism, with the European empires providing not only precedents and principles but also personnel. Liberal imperialism is both more deeply rooted in U.S. political culture and molded less by U.S. traditions than often thought.

That Walker should be viewed as a liberal imperialist might seem odd. Even after he conquered Nicaragua in 1855 and then sought to extend his rule to the rest of Central America, many of his contemporaries dismissed him and his men as nothing but international criminals bent on plunder. Indeed Walker's initial recruits were among the many U.S. citizens who invaded Latin America between the Mexican-American War and the Civil War. Because the invaders defied their government and violated U.S. law, they were widely denigrated as filibusters, which comes from the Spanish word for "freebooters" (*filibusteros*). And the filibusters of the 1850s did fit the pirate stereotype, as many were desperate (white) men seeking easy riches, violent thrills, and personal freedom.[4] Antebellum filibusterism gained such notoriety as it went against international efforts to criminalize nonstate violence.[5] Although the United States had spearheaded these efforts with its Neutrality Acts of 1794 and 1818, filibusters easily launched their ventures from U.S. soil. This reflected not only the weakness of the antebellum state but also filibusterism's popularity in a country enthralled with Manifest Destiny. After the 1848 conquest of California, U.S. expansionists increasingly championed filibusterism as a means to establish settler colonies abroad. All filibuster expeditions except Walker's failed to seize power; his was thus the only one to mutate into a movement of settler colonists. Yet the extreme violence that marred Walker's fall in 1857 only reinforced his image as a brutish rogue.

Present-day scholars, by contrast, tend to link the Walker episode with efforts of proslavery U.S. southerners to extend their illiberal institution to the tropics.[6] Buttressing this view is Walker's decree that relegalized slavery in Central America. He cemented his proslavery infamy with an 1860 book that equated his Nicaragua expedition with the spread of slavery.[7] Because Walker's account aimed to secure support from U.S. slaveholders for his (failed) attempt to reconquer Nicaragua, it both erases his long-standing Free Soil opposition to slavery's expansion and exaggerates the institution's role in his imperial venture of 1855–57.

For most of his reign, Walker and his followers instead identified their enterprise with the spread of democracy and free-labor capitalism. Walker's self-proclaimed empire certainly attracted U.S. southerners who maintained that democracy was for white people only and saw no contradiction in their efforts to spread liberty and slavery. Yet many more of his followers were northerners who not only opposed the expansion of slavery but also sought to uplift the Central American masses and free them from allegedly despotic elites. Hence Walker's movement enjoyed much support among ordinary Nicaraguans, including radicals fighting for democracy and social justice.

Walker's imperial project built on U.S. liberal traditions, especially the Jeffersonian ideal of a republican "empire of liberty" and the pro-statist American System of capitalist development. Yet it drew just as powerfully on the nascent liberal imperialism of European powers. This European influence reflected the view of antebellum officials and newspapers that Manifest Destiny was part and parcel of an international trend. As the pro-Walker *New York Herald* asserted in 1857:

Four great nationalities are simultaneously extending the benefits of civilization throughout the earth. The United States are carrying their social order and industrial energy to the decaying communities of Spanish America. England is opening Southern Africa, Australia, and a large portion of Asia to the lights of science and the ameliorating influences of commerce. France is . . . seeking to create new fields for the employment of industry in Northern Africa. Russia is . . . impressing upon the wandering hordes of Central Asia the elevating influences of civilization. . . . The remnants of the barbarous ages . . . are fast disappearing . . . and a newer generation is rising, to rule under more liberal and enlightened policy. The world is awakened to the great truth that the advance of each is best sought in the improvement of all among the family of nations.[8]

This antebellum valorization of imperial cooperation at a global scale challenges latter-day views that identify Manifest Destiny with "American exceptionalism."

While Walker and his leading men admired the liberal bent of French and Russian imperialism, they were mainly enthralled with the British civilizing mission in India. With good reason did the U.S. press coin the phrase *our Indian empire* to refer to Walker's Central American polity—a label that was quickly adopted by Latin American and European papers.[9] The appeal of British imperialism to Walker's men is puzzling at first glance. Like most agents of Manifest Destiny, Walker deemed the British the greatest threat to U.S. efforts to control Central America, which had long been a geopolitical hotspot due to its potential for an interoceanic canal that promised North Atlantic powers easy access to the fabled Asian market. In addition, Walker and his men never tired in denouncing the British for supporting their main Central American foes: local "aristocracies." Yet history shows that interimperial rivalries do not stop empires from learning from one other even if they made such comparisons in a selective way.[10] The Walker episode neatly reveals the now forgotten connections between Manifest Destiny and the rise of European liberal imperialism.

Reinforcing this link was Walker's dependency on European liberal émigrés, especially veterans of the failed revolutions that swept the Old World in 1848. These radicals arrived in the United States as committed imperialists and saw no contradiction in trumpeting what they called universal democratic republicanism and overseas U.S. expansion. Compared to Walker's U.S. followers, however, they upheld a more inclusive notion of Americanization based on cultural pluralism. The key role of European radicals in Walker's venture suggests that U.S. liberal imperialism began as a more cosmopolitan—and revolutionary—undertaking than it would become in the twentieth century.

Encountering European Liberal Imperialism

Walker (1824–1860) was attracted to Nicaragua mainly because the California Gold Rush of 1849 intensified U.S. efforts to construct an interoceanic canal across the Central American isthmus. The United States eventually built the canal in Panama (1904–14), yet in the mid-nineteenth century it deemed Nicaragua the more appropriate site. Walker thus embodied U.S. interest in annexing a country of great geopolitical importance—an interest rooted in the ideology of Manifest Destiny. But even before Walker set foot in Nicaragua, his expansionist outlook had also been shaped by European notions of liberal imperialism.

Because Walker evolved into the main U.S. symbol of slavery expansion following his 1857 expulsion from Nicaragua, it is easy to overlook his early embrace of European liberal imperialism. The Tennessee native steadfastly defended the South's "peculiar institution" yet opposed its spread from early on, largely for fear that it would unleash a U.S. civil war. His opposition was reinforced by the antislavery settings that marked much of his adulthood. After studying medicine in the abolitionist bastion of Philadelphia, the nineteen-year-old Walker spent the next two years (1843–45) in Europe, where he came to admire its brand of liberal imperialism as well as the democratic ideals that would drive the revolutions of 1848.[11]

That Walker's European sojourn greatly impacted his outlook becomes evident in his 1848–50 journalistic work for the *New Orleans Crescent*. A good example is his last editorial, which valorized the Old World's liberal principles (democracy, free trade, and "a more perfect and equitable social organization") but also stressed that "the people of the United States" had much to learn from European efforts to forge overseas settler colonies.[12] In fact Walker insisted that Manifest Destiny expansion by sea go hand in hand with that of the European powers. With the defeat of the 1848 revolutions, however, he believed that it fell to the United States to convert "the world to democracy."[13] And by "democracy" he meant not just republican rule and universal male suffrage but also the destruction of the privileges enjoyed by the "aristocrats" then ruling Europe and, in his mind, Latin America. It was this prodemocracy discourse that Walker invoked in explaining why the United States was destined to conquer the entire western hemisphere.

In 1850 Walker moved to California, where he continued to champion the liberal imperialism he had encountered in Europe. But the Golden State also turned him into a filibuster. Walker was inspired by the example of Count Gaston de Raousset-Boulbon, a veteran of the French colonization of Algeria who in 1852 led a failed invasion of French gold rushers against the Mexican state of Sonora under a banner of civilization and freedom.[14] A year later Walker sought to replicate the count's expedition with about two hundred U.S. adventurers. He even tried to entice Boulbon to join forces with him, to no avail.[15] Like the count, Walker aimed to create a private settler colony in a frontier region known for its gold and silver mines. He too failed miserably, with his group often on the run and enjoying little local support. The fiasco nonetheless turned him into a well-known filibuster—a fame that helps explain why he ended up in Nicaragua a year later. By then Walker had come to deem Central America a more propitious place for his imperial dreams.

If most U.S. filibusters were invaders, Walker and his men were invited to Nicaragua by leaders of its Liberal Party. His group was to help Liberals win the civil war they were waging against the ruling Conservatives; in exchange, the filibusters were promised vast tracts of uncultivated land. This offer reflected the long-standing desire of Liberals to promote the "Americanization" of their country, with many even hoping that Nicaragua would join the United States as a free state. (Central America had abolished slavery in 1824.) The recent U.S. conquest of Mexico's northern half hardly dampened Liberals' valorization of the "northern colossus" as their model state. On the contrary, they hoped even more strongly that U.S. annexation would both end the civil wars plaguing Nicaragua since independence and lead to the construction of a canal that would make their country "the emporium of the world."[16] Their pro-Americanism was reinforced by the California Gold Rush, which led thousands of U.S. adventurers to cross the isthmus. This transit became especially popular after the New York tycoon Cornelius Vanderbilt inaugurated his Nicaragua Line in 1851. While some U.S. travelers antagonized Nicaraguans, most fascinated the local population with what we now call the American Way of Life—an infatuation that helps explain why Walker's enterprise enjoyed local support.[17]

Yet Walker also profited from Nicaraguans' recent encounter with European liberal imperialists. Although Europeans had long sought to create private settler colonies in the region, such projects proliferated only after the Gold Rush drew as much attention to the isthmus as it had attracted in the seventeenth century. Reinforcing this boom was the anti-immigrant wave then sweeping the United States, for it pushed European colonization agents to train their eyes on Central America, which they deemed more welcoming. The Nicaraguan government signed contracts with French and German colonization companies seeking to create farming colonies in the country's frontier regions.[18] Nicaraguan officials eagerly courted these companies in the hope that the Europeans would bring "civilization" with them. Although none of the colonization projects was realized, they served as precursors for Walker's Department of Colonization, which organized the influx of U.S. settlers and whose leading members included Nicaraguans previously invested in European colonization.

European colonization projects also benefited Walker directly, as some of its members helped shape his enterprise. None was more critical to his fortunes than Bruno von Natzmer, a former officer in the Prussian Army. In 1851 the twenty-year-old aristocrat emigrated to Costa Rica with the Berlin Colonization Society for Central America, which was led by Baron Alexander von Bülow, a prominent exponent of the liberal imperialism then emerging in Germany.[19] Not by chance, then, did his society justify its colonization scheme by claiming that it was not only strengthening German influence abroad but also spreading "civilization" to nonwhite peoples.[20] Bülow's group planned for four thousand German families to join them each year, so that within twenty-five years their colony would have about half a million settlers. Their dream quickly clashed with reality, however, and the colony folded within a few years. While most colonists settled in the capital of San José, Natzmer joined the Costa Rican Army. In February 1855 he fled to Nicaragua to avoid trial for having embezzled money from his troops. When Walker arrived a few months later with fifty-nine filibusters, Natzmer was among the first to join his ranks and quickly became one of his most trusted intermediaries with Nicaraguans.[21]

Walker later wrote that he esteemed Natzmer for his military training, local knowledge, and ability to speak Spanish, English, and French.[22] But the Prussian also helped infuse Walker's project with German notions of settler colonialism that were more secular and cosmopolitan than those upheld by his U.S. followers, many of whom promoted a U.S.-centered vision of democracy embedded in the Protestant religiosity driving the country's Second Great Awakening. Indeed some Central Americans deemed the German civilizing mission more inclusive than Manifest Destiny, even if the latter had a stronger prodemocracy discourse. As Bülow's Costa Rican friends noted, German colonists were "more supple . . . than Yankees."[23] The adaptability of Europeans like Natzmer would prove valuable to Walker as he sought to consolidate his rule after seizing power in October 1855.

Walker's Liberal Empire

Thanks to local support, Walker became the only U.S. filibuster to rule a Latin American country. By the time a Central American army ousted Walker's group in May 1857, about twelve thousand U.S. colonists had settled in his realm, lured by the promise of rich mines and land bonanzas.[24] But even as Nicaragua filled up with the newcomers, Walker's rule continued to rest on Nicaraguans who hailed from all walks of life. What united them was their assumption that the foreigners were spreading U.S.-style democracy and progress. In hindsight, that idea seems unfathomable, for Walker's enterprise ended in a proslavery nightmare that brought unprecedented destruction to the isthmus. Yet Walker issued his slavery decree only toward the end of his rule, when the tide of the war began to turn against him. Moreover, his regime took no steps to implement the decree, leading many Nicaraguans to believe that it was merely a ploy to obtain funds from U.S. slaveholders.[25] The project that the Walker regime advanced with the greatest force was instead the liberal empire it pursued at the height of its power—an empire that was to span all of Central America.

The liberal bent of Walker's enterprise led prodemocracy reformers to join his ranks. This was true of his main Nicaraguan allies: upwardly mobile Liberal mulattoes struggling to forge a more democratic order against the ruling Conservative Party "aristocrats," who tended to self-identify as white. In particular, Walker came to depend on José María Valle, a popular caudillo (strongman) of humble origins whom local elites deemed a dangerous "communist" for having led the failed popular uprisings that shook the country in the late 1840s.[26] Like other Nicaraguan radicals, Valle justified his support for Walker by claiming that both were fighting for "true democracy."[27] Walker's liberal image also compelled prodemocracy adherents from the United States to flock to his realm. Among the most fascinating was Sarah Pellet, a fiery suffragist, temperance lecturer, and abolitionist who had worked with leading antebellum reformers such as Frederick Douglass, William Lloyd Garrison, and Lucy Stone. After spending two months in Nicaragua, Pellet returned to the United States, where she gave countless speeches defending Walker's efforts to spread "liberty."[28] Her message was echoed by his U.S. followers and his bilingual newspaper, *El Nicaraguense*, which was published in the filibuster capital of Granada.

Perhaps nothing better underscores local support for Walker's liberal project than the refusal of most Nicaraguans to support the Costa Rican invasion of April 1856. Fearing that Walker's group wanted to "seize all of Central America, exterminate its population and populate it with Yankees," Costa Rica invaded his realm with the expectation that Nicaraguans would rise up against the filibusters.[29] Yet few locals rallied to the Costa Ricans' cause, while Nicaraguan Liberal Party members helped Walker's men withstand the invaders. Costa Rican officials explained away their lack of local support by claiming that Walker had struck such fear into Nicaraguans that they not only were paralyzed but also considered the foreigners to be invincible.[30] A more honest assessment came from one of South America's most influential newspapers, *El Comercio* of Lima, Peru, which moaned that, even though "nobody believes it," Nicaraguans insisted that Walker's men were "universal patriots who had come to Nicaragua to civilize and moralize it."[31]

Much of Walker's local support rested on the promise of development that he and the U.S. colonists represented to Nicaraguans. At the heart of his rule stood a modernization project that has been eclipsed by the havoc his group would later wreak. Its most grandiose plan was to enable ocean steamers to cross the isthmus by constructing a railroad that would link both coasts. Unlike previous canal projects, the regime sought to create an interoceanic route that did not simply serve foreign shipping companies but would also provide local producers with better access to overseas markets. In addition, the regime undertook great efforts to develop the rural economy. While it prioritized the agro-export economy, it did not neglect the sector geared toward the internal market. The regime's modernization zeal also targeted urban centers, as when it sought to create a "new Granada" on undeveloped land.

Lack of funds and warfare prevented the Walker regime from realizing much of its modernization project. Still, it did enough to maintain Nicaraguans' confidence in its promise of development. The most noticeable outcomes were the rebuilding of war-torn towns and interdepartmental roads as well as the construction of new wharves. Yet the most enduring outcome consisted of land surveys and maps. These seemingly mundane tasks were key instruments of statecraft during the nineteenth century and greatly promoted economic development.[32] If Walker's surveyors first focused on frontier regions deemed most appropriate for colonization, they eventually moved to the country's most populated regions. Their work was cut short in September 1856, when a Guatemalan-Salvadoran invasion force reignited the Central American war. The German surveyors nonetheless produced the hitherto best topographical map of Nicaragua, which served as its official map until the first decades of the twentieth century.[33]

Like most modernization projects, that of Walker created tensions within local society. It ensured that thousands of U.S. settlers would make the journey to Nicaragua. And since those colonists seemingly embodied U.S. entrepreneurialism and innovation, they reinforced the faith of many Nicaraguans in Walker's promise of development. But if his modernization project helped shore up his support among ordinary Nicaraguans, it antagonized local elites, especially those afraid of losing farmland as a result of the surveys. These tensions broke out into the open in July 1856, when Walker launched his self-proclaimed revolution following the failed Costa Rican invasion.

As with most liberal revolutions of the era, Walker's sought to democratize the political system. Although this process led to his seizure of the presidency via a rigged election, it did introduce the direct vote. By shifting power from elite-dominated electoral colleges to communal authorities, the filibuster revolution gave popular sectors a new means with which to challenge elite power. Perhaps this helps explain why Walker retained the support of Valle and other local radicals fighting for democracy. These Nicaraguans helped radicalize the filibuster revolution by spearheading the confiscation of elite-owned estates. While they aimed to have the confiscation campaign benefit the rural poor, Walker wanted U.S. colonists to acquire the seized properties. The tension between both goals further destabilized the filibuster regime. Another source of tension was the regime's crusade to improve the "social virtues" and "moral duties" of the local masses by promoting antivagrancy laws, public hygiene, and temperance.[34] While U.S. reformers and elite Nicaraguans maintained that moral uplift was key to empowering the poor, their uplifting efforts reflected their condescension toward the poor and an unspoken desire to control them. Small wonder that Walker's revolution engendered much violence that contributed to his downfall.

European Underpinnings

The violence that marred the end of Walker's reign ensured that he and his men would be forever remembered as destroyers and plunderers. Their most infamous act was to burn Granada—one of the hemisphere's oldest cities—to the ground. But to reduce their enterprise to wanton violence would be to ignore how Walker's followers had sought to create a state capable of bringing about material progress. In many ways, their modernization efforts resembled those carried out by liberal regimes elsewhere in Latin America. The regime's focus on internal improvements and moral betterment also echoed the American System championed by the U.S. statesman Henry Clay and his Whig Party. According to El Nicaraguense, however, Walker's modernization project drew its greatest inspiration from European liberal imperialism. Even his transformation into the much acclaimed "Gray-Eyed Man of Destiny," who was to liberate Nicaraguan Indians from their local oppressors, built on a legend invented in the 1830s by British imperialists eyeing Nicaragua's Caribbean coast.[35]

Time and again, *El Nicaraguense* cited European cases to underscore that Walker's budding empire represented a broader trend in human history. While the paper followed many other antebellum expansionists in drawing on the ancient Greeks and Romans to justify Walker's imperial enterprise, its main models were contemporary forms of European expansion. It invoked the Russian case to show that the ideology of Manifest Destiny was not unique to the United States. Accordingly, the idea of "manifest destiny" was driving Russia's recent expansion, as evident in the Crimean War of 1853–56. By equating U.S. and Russian expansion, the paper could maintain that "all conquest comes from the North Southward, and will retain that direction until the mission of humanity is complete."[36] *El Nicaraguense*'s favorable view of Russian expansionism reflected the cultural affinity between two expanding continental empires.[37]

Still, the paper's main models were the sea-based empires that the British and the French had recently forged in Asia and Africa. It claimed that a key purpose of Walker's movement was to bolster the efforts of these European empires to civilize world regions that were populated by nonwhite races. Valorizing "the good that has always followed the expansive policy of France and Great Britain," *El Nicaraguense* insisted that the Walker regime was seeking nothing more than "the same path of regeneration in Central America, which has been productive of so much benefit in India, Africa, and islands of the sea, under the impulse of European expansion." It highlighted the economic benefits that the world would derive from such imperial cooperation: "The regeneration of Spanish America throws open to the communication and commerce of the world, twenty-five millions of people. . . . It brings into the market millions of acres of land adapted to the cultivation of the necessaries and luxuries of life, and thus cheapens living. . . . With cheap living famine is banished, and revolution goes with it. These are the fruits we promise to work out for Europe."[38] Political stability via free trade, the development of agro-export economies, moral uplift, and other liberal reforms—all these things, as *El Nicaraguense* stressed, linked Walker's project with the civilizing mission of European empires.

The filibuster paper clearly showcased these connections for strategic reasons. Above all, it sought to discourage the European powers from supporting the Central American war against Walker. In addition, the paper sought to bolster the regime's efforts to obtain European funding for its expensive modernization project. *El Nicaraguense* defended this courting of "the capitalists of Europe" by asserting, "We require a ship canal and certain railroads—we must have quartz machines and saw mills—all of which the State is too poor to build, and we must therefore solicit the aid of foreigners." And since Old World capital had helped fuel the recent expansion of the U.S. transport system, Walker's paper wondered, "Why should we not go direct to Europe?"[39]

Yet the connections that *El Nicaraguense* drew between Walker's imperial project and those of European powers also reflected actual similarities. If Walker's U.S. followers often claimed that his project was modeled after the expanding U.S. state, in reality his polity resembled more the overseas colonies of the British and the French, especially in its dependency on local collaborators. This similarity responded to the basic fact that both Walker's colonists and most European imperialists remained vastly outnumbered by the local population, whereas U.S. westward expansion entailed the rapid and massive immigration of settlers into sparsely settled regions.

Walker and other U.S. members of his regime valorized the European model precisely because they opposed Nicaragua's annexation to the United States. They knew that the incorporation of a large Catholic and nonwhite population into the Union would be fiercely opposed by U.S. nativists grouped in the powerful Know-Nothing Party. In addition, the escalating conflict over slavery's expansion into "Bleeding Kansas" made this an inopportune moment to seek annexation of another territory that might become a battleground between pro- and antislavery forces. But above all, annexation would have deprived Walker and his followers of their autonomy, for the history of U.S. continental expansion had shown them that annexed territories quickly came under the control of federal officials who ruled in a heavy-handed manner. In opposing annexation, Walker and his followers drew on the Jeffersonian idea of expansion, which called for U.S. colonists to create republics that would remain independent of the United States.[40] Just as important, they invoked the European path of expansion, which in their eyes promised greater self-rule than U.S. annexation.[41] For these reasons, the *New York Herald* contended that the Central American "countries cannot be brought into our Union. They can only be governed as India is governed."[42]

The *Herald* was hardly alone in claiming that Walker was forging a "new Indian empire" in Central America. Other U.S. observers believed that his regime would replicate the corporate empire that the British East India Company had carved out in India. After all, Walker's rise to power had been facilitated by U.S. agents of Vanderbilt's shipping company, which, thanks to its control of the Nicaraguan transit, exerted great influence over the country's affairs. Hence the *New York Herald* claimed that "the true North American policy in Central America is the successful British expedient of the East Indian Company."[43] Yet Walker proved to be anything but the pawn of Vanderbilt's company. In fact he confiscated all of its properties in Nicaragua—a brazen act that turned the tycoon into one of Walker's fiercest enemies.

Walker's regime was more bent on following the settler colonial path that the British and the French were then pursuing in places as different as Australia and Algeria. It created a Department of Colonization that was led by a scion of a Massachusetts family with old trading ties to the French colony of Guiana. In recruiting colonists and helping them settle in Nicaragua, the department built on the work of private Belgian, British, French, and German colonization companies that had previously sought to forge farming colonies in Central America. While the department focused its recruiting efforts in the United States, it also contacted European colonization agents as it was eager to have the Old World's "pauper population" migrate to Walker's realm.[44] Some agents were businessmen, such as Dr. Käsmann of Bremen (a leading port of emigration), who signed a contract pledging to send a "mass" of German colonists to Nicaragua.[45] Others were radical liberals who deemed Walker a kindred spirit, as was true of the Swiss physician Wilhelm Joos, who had participated in the French Revolution of 1848 and sought to establish a farming colony of five hundred Swiss families in the isthmus.[46] While the Central American war cut short the schemes of Käsmann and Joos, their cases highlight the European underpinnings of Walker's colonization project.

The filibuster army was another state institution that benefited from the imperial experience of Europeans. As one British observer noted, the filibuster chieftain attracted many "Frenchmen who had fought in Algeria [and] Englishmen who have been in our own artillery in the Crimea."[47] Some of Walker's soldiers had even more far-flung combat experiences, as was true of a veteran of the British war against the Xhosa in southern Africa and another who had fought in the Bengal Army of the British East India Company.[48] So great was Walker's trust in European imperial warriors that he handed over the army's command to the British-born Charles Frederick Henningsen, who had participated in the Russian campaign against Muslim tribes in the Caucasus.[49] Henningsen used his European military training to ensure that the filibusters became a better organized force, yet he could not prevent their ultimate defeat at the hands of a massive Central American military coalition.

The European influence on Walker's enterprise was further evident in the medical realm. A good example is the Jewish surgeon Israel Moses, who took charge of Walker's Medical Department and spearheaded the regime's public health campaign.[50] During his four-month stint in Nicaragua, the native New Yorker founded a military hospital, carried out medical experiments, devised vaccines to combat smallpox, and improved sanitary conditions in urban centers. As Walker's chief medical officer, Moses drew on the experiences of British and French army surgeons as well as on research conducted by European scientists on tropical diseases.[51] Much of his public health campaign focused on curbing the cholera epidemic then wreaking havoc in Walker's realm. Moses followed his European colleagues in believing that cholera was spread less by contagion than by unsanitary conditions, especially in poor neighborhoods. Hence his sanitary measures, too, targeted the lifestyle of the urban masses.

U.S. evangelical reformers in Walker's ranks also reinforced the European features of his liberal project. This was especially true of those whose outlook was shaped by the British missionary understanding of empire.[52] The activism of Walker's perhaps most outspoken reformer—the Massachusetts native Sarah Pellet—owed much to her education at Oberlin College, a Protestant hotbed of reform with long-standing missions in the British colonies of Jamaica and Sierra Leone.[53] The largest group of moral reformers in Walker's Nicaragua consisted of the military and civilian colonists who founded a chapter of the Sons of Temperance in Granada.[54] Then the main temperance society in the United States, the Sons had become increasingly connected with British settler colonialism, as evident in their recent expansion to Australia and Canada.[55] Even the chaplain of Walker's army (Reverend George May) had strong European ties: not only was he born in England but his father was trained at a British missionary college and later became pastor of New York City's Dutch Reformed Church, whose parent institution was deeply involved in Dutch overseas colonization.[56] Not surprisingly, Walker's realm also attracted Protestant missionaries. Among those most in contact with Nicaraguans was the Methodist David Wheeler, who had long worked for the American Bible Society in South America.[57] Ever since its founding in 1816, this New York–based organization had collaborated with the British and Foreign Bible Society to spread its liberal brand of evangelicalism across the globe.[58]

A diverse group of largely northern and antislavery reformers thus drew not just on U.S. traditions but also on European, especially British, imperial practices to help the Walker regime combat public immorality (drunkenness, gambling, promiscuity) and promote public health, education, and Protestantism.[59] Yet because they championed the Anglo-Saxon race as the "great moral redeemer of the world" that was destined to "control or absorb the entire human family," their moral crusade led the filibuster regime to more greatly emphasize racial differences between U.S. colonists and Nicaraguans.[60] If this differentiation was integral to Anglo-American liberal imperialism, it was also the backdrop for Walker's most notorious illiberal act: the relegalization of slavery.

Given Walker's current proslavery infamy, it is striking that his regime sought to emulate indentured labor systems identified with Europe's main antislavery powers: Great Britain and France. Those who knew Walker in Nicaragua were probably right to believe that his decree relegalizing slavery was a desperate gamble to appease two rival U.S. groups whose support he urgently needed as his rule began to crumble: wealthy slaveholders bent on torpedoing transatlantic efforts to encircle the South with antislavery polities, and those seeking to rid the United States of both slavery and its black population. For *El Nicaraguense*, the more viable solution to the problem of labor scarcity lay in the import of Chinese and Indian "coolies" (indentured workers), who were deemed not only productive and cheap but also "peculiarly adapted to the climate of Central America."[61] This was the solution that Great Britain had embraced to address the labor shortage plaguing its Caribbean colonies following the Slavery Abolition Act of 1833. In addition, Walker's regime urged France to bring from its African colonies "apprentices to the ports of Nicaragua, thus furnishing labor to the latter republic, and increasing the trade of French ships."[62] Both the coolie and apprenticeship systems marked European liberal imperialism of the era as they were forms of indentured servitude created under the guise of free labor. Walker's willingness to embrace them only bolstered the U.S. view that his Central American enterprise was "our Indian empire."

Of course, Walker's liberal project also departed from its European counterparts. Most palpably, the world-famous "king of filibusters" was poor at coaxing the U.S. government into supporting his venture. True, President Franklin Pierce, whose attorney general called Walker "a monomaniac, buccaneer, robber, and pirate," eventually granted diplomatic recognition to the filibuster regime—an act that greatly facilitated the flow of U.S. recruits and arms to Walker's realm.[63] In addition, the presence of U.S. warships in Nicaraguan ports undermined the Central American war against Walker and ensured that the filibusters were granted lenient surrender terms on May 1, 1857. Yet such state support paled to that enjoyed by private European imperial ventures of the era. If pro-Walker U.S. newspapers lamented that their hero did not receive the kind of aid that the British Crown was offering to the East India Company, a more appropriate example would be James Brooke, who had been ruling the Asian kingdom of Sarawak in Borneo since 1842 with the support of the British government and whose efforts to spread "civilization" to "the most perfidious, blood-thirsty and untractable of the native tribes" had impressed Walker well before he became a filibuster.[64]

For *El Nicaraguense*, however, the main difference separating Walker's republican empire from Europe's monarchic empires was that the former sought to spread democracy, while the latter did not.[65] Indeed British and French imperialism of the era excluded most colonized peoples from political participation, whereas the Walker regime sought to create a more democratic system that, in theory, gave unprecedented rights to the Nicaraguan masses. Walker even ordered his settler colonists to become Nicaraguan citizens. This peculiar form of imperial citizenship was undercut by filibuster racism but also presumed that Walker's U.S. colonists would ultimately constitute the majority of the population. Another key difference lies in the revolutionary thrust of Walker's project. If Great Britain and France tended to rule with the support of entrenched elites, the Walker regime unleashed a revolution against the local elite—mainly estate owners and rich merchants—in the name of the poor. This revolution failed miserably to bring freedom and equality to the masses. Still, the prospect of revolutionary change led many poor Nicaraguans to long maintain their faith in Walker.

Walker's Forty-Eighters

The filibuster revolution was spearheaded by Nicaraguan radicals of humble origins, such as Valle. But it was also driven by radical Europeans who were among the many non-U.S. natives in Walker's movement. About a third of the nearly twelve thousand U.S. residents who migrated to Nicaragua were born in Europe—a figure nearly three times larger than the foreign-born share of the U.S. population.[66] Moreover many had fought in the liberal revolutions of 1848. And it was these so-called Forty-Eighters and like-minded émigrés who greatly enhanced the liberal thrust of Walker's imperial enterprise.

Walker attracted many European liberals because they deemed him a kindred spirit. A number of Forty-Eighters in the United States certainly opposed the filibuster chieftain, denouncing him as a tool of the "slave oligarchy."[67] Yet many others viewed his enterprise as part of the global struggle that democrats were then waging against aristocrats who, as a pro-Walker Irish Forty-Eighter put it, "beggared, bled and starved the people."[68] One such émigré was the Swiss socialist Karl Bürkli, who would later play a prominent role in the First International. After failing to create a Fourierist colony near Dallas, Texas, Bürkli left for Nicaragua in January 1856, hoping it would be a better place for a "social democratic state."[69] Bürkli claimed to have been enticed by Walker's embrace of "socialist ideas" during his 1844 stay in Paris.[70]

That radical expatriates adopted Walker's cause had much to do with their belief that democracy was universal and could be spread by force. To be sure, nearly all émigré societies in the United States were organized along national lines and designed to rekindle the revolutionary struggle in their homelands. In consequence, groups ranging from the German Socialist Turners and French La Montagne to the Irishmen's Union, the Italian and Polish democratic societies, and the Fraternity of Hungarian and Slavic Exiles created their own militias to prepare themselves for the upcoming struggle. But just as the 1848 revolutions in Europe were interlinked, most émigré societies based in the United States collaborated with each other. They publicized their internationalism by jointly marching in street parades, waving the red flag that stood for "the solidarity and fraternity of nations," and singing the era's leading revolutionary hymn, "La Marseillaise."[71]

Initially their crusade for "universal democracy" targeted the monarchies that ruled Europe. By 1855 their revolutionary hopes had dimmed, as the old regimes proved more resilient than expected. Walker's conquest gave the émigrés' sagging spirits an unexpected boost, and many headed south in order to liberate the Central American masses from the yoke of local "aristocracies." Their first recorded departure occurred on February 25, 1856, when about one hundred French and German exiles sailed from New York.[72] Two days later another group left from New Orleans. Both groups sang "La Marseillaise" as they entered Walker's realm.[73] Liberal European émigrés continued to flock to Nicaragua until news of Walker's proslavery decree reached U.S. soil. Among the last to go were the more than one hundred French, Irish, German, and Polish émigrés who left New York on September 12, 1856, and the slightly smaller party of French and German exiles who departed from San Francisco a week later.[74]

These European émigrés served the filibuster regime in various ways. Some provided critical financial support, as was the case of the Granada-based merchant and banker George Beschor, a German Jew who had commanded revolutionary forces in Saxony.[75] Other Forty-Eighters furthered Walker's project of settler colonialism by taking their families with them and establishing new businesses in Nicaragua. Yet others strengthened Walker's enterprise by joining his army. They brought much military experience with them, for many had waged revolutionary warfare in their homelands. Few émigrés proved more important to Walker than the German officers who had served in monarchic armies before switching sides in 1848. Especially valuable were those who knew how to handle technologically sophisticated weapons, as was true of Adolph Schwartz, who led Walker's artillery division. This well-educated German typified the Forty-Eighters in Walker's ranks. Trained as an engineer, Schwartz had been an artillery lieutenant in the Army of the Grand Duchy of Baden when the revolution broke out. Like other junior officers, the then twenty-year-old joined the Revolutionary Army of Baden.[76] Following the revolution's defeat,

Schwartz moved to New York, where he worked as an architect and married a Baden native. In February 1856 Schwartz left his wife and two young children to join other exiles headed for Nicaragua.[77]

The case of Schwartz illustrates how European Forty-Eighters were critical to Walker's modernization agenda. He was part of a German-led group that carried out the all-important land surveys.[78] Their leader was the engineer Maximilian von Sonnenstern, a longtime officer in the Army of the King of Württemberg who was forced to migrate to the United States for participating in the revolution of 1848.[79] The other members of his surveying team were all German Forty-Eighters: they included the civil engineers Eugene Hesse and Max Ströbel, both of whom had recently worked for survey parties in the U.S. West.[80] Sonnenstern's reports reveal that he strongly supported the modernizing agenda of the filibuster regime. He also shared Walker's goal of promoting the region's colonization by European and U.S. immigrants, claiming that Nicaraguans were "not capable of improving this splendid country" and thus needed the influx of "an industrious and active population."[81]

Sonnenstern and Schwartz were among the many European radicals who had no qualms about championing Walker's imperial mission. That French émigrés would support Walker's endeavor should not surprise us. After all, the filibuster's goal of creating an empire in the name of civilization and democracy echoed the way French liberals and socialists had justified partaking in their country's brutal colonization of Algeria.[82] Yet even Forty-Eighters from Europe's nonimperial powers had long been committed imperialists. This was true of the largest group of liberal émigrés to join Walker: German expatriates. In 1848 many German revolutionaries had called for the creation of overseas settler colonies, especially in Latin America.[83] In their eyes, such colonies were essential to both the formation of liberal, democratic nations and the spread of "civilization" to the non-European world. They also invoked Manifest Destiny to argue that settler colonialism could promote democracy.[84] After the German revolutionaries fled to the United States, they maintained their belief in the need to spread democracy by force. They continued to advocate for overseas colonialism, albeit now as private, not state-sponsored undertakings—the very kind of imperial venture that Walker sought to realize in Central America.

If European radicals in Walker's ranks reinforced the revolutionary nature of his project, they strengthened its cosmopolitan thrust as well. And this was not just because they were non-U.S. natives but also because they challenged some of Manifest Destiny's most ingrained ideas. They tended to view U.S. expansion as a secular phenomenon and thus rejected the evangelical Protestantism espoused by many of Walker's U.S.-born followers, especially those affiliated with the moral reform movements then engulfing the United States.[85] Equally important, these European radicals did not follow most white U.S. expansionists in denigrating Latin America's mixed races. On the contrary, some even claimed that such "mixing of race" produced racial "greatness."[86] As a result, Walker's European radicals believed more strongly in granting political rights to the Central American masses than was typically the case with his U.S. followers. As much as these Europeans identified with the prodemocracy discourse and universalizing impulses of Manifest Destiny, they tended to have a more cosmopolitan view of it.

This view reflected the way Forty-Eighters had originally considered the United States to be a culturally plural nation, one that valorized both the Americanization of immigrants and the cultures of non-Anglo-Saxon whites.[87] Not surprisingly, their positive view of the United States changed after the Know-Nothing Party burst on the scene in the early 1850s. They now feared that the United States had come under the spell of bellicose nativists. Many went to Nicaragua in the belief that Walker's realm would be a better place to achieve a more inclusive form of Americanization. Ironically, then, the anticosmopolitan turn of antebellum society led Walker—the era's most famous agent of Manifest Destiny—to pursue an imperial project that was unusually cosmopolitan.

The cosmopolitan bent of Walker's enterprise would later be obscured by the violent authoritarianism marking the end of his Nicaraguan reign and his subsequent evolution into the U.S. South's main symbol of slavery expansion. But no matter how greatly Walker's antiliberal turn shocked his radical European supporters, some continued to believe in the viability of his original liberal project. As the prominent German Forty-Eighter Julius Fröbel asserted, had Walker stuck to his Free Soil program, his "federation of regenerated states of Hispanic-American origins . . . would have soon included Mexico and perhaps even California"—a federation in which, so Fröbel insisted, European liberal émigrés would have played a leading role.[88]

Conclusion

The European underpinnings of Walker's Nicaraguan enterprise suggests that a transimperial approach can help us more fully place the study of U.S. imperialism in world history. It is not enough to simply embed U.S. imperialism in a global context; we also need to trace the circulation of people, ideas, and things across distinct imperial terrains. Only by considering this circulation can we understand how Walker's European radicals sought to reshape Manifest Destiny's mission to redeem the world—and why U.S. liberal imperialism thus began as a more cosmopolitan and revolutionary undertaking than commonly assumed.

But as we extend transnational analysis to imperial formations, we need to be mindful of the selective ways in which rival empires seek to learn from each other. What is so telling about the connection that Walker's U.S. supporters made between his empire and British India is their refusal to see the similarities between the wars waged against both entities. The anti-imperial struggles in question were the Central American war that culminated in the expulsion of Walker's group in 1857 and the Indian Rebellion of the same year. Perhaps it was just a coincidence that both struggles took place at the same time. It is nonetheless revealing that they targeted empires that, in the eyes of Walker's supporters, enjoyed many commonalities. Unlike Walker's group, the British survived the anti-imperial revolt of 1857, partly by vigorously discussing the shortcomings of their own civilizing mission.[89] In sharp contrast, Walker's downfall did not fuel a public debate in the United States over the dismal failure of his largely northern followers to establish an antislavery "empire of liberty" in Nicaragua.

This U.S. refusal to reckon with the Walker episode would help doom the efforts of President Abraham Lincoln to solve the race and slavery questions fueling the Civil War by sending over four million African American settlers to Central America.[90] Lincoln's colonization scheme was famously lambasted by free blacks in the United States. But just as damaging was Central American hostility.[91] With Walker fresh in their minds, Central Americans shuddered when Lincoln's fellow Republicans stressed that the African American colonists would turn the isthmus into "our India."[92]

Just as recognizing the importance of transimperial connections can help us place U.S. imperialism in global context, so can keeping a close eye on events on the ground. Along with European precedents, principles, and personnel, local perspectives remain indispensable for grasping the nature, limits, and perils of U.S. efforts to impose its "great experiment of liberty" on other peoples.[93] Together, looking out and in reveals that American liberal imperialism has never been as exclusively American as it might seem.

NOTES

1. A different version of this essay is published in Michel Gobat, *Empire by Invitation: William Walker and Manifest Destiny in Central America* (Cambridge, MA: Harvard University Press, 2018). I am extremely grateful to Kristin Hoganson and Jay Sexton for their very helpful comments. Funding for this project was provided by the National Endowment for the Humanities (FA-54152-0), the University of Iowa Faculty Scholar Program, and the American Council of Learned Societies.

2. For a recent example, see Stephen Kinzer, *The True Flag: Theodore Roosevelt, Mark Twain, and the Birth of American Empire* (New York: Henry Holt, 2017).

3. See especially Jennifer Pitts, *A Turn to Empire: The Rise of Imperial Liberalism in Britain and France* (Princeton, NJ: Princeton University Press, 2005).

4. On U.S. filibusterism, see Robert May, *Manifest Destiny's Underworld: Filibustering in Antebellum America* (Chapel Hill: University of North Carolina Press, 2002); Amy Greenberg, *Manifest Manhood and the Antebellum American Empire* (Cambridge, U.K.: Cambridge University Press, 2005).

5. Janice Thomson, *Mercenaries, Pirates, and Sovereigns: State-Building and Extraterritorial Violence in Early Modern Europe* (Princeton, NJ: Princeton University Press, 1994).

6. E.g., Robert May, *The Southern Dream of a Caribbean Empire, 1854–1861* (Baton Rouge: Louisiana State University Press, 1973); Walter Johnson, *River of Dark Dreams: Slavery and Empire in the Cotton Kingdom* (Cambridge, MA: Harvard University Press, 2013).

7. William Walker, *The War in Nicaragua* (Mobile, AL: Goetzel, 1860).

8. "The New International Policy of the Four Great Powers of the World," *New York Herald*, June 2, 1857.

9. "The Nicaragua Meeting To-Night—Our Indian Empire and Directory," *New York Herald*, December 20, 1856; "Our India," *Boston Daily Atlas*, April 2, 1857; "Del 'Herald' de Nueva York," *Mercurio* (Valparaiso, Chile), April 15, 1857; "General Walker und die Filibusters in Central-Amerika," *Die Gartenlaube* (Leipzig, Saxony) 31 (1856): 41.

10. Ann Laura Stoler, "Tense and Tender Ties: The Politics of Comparison in North American History and (Post) Colonial Studies," *Journal of American History* 88, no. 3 (2001): 863.

11. For biographies of Walker, see Alejandro Bolaños Geyer, *William Walker: The Gray-Eyed Man of Destiny*, 5 vols. (Lake Saint Louis, MO: privately printed, 1988–91); Albert Carr, *The World and William Walker* (New York: Harper and Row, 1963).

12. "England and Her Colonies," *New Orleans Daily Crescent*, January 31, 1850.

13. "Foreign Policy of This Country," *New Orleans Daily Crescent*, October 10, 1849.

14. Delia González de Reufels, *Siedler und Filibuster in Sonora: Eine mexikanische Region im Interesse ausländischer Abenteurer und Mächte (1821–1860)* (Cologne, Germany: Böhlau Verlag, 2003), 140–41.

15. Bolaños Geyer, *William Walker*, 2:198.

16. No title, *Correo del Istmo* (León, Nicaragua), May 1, 1849.

17. On the Gold Rush's impact on Nicaragua, see Miguel Angel Herrera C., *Bongos, bogas, vapores y marinos: Historia de los "marineros" del río San Juan, 1849–1855* (Managua: Centro Nicaragüense de Escritores, 1999); Frances Kinloch Tijerino, *Nicaragua: Identidad y Cultura Política (1821–1858)* (Managua: Banco Central de Nicaragua, 1999); Gobat, *Empire by Invitation*, 12–45.

18. Friedrich Streber to unknown, Granada, August 10, 1850, MA-Ko 1-Kolonisation, Berliner Verein zur Zentralisation deutscher Auswanderung und Kolonisation bzw. Deutsche Kolonisationsgesellschaft für Zentralamerika 1849–93, Bremen Handelskammer Archiv; Norberto Ramírez to Ephraim George Squier, León, December 16, 1850, E. G. Squier Papers, Library of Congress.

19. Matthew Fitzpatrick, *Liberal Imperialism in Germany: Expansionism and National-ism, 1848–1884* (New York: Berghahn, 2008), 61–63; Herbert Schottelius, *Mittelamerika als Schauplatz deutscher Kolonisationsversuche, 1840–1865* (Hamburg, Germany: Christians Druckerei), 1939, 66.

20. *Entwurf des Statuts der Berliner Colonisations-Gesellschaft für Central-Amerika* (Berlin: G. Bernstein, 1849), 3, MA-Ko 1, Bremen Handelskammer Archiv.

21. Moritz Wagner and Karl Scherzer, *Die Republik Costa Rica in Central-Amerika* (Leipzig, Germany: Arnoldische Buchhandlung, 1856), 181–82, 346–58; Bruno von Natzmer to Comandante General, San José, February 5, 1855, Guerra 8639, Archivo Nacional de Costa Rica, San José (hereafter ANCR).

22. Walker, *The War in Nicaragua*, 68–69.

23. Wagner and Scherzer, *Die Republik Costa Rica*, 178.

24. This estimate was provided by the company that transported the emigrants to Nicaragua; see Testimony of Joseph N. Scott, April–May 1861, p. 102, claim 1, box 1, entry 436, Costa Rican Claims Convention of July 2, 1860, Record Group 76, U.S. National Archives.

25. P. Rouhaud to Ephraim George Squier, Greytown, March 28–31, 1857, roll 3, E. G. Squier Papers, Library of Congress.

26. Bradford Burns, *Patriarch and Folk: The Emergence of Nicaragua, 1798–1858* (Cambridge, MA: Harvard University Press, 1991), 145–59; Kinloch, *Nicaragua*, 101–41.

27. "El Coronel Valle de la fuersa expedicionaría del Medio Día," *El Nicaraguense* (Granada, Nicaragua), October 27, 1855.

28. "Lecture on Nicaragua," *Savannah (GA) Daily Morning News*, May 22, 1856; "Miss Sarah Pellet's Lecture on Nicaragua," *New Orleans Daily Picayune*, April 10, 1856; "Letter from Miss Pellett [sic]," *El Nicaraguense*, April 26, 1856.

29. President Juan Rafael Mora to Edward Wallerstein, San José, February 10, 1856, Legaciones y Consulados, 000560, caja Relaciones Exteriores (hereafter RREE) 001–005, exp. 5, ANCR.

30. Costa Rican Foreign Minister to Lafond, September 11, 1856, copiadores, no. 142, RREE, ANCR.

31. "Centro-América," *El Comercio*, September 10, 1856.

32. Matthew Edney, *Mapping an Empire: The Geographical Construction of British India, 1765–1843* (Chicago: University of Chicago Press, 1997); Raymond Craig, *Cartographic Mexico: A History of State Fixations and Fugitive Landscapes* (Durham, NC: Duke University Press, 2004).

33. *Mapa de la República de Nicaragua levantado por orden del gobierno por Maximilian v. Sonnenstern 1858* (New York: Kraetzer, 1858).

34. "Educacíon," *El Nicaraguense*, July 12, 1856.

35. Gobat, *Empire by Invitation*, 7.

36. "Pansclavism and Americanism," *El Nicaraguense*, January 5, 1856.

37. George Herring, *From Colony to Superpower: U.S. Foreign Relations since 1776* (New York: Oxford University Press, 2008), 228.

38. "Europe and America," *El Nicaraguense*, July 19, 1856.

39. "Two Lines of Policy," *El Nicaraguense*, March 22, 1856.

40. Peter Onuf, *Jefferson's Empire: The Language of American Nationhood* (Charlottesville: University of Virginia Press, 2000).

41. On how the U.S. territorial system of the era was apparently even more authoritarian than the British one that caused the American Revolution, see Julian Go, *Patterns of Empire: The British and American Empires, 1688 to the Present* (Cambridge, U.K.: Cambridge University Press, 2011), 47.

42. "The Commercial Effects of the Nicaragua Movement—Our New Indian Empire," *New York Herald*, December 23, 1856.

43. "More Patchwork Central American Diplomacy," *New York Herald*, December 9, 1856.

44. "Sentiment in the U States," *El Nicaraguense*, February 16, 1856.

45. Franz Hesse to Otto von Manteuffel, Cartagena, April 2, 1856, III. MdAI Nr. 7943, Geheimes Staatsarchiv Preussischer Kulturbesitz.

46. Sylva Brunner-Hauser, *Pionier für eine menschlichere Zukunft: Dr. med. Wilhelm Joos, Nationalrat 1821–1900* (Schaffhausen, Switzerland: Meili, 1983); "Ein neuer Kolonisator von Zentralamerika," *Der Kolonist* (Lichtensteig, Switzerland), July 12, 1856; "Zur Erläuterung des Spizeartikels der letzten Nummer," *Der Kolonist*, July 19, 1856.

47. Laurence Oliphant, *Patriots and Filibusters* (Edinburgh: Blackwood, 1860), 175.

48. "Lyster, William Saurin," in *Australian Dictionary of Biography*, http://www.adb.online.anu.edu.au/biogs/A050136b.htm.

49. Charles Brown, *Agents of Manifest Destiny: The Lives and Times of the Filibusters* (Chapel Hill: University of North Carolina Press, 1980), 366–67.

50. On Moses, who in 1855 helped found the Jews Hospital in New York (today Mount Sinai Hospital), see Gobat, *Empire by Invitation*, 123–24.

51. Israel Moses, "Military Surgery and Operations Following the Battle of Rivas, Nicaragua, April, 1856," *American Journal of Medical Sciences* 33, no. 65 (1857): 34.

52. On this British influence, see Emily Conroy-Krutz, *Christian Imperialism: Converting the World in the Early American Republic* (Ithaca, NY: Cornell University Press, 2015).

53. On Pellet, see Gobat, *Empire by Invitation*, 125–27.

54. Gobat, *Empire by Invitation*, 240.

55. Donald Beattie, "Sons of Temperance: Pioneers in Total Abstinence and 'Constitutional' Prohibition," PhD diss., Boston University, 1966, 103.

56. "May (Edward Harrison)," *Johnson's New Universal Cyclopaedia* (New York: Alvin Johnson, 1880), 3:369. On the lengthy involvement of the Dutch Reformed Church in overseas colonization, see C. R. Boxer, *The Dutch Seaborne Empire: 1600–1800* (New York: Knopf, 1965), 132–54.

57. Gobat, *Empire by Invitation*, 123.

58. Rebecca Bromley, "Distribution Abroad," Historical Essay no. 15, American Bible Society Archives (New York). On how antebellum U.S. missionaries used the British Empire to spread their ideals of Christianity and civilization abroad, see Conroy-Krutz, *Christian Imperialism*.

59. On this crusade, see Gobat, *Empire by Invitation*, 236–43.

60. "Races," *El Nicaraguense*, August 2, 1856.

61. "Coolies for Costa Rica," *El Nicaraguense*, May 10, 1856. See also "What Is Needed," *El Nicaraguense*, September 13, 1856.

62. Walker, *The War in Nicaragua*, 269.

63. Caleb Cushing, quoted in John M. Belolavek, *Broken Glass: Caleb Cushing and the Shattering of the Union* (Kent, OH: Kent State University Press, 2005), 267.

64. "Rajah Brooke," *New Orleans Daily Crescent*, January 17, 1850. On Brook as an agent of British liberal imperialism, see Gareth Knapman, *Race and British Colonialism in South-East Asia, 1770–1870* (New York: Routledge, 2016), 154–78.

65. E.g., "The Issue" and "Exceptional Filibusterism," *El Nicaraguense*, May 10 and August 2, 1856.

66. Register of the Army of the Republic of Nicaragua (muster roll, January 1857–April 1857), folder 120, Callander Fayssoux Collection of William Walker Papers, Tulane University; Michael Haines, "The Population of the United States, 1790–1920," in *The Cambridge Economic History of the United States*, vol. 2: *The Long Nineteenth Century*, edited by Stanley Engerman and Robert Gallman (Cambridge, U.K.: Cambridge University Press, 2000), 156.

67. "Manifest Destiny," *Der Pionier* (New York), May 4, 1856.

68. "The Nicaragua Filibusters," *New York Herald*, February 23, 1857.

69. Hans-Ulrich Schiedt, *Die Welt neu erfinden: Karl Bürkli (1823–1901) und seine Schriften* (Zurich: Chronos Verlag, 2002), 141–43.

70. Karl Bürkli, "Die sozialistische Expedition nach Texas," *Eidgenössische Zeitung* (Zurich), September 5, 1858.

71. E.g., "Republican Festival," *New York Times*, February 25, 1854.

72. "Two Hundred Filibusters Started for Nicaragua Unmolested," *Richmond (VA) Daily Dispatch*, February 27, 1856; "Rough Sketches from My Hammock and Knapsack of Camp Life in Nicaragua," *El Nicaraguense*, March 15, 1856.

73. "Our Nicaragua Correspondence," *New York Herald*, April 12, 1856.

74. *Wisconsin Banner und Volksfreund*, April 15, 1857.

75. George Beschor, "Bombardment and Incendiary of Greytown or San Juan de Nicaragua," San Juan del Norte, September 1860, folder 19, Samuel Smith Wood Papers, Yale University.

76. Klaus Hafner, ed., *Grossherzog Leopold von Baden: 1790–1852* (Karlsruhe, Germany: Badischen Landesbibliothek, 1990), 90.

77. A. Schwartz, "Ten Months in Nicaragua," *San Francisco Pictorial Magazine* 1, no. 1 (1857): 2; "New York, State Census, 1855," Ancestry.com, http://search.ancestry.com/search /db.aspx?dbid=7181; General Order Book, folder 111, order 12, Callander Fayssoux Collection.

78. Schwartz, "Ten Months in Nicaragua," 10.

79. Götz von Houwald, "¿Quién fue Maximiliano von Sonnenstern realmente?," in *Maximiliano von Sonnenstern y el primer mapa oficial de la República de Nicaragua*, edited by Orient Bolívar Juárez (Managua, Nicaragua: INETER, 1995), 1–5.

80. Henry Barrett Learned, "William Learned Marcy," in *The American Secretaries of State and Their Diplomacy*, edited by Samuel Flagg Bemis (New York: Cooper Square, 1963), 6:245; "Letter from the Secretary of the Treasury Communicating the Report of the Superintendent of the Coast Survey, Showing the Progress of That Work during the Year Ending November, 1849," in *Index to Executive Documents Printed by Order of the Senate of the United States during the First Session of the Thirty-First Congress* (Washington,

DC: Belt, 1850), 60; "The Mexican Boundary Commission," *Daily National Intelligencer* (Washington, DC), August 7, 1850.

81. "Topographical and Geographical Notices of the Department of Leon by M. Sonnenstern," *El Nicaraguense*, August 9, 1856.

82. Naomi Andrews, "'The Universal Alliance of All Peoples': Romantic Socialists, the Human Family, and the Defense of Empire during the July Monarchy, 1830–1848," *French Historical Studies* 34, no. 3 (2011): 473–502.

83. Fitzpatrick, *Liberal Imperialism in Germany*, 27–67.

84. Jens-Uwe Guettel, *German Expansionism, Imperial Liberalism, and the United States, 1776–1945* (Cambridge, U.K.: Cambridge University Press, 2012), 43–78.

85. E.g., Julius Fröbel, *Aus Amerika* (Leipzig, Germany: Deutsche Buchhandlung, 1857), 1:506–9, 521–22.

86. Julius Fröbel, *Aus Amerika* (Leipzig, Germany: Deutsche Buchhandlung, 1858), 2:609–10.

87. Alison Clark Effort, *German Immigrants, Race, and Citizenship in the Civil War* (Cambridge, U.K.: Cambridge University Press, 2013), 32–51; Daniel Nagel, *Von republikanischen Deutschen zu deutsch-amerikanischen Republikanern: Ein Beitrag zum Identitätswandel der deutschen Achtundvierziger in den Vereinigten Staaten 1850–1861* (St. Ingbert, Germany: Röhrig Universitätsverlag, 2012), 388–402.

88. Fröbel, *Aus Amerika*, 2:613.

89. Jill Bender, *The 1857 Indian Uprising and the British Empire* (Cambridge, U.K.: Cambridge University Press, 2016).

90. Eric Foner, "Lincoln and Colonization," in *Our Lincoln: New Perspectives on Lincoln and His World*, edited by Eric Foner (New York: Norton, 2008), 135–66.

91. Thomas Schoonover, "Misconstrued Mission: Expansionism and Black Colonization in Mexico and Central America during the Civil War," *Pacific Historical Review* 49, no. 4 (1980): 607–20.

92. *Speech of Hon. F. P. Blair, Jr. of Missouri, at the Cooper Institute, New York City* (Washington, DC: Buell and Blanchard, 1860), 7–8; Robert May, *Slavery, Race, and Conquest in the Tropics: Lincoln, Douglas, and the Future of Latin America* (Cambridge, U.K.: Cambridge University Press, 2013), 184.

93. In 1845 the *United States Magazine and Democratic Review* coined the term *manifest destiny* by stressing that it was the "manifest destiny" of the United States to spread its "great experiment of liberty" abroad.

4. EMPIRE, DEMOCRACY, AND DISCIPLINE:
THE TRANSIMPERIAL HISTORY OF THE SECRET BALLOT
Julian Go

In the first decade of the twentieth century, schoolchildren across the Philippine archipelago sat in their civics classes and read about a new electoral system that American colonial officials had established in the islands. "In order that the elections may be held with speed and accuracy," instructed one textbook, "the municipalities are divided by the municipal councils into election precincts, each of which must contain not more than four hundred voters." The passage continues:

> At least sixty days before the election the council appoints in each of the election precincts a place where the election shall take place. The council must supply this place with all the furnishings necessary for the proper conduct of the election. The room where the voting is to take place must contain one voting booth for every fifty voters in the district. . . . The booths must be placed behind a guard rail. The object of the booths and guard rail is to make the ballot secret. If spectators could observe the names of the candidates for whom an elector voted they might by threats or promises try to influence him to vote contrary to his wishes.[1]

The voting procedures painstakingly described in this textbook amount to a system known as the "secret ballot" system or, as the textbook pointed out, the "Australian ballot" system. Replacing earlier methods of voting that had been done publicly, the Australian ballot system enshrined secrecy as the principle of voting. This principle is manifest in nearly every democratic state in existence today, a "global norm" for democracies.[2]

But the system was not common in the early twentieth century; it was entirely new. The few municipal elections that had been held during Spanish rule in the Philippines were public, through methods such as *viva voce*. Secret voting through the Australian ballot system was not introduced until the U.S. occupation and the first municipal elections in 1899.[3] At that time the Australian system was just beginning to spread around the world. It made its first appearance in 1856 in Australia, when the Victorian Council passed the first known law calling for secret voting (which is why it is called the "Australian ballot" system). From there it spread to other parts of Australia, to England and Europe, and to the United States. Louisville, Kentucky, was the first U.S. city to model its electoral law after it, in 1888. In 1889 Massachusetts became the first state in the Union to adopt the system. It spread throughout the country thereafter, but even by 1910, when textbooks were teaching Filipino pupils about the Australian ballot system, the states of North Carolina, South Carolina, Georgia, and the territory of New Mexico had not yet adopted it. Nor had many other countries around the world.

This is puzzling. Why the Australian ballot system? And why was it introduced to the Philippines so early? The fact that it was introduced into the Philippines at all is itself a curiosity. The colonial Philippines was part of the American Empire. American officials appointed by the U.S. president wielded complete control over the Philippine colonial state. Elections and voting are not often associated with empire and colonialism, which are about coercion and suppression, not democracy and expressions of popular will. More curious still: the Australian ballot was also instituted in other American colonies. In U.S.-occupied Puerto Rico, American officials instituted it in 1900, just as their counterparts in the Philippines were doing so. Around the same time, U.S. military officials instituted the Australian ballot system in Cuba as well.

What was going on? One way to approach this curiosity is to dig deeper into the history of the Australian ballot system itself, tracing it as a *political technology*—a sociotechnical system of materials and procedures resulting from human knowledge and meant to impact political practice.[4] In this case, then, we are dealing with a technology of modern liberal democracy, and we can treat it analytically as we might treat any other piece of technology, namely, as something with diverse genealogical origins that travels across space and time and that maintains certain basic characteristics but also acquires novel meanings and functions as it is translated into new sociopolitical contexts. Global histories sometimes track the movement of people and ideas across transnational space, but let us here track the movement of a political technology—a technology integral to liberal political modernity. Doing so illuminates the peculiar relationship between ballots and U.S. Empire and foregrounds the colonial bases of political modernity and the transimperial development of modern democracy.

Technologies of Democracy

The Australian ballot system was a radical innovation. The system that the Victorian Council in Australia had been most familiar with before passing the law in 1856 was the English system, in which voting was animated by intense political rivalries. The voting started with rowdy speeches where "heckling, booing and cheering" were common. Voters had to walk through a succession of bars guarded by constables and were "mocked, jeered and applauded" as they made their way to the booth. They underwent a verbal examination and finally presented their choice orally.[5] Voting was public. Onlookers could hear and see who was voting for whom. After the election, poll books with the electors' names and their votes were often published.

The public nature of elections in England was intentional. Voting was conceptualized as a visible and public expression of status. When ideas about private voting had popped up in England earlier in the nineteenth century, critics dismissed them on the grounds that secret voting was "un-manly" and un-Protestant. Secrecy was associated with the "clandestine" and "feminine shroud of darkness" of the Catholic confessional.[6] It was even thought of as antithetical to democracy, "subversive of the public square itself," upending "open, reasoned argument." Secret voting was "a rebuke to enlightenment values."[7]

The introduction of state-printed paper ballots changed this system by introducing privacy. Even when ballots had been used in the old system in England or the United States, they were printed by political parties and marked in ways that made apparent who was voting for whom.[8] Or ballots were filled out in the presence of others, with little to no attempt at privacy. Under the new system created by the Legislative Council of Victoria, however, the ballots were all the same, printed at public expense by the state, and to be given at the voting place only to officials. Furthermore a sequestered space had to be provided, "into which the voter shall immediately retire, and there, alone and in private," mark their ballot. The identity of the voter was never to be made public.[9]

If private voting had previously been deemed undemocratic in England, the new private system in Australia was meant to make for a more perfect democracy, to ensure fair and honest elections by uprooting practices that had become seen as corrupt. Official ballots would thwart attempts by political parties to stuff ballot boxes. Secret voting would prevent bribery and intimidation: those who bribed or intimidated would never know whether or not voters actually voted their way. The Australian Ballot Association, which was the first society in Australia to promote the private ballot system, argued that such a system would ensure "the independent exercise of [the electors'] vote" and secure the "purity and freedom of election."[10]

The Australian ballot system, in sum, was a novel sociotechnical system devised to impact political practice. And like other technologies, it soon spread. From Australia it went to the United States and England and on to Belgium, Luxembourg, and Italy before spreading to nearly all democratic systems in the world. But the Australian ballot system was very much a political technology in other ways too. First, like those other markers of progress and political modernity, it was not the product of a single geographical site or location. Despite its name, it was only partly an Australian invention. It was an *intra-imperial* one and soon became *transimperial* as it moved to the United States and its Philippine colony. Second, exactly because it was a technology, it was multivocal. It could acquire various meanings and serve a variety of functions, some of which were less noble than ensuring the purity of elections.

From London to Australia and Back

Although the first secret ballot system became known as the Australian system, having come from New South Wales, it would be more precise to call it "the imperial ballot," for it was a product of actors and ideas that traversed the empire. The Australian bill had been drafted by Henry Samuel Chapman in the Victorian Legislative Council, but Chapman had been around. Born in London in 1803, he emigrated to Quebec in 1823. There he started a newspaper and subsequently visited Bath, England, in time to witness the first elections after the Reform Bill of 1832.[11] He served as an intermediary between the Legislative Assembly of Lower Canada and allies in the House of Commons, was a member of various commissions in England, and became imbued with the ideas of the English Philosophical Radicals before moving to New Zealand and then Victoria. Chapman thus came to Victoria already infused with the ideas of electoral reformers in the British Empire.

Prior to the Australian law, Philosophical Radicals like Jeremy Bentham and James Mill in England had been arguing that a private ballot system would prevent electoral corruption and temper the power of the aristocracy over government. Private voting, Bentham declared, would diminish the "joint yoke of the monarchy and the aristocracy upon the neck of the swinish multitude."[12] Chartists in England had also been advocating a private ballot system to curb the excessive and undue influence of the upper classes upon the electoral process. "The suffrage, to be exempt from the corruption of the wealthy, and the violence of the powerful, must be secret," contended Robert George Gammage in 1854. Middle-class liberal reformers and their representatives in the House of Commons took up the cause in the House from the Chartists.[13] Among these liberals was F. H. Berkeley, who put the ballot before the House every year between 1848 and 1866, failing each time.[14]

The movement for electoral reform in Australia was the direct outgrowth of these movements in the center of empire. Chapman identified himself as a Philosophical Radical. Before him, the main proponents of the secret ballot, such as those who founded and motivated the South Australian Ballot Association in 1851, were largely middle-class liberals who had been pushing to democratize the previously appointed legislative councils. Like middle-class advocates in England, they publicly supported principles that the Chartists had held dear, such as universal suffrage and the equalization of electoral districts.[15] Leading proponents included vocal Chartists such as E. J. Hawksley. And waves of immigrants to Australia from Great Britain and Ireland carried with them Chartist ideas and related political values, thereby infusing the secret ballot system with the same meanings that their English predecessors had.[16] While the avowed purpose of the ballot was to thwart corruption, proponents in Australia were particularly keen on the secret ballot system as a *class* project: a political technology to keep in check the power of the monarchy, landlords, and wealthy employers. Not only would the ballot system "prevent bribery" and "secure representation"; it would more specifically protect the poorer classes and working classes from being unduly influenced by their superiors.[17]

All of this evinces that the private ballot system was not purely Australian. It was an intra-imperial development, with diverse parts coming from a variety of sources to coalesce into a single system that was then dubbed the "Australian ballot." Still, Australia was indeed the originator, if only in the sense that it was the first place to institute the ballot. England did not do so until 1872 (directly inspired and animated by the Australian model).[18] But this raises another puzzle: Why was the movement for the secret ballot system successful in Australia rather than in England?

Part of the answer lies in Australia's comparably distinct social and political institutions. In England the movement had faced repeated failure because opposition had been consistently strong. Some opposed the ballot movement on ideological grounds: secrecy was "un-English."[19] But there was also *power*, plain and simple. For most of the early to mid-nineteenth century the very social and political elements whose influence the ballot system targeted—the monarchy, the aristocracy, and wealthy employers—controlled the state directly or through their allies in Parliament. The House of Lords had continually and fiercely resisted all proposals for a private ballot system; the small amount of support the ballot had received typically came from the House of Commons.[20]

Australia was different. While reformers in England faced opposition from the House of Lords, there was much less resistance in Australia. Most of the politicians in Australia were from the commercial and professional classes. There was no aristocratic legislative house, only legislative councils consisting of representatives of the middle classes and a smaller number of government officials with aristocratic orientations. In addition, the suffrage was larger in Australia than in England, incorporating many male Chartists.[21] It is thus notable that the only opponents of the secret ballot system in Australia were the small number of elite government officials on the Council.[22] The conservative aristocratic powers that had thwarted ballot reform in England had very little presence in Australia.

Yet if Australia lacked those conservative aristocratic elements, what was the need for the ballot at all? If the power of the conservative aristocratic establishment and its wealthy government allies was already minimal, why strive so hard to make voting secret and protect it against the tyranny of landlords, the government, or employers? Some opponents of the ballot in Australia argued this very same point. Secret voting was necessary in England to temper the influence of the powerful and corrupt, but in Australia voter intimidation at the hands of the wealthy was not as prevalent. "In England," announced one opponent of the ballot system at a public meeting, "a good deal of tyranny [is] exercised, but it [is] not so here."[23]

This suggests that there were other motivations behind the new system. The particularities of the Australian colonial context made ballot reform easier politically; they also gave the ballot movement a different meaning than that which had obtained in England. Reformers in Australia hitched to the new system the idea of Australian distinction. Evident in the proponents' discourse, for instance, are repeated references to "corruption" in England. At the Association's first meeting, James Allen reminded his peers that they had "by coming to this colony escaped many of the intolerable evils which oppressed their countrymen at home," so the ballot was necessary to fulfill that goal. Australia was a new world that would not repeat the metropole's mistakes. Against the claim that the secret ballot system was "unmanly and un-English," Nathanial Hailes retorted that this was all for the better. "Rotten boroughs, bull baiting and hanging the poor were once English—should South Australians rush to emulate England in these respects too?" Mr. Parkins, in one of the early meetings, announced similarly, "Un-English! If it were so, [I hope] to see many things yet more un-English into this colony."[24] An editorial in the newspaper *Argus* advocating the secret ballot recounted electoral corruption that brought England such "shame and disgrace." It concluded, "Let us learn to adopt [England's] virtues not her vices and crimes!" We should not "risk making the colonies a sordid old Britannia."[25]

The ballot reformers in Australia felt a strong sense of pride at casting off the oppression and weight of the past that was tied to the "mother country." The ballot system was to be a mark of their progressiveness, a sign of their distinction. It should "go forward to all the world," declared Dr. Eade at the first meeting of the Association in 1851, that "South Australia was the first of British colonies that adopted the safe and satisfactory system of voting by ballot."[26] In 1858, after Victoria had enacted the secret ballot system, Legislative Council member Thomas McCombie proudly wrote, "The objection often taken, that in America and France the ballot is not secret, is not tenable in Victoria."[27]

From Victoria to Louisville

The Australian ballot system first took hold in the United States in 1888. By 1891 thirty-two of the forty-two states had passed secret ballot laws.[28] All of these innovations were informed directly by Australia. The architect of the pathbreaking Louisville bill, Arthur Wallace, had come up with the legislation after first reading about the Australian law. Reformers such as Henry George and the members of the Philadelphia Civil Service Reform Association had long been advocating "the Australian ballot." Wigmore's *The Australian Ballot System* (1889) provided reformers with a digest of over thirty different statutes on the books for the secret ballot. Wigmore argued that Australia had "grasped the torch of progress," and Americans should do so too.[29]

What did the secret ballot mean in the context of the late nineteenth-century United States, which was no longer a British colony and where class and aristocratic discourse had been more muted? The general goal of undoing corruption that had partly animated Australians and the English was operative in the United States too. Elections in the United States had been rife with all manner of electoral chicanery: bribery, fraud, intimidation, and, where party ballots rather than oral votes were used, ballot manipulation. In New York City the machinery of Boss Tweed was exemplary: according to contemporary reports, his machine was able to buy city districts for $250 each.[30] Corruption was rife elsewhere too. Reports from Indiana found that for every five voters there was one man hired by political parties to purchase their vote.[31]

This corruption led U.S. reformers to favor the Australian ballot. The Republican reformers known as Mugwumps pursued the ballot as part of their larger program of curbing the excesses of party politics, establishing more efficient and honest city governance, and chipping away at the power of the party machines. In Louisville a series of electoral scandals had exposed the operations of the Democratic Party machine and its unelected bosses. State Representative Arthur Wallace led a reform group called the Commonwealth Club, which vowed to undo such corruption, leading to the implementation of the Australian system.[32] The key architect and proponent of the Massachusetts bill was Richard Henry Dana III, an "arch-mugwump" who had drafted the state's civil service law of 1883.[33] Henry George argued that only through a system of secret voting on government-printed ballots could the influence of money in elections be undone. Reformers within the political parties also came on board, supporting the Australian ballot system to preserve order in the lower ranks and discipline corruptors, as well as to save the expense of printing ballots and buying votes.[34]

There was another group besides the Mugwumps, however: labor. The first national party to put the Australian ballot on their platform was the United Labor Party, whose leader, Henry George, had long advocated for the Australian ballot. George ran for mayor of New York City in 1886 on the United Labor ticket. The party platform announced, "Since the ballot is the only means by which in our Republic the redress of political and social grievances is to be sought, we especially and emphatically declare for the adoption of what is known as the 'Australian system of voting,' in order that the effectual secrecy of the ballot and the relief of candidates for public office from the heavy expenses now imposed upon them, may prevent bribery and intimidation, do away with practical discriminations in favor of the rich and unscrupulous, and lessen the pernicious influence of money in politics."[35]

Some of the meanings and functions of the Australian ballot system were thus imported into the United States along with the system itself, but new twists were also turned. Consider studies on the effect of the institution of the Australian ballot upon voter turnout: all show that turnout most often decreased after the ballot system was instituted, often by as much as 26 percent.[36] The irony should not be lost: the Australian ballot was meant to perfect democracy, but in the United States its enactment limited it. One explanation for this outcome is that the decrease in voter turnout was intentional: the new ballot system was implemented to disenfranchise illiterate voters. The *viva voce* method, the statement of preference to a clerk, and color-coded party ballots had not required voters to read or write. The Australian ballot system changed this by requiring uniform government-printed ballots. Unable to read the names of the candidates, illiterate would-be voters could not vote.

The use of the ballot system to disenfranchise illiterates aligned nicely with Mugwumps' and other middle-class reformers' goal of halting the urban political machines. Those machines had long relied upon immigrants, many of whom were illiterate. The Australian ballot, noted the magazine editor George Gunton, was adopted to "eliminate the ignorant, illiterate voters" because "too many of our foreign-born citizens vote ignorantly."[37] But nowhere is the nefarious function of the new system more evident than in the American South, where white segregationists deployed the Australian ballot to suppress the African American vote. In the wake of the Fifteenth Amendment, southern Democrats had repeatedly sought ways to prevent African American voters from going to the polls. In 1891 the Arkansas State Legislature passed one of the first Australian ballot laws in the South, which included a clause that prohibited illiterate voters from receiving verbal help from friends or polling officials during voting. The result? African American illiterate voters stayed away. As one newspaper explained, when blacks "who could not read were told to go to the polls and vote, the majority of them declined . . . not caring to expose their inability to make out their tickets unassisted."[38]

Across the South various other additions to the original system were made to ensure its new function. Ballots typically contained dozens of names, and so in some cases the names of candidates on ballots were listed in random rather than alphabetical order. Florida, Tennessee, Virginia, and Maryland abolished party identifications on the ballot; Virginia printed ballots for congressional elections in Gothic letters.[39] In some states the "Repudiation party" was listed "in order to bewilder negroes who had been laboriously taught to recognize the word 'Republican.'"[40] In other states, strict time constraints were imposed upon voters, presumably to lessen the time that illiterates could spend on deciphering the words. Complex written instructions were also imposed, such as the instruction to mark a line across the candidates' name only three-quarters the length exactly. If not done properly, the validity of the ballot could be challenged.[41]

None of this was lost on critics. "American ingenuity," wrote Philip L. Allen in the North American Review, after reviewing some of the devious tactics to disenfranchise voters through the ballot, "has done much with the primitive Australian form."[42] In Arkansas the editor of the Gazette observed, "[The] average negro voter is decidedly inclined to vote, but lacks the necessary qualification of preparing a valid or legible ballot. . . . It has been estimated that perhaps three-fourths of them are incapable of preparing a ballot as required under the Australian system."[43] Certain proponents of the Australian ballot in the South were unabashed about it all. In 1892 this was a campaign song of the Democratic Party in Arkansas:

The Australian ballot works like a charm,
It makes them think and scratch,
And when a Negro gets a ballot
He has certainly got his match.
They go into the booth alone
Their ticket to prepare.
And as soon as five minutes are out
They have got to git from there.[44]

The Australian ballot suppressed voter turnout in the South more than anywhere else in the United States. While states like New Hampshire and Ohio saw a negative 1 percent change in voter turnout after the law, Arkansas saw a 21 percent decline, Alabama saw close to a 24 percent decline, and Virginia almost a 26 percent decline.[45] The racial component of this is clear. In Alabama the "Negro" vote for governor declined by at least 25 percent after the passage of the new ballot law; in Arkansas it declined by 46 percent, and in Louisiana by 65 percent.[46]

Evidently, when Mill had written that Americans did not need the secret ballot, he had underestimated American racism—and Americans' penchant for hitching new technologies to racial projects. And with this the reversal was complete: whereas the Chartists in England had originally deployed the secret ballot to chip away at aristocratic power in the service of the masses, the remnants of the American plantation aristocracy in the South found in the secret ballot a means to reinscribe its power at the expense of the masses—in this case, the black masses whose hard-won citizenship the southern establishment refused to countenance.

From Boston to Manila

In 1901 the American members of the Philippine Commission passed the first municipal code permanently establishing municipal governments in the islands. The Municipal Code required voters to use official ballots "provided in sufficient numbers by the provincial Governor" and to vote in a section of a room "cut off by a railing" in "secret."[47] The new municipal code instituted the

Australian ballot system for Filipinos by reproducing parts of the New York and Massachusetts laws that had been based upon the Australian bill. After the Municipal Code, the system was then extended to the elections for the first Philippine Assembly in 1907. As Philippine Supreme Court Justice George Malcolm later explained, the law for those elections was "a counterpart of the ballot laws almost universally adopted within comparatively recent times in the US, and is generally called by text writers the Australian ballot law."[48]

The system for secret voting was also instituted in American-occupied Cuba and Puerto Rico, thereby raising this question: What could the Australian ballot possibly mean in the margins of the American Empire? Disenfranchising illiterates and undesirables could not have been the goal in the Philippines because U.S. officials had already restricted the suffrage to literate and/or propertied resident males. So what was it all about?

As is well known, U.S. colonial officials in the Philippines and Puerto Rico put into action a program of "democratic tutelage" aimed at transforming the Philippine polity into the image of the officials' idealized vision of America's liberal-democratic state. That project involved constructing public schools, holding elections, and building local governments and national offices to provide a "practical political education" to the colonized elite in the "art of self-government."[49] Voting and elections were to be an important part of this educating process. Elihu Root, the U.S. secretary of war who oversaw the colonial administrations, described voting as the "greatest, most useful educational process."[50]

Part of this tutelary project was about legitimation: promising eventual self-government so as to win over the otherwise resistant elite while portraying U.S. colonialism as exceptional.[51] To be sure, military governor General E. Otis and the first and second Philippine Commission had been well aware that elections (with a restricted suffrage) would attract would-be and ongoing insurgents in the archipelago. "Ballots were much better and more effective than bullets," said one official in 1901.[52] But regardless of the motivation behind the project, why the Australian ballot system in particular?

It is useful to recall that many of the U.S. colonial officials in the Philippines had the mind-set of middle-class Mugwump and proto-Progressive reformers. Elihu Root, William Howard Taft, and other administrators had various ties to the reform movement at home.[53] Given this background, the democracy these colonial officials purported to transplant to the colonies was not just any type of democracy; it was the idealized liberal democracy of the American reformers that heralded as crucial "sovereign individuals," not "organic networks" formed through kin, ethnicity, or party machine.[54] This meant that one of the obstacles to democratic self-government in the Philippines pinpointed by U.S. officials was the Philippine social structure. Officials perceived a binary social structure of leaders and followers, elites and masses, and they castigated the former as despots or *caciques* (as they called them), that is, masters of rural land and labor who held tenants under their tyrannical sway. "The difficulty we find in the Filipino people," explained Taft, "is the ease with which an educated Filipino who has any wealth can control and oppress his own people."[55] Another official referred to this group as part of the "almost medieval system of privilege" that Americans should endeavor to "break up" in order to implant democracy in the islands.[56] And to top it all off, these caciques presumably used political office to perpetuate their power. "The politicians here are, with a few exceptions, venal and corrupt to the last degree," wrote Taft to his friend Henry Hoyt.[57]

In light of this we can see that the Australian ballot, rather than serving as a tool to disenfranchise undesirable voters, was part of a larger project to try to undo the power of the Filipino elite by preventing them from manipulating elections for their own ends. Civics texts were clear on how the Australian ballot system would not only prevent bribery and abuse but also prevent landlord-caciques from influencing the less powerful:

> Voting must be strictly secret. Sometimes a rich man may want some one elected because he thinks that man will do him favors. He may want the tenants on his land to vote for his candidate. They all know that man is not a good man for an official, but the influence of the rich man is strong and they are afraid to vote for a good man against their landlord's wishes. But when they can go into a small room by themselves and vote without any one being present, neither the rich man nor any one else can know how they voted. They can then vote for a good man without being afraid.[58]

George Malcolm, one of the American Supreme Court justices in the Philippines, wrote further: "The English Ballot Act, commonly known as the Australian Ballot System, is here in force. The privacy of the ballot, which is its most salient characteristic, is a valuable safeguard of the independence of the voter *against the influence of wealth and power*. The citizen must be allowed to vote for whom he pleases free from improper influences."[59]

In this sense, the American officials' motivation in the Philippines was not unlike that of their English Chartist and Australian predecessors: to curb if not undermine traditional aristocratic power. It is thus appropriate that American officials had referred to the Philippine social structure as a "medieval system": Filipino caciques were like aristocratic landlords whom the Philosophical

Radicals, Chartists, and Liberals in England had targeted through their electoral reforms. Taft did not hesitate to equate the "corruption" of the Philippine elite with aristocratic English politicians. The Filipinos, he said, "are tricky and uncertain as were the statesmen in the days of George the first and Queen Anne."[60]

Not only did officials classify the Philippines as a medieval system replete with aristocrats and landlords impeding the development of liberal democracy, but they also saw in the Philippines an ostensible ignorance, backwardness, and chaos that was putatively plaguing America's metropolises. In his 1901 essay "Democracy and Efficiency," Woodrow Wilson heralded "self-discipline" as the cornerstone of liberal democratic self-government, decrying what he saw as a lack of self-discipline in American cities. In those cities "the local machine and the local boss" rule, "voters of every blood and environment and social derivation mix and stare at one another at the same voting places," and "government miscarries, is confused, irresponsible, unintelligent, wasteful." Wilson then said that Filipinos and Puerto Ricans too lacked "self-discipline" and "self-control"; hence America's task was to give them the "discipline" they required to eventually rule themselves.[61]

As in the corrupt North American city, therefore, so too in the backward colony. American officials in the Philippines saw in their new colony the very sort of "boss-immigrant-machine complex" that they believed plagued American cities.[62] American officials equated the Filipino masses with the immigrants of American cities. Both ostensibly lacked the "ideas and aptitudes which fit men to take up . . . the problem of self-care and self-government."[63] Furthermore American officials equated the Filipino elite with the bosses leading the urban immigrant political machines. When explaining the situation to Congress, Governor Taft translated *cacique* as "boss" precisely, stating that in provinces like Cagayan, the "condition of affairs [is] caciqueism which, freely translated, means bossism."[64] The *Manila Times* advanced this view in a 1903 story about charges of bribery during the municipal elections: "The average Filipino is no novice at political wire-pulling. . . . He is just about as crafty in the art of politics as is the average American ward heeler and other political bosses." The writer summarized, "I shall not be surprised if I hear in the future that some Tomas or other, lately emigrated from the Philippines, has captured the votes of the largest ward in New York City over the head of some redoubtable Patrick."[65] Officials in the Philippines thus saw the ballot as part of a project to undo the power of a Filipino landed elite whom they equated with both feudal landlords and machine politicians. Through the private ballot system, recalcitrant elites were to be disciplined into democracy.

Still, the Australian ballot had other functions in America's overseas colonies that are worth considering. As in Australia, the Australian ballot system became a sign of attainment in the Philippines, though with different symbolic valences. On the one hand, American officials and residents in the archipelago enlisted the Australian ballot to mark out American exceptionalism. Americans often bragged of how their tutelary rule over the Philippines—with its politically modernizing and liberal trappings—was an exceptional political experience. They could thus hold up elections, and especially elections using the Australian ballot, as a mark of distinction. By employing the Australian ballot, Americans had given the colonial Philippines a shiny new political technology signifying progress and hence the benignity of American colonialism. After describing the electoral system in great detail, one civics textbook asserted, "This method of balloting is called the 'Australian ballot' and has been adopted in several of the most progressive states of the world."[66] A Philippine lesson book for the fourth grade said of the Australian ballot system, "It is one of the best laws that has ever been made."[67]

On the other hand, Filipino nationalists referred to the Australian ballot not to signify American benevolence but rather to signify why American rule should end. In 1916 Maximo Kalaw took up arguments being made that Americans had to further study conditions in the Philippines before determining that the Filipinos were deserving of self-government: "It is not . . . necessary for the American nation to know—and she can never thoroughly know—the minute details of Philippine conditions, in order to be able to settle, once and for all, the Philippine question. She did not have to know the characteristics and the skills of the people of Santiago de Cuba, or whether the city of Havana could honestly use the Australian ballot, before she declared that Cuba should be free and independent. It was enough to realize that an entire people were desperately fighting for liberty."[68] With the appropriate technology in place and the desire for liberty palpable, the Philippines too should be independent.

In later writings Kalaw argued that American rule had done its job. It had imparted democratic institutions, and time was now ripe for independence because "a more honest and efficient system of government has been established," involving "the principle of majority rule, equal opportunity for all, the Australian ballot system, the peaceful acceptance of electoral results, public office as a public trust, etc."[69] Kalaw thus concurred with his fellow nationalists who held that "President McKinley's ideal of teaching the people of the Philippines the art of self-government can now be best realized under an independent status."[70] In other words, the Philippines had all it needed from American rule, thank you very much—including the Australian ballot system. While American officials had boasted that their rule of the archipelago was special because it imparted modern democratic institutions in the Philippines, including the Australian ballot system, Kalaw and other nationalists held them to their word, using the ballot system as part of their discursive arsenal. This testifies to the transimperial deployment of this important technology of political modernity. But it also evinces the agency of the colonized subjects who deployed it.

The Transimperial Origins of Modern Democracy

We can now reach a better understanding of how and why the Australian ballot system was adopted relatively early in the Philippines, despite the fact that it was a colony, and despite the fact that colonialism and democracy are antithetical. The point is that the Australian ballot system did not amount to a system with a singular function or meaning. Like any technology, it was multivocal and could serve a range of purposes. It could be used as a mark of distinction, as in Australia; as a technology for checking the power of aristocrats, as in England; as a tool of exclusion or oppression, as in the American South and New York City; or as part of a disciplinary project in civilizing the uncivilized, as in America's tutelary empire. In all of these instances, the system assumed a similar form, but its purposes and meanings varied. Therefore, it is not surprising that an electoral device emerged in a colonial context. Because there is no single intrinsic function to such devices in the first place, there is nothing about them that is intrinsically opposed to colonial usages.

While we can better see the diverse purposes and meanings of the Australian ballot system, we can also see through them the diversity of empire. This is where a transimperial analysis is fruitful. By tracking a technology or an idea across and through empires—hence tracking it *transimperially*—we hold the thing constant while varying the context of its usages. This enables us to see something about those different contexts that we might not otherwise see. When we do this in a world of nation-states, we track things cross-nationally. We shine a light on social, political, or cultural differences that presumably align with national differences. When we track something transimperially, we track it through or across multiple empires. Doing so illuminates something about that diversity within and across empires; it also shows us the various projects of racialized power and fields of competition within and across those empires—not least with our case here, of the diverse and sometimes nefarious usages of the otherwise innocuous Australian ballot system.

There is also something substantive and not just methodological to note, for the Australian ballot system and its principles of secrecy have not only been important for the countries named here. They have been definitive of modern democracy. As Malcolm Crook explains, as the Australian system moved through the world, it became "upheld as a global ideal" and today "is commonly regarded as the natural complement to universal suffrage and democratic freedom"—so much so that the United Nations has taken the principle of secrecy to be a "self-evident tool of representative democracy."[71] Article 21 of its Universal Declaration of Human Rights declares, "The will of the people shall be the basis of the authority of government; this will shall be expressed in periodic and genuine elections which shall be by universal and equal suffrage and shall be held by secret vote or by equivalent free voting procedures."[72] No doubt, in the Australian ballot system lies one of liberal political modernity's origins. Yet that technology was neither a "national" nor a "colonial" invention. It did not exactly originate in one place to then spread throughout the world. Rather it was a technology that emerged across and through the space of empires: an Anglo-American transimperial invention whose history should remind us of the transimperial origins of America's political system—and of the modern world more broadly.

NOTES

1. Prescott F. Jernegan, *The Philippine Citizen: A Text-Book of Civics, Describing the Nature of Government, the Philippine Government, and the Rights and Duties of Citizens of the Philippines*, 3rd edition (Manila: Philippine Education Publishing, 1910), 100.

2. Malcolm Crook, "Reforming Voting Practices in a Global Age: The Making and Remaking of the Modern Secret Ballot in Britain, France and the United States, c. 1600–1950," *Past and Present* 212, no. 1 (2011): 199.

3. *Report of E. S. Otis, Commanding Department of the Pacific and 8th Army Corps, Military Governor in the Philippine Islands* (Manila: Bureau of Printing, 1899), 209.

4. On Foucault's concept of "technology," see Michael C. Behrent, "Foucault and Technology," *History and Technology* 29, no. 1 (2013): 54–104.

5. Frank O'Gorman, "The Secret Ballot in Nineteenth-Century Britain," in *The Hidden History of the Secret Ballot*, edited by Romain Bertrand, Jean Louis Briquet, and Peter Pels (Bloomington: Indiana University Press, 2006), 21.

6. Mark McKenna, *Building "a Closet of Prayer" in the New World: The Story of the Australian Ballot*, London Papers in Australian Studies (London: Menzies Centre for Australian Studies, 2002), 4.

7. David Gilmartin, "Towards a Global History of Voting: Sovereignty, the Diffusion of Ideas, and the Enchanted Individual," *Religions* 3 (2012): 413.

8. Tracy Campbell, "Machine Politics, Police Corruption, and the Persistence of Vote Fraud: The Case of Louisville, Kentucky, Election of 1905," *Journal of Policy History* 15, no. 3 (2003): 271.

9. Eldon Cobb Evans, "A History of the Australian Ballot System in the United States," PhD diss., University of Chicago, 1917, 85.

10. *South Australian Register*, January 28, 1851, 2.

11. R. S. Neale, "H. S. Chapman and the 'Victorian' Ballot," *Historical Studies: Australia and New Zealand* 12, no. 48 (1967): 506–21.

12. Jeremy Bentham, *Plan of Parliamentary Reform, in the Form of Catechism, with Reasons for Each Article* (London: John McCreery, 1817), clxxxii.

13. Ernest Scott, "The History of the Victorian Ballot," *Victorian Historical Magazine* 8, no. 1 (1920): 4–5.

14. McKenna, *Building "a Closet of Prayer" in the New World*, 16.

15. *South Australian Register*, January 28, 1851, 3.

16. Paul A Pickering, "A Wider Field in a New Country: Chartism in Colonial Australia," in *Elections: Full, Free and Fair*, edited by Marian Sawer (Sydney: Federation Press, 2001), 28, 42.

17. *Argus*, December 20, 1855, 5.

18. L. E. Fredman, *The Australian Ballot: The Story of an American Reform* (East Lansing: Michigan State University Press, 1968), 3–5.

19. Peter Brent, "The Australian Ballot: Not the Secret Ballot," *Australian Journal of Political Science* 41, no. 1 (2006): 40.

20. O'Gorman, "The Secret Ballot in Nineteenth-Century Britain," 24.

21. Robert Murray, *The Making of Australia: A Concise History* (Kenthurst, Australia: Rosenberg, 2014), 67.

22. *Argus*, December 20, 1855, 5.

23. *South Australian Register*, February 4, 1851, 4.

24. *South Australian Register*, February 4, 1851, 4.

25. *Argus,* December 12, 1855, 3.

26. *South Australian Register*, January 28, 1851, 3.

27. Crook, "Reforming Voting Practices in a Global Age," 221.

28. Crook, "Reforming Voting Practices in a Global Age," 227.

29. John Wigmore, *The Australian Ballot System as Embodied in the Legislation of Various Countries* (Boston: Boston Book Co., 1889), 1.

30. John E. Milholland, "The Danger Point in American Politics," *North American Review* 164, no. 482 (1897): 94.

31. Robert LaFollete Jr., "The Adoption of the Australian Ballot in Indiana," *Indiana Magazine of History* 24 (June 1928): 113.

32. Campbell, "Machine Politics, Police Corruption, and the Persistence of Vote Fraud," 271.

33. Fredman, *The Australian Ballot*, 36.

34. Alan Ware, "Anti-Partism and Party Control of Political Reform in the United States: The Case of the Australian Ballot," *British Journal of Political Science* 30, no. 1 (2000): 1–29.

35. John H. Hopkins, *A History of Political Parties in the United States* (New York: G. P. Putnam's Sons, 1900), 404.

36. Jac Heckelman, "The Effect of the Secret Ballot on Voter Turnout Rates," *Public Choice* 82, nos. 1–2 (1995): 111.

37. J. Morgan Kousser, *The Shaping of Southern Politics: Suffrage Restriction and the Establishment of the One-Party South, 1880–1910* (New Haven, CT: Yale University Press, 1974), 52.

38. Kousser, *The Shaping of Southern Politics*, 213.

39. Evans, "A History of the Australian Ballot System in the United States," 43.

40. Philip Loring Allen, "The Multifarious Australian Ballot," *North American Review* 191, no. 654 (May 1910): 609.

41. John Crowley, "The Secret Ballot in the American Age of Reform," in Bertrand et al., *The Hidden History of the Secret Ballot*, 60.

42. Allen, "The Multifarious Australian Ballot," 608.

43. John William Graves, "Negro Disenfranchisement in Arkansas," *Arkansas Historical Quarterly* 26 (1967): 214.

44. Graves, "Negro Disenfranchisement in Arkansas," 212–13.

45. Heckelman, "The Effect of the Secret Ballot on Voter Turnout Rates," 111.

46. Kousser, *The Shaping of Southern Politics*, 55.

47. Government of the Philippine Islands, *The Municipal Code and the Provincial Government Act, Being Act No. 82* (Manila: Bureau of Printing, 1905), 11.

48. Government of the Philippine Islands, *The Municipal Code and the Provincial Government Act*, 609.

49. Julian Go, *American Empire and the Politics of Meaning: Elite Political Cultures in the Philippines and Puerto Rico during U.S. Colonialism* (Durham, NC: Duke University Press, 2008), 20.

50. Go, *American Empire and the Politics of Meaning*, 28.

51. Julian Go, "The Provinciality of American Empire: 'Liberal Exceptionalism' and U.S. Colonial Rule," *Comparative Studies in Society and History* 49, no. 1 (2007): 74–108.

52. Bernard Moses, 1901, Philippine Diary, entry for February 27, 1901. Bernard Moses Papers, Bancroft Library, UC Berkeley.

53. Patricio Abinales, "Progressive Machine Conflict in Early Twentieth-Century U.S. Politics and Colonial State Building in the Philippines," in *The American Colonial State in the Philippines: Global Perspectives*, edited by Julian Go and Anne L. Foster (Durham, NC: Duke University Press, 2003), 148–81; Paul Kramer, "Reflex Actions: Colonialism, Corruption and the Politics of Technocracy in the Early Twentieth Century United States," in *Challenging U.S. Foreign Policy: America and the World in the Long Twentieth Century*, edited by Bevan Sewall and Scott Lucas (London: Palgrave Macmillan, 2011), 14–35.

54. John D. Buenker, "Sovereign Individuals and Organic Networks: Political Culture in Conflict during the Progressive Era," *American Quarterly* 40, no. 2 (1988): 187–204.

55. U.S. Senate, Committee on the Philippines, *Affairs in the Philippines: Hearings before the Committee on the Philippines of the United States Senate*, Senate Document No. 331, 57th Congress, 1st Session (Washington, DC: Government Printing Office, 1902), 51.

56. W. Cameron Forbes, *The Philippine Islands*, 2 vols. (Boston: Houghton Mifflin, 1928), 1:166.

57. William Howard Taft to Henry M. Hoyt, September 8, 1900, Clarence Edwards Papers, I, 1.16, Massachusetts Historical Society, Boston.

58. W. O. Beckner, "Studies in Civics for Fourth Grade Classes," *Philippine Education* 9, no. 6 (December 1911): 250.

59. George Malcolm, *The Government of the Philippine Islands: Its Development and Fundamentals* (Rochester, NY: The Lawyers Co-operative Publishing Co., 1916), 607–8, emphasis added.

60. Taft to Henry M. Hoyt, September 8, 1900.

61. Woodrow Wilson, "Democracy and Efficiency," *Atlantic Monthly*, March, 1901, 297.

62. Buenker, "Sovereign Individuals and Organic Networks," 188.

63. Matthew Frye Jacobson, *Barbarian Virtues: The United States Encounters Foreign Peoples at Home and Abroad* (New York: Hill and Wang, 2000), 193.

64. U.S. Senate Committee on the Philippines, *Affairs in the Philippines*, 51.

65. *Manila Times*, November 30, 1903, 1.

66. Jernegan, *The Philippine Citizen*, 100.

67. Beckner, "Studies in Civics for Fourth Grade Classes," 251.

68. Maximo M. Kalaw, *The Case for the Filipinos* (New York: Century, 1916), xii–xiii.

69. Kalaw, *The Case for the Filipinos*, 151–52.

70. Teodoro Kalaw, ed., *Epistolario Rizalino, vol. 1: 1877–1887* (Manila: Bureau of Printing, 1930), 150.

71. Crook, "Reforming Voting Practices in a Global Age," 199.

72. United Nations, "Universal Declaration of Human Rights," article 21, http://www.un.org/en/universal-declaration-human-rights. For a further discussion of secret voting today, see Romain Bertrand et al., "Introduction: Towards a Historical Ethnography of Voting," in Bertrand et al., *The Hidden History of the Secret Ballot*, 1–15.

5. MEDICINE TO DRUG: OPIUM'S TRANSIMPERIAL JOURNEY

Anne L. Foster

Both disease and opium long circulated throughout Southeast Asia without much restriction from colonial governments. Disease moved with relative freedom across borders and from person to person. In the nineteenth century, medical knowledge was just developing an understanding of contagion and how to promote prevention effectively. Governments were just beginning to take the first halting steps toward international public health and quarantine measures for the region.[1] For centuries opium use had followed disease. Often opium was a useful medicine rather than a recreational drug, since it offered effective symptom relief at a time when the *materia medica* provided few cures. Individuals and governments alike also profited from opium. Few perceived any reason, even if there had been capacity, to restrict its movement.

In the late nineteenth century, however, colonial governments in Southeast Asia increased their efforts to control both opium and the spread of disease. Colonial officials drew on new medical knowledge that diminished the medical usefulness of opium and were motivated by new ideas about the purpose of colonial rule. Strategies for control developed in a transimperial context. Sometimes this context was affirmative and celebrated: doctors and government officials developed transimperial relationships and took educational and professional journeys across borders. At other times, transimperial collaboration reflected the limits of colonial state power. The transimperial context in which opium policies and practices developed in the late nineteenth and early twentieth centuries demonstrates how the very measures colonial states took to shore up their power might undermine it and, simultaneously, how sharing power, which seemed to weaken or divide it, might make the state more resilient. Transimperial measures to control opium seemed, paradoxically, to both erase boundaries and reinscribe them as doctors and officials worked easily across borders, enacted measures to control opium crossing borders, and observed those measures being evaded.

More generally during the late nineteenth century, as imperial states grew in scope and reach, they attempted to extend their control of bodies, promote public health, and enforce borders by taxing and enumerating commodities. But they constantly confronted the limits of their power; each new enforcement created additional resistance. This is the dilemma of late imperialism. The system looked robust, as imperial states honed instruments of surveillance and control, encouraged more extensive and technologically advanced plantation agriculture and extractive technology, fully embraced participation in a global economy, and neatly, it appeared to them, balanced enticements for indigenous elites who cooperated with increasingly harsh repression of resisters. The imperial state appeared to have enduring power.[2]

But as the collapse of the global imperial system in the aftermath of World War II indicates, imperial states were brittle. Even around the turn of the twentieth century, many colonial officials sensed that the challenges facing the system might be greater than the resources it had available to protect itself. This sense of looming challenge combined with improved technologies of travel and communication to encourage colonial officials to collaborate with one another to shore up the imperial system. In highly visible venues, such as the growing numbers of international conferences and the League of Nations, and in less visible ones, such as regular visits of colonial officials with their counterparts elsewhere, educational circuits, joint policing and surveillance, and sharing of publications, colonial officials learned from one another, forged some policies in common, and exchanged information about threats.[3]

Scholarly attention to this work is modest and so far has focused, not surprisingly, on how colonial officials collaborated in their responses to cross-colonial threats to the imperial system, most notably from revolutionaries, especially those inspired by political or religious ideologies not linked to a given nation-state. As we see in this volume too, the mobility of labor and capital and boundary-crossing trade have also invited attention to the ways competition and collaboration shaped a common imperial system. Scholarship in these areas is sufficiently developed to facilitate attention to the more quotidian aspects of life that also contributed to transimperial collaborations. Ideas about health, medicine, and opium developed in a transimperial context during the late nineteenth and early twentieth centuries.[4] For colonial states, the challenge came from the imperative to control opium and disease, neither of which could easily be prevented from crossing borders and both of which had potential to undermine the health of empire.[5] The transimperial movement of disease and drug prompted transimperial responses, similar policies, and circulation of knowledge and personnel.

Before 1890 few people questioned opium's central role in the medicine chest, the government's revenue, and the social life of Asian colonies. In 1890 germ theory was just beginning to prompt changes in hygienic practices that allowed safe surgery as well as clean water supplies. Antibiotics were not yet invented; aspirin was a few years in the future. Vaccines existed, but for few illnesses, and were not yet globally adopted.[6] The late nineteenth-century world was one in which people everywhere were highly likely to spend a good portion of their life ill and in pain, with little effective medical relief other than opium. In Southeast Asia opium for centuries had been an important medicine to alleviate aches and pains, from headache to the effects of cancer; to reduce symptoms of malaria; and, through what today is usually considered an unwelcome side effect (constipation), to bring relief from dysentery and other stomach ailments.[7]

Before European imperialism, few people in Southeast Asia smoked opium purely for pleasure. Europeans found that opium served empire well, however. It was a consumer good that manufactured its own demand. Providing opium to workers in dangerous and difficult jobs, such as tin mining, clearing land for plantations, and dock work, meant workers worked harder and longer than would ordinarily be possible and were reluctant to leave their supplier-employer. And since European governments maintained a monopoly over the legal import of opium and controlled the right of sale, it was highly profitable. In the late nineteenth century European colonial governments in Southeast Asia derived at least 15 percent and as much as 50 percent of their revenue from opium.[8] Even as opium seemed an integral part of the fabric of medical practice, economics, and society in colonial Southeast Asia, anti-opium sentiment grew in each colony, especially after the 1880s. Because many of the first anti-opium activists embraced a number of reforms or were missionaries, historians have not much questioned why anti-opium activism gained traction at this time, resulting in ever-increasing regulation during the first part of the twentieth century.[9]

One explanation has been offered: the changing nature of the regular opium consumer, from a sympathetic and deserving user to a frightening and alien addict. David Courtwright has painted a compelling picture of the transition in the United States, noting that the mid-nineteenth-century addict was usually presented as a Civil War veteran addicted to opium because of the physical, and perhaps psychic, pain resulting from military service, or a middle-class white woman who took a little laudanum to deal with the stresses of daily life. By the early twentieth century the prevailing image in the United States of an opium user was more threatening: an ethnic Chinese man smoking opium in the alien space of an opium den and luring innocent white women to immoral behavior there.[10] The death of Civil War veterans removed the most valorous user of opium in the United States and suggests why it was easy to perceive opium users differently in that country. It does less to explain the concurrent transition in other parts of the world. Anti-opium activists worked to change the image of an opium user from benign or pitiable to menacing or degenerate. They succeeded in part because the perceived "legitimate medical use" of opium declined, and recreational use therefore appeared to increase.

In colonial Southeast Asia, existing distinctions between methods of consumption reinforced new understandings of the appropriate medicinal use of opium. Europeans used opium for medical purposes and took it in laudanum or pill form; smoking opium was reserved for pleasure and was a transgressive act for Europeans. Ethnic Chinese and indigenous peoples traditionally consumed opium by smoking, whether for a medicinal or a recreational purpose. Europeans historically tolerated opium smoking by Asians, criticizing it only when Asians were addicted and unable to fulfill work or family duties. Beginning in the 1890s, however, anti-opium activists argued with growing success that opium smoking was always harmful, disregarding traditional medical uses.[11]

At the turn of the twentieth century both medicine and public health began to develop in ways that sharpened the distinction between types of opium consumption. Doctors and public health providers learned from each other across imperial boundaries, increasingly thinking of themselves as practitioners of "tropical medicine," expert in diseases of whole regions, rather than merely serving within a particular colony or country.[12] Knowledge of disease, of measures to prevent it, and of the treatment for it circulated throughout the region. As these health-care providers began to believe themselves better able to prevent and cure disease, they were less likely to see opiates as an appropriate response except in limited circumstances. P. N. Gerrard, author of a widely circulated pamphlet titled *On the Hygienic Management of Labour in the Tropics*, practiced in the Federated Malay States. His pamphlet referred to practices he had learned from people he viewed as colleagues in Sumatra and Ceylon, including a fellow British physician who oversaw Dutch rubber plantations in

Sumatra. His pamphlet circulated throughout the region, providing guidance to plantation managers in a variety of imperial settings. Gerrard did advocate some use of opiates, mostly the patent medicine chlorodyne, to treat dysentery and diarrhea. But this recommendation always came at the end of discussion of a disease, after pages of how to prevent disease through proper siting of housing, provision of clean water supplies, encouragement of mosquito netting, and other public health measures.[13] In his pamphlet opiates were the response to the failure of modern medicine.

At the end of the nineteenth century, modern medicine and public health innovations in hygiene promised a much healthier environment. Imperial governments, both to fulfill the civilizing mission which they increasingly used to justify their rule and to ensure a reliable workforce and unfettered circulation of goods, worked to facilitate these innovations. They began the process of improving water delivery and sewage disposal.[14] They pursued initiatives to clean up cities and provide more healthy urban environments.[15] They began funding health clinics and training indigenous health-care providers.[16] And they exchanged information among colonial officials about the best implementation strategies, visiting one another and adapting and critiquing the policies of other imperial powers.[17] One result of these initiatives was supposed to be a healthier population, relying on "modern" medicine and less frequently using traditional remedies such as opium. Ordinary Southeast Asians, however, had little access to these modern innovations. Modern sewer systems existed in only a few cities, and usually in only parts of those.[18] And as William Collins, a participant in many of the opium conferences of the early twentieth century noted, in many parts of Asia "thousands of the population never come into contact with a medical man." Collins was mindful of the harm opium could cause but cognizant of the uneven distribution of care. He quipped that "these drugs" did not seem to "lose their efficacy because they [were] not prescribed or administered by a registered medical practitioner."[19] The few truly effective medicines, such as pharmaceutical quinine, were too expensive for almost all Asians.[20] Ideas about what was an appropriate medicine had begun to change, but people's access to that standard of care lagged behind.

Learning from One Another

The critique of opium's pervasive role in society took hold throughout Southeast Asia beginning in about 1890, in part because doubts about its legitimate medical use began to surface. Even if few people had access to the range of public and private health innovations that would prevent the conditions for which opium was commonly used, the existence of those methods began to undercut opium's status as useful medicine. The critique also developed in a transimperial context, in which anti-opium reformers, government officials, and health professionals all traveled to, reported on, and learned from other imperial powers. The colonial government in the Netherlands Indies was the first to send a representative to another colony with the explicit purpose of learning about opium policy. Concern about corruption and smuggling prompted by the distribution method for opium had led to an internal investigation and some policy changes as early as the 1860s, but corruption remained. In the late 1880s, when Dutch officials had come to the conclusion that they might need to adopt a new distribution system, they decided to send W. P. Groeneveldt, a Dutch member of the colony's advisory council and an expert on China, to French Indochina to study their government monopoly system.

The study trip, made in early 1890, displayed the trappings of both international relations and the common imperial mission of these colonial neighbors. The state-to-state relationship was evident in the official letter requesting that Groeneveldt, the official heading the small delegation, be permitted to conduct this study and be given courtesies of information and introduction to appropriate French and Vietnamese officials. After the visit, too, the Dutch government awarded the prestigious Order of the Netherlands Lion to the top French officials who had helped Groeneveldt, in "accordance," as one historian wrote "with international courtesies."[21] Both the language of the report and the policy recommendations emphasized the close comparisons of conditions in the two colonies made by Dutch officials and reflect Groeneveldt's perception that because the French and Dutch tasks were essentially similar, the Dutch could build easily on French policy innovations. The French, for instance, had lowered the price of opium in an effort to undercut smuggling, leading to an apparent increase in the number of smokers, so Groeneveldt recommended against this approach and in favor of a strong antismuggling police force. Soon after the report appeared, the Dutch adopted an opium monopoly in Java and Madura, modeled on the one operating in French Indochina.

The Dutch had little concern about levels of opium consumption but worried about corruption associated with opium sales. In 1890 policy was not yet driven by a critique of opium smoking or arguments that the colonial governments should stop selling opium in order to protect indigenous people's welfare. Groeneveldt made nearly no effort to distinguish between what later came to be called "legitimate" medical use and other uses. His sole attention to opium as medicinal was in observing that some "Annamite doctors" prescribe it for "intestinal ailments" to "excellent effect" and, in the conclusion to the study, the observation that opium is a "stimulant" and, when used properly, has beneficial effects for the consumer.[22]

Groeneveldt paid little attention to the effects of consumption, but worries about corruption and smuggling of opium prompted a broader discussion of the issue in the Indies both before and after he made the study trip. In a widely circulated pamphlet, an apothecary named J. Haak noted that the opium ordinary people purchased through the existing opium farm system had a widely varying morphine content. People who used farm opium for a medical purpose could not tell if the amount of opium they had purchased was sufficient for their needs, or perhaps too strong and likely to promote addiction. As an apothecary, he had a professional interest in encouraging people to purchase medicines from professionals, but in his pamphlet he argued for adoption of the government monopoly system so that opium could be produced more scientifically, resulting in more consistent morphine contents.[23] The Dutch debate was the first to take place within a transimperial context for assessing how to approach opium distribution, and it hinted at the ways future criticism of opium consumption would rest on distinctions between legitimate medical uses and more problematic recreational uses.

An Imperial Inquiry and Its Regional Consequences

In Britain, however, a broad critique of opium use had existed for some years. This critique initially reflected perceived problems with opium use in England. Press attention to high infant mortality associated with overuse of opiates by infants and children prompted government inquiries and was at least partially responsible for the 1868 Pharmacy Act, an early effort to medicalize and thereby restrict opiate use.[24] In 1874 reformers and missionaries founded the Society for the Suppression of the Opium Trade, initially focused on ending the opium trade from British India to China. Debates in Britain, and among British colonial officials, reveal the growing clash of perceptions about appropriate use of opium, particularly regarding whether opium smoking and eating could be considered medicine or were always recreational. British sales of opium in China so obviously fed recreational consumption that the Society for the Suppression of the Opium Trade gained traction in public opinion for their critique of British opium policy, and by the early 1890s had sufficient influence to demand a massive parliamentary study of the opium problem. This 1893–94 inquiry focused primarily on British involvement in the opium trade between India and China. In an effort to demonstrate the broader ill effects of a British imperial policy resting on production (in India) and sale (in China, in the rest of the

British Empire, and in other Asian empires) of opium, the inquiry extended to the rest of Asia.

The inquiry team sent questionnaires to British consular representatives in French Indochina and the Netherlands Indies, asking primarily for amounts consumed and distribution methods. Their survey also contained a question about whether users typically became addicts, and one about the effects of opium usage on "public health." In Indochina the acting British consul, J. L. O'Connell, answered the questions directly, claiming that most users "become slaves to the habit" and that the effect on public health was "prejudicial, especially on Europeans."[25] The acting British consul in Batavia, A. F. MacLachlan, solicited a report from the Dutch government, which directed a response through their consul in Calcutta. The Dutch report provided more detail about amounts and distribution and preparation methods, but completely evaded the questions on addiction and effects on public health.[26]

The Commission visited only India, but while there interviewed people of many different nationalities and experiences, including doctors, missionaries, merchants, and business owners, from India, Britain, China, the United States, and Europe. And to gain knowledge about the experience in the rest of the Asian colonies, the Commission sent a list of questions to the governors of Hong Kong and the Straits Settlements. The governor general of the Straits Settlements received a list of eighteen questions and consulted with thirty-five men, many of them local officials but also physicians, businessmen, and religious leaders. Almost all of them (twenty-nine) had European names. Of the remaining six, four had Chinese names, and two were identified as prominent Muslims, meaning Malay in ethnicity.[27] As a group they were sanguine about opium use in the colony, believing most opium smokers to be moderate users, and reporting there was no resentment in the colony about the British opium policy. They also reported that both Chinese and Malay inhabitants tended to believe in the medicinal powers of opium and to see it as necessary. This report focused exclusively on opium consumed by smoking, thereby allowing the respondents to evade the topic of European opium consumption and exploring only slightly the question of opium as medicine. Overall, although a few respondents opposed opium smoking as a matter of principle, the majority of those questioned favored the current opium system, and their answers reflected their desire that it not be questioned.[28] Europeans in the colony assuredly did consume medicinal opium, possibly in ways that were also recreational, so the fact that in this report such consumption was not even seen as, let alone reported as, opium use demonstrates that there was a perception, as yet not much voiced, that there were legitimate medical uses for opium and that there were other kinds of uses, possibly not legitimate.

The Commission also explored opium policy in Burma by interviewing several British colonial officials and private citizens who lived in Burma when the Commission was in India. Britain had only recently (in 1886) extended its rule over the northern part of Burma, where opium historically had been grown. After 1886 it appeared that opium consumption throughout the colony increased, and especially that ethnic Burmans in lower Burma, who were believed not to have a tradition of recreational opium consumption, had started to smoke and were becoming addicted in large numbers. A new law was coming into effect in 1894, forbidding ethnic Burmans from smoking opium recreationally after that date, allowing existing consumers of opium who registered with the government to continue to purchase opium from government opium shops and stipulating who was licensed to distribute medicinal opium.[29] This approach of registering existing users, disallowing new recreational users, and permitting medicinal use provided a model for nearly all the colonial governments in Asia during the next fifteen years. The most significant variation came in how colonial officials defined appropriate medical use.

As the Burmese law demonstrated, the British definition was broad. Among those licensed to possess significant quantities of opium for distribution and provide it to others were British doctors and pharmacists as well as any doctor with a degree from an Indian medical school or qualified under the English Medical Acts, meaning nearly all doctors in the colony. The rationale provided by the British government for this broad licensing: "There is no danger that gentlemen of this class will deal in opium illicitly."[30] The testimony did not touch on what kinds of medical conditions called for opium. British law also permitted tattooers to possess a large amount of opium for distribution, since they needed to relieve pain.[31] Although British law made a distinction between recreational and medicinal use of opium, and approved the latter more than the former, it did not provide strict guidance about what constituted an appropriate medical use or specify that some preparations of opium were medicinal and others recreational. British officials justified the policy in part by the need for Asians to be able to follow traditional medical practice, especially since few had access to modern health care. In a 1904 report, for example, which often emphasized the difficulties in controlling illicit traffic in opium, W. J. Keith, secretary to the financial commissioner of Burma, concluded, "There is in Burma as elsewhere a distinction between abuse and use." In Burma, however, the medicinal use was more extended than in some other places, since "the habitual use of the drug as a preventive of fever and dysentery [was] practically a necessity to the dwellers on the sea-coast and in or near the hills and to fisherman in the delta."[32] Keith echoed a common British sentiment: controlling access to opium was a legitimate activity of government but needed to be done in ways appropriate to the specific circumstances in an area. After 1894 the debate among leaders of countries in Asia increasingly revolved around the question of the nature of legitimate medical use, and not whether there was a distinction between medicinal and recreational use.

The massive investigation done for the British Royal Commission, with the reports and transcripts of interviews running to seven volumes, had no significant immediate policy result in Britain, which continued to support trade in opium with China and to sell opium in its Asian colonies. The pro-opium opponents of the inquiry succeeded both in protecting the opium trade and in focusing the bulk of testimony on India and China. But the wide range of the British Empire in Asia, and the public, voluminous nature of the evidence gathered by the inquiry, meant that its evidentiary base and conclusions, as well as the debates in the testimony, supporting evidence, and results about the usefulness and effects of opium consumption, had a broader audience than just the British Parliament. The anti-opium forces redoubled their efforts, particularly working to attract doctors to their side since the testimony of physicians during the Royal Commission that opium was relatively harmless seemed to have been damaging to their cause. Anti-opium publications such as *Friend of China* (British) and *Opiumvloek* (Dutch) expanded their efforts, but the most important lead was taken by missionaries in China and their supporters.

A group of British, American, and Chinese physicians in China came together in 1896 to form the Anti-Opium League in China. One of their first acts was to send a questionnaire to all the physicians in China they could identify. The respondents, numbering slightly more than one hundred, were nearly all English, American, or Chinese, but there were significant numbers of Scottish respondents and some Canadians, Irish, and Germans as well. Not surprisingly, given the source of the questionnaire, no one had anything positive to say about the consumption of opium. At best, comments noted that consumers with sufficient funds could stave off ill effects longer than those who were poor.[33] The survey phrased its medical questions in a leading way. One asked whether smoking opium worked as a prophylactic against malaria, fever, or rheumatism, another whether local Chinese believed it to be a prophylactic, and then finally whether Chinese medical practitioners prescribed opium smoking for chronic illnesses, and if so, did it provide relief. The questions asked only about smoking opium, not the methods of opium use common to Europeans and Americans. Part of drawing the sharp line between inappropriate and appropriate use was putting the practice of smoking into the purely recreational category. Nearly three-quarters of respondents said opium was not a prophylactic, and nearly two-thirds said the Chinese did not believe it was, but in each case about one-quarter did not answer this question. Nearly everyone said that Chinese practitioners did recommend or prescribe opium, but equally reported that relief was only temporary.[34] These answers could easily have been given by physicians who were neutral or favorable to opium, since they reflected the contemporary medical knowledge that opium was useful for treating symptoms but neither prevented nor cured disease. When deployed by physicians, however, this rhetorical strategy, of deemphasizing its usefulness as a medicine and emphasizing the addictive nature of the drug, was persuasive. During the 1890s European colonial governments had begun to control distribution of opium to prevent corruption and had taken the first halting steps toward modern sanitation and medical facilities, which would decrease widespread palliative use of opium. Colonial governments were not, however, taking steps to eradicate nonmedicinal use. Activists, like those in the Anti-Opium League, prepared to challenge that complacency.

Opium and U.S. Rule in the Philippines

The first president of the Anti-Opium League of China, H. C. DuBose, was an American missionary who was also turning his attention to the new U.S. colony in the Philippines. DuBose used his contacts with U.S. politicians as well as other missionaries in the region to advocate against opium and alcohol for the Philippines soon after the United States acquired it as a colony. In 1899 DuBose, who had been born in South Carolina, wrote to John McLaurin, that state's junior senator, to encourage him to oppose plans to allow sale of opium in the Philippines.[35] McLaurin, though a Democrat, had recently sided with the Republicans in voting to ratify the Treaty of Paris, ending the war with Spain and annexing the Philippines. DuBose seems to have hoped that the ruling Republicans would listen to their new supporter on the Philippines. His letter was passed to the departments of state and war and prompted a debate about the proper policy. In the midst of many competing and urgent priorities in U.S. colonial policy in 1899–1900, however, U.S. officials defaulted to the same opium policy for the Philippines that existed in the United States: no regulation other than an import tax. This approach seemed simple and likely to bring in revenue.[36]

American missionaries in the Philippines took up the anti-opium cause from their compatriots in China, lobbying President Theodore Roosevelt and Secretary of War Elihu Root through their churches and reform groups in the United States, as well as directly lobbying Governor General William Howard Taft.[37]

In 1903 they delayed implementation of an opium farm system, modeled on the previously common system in European colonies of Southeast Asia. They also pressed successfully for a commission that would travel to Asian countries to study the systems in place and recommend a policy for the United States.[38] This commission consisted of Reverend Charles H. Brent, Episcopal bishop of Manila; Edward C. Carter, commissioner for public health; and Jose Albert, a physician from Manila. Although two of the three commissioners were medical experts, the investigators focused more on recreational than medical usage.

This U.S. commission pursued an ambitious transimperial learning project in an effort to decide about the best opium policy for the Philippines. Progressives in the Roosevelt administration approached difficult policy decisions by first studying the problem and how others had approached it. This impulse fit well with the growing tendency in colonial Southeast Asia for imperial officials to see themselves as engaged in a common endeavor and to share books, advice, and information, as well as build personal relationships. The trip was an extensive one, lasting from mid-August 1903 to early January 1904, with additional interviews in the Philippines in February 1904. Commissioners visited, in this order, Hong Kong (for organizational purposes), Japan, Formosa, China (Shanghai), Hong Kong, French Indochina (Saigon), Singapore, Burma, and Java. In each place they met with local officials and sometimes with doctors, local businessmen, and religious leaders. The official report of the commission praised "foreign officials and representatives of the American Government" who provided "interested, prompt and efficient aid." They noted that commission members were "conscious of the wider aspect of the problem" and hoped this report would "be the starting point of a new investigation in other countries."[39] Despite the differences in goals for opium policy, officials in each country wanted to improve their ability to control the opium trade and to learn about medical innovations and how to combat abuse.

The report's findings and recommendations section starkly contrasted appropriate "medicinal" use of opium with harmful recreational use. The commissioners held up as a model the strict prohibition in Japan, where even the gear for smoking opium was distributed only by pharmacists and only with a doctor's prescription. Even though most Europeans interviewed by the commission noted that opium was used in Southeast Asia in ways that blurred the distinction between medicinal and recreational use, the American commissioners tried to draw a strict line. They had been charged with investigating opium in other countries in order to "reduce and restrain the use of opium" in the Philippines.[40] This investigation was not open-ended, then, but was meant to figure out how to best limit opium use. Perhaps because of this mandate, the commissioners did not ask searching questions about the nature and effectiveness of medicinal use. But their questions and findings reflected the still confused thinking about the medicinal role of opium.

Some parts of the report grudgingly presented opium as useful. In the findings on China, the report noted, "We administer morphine to relieve pain. The life of the indigent Chinese coolie is pain, caused by privation. The opium sot is an object of pity rather than of contempt."[41] The pity was mixed with blame, though. This part of the report echoed American missionary critiques of the lack of healthy food and sport in China and of the economic and political structure of society, which perpetuated stultifying inequality, to the detriment of rich and poor alike.[42] The report also explained that people who lived in the "unhealthful districts" of Java might use opium at higher rates, and Burma had more casual rules about opium in order to combat malarial chills and due to their tradition of extensive tattoos. Tattooers were allowed to distribute opium in the same way as medical professionals.[43] These conditions may have justified opium use, but they were problems to be solved, not acceptable over the long term.

Transcripts of interviews at the various stops suggest the commissioners had little interest in exploring medicinal needs or the ways in which opium was used that may have had medicinal purposes. The specific questions differed from person to person, but the main subjects of interest were whether moderate opium use was possible, whether opium use always caused serious harm, whether opium or alcohol use was worse, and the differences in opium use among different ethnic groups. Commissioners commonly asked about the insurability of opium users (for life insurance) as well. They did speak to at least one doctor in most of the places they visited, but rarely asked different questions of the doctors than of government officials, missionaries, and businessmen.

Sometimes medical issues came up in the midst of answers to these other questions. In Singapore, Mrs. Blackstone, a member of the Woman's Christian Temperance Union, testified that opium was used "very largely" among women, who "begin taking it as a medicine, but it gets such a hold on them that they can not give it up." Asked about whether children were given opium, she replied that it was given to European and Chinese children, "as paregoric is," to help them sleep.[44] With no further elaboration of either of these statements, the report left the line between medicinal and recreational use of opium unclear. What illness or injury prompted the women to take opium long enough to become addicted? And was Mrs. Blackstone unaware that paregoric contained opium? Respondents in Burma were most likely to mention the need for opium as a response to malaria and call it necessary.[45] As with earlier reports, the method of consumption seemed to matter in assessments regarding when opium was a medicine. Paregoric and other tinctures were acceptable; smoking was not; recent increases in cases of injected morphia prompted universal concern among interviewees.[46]

No definitive picture of opium consumption and its effects could be painted by relying on the testimony gathered for this report. Those interviewed disagreed wildly about the percentage of people who smoked, the immediate and long-term effects, the methods for controlling access, and the effectiveness of existing laws. Nearly everyone did agree, however, that government policies should focus on reducing overall consumption of opiates and increasing medical oversight. The Philippine Commission agreed. It argued that where the habit of opium smoking was well-established, immediate prohibition was impossible. In their 1905 report they recommended a government monopoly registration of opium smokers and gradual movement toward prohibition, "except for medical purposes," within three years.[47] These policies borrowed heavily from similar ones in effect in Formosa and the Netherlands Indies. As with those plans, it left the definition of medical purposes vague, perhaps deliberately so.

The Philippines did adopt the recommendation for prohibition of opium within three years, and by 1908 Philippine local law and U.S. federal law combined to prohibit use of opium in the Philippines except under a doctor's prescription. The Philippine government did not adopt a government monopoly during the 1905–8 period. That level of government bureaucracy was deemed too complicated, especially for such a short time. Anti-opium forces also decried the possibility of the government's directly selling opium, making it clear that the political consequences of an opium monopoly would be negative.[48] Passing a law to prohibit opium use was simple; prohibiting opium use was not. In 1907, the last year opium could be freely imported into the Philippines (subject only to a high tariff), imports reached record levels of more than 728,000 pounds. And already in early 1909 James F. Smith, governor general of the Philippines, stated that it would be "very difficult to enforce prohibition" without the "aid" of other countries. U.S. officials perceived a need for a regional solution to the opium problem and invited states having "possessions and direct interest" in the region to jointly investigate the issue.[49] This resulted in the 1909 Shanghai Commission, which brought together the most significant opium-producing and -consuming nations. The Commission's task was to investigate and share information about opium consumption and control, but attendees believed that it was a likely first step toward a convention or treaty. They therefore negotiated carefully to preserve and advance imperial interests, one of the most important of which was the right to define legitimate medical use.

Hints of the disputes that would emerge during the course of the conference about medical use appeared in the information countries chose to include (or not include) in their reports for the Commission and in the composition of the delegations. The United States, Japan, and China all included medical doctors among their delegates. Britain, France, the Netherlands, and Portugal included only consular and colonial officials, the latter mostly from the opium bureaus or tax departments.[50] The instructions for the investigatory reports did not include requests for any information about medical use of opium, and nearly no country included that information. This Commission, which might have been expected to represent the culmination of the growing global understanding of the benefits of modern medicine, the appropriate limits on the use of opiates, and the myriad ways that improvements in infrastructure and public health could improve health more than distribution of opiates, instead revealed that colonial powers would still assert the unique needs of their own empires when necessary. Dr. Hamilton Wright, an anti-opium activist and head of the U.S. delegation, attempted several times to get agreement on a resolution restricting opium to "legitimate medical use." Sir Cecil Clementi Smith, head of the British delegation, skillfully deflected and avoided this discussion for most of the conference but in the end was forced to directly state the British position: "To put it perfectly plainly, and to be entirely frank, the British Delegation is not able to accept the view that opium should be confined simply and solely to medical uses."[51] Wright and Clementi Smith retired to a private conference, returning with a resolution flexible enough to earn unanimous approval. It called for "gradual suppression" and noted that "use of opium in any form otherwise than for medical purposes [was] held by almost every country to be a matter for prohibition or for careful regulation."[52] Each country could interpret this language in its own way, as was the intention, but claim to be working toward a common goal.

The 1909 Shanghai Opium Commission revealed both the limits of the transimperial process of learning, exchange, and collaboration that had occurred in colonial Southeast Asia since 1890 regarding opium, and the ways in which that transimperial process would change after 1910 under the commitment to "gradual suppression." Even as British colonial officials such as Clementi Smith asserted Britain's right as a sovereign imperial power to define legitimate medical use for its colonial subjects, opium, and the disease symptoms for which opium offered relief, remained stubbornly resistant to control by the imperial state. The resolution calling for gradual suppression concluded by noting "the desirability of a re-examination of their systems of regulation in the light of the experience of other countries dealing with the same problem."[53] Since 1890 colonial officials in Southeast Asia had been doing just that, sharing knowledge of disease, medicine, and appropriate regulations for opium. In the aftermath of the U.S. decision to pursue prohibition, and of the other imperial powers to endorse gradual suppression, the transimperial threat posed by opium shifted. When imperial officials claimed subjects still needed access to opium to combat malaria or dysentery, they invited criticism of their insufficient public health measures. Smuggling threatened state authority, not just opium farmers' profits. These threats prompted ever closer collaboration, especially intelligence sharing about smugglers, even while imperial officials disagreed about how best to control opium for the benefit of their subjects.

NOTES

1. Mark Harrison, *Contagion: How Commerce Has Spread Disease* (New Haven, CT: Yale University Press, 2012). See especially chapter 7, 174–210.

2. A selective list of some of the works that have most informed my thinking about the late imperial state include Tony Ballantyne and Antoinette Burton, "Empires and the Reach of the Global," and Emily S. Rosenberg, "Transnational Currents in a Shrinking World," both in *A World Connecting, 1870–1945*, edited by Emily S. Rosenberg (Cambridge, U.K.: Cambridge University Press, 2012), 285–434, 815–998; Alfred W. McCoy, *Policing America's Empire: The United States, the Philippines and the Rise of the Surveillance State* (Madison: University of Wisconsin Press, 2009); Rudolf Mrazek, *Engineers of Happy Land: Technology and Nationalism in a Colony* (Princeton, NJ: Princeton University Press, 2009); James C. Scott, *Seeing Like a State: How Certain Schemes to Improve the Human Condition Have Failed* (New Haven, CT: Yale University Press, 1999); Eric Tagliacozzo, *Secret Trades, Porous Borders: Smuggling and States along a Southeast Asian Frontier, 1865–1915* (New Haven, CT: Yale University Press, 2005).

3. The essays in Julian Go and Anne L. Foster, eds., *The American Colonial State in the Philippines: Global Perspectives* (Durham, NC: Duke University Press, 2003) remain indispensable. See also Aidan Forth and Jonas Kreienbaum, "A Shared Malady: Concentration Camps in the British, Spanish, American and German Empires," *Journal of Modern European History* 14, no. 2 (2016): 245–67; Daniel E. Bender and Jana K. Lipman, *Making the Empire Work: Labor and United States Imperialism* (New York: New York University Press, 2015); Alfred W. McCoy and Francisco Scarano, eds., *Colonial Crucible: Empire in the Making of the Modern American State* (Madison: University of Wisconsin Press, 2009). From a somewhat different perspective, see J. P. Daughton, "Behind the Imperial Curtain: International Humanitarian Efforts and the Critique of French Colonialism in the Interwar Years," *French Historical Studies* 34, no. 3 (Summer 2011): 503–28.

4. Warwick Anderson has pioneered work on disease and empire in comparative perspective. See especially "The Colonial Medicine of Settler States: Comparing Histories of Indigenous Health," *Health and History: Journal of the Australian and New Zealand Society for the History of Medicine* 9, no. 2 (2007): 144–54, and Warwick Anderson and Hans Pols, "Scientific Patriotism: Medical Science and National Self-Fashioning in

Southeast Asia," in *Endless Empire: Spain's Retreat, Europe's Eclipse, America's Decline*, edited by Alfred W. McCoy, Josep Fradera, and Stephen Jacobson (Madison: University of Wisconsin Press, 2012), 265–72. See also Robert Peckham and David M. Pomfret, eds., *Imperial Contagions: Medicine, Hygiene, and Cultures of Planning in Asia* (Hong Kong: Hong Kong University Press, 2013); José Amador, *Medicine and Nation Building in the Americas, 1890–1940* (Nashville, TN: Vanderbilt University Press, 2015); Anne-Emanuelle Birn and Theodore M. Brown, eds., *Comrades in Health: U.S. Health Internationalists, Abroad and at Home* (New Brunswick, NJ: Rutgers University Press, 2013).

5. The spread of plague in Asia in the late nineteenth century provides a dramatic example. See Robert Peckham, "Infective Economies: Empire, Panic and the Business of Disease," *Journal of Imperial and Commonwealth History* 41, no. 2 (2013): 211–37.

6. Most histories of medicine focus on discovery, not adoption, of new techniques and drugs. The historian of medicine Roy Porter rightly called the mid-nineteenth-century insights about bacteriology "one of medicine's few true revolutions," but it took decades for the benefits to be globally dispersed. Roy Porter, *The Greatest Benefit to Mankind: A Medical History of Humanity* (New York: Norton, 1997), 428.

7. Carl A. Trocki, *Opium, Empire and the Global Political Economy: A Study of the Asian Opium Trade, 1750–1950* (New York: Routledge, 1999), 13–26.

8. Trocki, *Opium, Empire and the Global Political Economy*, 137–52; Anne L. Foster, "Opium, the United States and the Civilizing Mission in Colonial Southeast Asia," *Social History of Alcohol and Drugs* 24, no. 1 (Winter 2010): 8–9.

9. For discussion of rising anti-opium sentiment, see James R. Rush, *Opium to Java: Revenue Farming and Chinese Enterprise in Colonial Indonesia, 1860–1910* (Ithaca, NY: Cornell University Press, 1990), 198–241; Carl A. Trocki, *Opium and Empire: Chinese Society in Colonial Singapore, 1800–1910* (Ithaca, NY: Cornell University Press, 1990), 183–219; Ashley Wright, *Opium and Empire in Southeast Asia: Regulating Consumption in British Burma* (New York: Palgrave Macmillan, 2014).

10. David T. Courtwright, *Dark Paradise: A History of Opiate Addiction in America* (Cambridge, MA: Harvard University Press, 2001), 35–84.

11. See, for example, the discussion of opium smoking in Joshua Rowntree, *The Imperial Drug Trade* (London, 1905), 139–46.

12. Deborah Neill, *Networks in Tropical Medicine: Internationalism, Colonialism, and the Rise of a Medical Specialty, 1890–1930* (Stanford, CA: Stanford University Press, 2012), 12–43.

13. P. N. Gerrard, *On the Hygienic Management of Labour in the Tropics* (Singapore: Methodist Publishing House, 1913), xi–xiv, 1–28. Using an opiate for dysentery is mentioned on 25; for diarrhea on 28.

14. Warwick Anderson's *Colonial Pathologies: American Tropical Medicine, Race and Hygiene in the Philippines* (Durham, NC: Duke University Press, 2006) is the most succinct introduction. See also Brenda S. A. Yeoh, "Urban Sanitation, Health and Water Supply in Late Nineteenth and Early Twentieth-Century Colonial Singapore," *South East Asia Research* 1, no. 2 (September 1993): 143–72.

15. Robert Peckham, "Hygienic Nature: Afforestation and the Greening of Hong Kong," *Modern Asian Studies* 49, no. 4 (July 2015): 1177–209; David Brody, "Building

Empire: Architecture and American Imperialism in the Philippines," *Journal of Asian American Studies* 4, no. 2 (June 2001): 123–45.

16. For example, see Laurence Monnais-Rousselot, "La médicalisation de la mère et de son enfant: L'exemple du Vietnam sous domination française, 1860–1939," *Canadian Bulletin of Medical History* 19, no. 1 (Spring 2002): 113–37; Penny Edwards, "Bitter Pills: Colonialism, Medicine and Nationalism in Burma, 1870–1940," *Journal of Burma Studies* 14 (2010): 21–58; Liesbeth Hesselink, *Healers on the Colonial Market: Native Doctors and Midwives in the Dutch East Indies* (Leiden, Netherlands: KITLV Press, 2011).

17. Although about a slightly later time period, see Tomoko Akami, "A Quest to Be Global: The League of Nations Health Organization and Inter-colonial Regional Governing Agendas of the Far Eastern Association of Tropical Health, 1910–1925," *International History Review* 38, no. 1 (2016): 1–23; Tomoko Akami, "Imperial Politics, Intercolonialism, and the Shaping of Global Governing Norms: Public Health Expert Networks in Asia and the League of Nations Health Organization, 1908–1937," *Journal of Global History* 12, no. 1 (2017): 4–25. See also Bernard Hillemand and Alain Ségal, "Les six dernières conferences sanitaires internationales 1892 à 1926: Prémices de l'Organisation Mondiale de la Santé (O.M.S.)," *Histoire des sciences médicales* 48, no. 1 (2014): 131–38.

18. Matthew Gandy, "The Bacteriological City and Its Discontents," *Historical Geography* 34 (2006): 14–25, esp. 18–22.

19. William J. Collins, *The International Opium Convention: Drugs and Legislation* (London: J. Bale, Sons and Danielson, 1912), 14.

20. Daniel R. Headrick, "The Tools of Imperialism: Technology and the Expansion of European Colonial Empires in the Nineteenth Century," *Journal of Modern History* 51, no. 2 (June 1979): 145–47. Headrick claims that by the 1830s, quinine was inexpensive enough to be in general use. That was true for Europeans, but not for most Asians. See Michitake Aso, "Patriotic Hygiene: Tracing New Places of Knowledge Production about Malaria in Vietnam, 1919–1975," *Journal of Southeast Asian Studies* 44, no. 3 (October 2013): 426–28.

21. Biographical information about Groeneveldt from Marinus Willem de Visser, "Levensbericht van Willem Pieter Groeneveldt," *Jaarboek van de Maatschappij der Nederlandse Kunde, 1916* (1916), *Digitale bibliotheek voor de Nederlandse letteren*, http://www .dbnl.org/tekst/_jaa003191601_01/_jaa003191601_01_0016.php. Information about the trip itself from Koos Kuiper, "Du Nouveau sur la mystérieuse mission de Batavia à Saigon en 1890," *Archipel* 77 (2009): 27–44; this information from 35–36.

22. W. P. Groeneveldt, *Rapport over het Opium-Monopolie in Fransch Indo-China* (Batavia, Netherlands Indies: Landsdrukkerij, 1890), 86–87, 115. The Dutch word is *matig*, which means "temperately" or "moderately."

23. J. Haak, *Opium Regie met Normaal Tandjoe* (Samarang, 1889). In the 1880s and 1890s the budding anti-opium movement in the Netherlands Indies focused on ending the opium farm system and moving to a system of government monopoly, not on ending opium consumption. A popular anti-opium novel published in 1886 (translated into English in 1888), *Baboe Dalima*, dramatically features the effects of opium farm corruption on the lives of innocent Dutch and Javanese but does not call for prohibition of opium use. The Anti-Opium Bond, established in 1889, was the vanguard of popular anti-opium

activism in the Netherlands and Netherlands Indies, and also initially merely advocated ending the opium farm.

24. Virginia Berridge, *Opium and the People: Opiate Use and Drug Control Policy in Nineteenth and Early Twentieth Century England* (London: Free Association Books, 1999), 97–105, 120–22.

25. Great Britain, *First Report of the Royal Commission on Opium*, vol. 5: *Appendices* (London, 1894), 345.

26. Great Britain, *First Report of the Royal Commission on Opium*, 5:344.

27. Nearly all those with European names appear to have been British, although origins are not always possible to determine from the information provided. Of the four people with Chinese names who were interviewed, three were then, or had previously been, opium farmers.

28. Great Britain, *First Report of the Royal Commission on Opium*, 5:145–84. This is the whole section on the Straits Settlements, with the report on 145–54, and enumeration and summary of witness statements on 154–84.

29. Wright, *Opium and Empire in Southeast Asia*, especially chapters 2 and 4.

30. Great Britain, *First Report of the Royal Commission on Opium*, vol. 2: *Minutes of Evidence* (London, 1894), 490.

31. Great Britain, *First Report of the Royal Commission on Opium*, 2:492–93.

32. W. J. Keith, "Report on the Working of the Revised Arrangements for the Vend of Opium in Lower Burma during the year ended 31st March 1904" (Rangoon, Burma, November 1904), IOR/V/24/3127, India Office Records, British Library, London.

33. William Hector Park, compiler, *Opinions of over 100 Physicians on the Use of Opium in China* (Shanghai: American Presbyterian Mission Press, 1899), vii–xii, 1–8. Interestingly, the chart listing where people came from also listed where they received their medical education. Most people, but not all, were educated in or near their home country.

34. Park, *Opinions of over 100 Physicians*, 34–40.

35. Rev. H. C. DuBose to Senator John McLaurin, extracted in memorandum, September 23, 1899, file 1023–1, entry 5, RG 350, National Archives and Records Administration, College Park, Maryland.

36. This development is discussed in Anne L. Foster, "Models for Governing: Opium and Colonial Policies in Southeast Asia, 1898–1910," in Go and Foster, *The American Colonial State in the Philippines*, 96–97.

37. There was a rudimentary press campaign, especially in religious periodicals. See, for instance, Wilbur F. Crafts, "Capital News from a Reformer's Viewpoint: McKinley and Missions," *The Advance*, May 10, 1900, 671. Crafts was the author of a popular, multiedition book advocating temperance for "native races." The 1900 edition of the book focused on the evils of alcohol in the Philippines under U.S. rule. Wilbur F. Crafts, *Protection of Native Races against Intoxicants and Opium* (Chicago, 1900), 186–206.

38. As discussed in Foster, "Models for Governing," 98–99, both personal lobbying and a massive telegram campaign shaped this decision.

39. U.S. Congress, Senate Committee on the Philippines, *Message of the President, transmitting the report of the committee appointed by the Philippine Commission to investi-*

gate the use of opium and traffic therein, Senate Doc. 265 (Washington, DC, 1906), 19–20 (hereafter *Traffic in Opium*).

40. *Traffic in Opium*, 21.

41. *Traffic in Opium*, 29.

42. For example, see Stefan Hübner, "Muscular Christianity and the Western Civilizing Mission: Elwood S. Brown, the YMCA, and the Idea of the Far Eastern Championship Games," *Diplomatic History* 39, no. 3 (June 2015): 532–57.

43. *Traffic in Opium*, 42–44.

44. *Traffic in Opium*, 100–101.

45. *Traffic in Opium*, 117, 122.

46. The final set of questions for the longer interviews was almost always about morphia, and the increased use of that preparation of the drug was universally condemned.

47. *Traffic in Opium*, 50–51.

48. See the discussion of this debate and decision in Anne L. Foster, "Opium, the United States, and the Civilizing Mission in Colonial Southeast Asia," *Social History of Alcohol and Drugs* 24, no. 1 (Winter 2010): 12–15.

49. James F. Smith to Charles Denby (U.S. consul in China), February 19, 1909, entry 33, in RG 43, Records of International Conferences, Commissions and Expositions, National Archives and Records Administration. See the broader discussion in Anne L. Foster, "Prohibition as Superiority: Policing Opium in South-East Asia, 1898–1925," *International History Review* 22, no. 2 (June 2000): 260–64.

50. It appears that both Germany and Austria-Hungary also had medical professionals as delegates, but those men were simultaneously the consular officials for their countries in China, so it seems unlikely they were chosen for their medical expertise. International Opium Commission, *Report of the Proceedings*, vol. 1 (Shanghai, 1909), 3–6.

51. International Opium Commission, *Report of the Proceedings*, 1:46–50. The Chinese and Japanese delegations supported the United States, while the French, Dutch, Portuguese, and Siamese delegations supported the British position on this matter.

52. International Opium Commission, *Report of the Proceedings*, 1:61.

53. International Opium Commission, *Report of the Proceedings*, 1:61.

PART III. GOVERNING STRUCTURES

6. ONE SERVICE, THREE SYSTEMS, MANY EMPIRES: THE U.S. CONSULAR SERVICE AND THE GROWTH OF U.S. GLOBAL POWER, 1789–1924

Nicole M. Phelps

In the long nineteenth century, the U.S. Consular Service (USCS) helped to enmesh the United States in a global network of trade dominated by the great imperial powers and concentrated in the world's major port cities. Working alongside one another in these cosmopolitan cities, consular officials representing governments from all over the globe advanced national and imperial interests by collecting customs duties for government coffers and protecting state sovereignty by restricting and channeling flows across geographic borders (see table 6.1). Yet consular officials also played a significant role in knitting the imperial world system together by smoothing the cross-border travels of goods, capital, and people. To this end, consular officials at major ports provided routine paperwork that could be trusted by other border officials. They also helped governments, commercial interests, and individuals cope with jarring disruptions to these flows, from natural catastrophes and shipwrecks to illnesses and other personal misfortunes. Their work was the stuff of both transnational and transimperial connections.

This major port-based consular system was distinct from the nineteenth-century diplomatic system, which was based in imperial and national political capitals. Some of those political capitals were also major ports, but diplomatic and consular officials operated separately and had distinct functions. Indeed most governments had separate diplomatic and consular institutions in the nineteenth century, and the United States was ahead of the curve when it combined the USCS with the diplomatic service to create the U.S. Foreign Service

TABLE 6.1. Cities with the Most Consular Officials, c. 1897

City	Number of Consular Officials
London	25
New York City	25
Liverpool	24
Marseilles	24
Hamburg	24
Paris	23
Berlin	23
Genoa	23
Antwerp	23
Lisbon	23
Barcelona	23
Cadiz	23
Glasgow	22
Havre	22
Bremen	22
Malaga	22
Christiania (Oslo)	22
San Francisco	22
Cardiff	21
Copenhagen	21
Amsterdam	21
Naples	21
Palermo	21
Venice	21
Ghent	21
Havana	21
Valencia	21
Boston	21
Liege	20

Source: Data from National Archives and Records Administration, specifically the various country files in collection 19: Reports on the Consular Service of Foreign Countries, 1897, Inventory 15, Record Group 59, General Records of the Department of State, NARA; the DOS-created ledger that is Volume 2 in 883: Analyses of Reports on Consular Establishments of Foreign Powers, 1907, Inventory 15, NARA; and the section of the *Register of the Department of State* that lists foreign consular posts in the United States.

in 1924. Diplomats dealt with high politics and representational functions, and governments were limited by international norms and laws to establishing one embassy or legation per empire or country.[1]

Consular officials, on the other hand, dealt with the everyday practicalities of keeping people, goods, and capital moving through the proper channels across national and imperial borders. Bilateral treaties allowed them to be posted wherever there was a perceived need, and the norm of fee-based remuneration and relatively low salaries facilitated their proliferation in the long nineteenth century (see figure 6.1). Consular agents provided official representation not only in Europe but also in colonial entrepôts. The major port consular system was open to any government that wanted to engage in trade and was willing to abide by the rules and norms that had been initially developed in Europe. This consular system, with its emphasis on trade and aid to sailors and other travelers, is what comes to many people's minds when they think of consuls, and in the relatively sparse literature on consuls, it is what gets much of the attention.[2]

But in the long nineteenth century, this relatively open system of major port consular posts coexisted with two other consular systems that were far more exclusive. One of these systems operated in what the U.S. Department of State (DOS) referred to as "non-Christian countries," including the Ottoman Empire and China.[3] Its defining feature was extraterritoriality, with sending governments having the right to exercise direct jurisdiction over their citizens or subjects in the host country. This system was explicitly unequal because the "non-Christian" governments did not have reciprocal rights in Europe or the Americas. It relied on interimperial cooperation for its maintenance. In the U.S. case, it also relied on cooperation with local employees to overcome significant language barriers. This consular system was especially fragile and prone to corruption because only a few people had the linguistic and cultural expertise to participate in and oversee this particular matrix of power and dependence. Nonetheless, like the major port consular system, it advanced U.S. interests and power.

The third consular system was that of informal empire. In this system the rules of the major port system applied, rather than extraterritoriality. However, unlike in the major ports, only one government had a consular presence. The usual effect was to forge a bilateral relationship between the sending government and the host locality that sidelined imperial and national governments, but these consular posts could also help to generate interimperial alignments. The U.S. government used its consular service to gain access to rival empires and

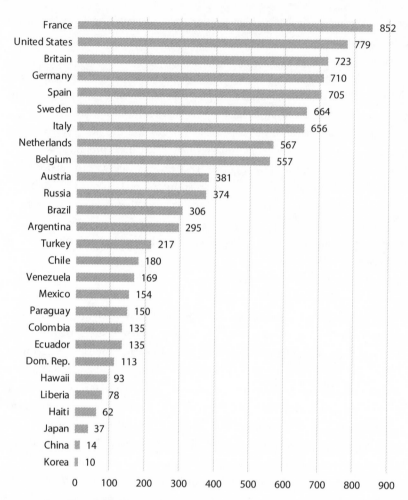

FIGURE 6.1. Size of consular services, 1897.
Source: See note 6.

to strengthen its official and commercial presence more than other governments did, particularly in the period between the U.S. Civil War and World War I (see table 6.2). A significant number of these informal empire posts were in Central America and the Caribbean, where, it should be noted, there was less formal empire with which to contend. Even more of these posts were in the British Empire, however, and especially in Canada. These posts were often operated by British subjects. In addition to expanding the U.S. economic foothold in the British dominion, USCS officials created and embodied an alignment of British

TABLE 6.2. Consular Services with the Most "Informal Empire" Posts, c. 1897

Country	Informal Empire Posts*	Total Consular Posts	Percentage of Informal Empire Posts
United States	197	779	25
Spain	115	705	16
Sweden	86	664	13
Italy	78	656	12
France	100	852	12
Argentina	33	295	11
Britain	70	723	10

*"Informal empire posts" are defined as those at which only one government is represented.
Source: Data from National Archives and Records Administration, specifically the various country files in collection 19: Reports on the Consular Service of Foreign Countries, 1897, Inventory 15, Record Group 59, General Records of the Department of State, NARA; the DOS-created ledger that is Volume 2 in 883: Analyses of Reports on Consular Establishments of Foreign Powers, 1907, Inventory 15, NARA; and the section of the *Register of the Department of State* that lists foreign consular posts in the United States.

and American interests that contributed to the post–Civil War rapprochement between the two countries.

The three consular systems, supplemented at times by the diplomatic system, furthered the transborder flow of people, goods, and capital that, in turn, generated U.S. economic, political, and cultural power. The United States used that power to acquire colonies, build an informal empire, and cooperate on an equal footing with other imperial powers to preserve and expand imperial structures. The fact that the USCS operated within the three different systems with an annual average of 713 posts in operation across the globe in the period from 1872 to 1906 made for an unwieldy institution that was difficult to govern from the center in Washington.[4] The USCS functioned relatively well, especially when its officials stayed at their posts long enough to acquire crucial knowledge of local conditions and gain experience with the specific consular functions required there. A significant reform effort in 1906 produced major changes that emphasized national sovereignty and knowledge of uniform, DOS-centered bureaucratic practices rather than inter- and transimperial cooperation and local knowledge, but by that point the United States had already reaped the benefits of those more cooperative nineteenth-century consular efforts.

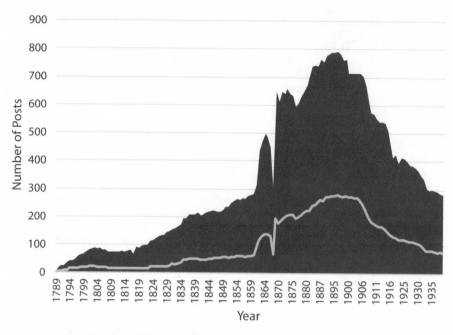

FIGURE 6.2. Number of U.S. Consular Service posts by year, 1789–1939. The light line indicates the number of posts in the British Empire and Commonwealth. Based on data from the *Register of the Department of State* and its successors, the *Official Register of the United States*, and Smith's *America's Diplomats and Consuls of 1776–1865*. Source: See note 4.

The Growth of the U.S. Consular Service to 1856

The USCS was not consistent in size, geographic distribution, or personnel structure over the long nineteenth century, nor did it engage consistently in the major port, extraterritorial, and informal empire consular systems. The history of the USCS can be broken into four periods: two periods of relative stability, from 1789 to 1856 and 1872 to 1906, and two periods of change, between 1856 and 1872 and 1906 to 1924. Trans- and interimperial engagement was most pronounced in the 1872 to 1906 period, when the USCS was actively engaged in all three consular systems and British and American interests intermingled more intensely, especially in Canada.

From 1789 to 1856 the USCS was characterized by a steady growth in size and a primary engagement with the major port system (see figure 6.2). In 1790 there were nineteen posts across the globe: Canton (Guangzhou) in China; Marrakesh, Mogador, and Tangier in the Barbary States; Lisbon in Portugal, and Fayal and Funchal in the Azores and Madeira, respectively; Bordeaux, Havre,

Marseilles, Nantes, and Rouen in France; the Free and Hanseatic City of Hamburg; London, Liverpool, Cowes, and Dublin in the British Isles; Cap-Haitien and Martinique in the French Caribbean; and Paramaribo in Dutch-controlled Surinam. By 1856 there were 269 posts, with a particular concentration around the Mediterranean. The British Empire hosted 62 posts, or 23 percent of the total, including 7 posts in Canada.

The growth of the service reflected the expansion of the U.S. economy and the importance of maritime trade and customs duties to the federal budget, but its pace and placement also reflected domestic political constraints on official U.S. interactions with the wider world. Generations of politicians took George Washington's 1796 Farewell Address advice to heart and minimized political engagement with European empires, keeping the Washington-based DOS staff and the diplomatic service small. President Washington had also advised commercial expansion, though, and that enabled the growth of the USCS. Many American politicians hoped to break into European-based mercantile empires via trade rather than diplomacy, and the exchange of consular officials was much easier and less expensive than exchanging diplomats.

Before 1856 consular officials were much less expensive than diplomats because they did not receive government salaries. They worked for fees, and so a consular official's income could vary dramatically depending on where he was posted.[5] The fee system—which other governments also employed—was vulnerable to corruption, as standard prices were rarely published and the DOS and Treasury did not yet pay careful attention to the accounts.[6] Before 1856 consular officials were also allowed to engage in their own private business pursuits. Part of the compensation of the job was the prestige of the title in the local community and the possibility of improved access to commercial information, but the most significant advantage may have been the convenience of not needing to seek out a consular official to complete the paperwork necessary for the transborder shipment of goods and people.

Despite the lack of financial remuneration, the functions performed by consular officials were essential to the movement of goods, capital, and people across imperial and national borders. Indeed the need for consular services was so great that it outweighed concerns about the nationality of the people performing them, and governments—including that of the United States—frequently appointed citizens or subjects of other governments to consular posts in an effort to make sure the necessary work got done. The work of enabling global flows was fundamentally cooperative.

Before 1856 there was one place where U.S. consular officials received government salaries: the Barbary States.[7] There European and American activities were governed by the capitulation system, which had been formalized between the Ottomans and the French in 1500, largely out of a European desire to protect Christians from Islamic rule. European and American governments—as represented by consular officials—exercised direct jurisdiction over their subjects or citizens, shielding them from the host government. This was not a reciprocated right: Ottoman consular officials did not have extraterritorial privileges in European and American countries. For states with extraterritorial privileges, an effective judicial system required a jail, a court with a salaried marshal, and usually at least one reliable—one might substitute "salaried" for "reliable"—interpreter. In the USCS the marshal and interpreter could be paid directly by the U.S. government, but the expenses of the jail and the court came out of the consular official's salary.

The basic USCS approach to exercising extraterritorial rights was later copied in other, similar places. After establishing relations with the Ottoman government in 1830, the U.S. government operated a consular court in Constantinople. Following the 1844 Treaty of Wangxia, the USCS grew its presence in China, operating courts at various times in Amoy (Xiamen), Chinkiang (Zhenjiang), Foochow (Fuzhou), Hankow (Hankou), Shanghai, Swatow (Shantou), and Tientsin (Tianjin). There was a consular court in Bangkok, Siam, from 1856 to 1921, and the extraterritorial system was extended to Japan from 1858 to 1899.[8] The USCS presence in the Barbary States, Ottoman Empire, China, and Japan was not limited to posts with consular courts. Consular officials in posts without extraterritorial courts funneled cases to the courts as needed. Depending on their specific location, these other officials participated in the trade-focused activities of the major port and informal empire systems or concentrated their efforts on protecting American (and, at times, European) Christian missionaries and their converts, helping to carve out a distinct legal and cultural status for these individuals in the host country.[9]

Everywhere the USCS participated in the extraterritorial system, it followed in the steps of European imperial powers that had gone before, and cooperation among those powers was crucial in keeping the system of sharp inequalities in place. Even as they exercised the privileges of extraterritoriality, however, USCS personnel were dependent on locals for the operation of the system, because the United States did not produce sufficient numbers of Americans who were fluent in Ottoman Turkish, Arabic, Chinese, Japanese, or Thai. The DOS introduced a "student interpreter" program in 1906 in an effort to build linguistic capacity, but supply rarely kept up with demand, and those U.S. efforts paled in comparison with the training provided by other governments through institutions like the Austrian Consular Academy or the on-the-ground training afforded to British and French colonial officials. Although local employees helped the USCS overcome its language deficiencies everywhere where English was not the primary language, the deficit was greater in the extraterritorial countries. The combination of interimperial cooperation to enforce the inherent inequality of the extraterritorial system and the USCS dependence on locals for that system's daily operation made for a particularly fragile system that was vulnerable to corruption. A variety of generally successful anticorruption reforms in the USCS over the course of the nineteenth century had the least impact in extraterritorial posts, especially in China.[10]

The Civil War and the Transimperial Service, 1856 to 1906

The expansion of the extraterritorial system in to China, Japan, and Siam coincided with a variety of other changes in the USCS that fundamentally altered the institution and its relationship to imperial power. The combination of reform legislation in 1856 and the Civil War from 1861 to 1865 prompted significant change, including a sharp increase in the overall size of the service and a marked expansion into the British Empire. Throughout the 1856–72 transition period and on to 1906, the emphasis in the USCS remained on cooperation: maintaining cross-border flows was more important than expressions of national sovereignty.

The 1856 reforms were designed to improve the quality of the USCS by reducing corruption and expanding the pool of potential candidates; they were a first step on the road to professionalization. The chief reform was to remove some posts—especially the most lucrative ones in the major ports—from the fee system and instead provide those consular officials with a government salary. Those salaried officials were no longer allowed to engage in private business.[11] The fees they collected needed to be accounted for in detail, and any fees beyond $250 per quarter had to be forwarded to the Treasury. The 1856 legislation tied ranks and salaries to specific posts. London, for example, was a consulate general at the maximum salary of $7,500 per year, and Leipzig was a consulate at $1,500 per year.[12] As it had before 1856, the Senate confirmed nominees for specific posts, rather than to ranks, so they could not be moved from post to post without additional Senate confirmation. Salaried posts were supposed to go to U.S. citizens, but the legislation allowed the employment of non-U.S. citizens when necessary.

As the 1856 legislation—and the augmented paperwork it required—was being implemented, the Civil War began. The Union needed friends on the ground all over the world to monitor and hopefully scuttle Confederate attempts to secure supplies and diplomatic recognition. Embracing their belief in the potential of the federal government and benefiting from the absence of southerners in Congress, the Union government roughly doubled the size of the USCS, from 282 posts in 1860 to 497 in the peak war year of 1864 (see figure 6.2). Some of this was done by creating more salaried positions, but the bulk of it was done by adding scores of "consular agents" to the ranks. Agents worked for fees and could pursue private business interests. They had to be U.S. citizens only when it was practical; usually it was not. They also did not have to be confirmed by the Senate, so appointing them was easy, and they were largely immune from the patronage system.[13] With little incentive to replace them, agents often remained in their posts for years, providing substantial institutional stability and local knowledge.[14] In essence, employing agents allowed for the combination of the flexibility of agents with the stricter administrative practices of the 1856 reform, continued USCS engagement with all three consular systems, and the possibility of developing large stores of local knowledge.

The war swelled the USCS all over the world, but the most dramatic increases were in the Portuguese and British empires. The USCS bloomed in the Portuguese Empire, with the five posts in 1860 surging to thirty-six posts during the war and then falling to a postwar annual average of nineteen posts in operation. The wartime expansion was not spread evenly throughout the empire: it was concentrated on the European mainland and in the Azores. This arrangement certainly made it difficult for Confederate ships to enter the Mediterranean unobserved. The bulk of the posts were agencies operated by Portuguese subjects, raising the question of their motivations. Potentially the Union tapped into networks of observers who had been aiding in the enforcement of the ban on Portuguese slave trading and activists who advocated for the extension of Portugal's 1761 abolition of slavery in the metropole to the entire empire; that extension came in 1869.[15]

As it had in Portugal, the USCS presence in the British Empire expanded during the Civil War. Unlike Portugal, however, that expansion was sustained and even increased after the war ended. In the British Isles, sixteen new posts were created during the war, joining the twenty-nine that already existed. In the British Caribbean, the Antipodes, and Africa, the USCS presence grew, from twenty total posts to twenty-nine. The most dramatic change, though, came in Canada, where the eight posts that had been created since the establishment of a post at the major port of Halifax in 1830 were joined by forty-four wartime posts. Immediately following the war, there was an initial effort to reduce the size of the USCS again, but the Ulysses Grant administration opted to reverse that trend, keeping the service large. In the period of relative institutional stability from 1872 to 1906, the USCS averaged 713 posts in operation globally in any given year. An average of 247, or nearly 35 percent, were in the British Empire, and an average of 116, or nearly 16 percent of the total, were in Canada (see table 6.3). In terms of numbers, the peak USCS penetration of the British Empire came in 1896 and 1899, when 136 posts were operational in Canada.[16]

This extensive network of posts allowed for voluminous exchange of people, goods, and capital between the British Empire and the expanding U.S. empire, integrating their economies, aligning their interests, and contributing to the postwar rapprochement and subsequent "special relationship."[17] The considerable number of British subjects who operated USCS posts as agents carried this alignment even further, making them embodiments of transimperial cooperation.[18] The British subjects in the USCS were not matched by a network of Americans serving as British consular officials, nor were there a comparable number of British consular posts in the United States and its empire. The massive U.S. consular presence in Canada tipped into the realm of U.S. informal empire. From the comparative data available, it appears that no other government had such dense consular representation anywhere. The USCS did not have such a presence even in its southern neighbor, Mexico, where posts were distributed across states rather than concentrated at the border.[19]

Consular Functions, 1872–1906

By looking at activity in USCS posts in Canada in the 1872–1906 period, we can see what consular officials at major ports and informal empire posts did on a day-to-day basis to keep people, goods, and capital flowing across imperial and national borders. Consular officials needed to strike the right balance between keeping the system moving and making sure that the government's sovereign rights—including its right to have borders—were respected. Ultimately they occupied positions of trust, providing documentation and information that other people—be they U.S. or foreign officials or private citizens—could use to shape the transborder flows of interest to them.

Certainly one of the two major port system functions—aid to seamen—was important along the Canadian coasts and presumably on the Great Lakes as well. Seamen who developed health problems too severe to allow them to remain on board ship were entitled to food, clothing, shelter, and medical treatment at U.S. government expense, organized by consular officials, if they were U.S. citizens or in service on U.S. vessels. Expenses for the relief of seamen were supposed to be recorded in a dedicated account ledger and submitted quarterly to the Treasury. The effects and bodies of those who died fell to consular officials, who either worked with executors or arranged the logistics of burial and sale of effects themselves.[20] Consular officials also helped to monitor and

TABLE 6.3. Locations of U.S. Consular Posts in Canada, 1872–1906.

Alberta
Calgary
Lethbridge

British Columbia
Chemanius
Cumberland
Fernie
Nanaimo
Nelson
Rossland
Union Bay
Vancouver (Granville)
Victoria

New Brunswick
Bathurst
Campbellton
Campobello Island
Edmundston
Frederickton
Grand Manan
McAdam (Junction)
Moncton
Miramichi (Newcastle)
Richibucto
St. Andrews
St. George
St. John*
St. Stephen
Woodstock

Newfoundland
Bay Bulls
Harbor Grace
Port-aux-Basques
St. John's*
St. Vincent

Nova Scotia
Annapolis Royal
Antigonish
Arichat
Barrington
Bridgewater

Canso
Cheverie
Cornwallis
Cow Bay
Digby
Glace Bay
Guysborough
Halifax*
Kempt
Kingsport
Lingan
Liverpool
Lockport
Louisburg
Lunenburg
North Sydney
Parrsboro
Pictou*
Port Hastings
Port Hawkesbury
Port Joggins
Pugwash
River Herbert
Shelbourne
Sydney*
Windsor
Wolfville
Yarmouth

Manitoba
Deloraine
Emerson
Gretna
Wakopa
Winnipeg

Ontario
Amherstburg
Arnprior
Barrie
Belleville
Brantford
Brockville
Carleton Place

Chatham
Clifton
Clinton
Coburg
Collingwood
Cornwall
Courtwright
Deseronto (Mill Point)
Duart
Elliot Lake (Algoma)
Fort Erie
Fort William
Galt
Gananoque
Goderich
Gore Bay
Guelph
Hamilton
Kenora (Rat Portage)
Kingston
Lindsay
London
Midland
Morrisburgh
Napanee
Niagara Falls
North Bay
Orillia
Oshawa
Ottawa
Owen Sound
Palmerston
Paris
Parry Sound
Peterborough
Picton
Port Hope
Port Rowan
Port Stanley
Prescott
Sarnia (Port Sarnia)
Sault Ste. Marie
Smith's Falls

TABLE 6.3. (*Continued*)

St. Catherines	**Quebec**	Montreal*
St. Thomas	Arthabaska	Paspebiac
Stratford	Cabano	Point Levi
Sudbury	Chicoutimi	Potton
Thunder Bay (Port Arthur)	Clarenceville	Quebec City
Toronto*	Coaticook	Rimouski
Trenton	Cookshire	Riviere du Loup
Wallaceburg	Coteau-du-Lac	Sherbrooke
Walton	Farnham	Sorel
Waterloo	Frelighsburg	St. Hyacinthe
Waubaushene	Gaspé*	Saint-Jean-sur-Richelieu
Whitby	Georgeville	(St. John's)
Wiarton	Grand Mère	Stanbridge East
Windsor	Grenville	Stanstead (Junction)
Wingham	Hemmingford	Sutton
	Hereford	Trois-Rivières (Three
Prince Edward Island	Hinchinbrook	Rivers)
Alberton	Hochelaga (and Longeuil)	Vallee-Jonction (Chaud-
Cascumpec	Huntington	iere)
Charlottetown*	Lachine	Victoriaville
Georgetown	Lacolle	
Souris	Levis	**Saskatchewan**
St. Peter's Bay	Lineboro	North Portal
Stanley's Bridge	Magdalen Islands	**Yukon**
Summerside	Megantic	Dawson City

Note: A U.S. consular official was posted to these places at some point in the 1872–1906 period. Posts marked with an * were opened before 1861. The list reflects present-day, rather than historical, town and province names. An interactive map is available at Google, "U.S. Consular Posts in Canada and Mexico, 1872–1906," https://drive.google.com/open?id=1G3VT_rscp6jHmz8LXsUXz7PMmRc&usp =sharing.

Source: Statistics regarding service size and post placement are derived from the annual *Register of the Department of State*, which began in 1869, and its successors, the *Foreign Service List* and *Key Officers of Foreign Service Posts*; Walter Burges Smith, *America's Diplomats and Consuls of 1776–1865: A Geographic and Biographic Directory of the Foreign Service from the Declaration of Independence to the End of the Civil War* (Arlington, VA: Center for the Study of Foreign Affairs, 1986), which is drawn primarily from the DOS's file of consular cards, supplemented by other sources; and the U.S. government's *Official Register of the United States*, which was published on a roughly biannual and then annual basis from 1816. These sources are almost entirely in agreement when it comes to Senate-confirmed and/or salaried posts. Data on agencies are more elusive, as the *U.S. Register* listed them only during some administrations. To the best of my knowledge, none of these sources was published in 1890 and 1904, and in 1921, 1922, 1923, and 1924 the *U.S. Register* refers people to the *DOS Register* for the full DOS listing, but the *DOS Register* was not published in those years.

regulate labor conditions aboard vessels, refereeing complaints and ensuring wages were paid in a manner consistent with U.S. law and the ship's articles. They checked to make sure that the people who were supposed to be aboard a ship actually were aboard, guarding against unlawful death, impressment, desertion, and stowaways.[21]

Consular officials' certification of the list of people aboard a ship was one of the many documents a ship's master needed so the vessel could clear U.S. Customs upon arrival in the United States. Preparing people and goods to go through U.S. Customs was the other fundamental consular function in the major port system. Consular officials, along with the Revenue Cutter Service, combined with the Customs Service to form and police the commercial borders of the United States.[22] This trio of institutions was created early in the government's history and was well funded, seeing as they ensured the collection of customs duties, which formed the main source of federal revenue prior to the introduction of the income tax in 1913.

In terms of paperwork, the bare minimum needed to bring more than $100 worth of goods into the United States was an invoice and a shipper's declaration, both certified by a U.S. consular official. Invoices had to be triplicate originals, one copy staying in the consular archives, the second going with the shipper, and the third posted by the consular official to the collector of customs at the intended port of entry; the collector's copy was supposed to arrive before the actual goods. In some cases additional certified materials could be required, such as product samples—also to be collected in triplicate—documentation of disinfection, and special declarations regarding artworks. In certain circumstances the packaging in which goods were transported also needed separate paperwork, and consuls were supposed to attest that the labels stating goods' place of origin and/or manufacture were accurate. Consular officials who suspected wrongdoing in any of this were supposed to gather evidence and forward it to the customs officer, who would decide whether something illegal had been done; in the most flagrant, clearcut cases, consular officials could refuse to issue the necessary certified documents.[23]

Goods that moved from place to place outside the United States before they entered it typically required documentation from the consular officials in each stopping place along the route. Those stops could be intentional, but they could also be accidental. For instance, if a ship had to put into a port because of a storm, the consular official at that port could provide a certified form that explained the circumstances and ensured that the shippers did not face extra duties as a result of their unexpected stop. Consular officials were the ones to document the journey of goods—and people—in ways that could be understood and trusted by U.S. officials at the border.

The U.S.-Canadian trade relationship did have unique features that influenced the number and placement of uscs posts. The 1872–1906 period was a time in which Canadian goods did not enjoy free access to the United States or lower tariff rates, and high, Republican protectionist tariffs were in effect for much of the time. These policies incentivized U.S. authorities to make sure the necessarily high volume of Canadian goods entering the United States did so legally. The 1871 Treaty of Washington complicated matters because it allowed the duty-free transshipment of certain British and Canadian goods through specified U.S. ports of entry, as well as mutual duty-free transshipment rights along the waterways that connected the Great Lakes and the Atlantic.[24] Although some goods were allowed to move along these paths duty-free, shippers needed the paperwork to prove they had the right to do so. The movement of goods from Canada to the United States by rail was also governed by a special set of rules. Consular officials were allowed to seal railroad cars at inland posts in Canada—in Stratford, Ontario, for example—and provide them with the necessary paperwork so they could travel all the way to inland U.S. Customs entry points such as St. Louis, Missouri, without stopping at the geographic border between the two countries.[25] This system contributed to the proliferation of posts, especially in southern Ontario, and it reduced the challenges of integrating the Canadian and U.S. economies, helping to align Anglo-American interests.

Inanimate objects were not, of course, the only things that had to go through U.S. Customs. The trade in animals across the U.S.-Canadian border was also substantial, and consular officials inspected, quarantined, and certified those animals according to U.S. law, which varied by the species of animal and the purposes for which the animal would be used in the United States.[26] Providing a large number of consular posts, rather than trying to move large quantities of animals across at a few places, may have aided in keeping the animals well-nourished and healthy.

Animals also accompanied immigrants across the border. There was a special form to certify that teams of animals used to transport migrants and their personal belongings were allowed to cross duty-free, though any horses involved that had been or would be used for racing were not exempt from duties.[27] It is not hard to imagine that consular officials located right at the border provided paperwork to people who had tried to enter the United States and failed, not knowing what documents they actually needed to get themselves and their belongings across the border.

As the U.S. federal government developed new, exclusionary immigration laws and an institutional apparatus to enforce them, consular officials were called upon to assist. They had already been providing weekly health and sanitation reports to the Treasury Department so the Marine Hospital Service—reformed and strengthened in 1871—could establish quarantines. With the introduction of the Chinese Exclusion Act in 1882, passports were required for the select categories of Chinese people who could enter the United States, and consular officials provided one route by which passports could be obtained. Consular involvement in the inspection of potential migrants and the issuing of passports and visas intensified as exclusionary laws multiplied, with the most significant growth in this area coming after 1906.[28] Migration-related consular work was particularly heavy at the major points of entry into Canada, where U.S. consular officials provided services for both U.S. citizens and non-U.S. citizens who aimed to travel through Canada to the United States. USCS personnel worked alongside significant numbers of other countries' consular officials at Montreal, Halifax, St. John (New Brunswick), Toronto, Quebec City, Vancouver, St. John's (Newfoundland), and Victoria.[29]

People also crossed the border in the other direction for a variety of reasons. The relative ease of crossing from the United States into Canada and the lack of a comprehensive extradition treaty encouraged American fugitives to flee to Canada, and consular officials participated in efforts to track them down.[30] Unlike U.S. consular officials operating in the extraterritorial system, those posted to Canada and most other countries did not have any judicial authority over U.S. citizens in the area. They could render assistance to U.S. citizens who were arrested, which might include monitoring prison conditions or recommending a local attorney, but the DOS cautioned consular officials against taking more dramatic steps.[31] In practice, consular officials often advised people who had been released pending trial to leave the country, thus eliminating the need to mount a defense.[32]

Tourism also drew Americans to Canada, though it is not clear that any USCS posts were created to deal primarily with tourists, as was the case with European spa towns like Carlsbad in Austria. At those European posts, consular officials were frequently called on to put their foreign-language and social skills to work to smooth over disputes regarding hotel bills and similar matters. Americans undoubtedly got into the same kind of arguments in Canada, but, outside Quebec, language was less of an issue. Throughout the 1872–1906 period, the Thousand Islands and Niagara Falls were certainly tourist draws, and, as time went on, destinations served by the Canadian Pacific Railway and its related luxury hotels drew more visitors, especially to the Canadian Rockies and Pacific coast.

Consular officials were frequently visited by U.S. citizens who had come to Canada looking for work, were traversing Ontario as the shortest route between New England and Michigan, or, around 1896, were attempting to enrich themselves via the Klondike gold strike. If they fell into financial difficulties, they often asked consular officials for assistance. Officials often helped, though they did so from their own resources; unlike most European governments, the U.S. government did not have a public fund for this purpose. The U.S. government did, however, have a public fund for paying pensions to Civil War veterans, widows, and orphans. Consular officials participated in that system by hearing and certifying the required annual oath from those pensioners living abroad that proved they were still alive. They helped connect recipients with the correct authorities in the United States, frequently putting in a good word for applicants—who would, of course, be a continued drain on the consular official's personal finances if they remained in the district. They also helped to answer questions about pensions and smooth over problems that arose through unexpected circumstances that were no fault of the pension recipient.[33]

Just as members of the public could call on consular officials with questions or problems, so too could U.S. government agencies. These could be one-time requests, such as the query from the U.S. Department of Agriculture (USDA) about whether Pilsner beer had to be made in the Bohemian town of Pilsen, Austria, to be legitimately called Pilsner.[34] Consular officials also provided regular flows of information upon which U.S. government agencies acted. The Treasury received monthly reports on currency values, and the USDA received reports on local agricultural conditions, also monthly and frequently with accompanying samples of plants and seeds. The DOS received annual reports on local commercial conditions for publication in *Commercial Relations* and encouraged monthly reports for inclusion in its *Consular Reports* series.

These commercial reports were made available to the public in the hopes that they would help stimulate trade, providing businesses with news of potential opportunities to seize and pitfalls to avoid. Consular officials at major ports and especially at informal empire posts were also supposed to actively promote trade by cultivating relationships with locals. How specific officials attempted this depended on individual circumstances, but one common approach was to maintain a publicly accessible library of U.S. commercial publications, especially trade journals and directories. In some consulates the library was large enough to be a formal reading room; others were far more modest.

It is difficult to measure the effectiveness of consular trade promotion activities, but scholars have typically found them wanting.[35] It is worth bearing in mind, however, that a U.S. consular official's very presence in a locality could raise awareness of the possibility of trade with the United States. Much more important, the presence of the consular official lowered the costs associated with that potential trade by being on hand to provide all the necessary paperwork and, hopefully, to answer questions about American markets, tastes, and regulations. In Canada—especially Anglophone Canada—where knowledge of language, culture, markets, and financial systems was shared across the border, or at least easy to come by, ready access to consular officials significantly reduced the remaining, largely bureaucratic obstacles to trade, facilitating the integration of key aspects of the Canadian and U.S. economies.[36] USCS efforts helped to orient the Dominion of Canada toward the United States rather than its imperial metropole in Britain.

Reforms and Nationalization, 1906–1924

Having consular officials close at hand made it easier for people to access the services they provided and enhanced the U.S. government's ability to exercise its full sovereign rights. However, with nearly eight hundred posts operating in any given year, a staff of citizens and noncitizens with relatively frequent turnover, and the unique demands and geographies of the major port, extraterritorial, and informal empire systems, the USCS was difficult for the Consular Bureau and the rest of the Washington-based DOS staff to keep track of, let alone actively manage. That the service functioned at all was something of a minor miracle, especially given the lack of training and instruction for consular officials. Like most of the world's nineteenth-century consular services, the USCS muddled through with an army of the willing, despite the fact that serving resulted in financial hardships for many officials. Individual officials may not have benefited much financially, but the United States benefited tremendously from consular officials' labor and local knowledge. Through USCS engagement in major port-based trade, penetration of "non-Christian countries" via the system of extraterritoriality, and the cultivation of an informal empire, the United States expanded its political, economic, and cultural reach across the globe by the end of the nineteenth century.

Having accomplished that global expansion, the United States was the first major power to reform its consular service so as to make it smaller and more responsive to the center of government authority. While the British, French, and German consular services continued with modest growth and the Italian and Austrian services initiated substantial expansions designed to maintain connections with their migrants abroad, the 1906 reform legislation in the United States began a gradual contraction in the number of consular posts (see

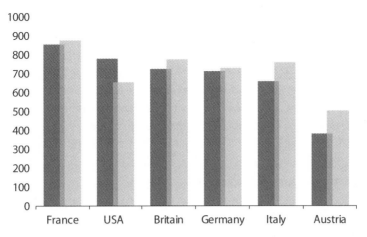

FIGURE 6.3. Size of select countries' consular services, 1897 and 1907. Source: See note 6.

figure 6.3).[37] The 1906 reform also began to erode the sense of three distinct consular systems, and, with the 1924 Rodgers Act, the distinct roles for the consular service and the diplomatic service were erased entirely in favor of a single U.S. Foreign Service. The reforms were undertaken in the name of professionalization and efficiency, not nationalization, but in practice they had a nationalizing effect, removing non-U.S. citizens from the ranks and emphasizing rotation among posts rather than the cultivation of local knowledge and relationships. From the perspective of DOS officials in Washington, the USCS did become more efficient. Those efficiencies, however, relied on a combination of technological changes—themselves partially a result of consular labor—and the concentration of political, economic, and cultural power that nineteenth-century consular officials had been so instrumental in achieving. Out of choice or necessity, people in need of consular services had to bear greater costs in reaching U.S. consular officials rather than relying on those officials' proximity.

The most important aspect of the 1906 reform law was the creation of consuls general at large (CGALS). The five CGALS were each assigned to a specific region of the world, and they traveled from post to post, gathering information on employees and local practices, instructing consular officials in the performance of their duties, and making recommendations to the DOS about promotions and severances, post closures, and other changes to consular practices. This system of inspection was designed to be permanent, as opposed to the handful of ad hoc inspection tours that had been done since the Civil War.[38] It was the most effective tool the DOS had yet possessed for fostering uniformity of practice and scrupulous attention to directions from Washington. The CGALs preached esprit de corps and the adoption of state-of-the-art scientific management practices, with an eye toward being able to move consular officials from post to post smoothly. The CGALs envisioned a USCS in which consular officials were much more clearly agents of the DOS rather than people of indifferent nationalities who worked to keep goods and people moving through specific places.

The chief casualties of the 1906 reforms were consular agents. The CGALs recommended raising some agencies to salaried consulates. By this point, salaried offices were almost entirely in the hands of U.S. citizens, and non-U.S. citizens would not be hired for new salaried positions, so a few agents were out of a job. The CGALs recommended closing some agencies, either because they were no longer needed or because they thought the incumbent was not doing a satisfactory job and there was no reasonable prospect of finding a U.S. citizen to take over the agency. More research into these closures is needed, but it appears that agents who were not regarded as Anglo-Saxons were immediately let go, regardless of the length or quality of their service. By contrast, agents in Canada—many of whom had been serving since the Civil War or shortly thereafter—were left in place until they chose to retire or they died. Besides post status changes and closures, several agents quit their jobs after the CGALs criticized their work or demanded that they do more—without, of course, receiving any additional financial compensation for their expanded efforts.[39]

World War I accelerated the process of standardization and efficiency, eradicating many of the long nineteenth century's norms surrounding the exchange of personnel and dealing a death blow to the capitulation-based system of extraterritoriality. The experience of performing emergency consular services for many of the world's governments during the war encouraged DOS officials to value efficiency—and border control—to an even greater extent.[40] Beyond the collapse of the German, Austrian, Russian, and Ottoman empires, World War I had a profoundly destabilizing effect on European empires, even as they expanded to encompass more territory, particularly in the Middle East. The war destabilized the U.S. empire as well, prompting a complete overhaul of its citizenship and immigration laws.[41] Nation-states gradually replaced empires as the main constituent actors in "international" affairs, and politicians—especially American politicians—emphasized the equality of those nation-states in their rhetoric.[42] The symbolism surrounding diplomats was repurposed to meet the demands of this new system, particularly through the elimination of ranks for chiefs of diplomatic missions; everyone was now an ambassador. After the

Rodgers Act merged the USCS and diplomatic service in 1924, some consulates remained open, but as extensions of embassies, not as distinct institutional spaces. Among career U.S. Foreign Service officers, the "consular track" that emerged in the twentieth century did not include trade at all; instead it emphasized passports, visas, and emergency aid to U.S. citizens abroad. Officials who had worked to minimize the obstacles presented by borders in the long nineteenth century's global imperial system devoted ever more effort to border maintenance in the twentieth century's nation-state system.

NOTES

This research was supported by a University of Vermont College of Arts and Sciences Faculty Research Support Award and a Coor Collaborative Fellows Grant from the UVM Humanities Center. Many thanks to Daniella Bassi, Natalie Coffman, Kiara Day, and Sarah Holmes, who assisted with data formatting.

1. On other countries' consular service, see Jörg Ulbert and Lukian Prijac, eds., *Consuls et Services Consulaires Au XIXe Siecle = Die Welt Der Konsulate Im 19. Jahrhundert = Consulship in the 19th Century* (Hamburg, Germany: DOBU, 2010); Ferry de Goey, *Consuls and the Institutions of Global Capitalism, 1783–1914* (London: Pickering and Chatto, 2014); Rudolf Agstner, *Austria (-Hungary) and Its Consulates in the United States of America since 1820: "Our Nationals Settling Here Count by the Millions Now"* (Zurich: LIT Verlag, 2012); D. C. M. Platt, *The Cinderella Service: British Consuls since 1825* (London: Longman, 1971). On the culture of nineteenth-century diplomacy, see Nicole M. Phelps, *U.S.-Habsburg Relations from 1815 to the Paris Peace Conference: Sovereignty Transformed* (New York: Cambridge University Press, 2013), chapters 1 and 2.

2. See note 1, especially de Goey, *Consuls and the Institutions of Global Capitalism*. On the USCS, see Charles Stuart Kennedy, *The American Consul: A History of the United States Consular Service, 1776–1924*, revised 2nd edition (Washington, DC: New Academia, 2015). For an account that encompasses more than trade, see Bernadette Whelan, *American Government in Ireland, 1790–1913: A History of the US Consular Service* (Manchester, U.K.: Manchester University Press, 2010).

3. U.S. Department of State (hereafter cited as DOS), *Regulations Prescribed for the Use of the Consular Service of the United States* (Washington, DC: Government Printing Office, 1896).

4. Statistics regarding service size and post placement are derived from the annual *Register of the Department of State*, which began in 1869, and its successors, the *Foreign Service List* and *Key Officers of Foreign Service Posts*; Walter Burges Smith, *America's Diplomats and Consuls of 1776–1865: A Geographic and Biographic Directory of the Foreign Service from the Declaration of Independence to the End of the Civil War* (Arlington, VA: Center for the Study of Foreign Affairs, 1986), which is drawn primarily from the DOS's file of consular cards, supplemented by other sources; and the U.S. government's *Official Register of the United States*, which was published on a roughly biannual and then annual basis from 1816. These sources are almost entirely in agreement when it comes to Senate-confirmed

and/or salaried posts. Data on agencies are more elusive, as the *U.S. Register* listed them only during some administrations. To the best of my knowledge, none of these sources was published in 1890 and 1904, and in 1921, 1922, 1923, and 1924 the *U.S. Register* refers people to the *DOS Register* for the full DOS listing, but the *DOS Register* was not published in those years.

5. In the long nineteenth century, consular officials were men. On occasion wives and daughters might fill in or assist, and after midcentury women might have clerical positions, but the positions listed in official registers were all held by men.

6. Data on other countries' services come from the various files in 19: Reports on the Consular Service of Foreign Countries, 1897, Inventory 15, Record Group 59: General Records of the Department of State, U.S. National Archives and Records Administration, College Park, Maryland (hereafter cited as NARA); the DOS-created ledger that is Volume 2 in 883: Analyses of Reports on Consular Establishments of Foreign Powers, 1907, Inventory 15, NARA; and the section of the DOS *Register* that lists foreign consular posts in the United States. See also note 1.

7. The U.S. government established relations with Morocco in 1786. Treaties with Algeria, Tripoli, and Tunis followed in 1795, 1796, and 1797, respectively.

8. The U.S. and Siamese governments opened relations in 1833, but that original treaty did not include extraterritorial provisions.

9. Ruth Kark, *American Consuls in the Holy Land, 1832–1914* (Detroit, MI: Wayne State University Press, 1994).

10. The lack of change in China resulted in special investigations that were not paralleled in other parts of the world. See, for example, 136: Reports of Treasury Agents on U.S. Consulates, 1870–1873; and 889: Records relating to Charges against John Goodnow and Robert McWade, 1902–1906, both in Inventory 15, NARA.

11. Officials on "Schedule B" drew salaries between $1,500 and $7,500, depending on the post, and they could not engage in private business. Those on "Schedule C" drew significantly smaller salaries—not more than $1,000—and could still engage in business.

12. In addition to consulates general and consulates, there were a handful of freestanding vice consulates, commercial agencies, and consular agencies. Consuls general were nominally in charge of lesser consular officials in their country or empire, but that does not appear to have been universally observed.

13. For descriptions of the types and qualifications of consular officials, see DOS, *Regulations*, 4–18.

14. In 1903 the 376 agents for which appointment data are available had served an average of nine years at post; 55 of them had been at their post for twenty years or more. The average length of service would likely be longer if the 1872–1906 period is considered as a whole, because many of the agents who signed on during the Civil War or in the 1870s had died shortly before 1903 after serving for decades. DOS, *Register* (1903).

15. The Portuguese government banned its slave trade north of the Equator in 1815 and south of the Equator in 1842.

16. See note 4.

17. Entry points into the scholarship on Anglo-American relations include Stuart Anderson, *Race and Rapprochement: Anglo-Saxonism and Anglo-American Relations,*

1895–1904 (Rutherford, NJ: Fairleigh Dickinson University Press, 1981); Kathleen Burk, *Old World, New World: Great Britain and America from the Beginning* (New York: Atlantic Monthly Press, 2008).

18. In 1903 there were 148 British subjects serving in the USCS, of which 139 were agents; 124 were serving in the British Empire, and 120 of those were agents. Of those in the British Empire, 58 were in Canada and 31 were in the British Isles. DOS, *Register* (1903). The figures here include the few people whose place of birth was listed, but not their place of appointment; their citizenship status is not entirely clear, but they have been counted as what is most likely.

19. See note 6. An interactive map of U.S. posts in Canada and Mexico is available at Google, "U.S. Consular Posts in Canada and Mexico, 1872–1906," https://drive.google .com/open?id=1G3VT_rscp6jHmz8LXsUXz7PMmRc&usp=sharing.

20. Consular officials performed these services for U.S. citizens who were not seamen as well. DOS, *Regulations*, 154–64.

21. DOS, *Regulations*, 61–141. On consular management of shipboard labor, see Matthew T. Raffety, *The Republic Afloat: Law, Honor, and Citizenship in Maritime America* (Chicago: University of Chicago Press, 2013); Brian Rouleau, *With Sails Whitening Every Sea: Mariners and the Making of an American Maritime Empire* (Ithaca, NY: Cornell University Press, 2014).

22. Although not mentioned by the authors, consular officials could be characterized as part of the "government out of sight" or the "outward state." Brian Balogh, *A Government Out of Sight: The Mystery of National Authority in Nineteenth-Century America* (Cambridge, U.K.: Cambridge University Press, 2009); Andrew Wender Cohen, "Smuggling, Globalization, and America's Outward State, 1870–1909," *Journal of American History* 97, no. 2 (2010): 371–98.

23. DOS, *Regulations*, 276–317. See also Robert E. May, "Culture Wars: The U.S. Art Lobby and Congressional Tariff Legislation during the Gilded Age and Progressive Era," *Journal of the Gilded Age and Progressive Era* 9, no. 1 (2010): 37–91.

24. Great Britain and the United States, Treaty of Washington (1871), articles 29–30.

25. DOS, *Regulations*, 298–99.

26. DOS, *Regulations*, 153, 300–301. See also Kristin L. Hoganson, "Meat in the Middle: Converging Borderlands in the U.S. Midwest, 1865–1900," *Journal of American History* 98, no. 4 (2012): 1025–51.

27. DOS, *Regulations*, 301.

28. DOS, *Regulations*, 49–61.

29. In 1897 there were at least fifteen countries with consular posts in Montreal; Halifax, St. John, and Toronto had eleven; Quebec City had ten; Vancouver had nine; and St. John's and Victoria had seven each. 19: Reports on the Consular Service of Foreign Countries.

30. Katherine Unterman, "Boodle over the Border: Embezzlement and the Crisis of International Mobility, 1880–1890," *Journal of the Gilded Age and Progressive Era* 11, no. 2 (2012): 151–89.

31. DOS, *Regulations*, 166–67.

32. For examples, see Phelps, *U.S.-Habsburg Relations*, chapter 3.

33. In 1903 the DOS surveyed its consular officials about requests for aid. The responses are contained in 885: Reports of Consuls on Aid to U.S. Citizens, 1903, Inventory 15, NARA. See also DOS, *Regulations*, 178–79.

34. According to the Austrians, it did need to come from Pilsen (Plzeň). Acting Secretary of Agriculture to Secretary of State, Washington, April 6, 1911, file 611.634/3, decimal file 1910–29, NARA.

35. See, for example, de Goey, *Consuls and the Institutions of Global Capitalism*; David M. Pletcher, "Rhetoric and Results: A Pragmatic View of American Economic Expansionism, 1865–89," *Diplomatic History* 5, no. 2 (1981): 93–106.

36. In *Consuls and the Institutions of Global Capitalism*, de Goey argues that, in general, nineteenth-century consuls fed global capitalism by reducing transaction costs.

37. See note 6.

38. CGAL reports and correspondence are spread throughout the DOS archives; a key collection is 865: Inspection Reports on Foreign Service Posts, Inventory 15, NARA. Earlier, ad hoc inspection reports can be found in files 869–872, Foreign Service Inspection Records; and in 136: Reports of Treasury Agents on U.S. Consulates, Inventory 15, NARA.

39. See, for example, the numerous recommendations and responses contained in 874: Correspondence of Inspector Alfred L. M. Gottschalk, Inventory 15, NARA.

40. Phelps, *U.S.-Habsburg Relations*, chapter 3.

41. Christopher Capozzola, "Legacies for Citizenship: Pinpointing Americans during and after World War I," *Diplomatic History* 38, no. 4 (2014): 713–26.

42. On the transition to a new nation-state system, see Eric D. Weitz, "From the Vienna to the Paris System: International Politics and the Entangled Histories of Human Rights, Forced Deportations, and Civilizing Missions," *American Historical Review* 113, no. 5 (2008): 1313–43; Erez Manela, *The Wilsonian Moment: Self-Determination and the International Origins of Anticolonial Nationalism* (Oxford: Oxford University Press, 2007); Phelps, *U.S.-Habsburg Relations*.

7. TRANSIMPERIAL ROOTS OF AMERICAN ANTI-IMPERIALISM: THE TRANSATLANTIC RADICALISM OF FREE TRADE, 1846–1920

Marc-William Palen

"The clear connection between the anti-imperialist movement and earlier movements for liberal reform has never received much attention," Christopher Lasch observed sixty years ago. Despite the distance of time, his observation still remains remarkably salient today. Most scholarship on the American Anti-Imperialist League (AIL, 1898–1920) has continued to focus narrowly on the period between its founding in 1898 during the Spanish-American War and the end of the U.S. war in the Philippines in 1902. This chronological narrowing not only sidelines the continued anti-imperial activities of the AIL leaders in the years that followed; it also hides U.S. anti-imperial efforts to thwart transimperial projects in Africa, the Caribbean, and the Asia-Pacific in the decades that preceded the formation of the AIL.[1]

Considering that historians have long associated free trade with late nineteenth- and early twentieth-century Anglo-American imperialism, this story begins at what, at first sight, might seem an unlikely starting point: the mid-nineteenth-century Anglo-American free-trade movement. Although this probably brings to mind imperial ambitions of worldwide market access, meaning access to an entire imperial world system, free-trade ideas in fact spurred U.S. anti-imperialism at the turn of the twentieth century. Going well beyond opposition to mercantilist policies intended to benefit particular empires, they contained a far larger imperial critique. Paying closer attention to the free-trade ideas that spurred turn-of-the-century American anti-imperialists can help us locate what Jay Sexton and Ian Tyrrell recently described as "the lost cosmopolitanism of anti-imperialist adherents in the late nineteenth and early twentieth centuries."[2]

The economic cosmopolitan motivations of American anti-imperialists have been either misrepresented or marginalized or both.[3] Recent scholarship on American anti-imperialist ideologies has tended to focus on culture and politics rather than economics.[4] The older Wisconsin School of diplomatic history did place due importance upon the economic ideas of AIL leaders. However, using a New Left brush, the Wisconsin School took the opportunity to paint the leading turn-of-the-century anti-imperialists as informal imperialists. Wisconsinite scholars deemed all forms of U.S. economic expansion— including peaceful, noncoercive foreign market expansion—as imperialistic. Even the widespread pacific AIL advocacy of free-trade internationalism struck these scholars as an example of what the Wisconsin School founder, William Appleman Williams, described as "imperial anti-colonialism."[5] This New Left rebranding thereby hid the extent to which the era's leading anti-imperialists opposed not only formal imperialism but also informal economic imperialism.[6]

This essay argues that the AIL leadership's widespread subscription to free-trade ideas, emanating from the metropolitan heart of the British Empire, underpinned their anti-imperial moralism. The British-born free-trade ideas of the 1830s and 1840s—what Richard Huzzey calls "the moral economy of free trade"—conditioned the institutions and ideas of American anti-imperialism from the mid-nineteenth to the early twentieth century, when the U.S. imperial project came to encompass large swaths of the Caribbean and the Asia-Pacific formerly under the sway of the Spanish Empire.[7] Businessmen and nationalists in the former Spanish colonies, desiring to control their own tariff policies and to have free access to the U.S. market, thereupon embodied the broader anti-imperialist critique of U.S. protectionist imperialism. American anti-imperial activism, intersecting as it did with the British, Spanish, and U.S. empires, must therefore be understood as a transimperial phenomenon. As Michael Cullinane demonstrates, the U.S. anti-imperialist movement was far from a purely domestic affair; strong transatlantic ties connected American anti-imperialists with their European counterparts.[8] But this anti-imperial story is incomplete without a study of AIL leaders' commitment to British free-trade ideas. Their economic cosmopolitanism—their conviction that free-trade internationalism laid the economic foundations for world peace and prosperity—was a crucial component of what Leslie Butler describes as the AIL's "progressive Anglo-American tradition."[9] Their subscription to British free-trade ideas was thus also in part an attempt to counter the widespread prevalence of Anglophobia and empire-building among the Republican Party's protectionist majority.[10] Considering the Anglophilia of most of the AIL leaders, the transatlanticism of their economic beliefs should come as little surprise. It should be less surprising still considering that economic ideas had long been entwined with Anglo-American anti-imperial debates.[11]

Misrepresentations of both the turn-of-the-century American political economy and the ill-named Open Door Empire as free trade in character have hidden the radical nature of anti-imperialists' economic cosmopolitanism.[12] The predominance of economic nationalist ideas and policies in late nineteenth- and early twentieth-century American trade politics underpinned the GOP's push for an American Closed Door Empire and informed the British-influenced free-trade critique of U.S. colonialism. Whereas Britain had turned to free trade at midcentury, protectionist ideas and policies triumphed in the United States from the 1860s onward.[13] From the crucible of the Civil War, the Republican Party emerged as the party of economic nationalism. It dominated the executive branch of government for more than half a century. Only two Democrats, Grover Cleveland (1885–89, 1893–97) and Woodrow Wilson (1913–21), held the presidency during the seventy-two-year period between 1861 and 1933. The GOP also controlled a good portion of the Supreme Court and Congress for much of this time, including both houses of Congress between 1897 and 1911, the era's most significant period of U.S. colonial expansion and policymaking.[14] The resulting protectionist makeup of the U.S. imperial economic system in the late nineteenth and early twentieth centuries catalyzed the economic cosmopolitanism of American anti-imperialists.

American anti-imperial understandings of protectionist economic policies were shaped by a British anti-imperial free-trade tradition stretching back to the late eighteenth century. Writing *The Wealth of Nations* (1776) amid the outbreak of the American Revolution, Adam Smith had condemned mercantilist protectionism for breeding state-sponsored monopolies and for drumming up nationalistic support for expensive and unnecessary colonial enterprises.[15] Smith's mid-nineteenth-century disciples in Europe and North America, most notably the British radical politician Richard Cobden (1804–1865), developed this connection further, drawing a direct ideological line between economic nationalism and imperialism, and, conversely, economic cosmopolitanism and anti-imperialism.[16] In 1962 the historian Oliver MacDonagh termed this ideological confluence of economic cosmopolitanism, peace, and anti-imperialism within Britain "the anti-imperialism of free trade."[17] This Anglo-American Cobdenite anti-imperial tradition was rich, giving birth to the even more radical free-trade ideas of the American political philosopher Henry George in the

1870s and 1880s. These same free-trade ideas, crisscrossing the Atlantic between the 1840s and the First World War, animated anti-imperial opposition to the American Empire.

Transimperial Emergence of the Economic Cosmopolitan Critique of Imperialism

The economic cosmopolitan critique of imperialism made its controversial entry into mainstream British politics in the 1830s and 1840s. Its arrival was an internationalist offshoot of the era's British free-trade movement. Spearheading both was the Liberal radical parliamentarian, Manchester manufacturer, abolitionist, and peace activist Richard Cobden. He and the other leaders of the Anti–Corn Law League (ACLL), active from 1839 to 1846, set out to eliminate Britain's protective tariffs on foreign grain for three key reasons: to provide cheap bread to the starving masses, to undermine the undue political influence of the country's militant landed elite, and to create a more peaceful world. Building upon the pacific internationalist elements of Smith's *The Wealth of Nations* and David Ricardo's theory of comparative advantage, Cobden and his disciples—known as Cobdenites or the Manchester School—believed that creating a globally integrated marketplace through free trade would eliminate the main political and economic causes of war and imperial expansion. Following the termination of the Corn Laws in 1846, Cobden and his followers set out to spread his anti-imperial gospel of free trade to the rest of the world. Cobden himself became an outspoken critic of British imperialism and a leader of the midcentury international peace movement, as did many of his disciples within the rising American Empire.[18]

Beyond the borders of the United Kingdom, Cobden's economic cosmopolitanism found its most numerous subscribers in the American Northeast. These American Cobdenites were involved in myriad transatlantic reform movements throughout the mid-nineteenth and early twentieth centuries, including the closely related international peace, anti-imperialist, and abolitionist movements.[19] Cobden's American free-trade disciples included abolitionists from Boston and New York City like William Lloyd Garrison, Charles Sumner, William Cullen Bryant, and Henry Ward Beecher. For these abolitionists, free trade was thought to be the next peaceful and prosperous step in the emancipation of mankind, whereas protectionism shackled consumers and laborers to the dictates of special interests, fostering in the process monopolies and geopolitical tensions that too often led to militarism and war.[20] In the 1850s this radical minority of northeastern Cobdenites supported the newly formed Republican

Party, owing to its ideological dedication to free labor, free soil, and antislavery. The members of the Republican Party's Cobdenite minority were well aware that they were outnumbered by the party's economic nationalists, but they were not put off; freeing American slaves was a more immediate priority than freeing American trade.

When the U.S. Civil War broke out, the primary underlying cause of slavery was initially obfuscated across the Atlantic. As a result, Cobden and other British abolitionists were at first confused about its causes; the North's initial unwillingness to make emancipation a war aim made it seem to many Britons as though the conflict pitted a free-trade South against a protectionist North. This common British misperception was corrected by 1863, owing to the propaganda efforts of various transatlantic Cobdenites and Lincoln's Emancipation Proclamation.[21] Upon the war's end in 1865, these independent Republican free-traders, seeing direct parallels between themselves and the small but well-mobilized ACLL in Britain, hoped to duplicate British free-traders' successes.[22]

The Cobdenite free-trade-and-peace movement in the United States picked up pace immediately following the U.S. Civil War, with the founding of London's Cobden Club. The Club was established soon after Cobden's 1865 death, and one of its goals was to overturn the American protectionist system. More broadly, the Club desired world peace through international arbitration, noninterventionism, and free trade. The Cobden Club's pacific global economic vision was enshrined in its motto: "Free Trade, Peace, and Goodwill among Nations."

In emulation of the ACLL, the American Free Trade League (AFTL) was established in New York City just after the Civil War in order to spread Cobdenism to the United States. Its founders (or marquee members) included the abolitionists William Cullen Bryant, editor of the *New York Post*; Horace White, editor of the *Chicago Tribune*; the Ohio politician Jacob D. Cox; and Boston's Edward Atkinson. In the decades that followed, regional affiliates of this first national American Cobden Club popped up across the American North and West. The AFTL's "Declaration of Principles" declared free trade to be "the natural and proper term in the series of progress after Free Speech, Free Soil and Free Labor." The AFTL's monthly newspaper, *The League*, was named after the ACLL's circular, and the AFTL newspaper took for its motto a line from Cobden: "Free-Trade: The International Common Law of the Almighty." In 1868 *The League*, rebranding itself *The Free-Trader*, saw its circulation jump from four thousand to sixteen thousand between 1869 and 1870 alone, and its articles reportedly made their way to "nearly every newspaper in the United States."[23] As it grew in influence, the AFTL continued to work closely with London's Cobden Club. The Club's international membership roles, in turn, swelled with the addition of large numbers of AFTL members.[24]

David Ames Wells, an economist and independent Republican, soon took charge of the post–Civil-War Cobdenite movement in the United States. Following a trip to England in the late 1860s, Wells, a protectionist, had come around to the belief that universal free trade was "in accordance with the teachings of nature" and was "most conducive to the maintenance of international peace and to the prevention of wars."[25] He became president of the AFTL in 1871 and was deputized as the American secretary of the London Cobden Club not long after.

Under Wells's leadership, the AFTL quickly developed a nationwide propaganda campaign. Henry Ward Beecher, Edward Atkinson, William Lloyd Garrison, and the legalist David Dudley Field, among others, lent the American free-trade movement gravitas and publicity with their AFTL-sponsored speaking tours across the country. Other notable early AFTL members included the transcendentalist Ralph Waldo Emerson; Reverend Joshua Leavitt, founder of the Liberty Party; the founding editor of the *Nation*, E. L. Godkin; and a young journalist from San Francisco named Henry George.[26]

A desire to ease Anglo-American tensions helped motivate transatlantic Cobdenite peace and anti-imperial efforts, especially when it came to Canadian-American relations. Cobdenite critics of imperialism and war shared a desire to end Canadian-American conflict, which loomed large in the years after 1865 thanks to Fenian radicalism and calls for U.S. annexation, by liberalizing trade between the British settler colony and the United States.[27]

A British émigré named Goldwin Smith took a lead role in the North American free-trade-and-peace movement. The English-born radical journalist and Cobden Club member had been the Regius Professor of Modern History at Oxford before immigrating to the United States in 1868 to teach at Cornell University. Finding the anti-British sentiment of the times too much to handle, Smith moved to Toronto three years after his American arrival.[28] There he became probably the most outspoken Cobdenite advocate of devolving the British Empire through the emancipation of its colonies while maintaining informal free-trade relations. Pro-imperial opponents dubbed this the "Manchester Colonial Theory."

Thanks to Smith's efforts, the Cobdenite Manchester School's call for devolving imperial control over the colonies had become popular in Canada at mid-century. Smith was among the most prominent within the Manchester School in criticizing the British Empire for being atavistic, undemocratic, and unnecessarily expensive. He and others of the Manchester School instead advocated for the empire's devolution and dissolution, which earned them the moniker "Little Englanders." They proposed that the ties between the motherland and her colonies could peacefully and profitably be maintained through free trade, free migration, and friendly relations.[29] As early as 1863 Smith had advocated for greater political and fiscal autonomy for the empire's settler colonies, and he became a vocal proponent of Canadian independence. After Canadian confederation in 1867, Smith became the leader of the Canadian movement for commercial union between Canada and the United States. For Smith, it was only natural that the two countries should become economically integrated, considering their already strong trade links, alongside their common Anglo-Saxon heritage and geographic proximity.

Smith found numerous free-trade-and-peace allies among America's Cobdenite Anglophiles. The AFTL lobbied on behalf of Canadian-American trade reciprocity, and David Ames Wells, William Cullen Bryant, Arthur Latham Perry, and Cyrus Field also lent their support to the short-lived American Commercial Reciprocity League, with the aim of informing U.S. public opinion about the potential benefits of Canadian-American trade liberalization. In his popular book *Protection or Free Trade* (1886), Henry George, an AFTL and Cobden Club member, similarly advocated for Canadian-American free trade, "fraternity and peace" to counter the era's "spirit of protectionism . . . national enmity and strife."[30] These North American Manchester School efforts claimed tangible success in the late 1880s when the Canadian Liberal Party endorsed American commercial union in its party platform. Canada's protectionist Conservative Party instead supported closer trade ties within the British Empire through a policy of imperial trade preference. Following Republican passage of the protectionist McKinley Tariff of 1890 (which excluded Canada from establishing reciprocal trade with the United States), the Conservatives narrowly came out on top in Canada's 1891 federal election, resulting in further Canadian-American trade disputes and mutual fears of military invasion by one side or the other for decades to come.[31]

In the Caribbean sphere, American Cobdenite leaders similarly opposed the Republican Party's imperial designs on annexing Santo Domingo in the 1870s and 1880s. In 1870 the former Ohio governor and AFTL cofounder Jacob D. Cox resigned as President Ulysses S. Grant's interior secretary over the annexation issue; Charles Sumner was forced out of his chairmanship of the Senate Foreign Relations Committee owing to his opposition; and David Wells was fired from his position as special commissioner of the revenue.[32] When the Republicans again raised the specter of annexation in the early 1880s, New York City's R. R. Bowker asked why the United States should not instead try to gain access to the markets of Santo Domingo "without the cost of annexation" through the anti-imperialism of free trade? And why limit U.S. market expansion just to Santo Domingo, when the United States might also trade freely with South America, Canada, the whole world even, thereby making America "the apostle among nations of the gospel of 'peace on earth, good-will among men'"?[33]

New Left scholars have portrayed calls like Bowker's for free trade with Santo Domingo and the world as bids for informal imperialism. Through a neo-Marxist lens, all forms of foreign market expansion appeared imperialistic, regardless of the tactics, ideologies, or policies involved in expanding U.S. trade abroad. But Bowker did not join with the economic nationalists of the Republican Party in calling for coercively opening up the markets of the world; rather he suggested that the U.S. adopt free trade as an anti-imperial policy for peaceful market expansion through mutual "good will." Much as MacDonagh argued for British Cobdenites, the U.S. Cobdenite espousal of the anti-imperialism of free trade should not be misconstrued as informal imperialism.

That said, some American anti-imperialists did gaze upon the British Empire with rose-tinted glasses owing to their Anglo-Saxonist leanings. For some of the most extreme Cobdenite Anglophiles, their belief in the superiority of what they considered to be a shared Anglo-Saxonism informed their belief that British free trade was good not only for the United States but also for the world. This meant that even as American anti-imperialists demonstrated a critical awareness of the Republican Party's imperialism of economic nationalism, they sometimes turned a blind eye to the coercive implementation of British free-trade imperialism in places like India and South America.[34] But such instances were exceptional cases rather than the rule. As David Patterson notes, by and large "while they admired the British tradition of liberty and British achievements in literature, commerce, and industry, they had little sympathy with British imperialism." They were careful to distinguish "between its 'false' imperialistic tradition of Benjamin Disraeli, Joseph Chamberlain, and Cecil Rhodes and the 'true' England of Richard Cobden, John Bright, John Morley, and William Gladstone, all anti-imperial Liberals."[35]

Inspired by these British anti-imperial Liberals, American Cobdenites were able to steer American anti-imperial policies more directly during the two nonconsecutive Democratic administrations of Grover Cleveland (1885–89, 1893–97). President Cleveland surrounded himself with American Cobdenites as cabinet appointments (including his secretaries of state, war, agriculture, treasury, and the interior) and as unofficial economic advisors. As a result, Cleveland's administrations sought out more amicable Anglo-American relations and demonstrated a clear Cobdenite propensity for foreign policy noninterventionism and trade liberalization to create a more peaceful world order.

The new administration's anti-imperial leanings became evident almost as soon as Cleveland entered the White House in 1885 through its opposition to Republican imperial projects in Latin America, Africa, and the Asia-Pacific. In Latin America, for example, whereas Republican economic nationalists like James G. Blaine of Maine—the Republican presidential nominee in 1884—sought U.S. imperial control over any canal attempts in Central America, Cleveland and his cabinet opposed the Republican Party's planned construction of a Nicaraguan canal and the annexation of the territory surrounding it.[36] Cleveland's protectionist opponents were quick to attack his administration's early Cobdenite anti-imperial tendencies and pro-British sympathies.

With regard to Africa, Cleveland and his Cobdenites continued their opposition to coercive Republican imperialism by distancing the United States from the previous administration's imperial designs in the Congo, where the issue of free trade once again played a controversial role. American Cobdenites looked askance upon the 1884 Berlin Conference resolutions and their implications for possible U.S. territorial annexation and political entanglements in Africa, despite attempts by proponents of the imperialistic resolutions to couch the initiative in free-trade verbiage.[37] In 1885 Cleveland and his cabinet were quick to revoke U.S. recognition of the Berlin Treaty and refused to submit it for congressional approval.[38]

In the Asia-Pacific, Cleveland's Cobdenite anti-imperial approach once again contrasted with that of his Republican counterparts when, in a January 1887 special message to Congress, Cleveland "insisted that autonomy and independence of Samoa should be scrupulously preserved." At the Washington Conference held later that year, Cleveland's Cobdenite secretary of state, Thomas Bayard, fought for Samoan independence, insisting that "the independence and autonomy" of Samoa "be preserved free from the control or preponderating influence of any foreign government." Cleveland thereafter attempted to devolve American informal influence entirely from Samoa during his second administration.[39] Upon entering the Oval Office for a second term in early 1893, Cleveland also reversed his Republican presidential predecessor's recent attempts to annex Hawai'i. The Cobdenite Carl Schurz lobbied the cabinet against annexation, and Roger Q. Mills denounced annexation in the Senate. Pro-free-trade news outlets like the *New York World*, the *New York Times*, the *New York Evening Post*, and the *Nation* castigated Hawai'i's U.S.-dominated "Sugar Trust" for fomenting the annexationist agitation.[40] From the Congo to Samoa to Hawai'i, Cleveland's Cobdenites had begun implementing the anti-imperialism of free trade.

When Cleveland's Cobdenites denied the Republican economic nationalists their colonial prizes in the Asia-Pacific, they took aim at the cabinet's

British-influenced anti-imperialism of free trade. Senator Henry Cabot Lodge (R-MA) railed against the Democratic Party's abandonment of its once great Jeffersonian legacy of territorial expansion. He charged the Cleveland administration with conspiring "to overthrow American interests and American control in Hawaii" and "to abandon Samoa." The Democratic leadership had "been successfully Cobdenized." This was "the underlying reason for their policy of retreat," Lodge asserted. "We have had something too much of these disciples of the Manchester school." Theodore Roosevelt, Lodge's protégé, privately expressed similar sentiments to Lodge: "As you say, thank God I am not a free-trader. In this country pernicious indulgence in the doctrine of free trade seems inevitably to produce fatty degeneration of the moral fibre." He also suggested that the incarceration of the pro-free-trade, "peace at any price" editors of the *New York Evening Post* and the *New York World* would bring him "great pleasure."[41]

Roosevelt and Lodge's protectionist worries about the demise of the American imperial spirit proved to be unwarranted. The timing of the U.S. declaration of war against the Spanish Empire soon after William McKinley, the GOP's "Napoleon of Protection," moved into the White House and the Republicans gained control of both houses of Congress in 1897 was no coincidence. The subsequent colonial spoils catalyzed renewed anti-imperial mobilization from American economic cosmopolitans.

The Anti-Imperialism of Free Trade's Transimperial Crossings

The anti-imperialism of free trade crossed into the transimperial terrain of the Spanish Empire in 1898. The AIL, founded by American Cobdenites soon after the outbreak of the Spanish-American War, became the country's most visible U.S. anti-imperialist organization, with local chapters spread throughout the country. Historians long have noted that the anti-imperialists of 1898 were a diverse group. But AIL officers were connected by the underappreciated common denominator of the transimperial free-trade movement. Tracing the history of the American Cobdenite free-trade movement illuminates how the vast majority of AIL officers were free-traders involved in a variety of Cobdenite free-trade-and-peace organizations (see figure 7.1). Their subscription to peaceful economic cosmopolitanism was, for many of them, foundational to their anti-imperial activism. They opposed the formal American colonial acquisitions obtained from the Spanish Empire in the Caribbean and the Asia-Pacific, as well as the subsequent informal coercive protectionist policies that the GOP forced upon Cuba and the formal U.S. colonies of Puerto Rico, Hawai'i, and the Philippines.

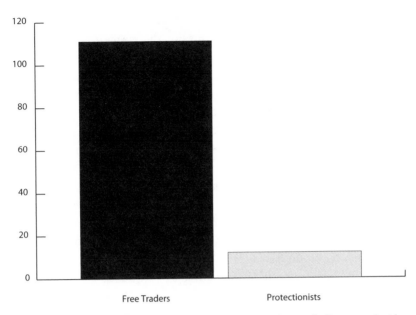

FIGURE 7.1. The economic cosmopolitanism of the AIL. The graph illustrates the ideological prevalence of free trade among the officers of the AIL. Courtesy of the author.

An ideological adherence to Cobdenite free-trade principles, particularly its close association with peace and anti-imperialism, moved AIL leaders to action after 1898. Their anti-imperialism of free trade was put on further display in their post-1898 opposition to the informal and formal economic dimensions of what April Merleaux calls the "U.S. sugar empire."[42] Beginning with the 1901 *Downes v. Bidwell* decision, the U.S. Supreme Court legalized the protectionist framework of the American closed door empire by allowing the federal government to levy tariffs against the country's own colonies so as to insulate domestic U.S. sugar growers from competition with the empire's newly acquired sugar-producing colonies. American Cobdenites unsuccessfully opposed this economic nationalist imperial legislation. For example, Erving Winslow, an officer of both the AIL and the AFTL, was quick to castigate the Supreme Court decision because it meant that not just Puerto Rico but also the Philippines would remain "outside the Constitution" and their tariff rates "subject to the arbitrary power of Congress."[43] AIL leaders continued to oppose subsequent instances of informal U.S. imperialism in the Caribbean. In 1915, for example, Jane Addams, an AIL officer, led the Woman's Peace Party, a women's suffrage and free-trade-and-peace organization, against the Wilson administration's attempt to coerce Haiti into signing a treaty granting twenty years of U.S. control over its finances and customs.[44]

Opposition to U.S. closed-door imperialism expanded into an even broader transimperial phenomenon once local critics among the former colonies of the Spanish Empire joined the free-trade fight. Cubans and Filipinos were among the loudest in voicing their dissent against U.S. imperialism of economic nationalism.

Cuba became an informal American colony after the island gained ostensible independence from Spain in 1898. The question of Cuban-American trade reciprocity soon followed. In 1902 it became one of the most hotly debated issues in Congress. Republican imperialists, at odds with both the AIL and anti-expansionists within their own party, wanted to implement protectionist reciprocity and control the island's finances and foreign trade. Cuban nationalists instead lobbied Congress for Cuban-American trade liberalization and greater local autonomy over the island's tariff policy. To this end, Luis V. de Abad, representing the tobacco interests and "all the laboring classes" of Cuba, asked the U.S. House Committee on Reciprocity with Cuba for a substantial decrease of the duties on Cuban cigars and raw tobacco. He argued that these protective tariffs were artificially lowering profits and creating unemployment on the island, added to which, "under the United States tariff it has been impossible for us to go into any foreign market." Luis V. Placé from Havana, representing a prominent group of Cuban merchants called the Corporaciones Económicas, argued, "As a Cuban I would like to give the United States free trade. The whole of American products imported into Cuba ought to be free. . . . The proper solution of the Cuban problem is virtually free trade with both countries." He also expressed his awareness of the issue's imperial power dynamics: "I ask for free trade on the understanding it is for you to grant it; we beg."[45]

The final version of the reciprocity treaty was a far cry from the free-trade version requested by the AIL, Cuban merchants, and independence leaders, as it ended up providing only a 20 percent discount on U.S. tariff rates. Disillusioned independence leaders like Juan Gualberto Gómez, head of Cuba's Liberal Party and an ally of José Martí in the Cuban independence movement, came out in opposition to reciprocity in its final form because, according to Mary Speck, the U.S. "had shown so little commitment to free trade." Other Cuban nationalists, however, gave their pragmatic support to the treaty, warning that to do otherwise would risk U.S. annexation. To them the message was clear: Cubans must either embrace informal U.S. imperialism through protectionist reciprocity or risk formal U.S. colonialism.[46]

A handful of years later, the side effects of the Republican Party's closed-door policy toward the Philippines were beginning to show. The U.S. government's protectionist policies were creating high prices on basic necessities, harming poverty-stricken Filipino consumers and various local businesses.[47] The protectionist policies soon sparked Filipino nationalist protests. On July 11, 1908, a large gathering took place in Manila "to endorse the mass petition for the free entry of Philippine goods to American markets . . . prompted by the apparent indifference of the U.S. Senate" to the ill effects of its colonial protectionist policies. Three hundred Filipino businessmen convened what became the Philippines's first Committee on Free Trade. Its officers included pro-independence advocate Pedro Guevera, a future member of the Philippine Congress (1909–12, 1916–22) and the Nationalist resident commissioner for the Philippines (1923–36), and Don Luis Hidalgo, a trade unionist and cofounder, in 1903, of the Chamber of Commerce of the Philippines. Similar meetings were held across the islands, resulting in the signatures of thousands of supporters.[48] The GOP's turn-of-the-century protectionist imperial policies thus garnered substantial opposition not only from the AIL but also from nationalists in Cuba and the Philippines.

Free-Trade Radicalism's Anti-Imperial Networks

The transimperial dimensions of this anti-imperial story become even more visible with closer examination of the Cobdenite ideas at play. Digging deep into the economic cosmopolitanism of the AIL reveals that free-trade ideas crossed the Atlantic in both directions. One particular Cobdenite offshoot was the free-trade ideology that became known in the United States as the single tax or Georgism, named after the American journalist and political economist Henry George. George's ideas crisscrossed U.S. and British imperial boundaries, becoming the leading vein of U.S. free-trade thinking to influence British Cobdenites.

The positions of George's followers on both sides of the Atlantic concerning free trade, anti-imperialism, and peace became even more radical than those of the more orthodox followers of the Manchester School. George first formulated his single tax theory—which held that a country could derive all of its revenue through a direct tax on the potential value of land—in his internationally best-selling book *Progress and Poverty* (1879). This single tax on land, according to George, was a panacea that would at once provide a steady revenue stream for local and federal governments, discourage land monopolization by incentivizing land development, and eliminate the need for all other forms of direct and indirect taxation, including tariffs. For George and his followers on both sides of the Atlantic, eliminating land monopolies and all other barriers to trade would undermine the economic causes of imperialism and war and thus bring prosperity and peace to the world.

George considered his land tax proposal a natural outgrowth of the transatlantic Cobdenite free-trade-and-peace tradition. Indeed land reform had long been tied to Cobdenism, as George and his transatlantic disciples were keen to emphasize. In 1898, for example, amid scathing critiques of President McKinley's warmongering and autocratic maneuverings, the second issue of the newly launched Georgist publication the *Public* emphasized the movement's Cobdenite connections.[49] Georgists maintained their strong opposition to American colonialism through the *Public* and in their involvement in the AIL.[50]

George himself had converted from protectionism to Cobdenism in the 1860s, at which point he put his faith "in the international law of God as Cobden called free trade." George became an American member of the Cobden Club in 1881, taking an active role in various American Cobden Clubs, including the AFTL and the New York Free Trade Club. Following his conversion to Cobdenism, he aligned himself politically with the independent Republican Cobdenites who became known as Mugwumps after they threw their support behind Cleveland in the 1884 presidential election. He praised Cleveland's 1887 message to Congress as "a manly, vigorous, and most effective free-trade speech" and stumped for Cleveland's reelection amid the "Great Debate" of 1888.[51] George also supported Cleveland's 1892 presidential run, predicting to his friend and single tax disciple Louis F. Post that a world united "in the bonds of commerce and its guarantee of peace among the nations" was now near at hand.[52]

Following the 1879 publication of *Progress and Poverty*, George and his growing transatlantic following argued that Georgism was a natural extension of Cobdenism. Because of this, his single tax theory found an even stronger reception within Free Trade England than it did in Protectionist America. George himself spent a great deal of time during the 1880s traveling between the United States and Great Britain in an effort to popularize his free-trade ideas. The first British edition of *Progress and Poverty* appeared in 1881. It sold 100,000 copies within three years, spurring George to claim that his book had "circulated in Great Britain as no economic work had ever circulated before." His arrest and imprisonment during an 1881 visit to Ireland as a reporter for the *Irish World* only lent his ideas more transatlantic notoriety and sympathy in advance of his subsequent lecture tours in Britain. His radical ideas swept across Great Britain from the early 1880s onward, and modified versions of his single tax theory were adopted by Liberal and Labour Party platforms at the turn of the century.[53] Jane Cobden—a daughter of Richard Cobden and active in Britain's turn-of-the-century anti-imperial, Irish home rule, free trade, and women's suffrage movements—was among those sympathetic to Georgism. She connected the single tax movement to her father's midcentury push for "free trade in land," as did other British Cobdenites fired up by George's single tax philosophy.[54]

Even though Georgism was too radical for some orthodox Cobdenites in the United States, the two wings remained wedded to the transatlantic anti-imperialist struggle. Their internal differences over fiscal reform stemmed mainly from the fact that the Georgist position took an even more absolutist stance on free trade than did the Cobdenite doctrine that inspired it. In particular, where orthodox Cobdenites supported indirect taxation through minimal tariffs for revenue purposes only, George's new proposal suggested that all tariffs—and every other form of taxation, for that matter—ought to be replaced by a single direct tax on the estimated value of land. Georgists thus expounded a more absolute commitment to free trade than orthodox Cobdenites. Nevertheless, despite their differences in degree concerning free-trade cosmopolitanism, the two Cobdenite camps stood side by side in their common causes of anti-imperialism and peace through the AIL and other anti-imperialist and peace organizations between 1898 and 1920.

The transimperial ties between Cobdenite anti-imperialists on both sides of the Atlantic grew substantially with the addition of George and his disciples, and were strengthened further through the efforts of AIL officers Lucia and Edwin D. Mead. Lucia was, according to John M. Craig, "an uncompromising adherent to 'free trade' economic theories" and opposed U.S. colonialism, navalism, and the Monroe Doctrine. Edwin was a member of the New England Free Trade League and the American Peace Society, a cofounder of the Twentieth Century Club, and director of the World Peace Foundation upon its founding in 1910. Lucia and Edwin's peace internationalist worldviews crystalized following a trip to England in 1901, where they met with pro-Boer editor William T. Stead and British Cobdenite J. A. Hobson.[55] Hobson's critiques of the Boer War had a sizable impact upon Lucia and Edwin's subsequent anti-imperial critiques; Lucia described their private meetings with Hobson and other British anti-imperialists as an "intellectual Thanksgiving."[56]

Soon thereafter, in late 1902, Edwin's Twentieth Century Club in Boston invited Hobson and a fellow British anti-imperialist, George H. Perris, to lunch with the members of the New England branch of the AIL, just as Hobson's *Imperialism: A Study* was making its transatlantic debut.[57] Hobson again addressed the AIL in 1903. Perris, an antimilitarist and absolute pacifist, likewise furthered transimperial ties through his anti-imperialist lecture tour that took him to seven U.S. cities. The American Peace Society's publication *The Advocate of Peace* reported that Perris's last lecture, at Cooper Union in New York, attracted around one thousand attendees.[58] It was also more than coincidental that Hobsonian critiques of U.S. financial imperialism became more pronounced at AIL meetings and in American anti-imperial writings during and after Hobson and Perris's U.S. visit.[59] Nor did Hobson shy away from criticizing the U.S. protectionist system in the years to come.[60]

Even as more orthodox Cobdenites like Hobson strengthened the lines of communication within the transatlantic anti-imperial movement, Georgist Cobdenites were working across Anglo-American imperial boundaries to argue for anti-imperial policies. The propagandistic efforts of Joseph and Mary Fels, for example, built upon these anti-imperial networks following their relocation to London from Philadelphia. Joseph, a wealthy retired U.S. soap manufacturer and AIL officer, and his wife, Mary—a radical suffragist and peace advocate who eventually became the editor of the anti-imperial Georgist publication the *Public*—provided the single tax movement in Britain with much-needed financial bolstering at the turn of the century. Georgist reformers in Britain were among the main recipients of the Felses' international largesse, leading to the formation of the United League for the Taxation of Land Values (as the Georgist movement was known in Britain), as well as numerous local chapters scattered throughout the British Empire. The League sought to spread George's land policies throughout the British colonies and thereby break up the land monopolies of the empire's aristocratic elites. Writing from London, Joseph laid this out in an open letter to Andrew Carnegie in 1910 entitled "Free Trade and the Single Tax vs. Imperialism." In it, Joseph argued that "if conditions of absolute free trade had prevailed," there would have been no Russo-Japanese War and no need for U.S. control of the Philippines: "If Japan maintained no custom houses, the power that would try to rob her of her independence would have nothing to gain and very little to lose. Henry George made this clear in his *Protection or Free Trade*. . . . The interests which dragged the United States into the disgraceful Philippine adventure would not and could not have succeeded in doing so, had not the existence of land monopoly at home made it evident that the same institution would surely be continued by our government in the Philippines." The unnatural "need of foreign markets," he continued, "which is so frequently used as an argument to justify wars of criminal aggression is a 'need' that would not be felt if the aggressing nation enforced justice at home" through adoption of the single tax and absolute free trade with the world.[61] As Mary similarly described it in 1916, just before taking part in the transatlantic travails of the Ford Peace Expedition, free trade through Georgist land reform would undermine colonialism by dismantling imperial demands for foreign markets and transportation networks wrought from protective tariffs.[62]

Anti-imperial and peace leaders like Joseph and Mary Fels thus believed that Georgism would undermine imperial expansion in three key ways. First, developing land to maximum efficiency would increase the global supply of raw materials, thereby undercutting a principal driver of imperial expansion. Second, it would undermine the militant influence of the landed aristocracy, a long-held goal of Georgists and orthodox Cobdenites alike. Third, absolute free trade would eliminate the market inefficiencies wrought from protectionism and monopolies, which they believed to be another key force behind the imperial search for foreign markets.

Conclusion

It may seem ironic that some of the leading anti-imperialist theories in the turn-of-the-twentieth-century United States came from the leading empire of the day, but transimperial crossings were never limited to strategies of imperial rule; they also advanced anti-imperial dissent. Transatlantic free-trade cosmopolitanism—whether orthodox Cobdenism or its more radical Georgist variant—fueled a major strain of Anglo-American anti-imperialism from the 1840s until the AIL's dissolution in 1920. The vast majority of AIL officers were Cobdenite free-traders, influenced by British anti-imperialist thought. In a time of U.S. political, military, and economic assertion, they drew on principles expounded by British radicals.

The anti-imperialism of free trade was a transimperial phenomenon that came to encompass the British, American, and Spanish empires. Especially in the British Empire and its rising American associate, Cobdenites struggled to replace the economic logic that undergirded imperialism with the free-trade principles they believed would undermine empire and foster peace. This association of free trade with anti-imperialism was also embraced by businessmen, consumers, and nationalists within U.S. colonies in the Caribbean and Asia-Pacific following the Spanish-American War. Traveling across imperial boundaries, anti-imperial economic theories sought to undo the world that had produced them.

NOTES

1. Christopher Lasch, "The Anti-Imperialists, the Philippines, and the Inequality of Man," *Journal of Southern History* 24 (August 1958): 330n28; Adam Cooke, "'An Unpardonable Bit of Folly and Impertinence': Charles Francis Adams Jr., American Anti-Imperialists, and the Philippines," *New England Quarterly* 83 (June 2010): 313–38; Robert L. Beisner, *Twelve against Empire: The Anti-Imperialists, 1898–1900* (New York:

McGraw-Hill, 1968); Frank Freidel, "Dissent in the Spanish-American War and the Philippine Insurrection," *Proceedings of the Massachusetts Historical Society* 81 (1960): 167–84; Fred H. Harrington, "The Anti-Imperialist Movement in the United States, 1898–1900," *Mississippi Valley Historical Review* 22 (September 1935): 211–30; John M. Gates, "Philippine Guerillas, American Anti-Imperialists, and the Election of 1900," *Pacific Historical Review* 46 (February 1977): 51–64; Gerald E. Markowitz, ed., *American Anti-Imperialism 1895–1901* (New York: Garland Library of War and Peace, 1976); Erin Leigh Murphy, "Anti-imperialism during the Philippine-American War: Protesting 'Criminal Aggression' and 'Benevolent Assimilation,'" PhD diss., University of Illinois at Urbana-Champaign, 2009; Daniel Schirmer, *Republic or Empire: American Resistance to the Philippine War* (Cambridge, MA: Schenkman, 1972); Richard E. Welch Jr., *Response to Imperialism: The United States and the Philippine-American War, 1899–1902* (Chapel Hill: University of North Carolina Press, 1979); Richard E. Welch Jr., "American Atrocities in the Philippines: The Indictment and the Response," *Pacific Historical Review* 43 (May 1974): 233–53; James A. Zimmerman, "Who Were the Anti-Imperialists and the Expansionists of 1898 and 1899? A Chicago Perspective," *Pacific Historical Review* 46 (November 1977): 589–601; Jim Zwick, "The Anti-Imperialist League and the Origins of the Filipino-American Oppositional Solidarity," *American Journal* 24 (Summer 1998): 64–85.

2. Ian Tyrrell and Jay Sexton, eds., *Empire's Twin: U.S. Anti-Imperialism from the Founding Era to the Age of Terrorism* (Ithaca, NY: Cornell University Press, 2015), 16.

3. Lasch even went so far as to assert that American anti-imperialists ignored the imperialists' economic policies and ideas ("The Anti-Imperialists, the Philippines, and the Inequality of Man," 322).

4. Tompkins notes briefly that "there was a logical correlation between their free-trade views and their anti-imperialism, as there had been for Cobden and Bright, by whom they were also influenced in both respects." E. Berkeley Tompkins, "The Old Guard: A Study of the Anti-Imperialist Leadership," *Historian* 30 (May 1968): 375. See also E. Berkeley Tompkins, *Anti-Imperialism in the United States: The Great Debate, 1890–1920* (Philadelphia: University of Pennsylvania Press, 1970); David Patterson, *Toward a Warless World: The Travail of the American Peace Movement, 1887–1914* (Bloomington: Indiana University Press, 1976), 74, 80. Cultural and political studies include Michael H. Hunt, *Ideology and U.S. Foreign Policy* (New Haven, CT: Yale University Press, 1987); Eric T. Love, *Race over Empire: Racism and U.S. Imperialism, 1865–1900* (Chapel Hill: University of North Carolina Press, 2004); Gill H. Boehringer, "Black American Anti-Imperialist Fighters in the Philippine American War," *Black Agenda Report*, September 15, 2009; Brandon Byrd, "To Start Something to Help These People: African American Women and the Occupation of Haiti, 1915–1934," *Journal of Haitian Studies* 21 (2015): 127–53; Kristin L. Hoganson, "'As Badly Off as the Filipinos': U.S. Women's Suffragists and the Imperial Issue at the Turn of the Twentieth Century," *Journal of Women's History* 13 (Summer 2001): 9–33; Erin Leigh Murphy, "Women's Anti-imperialism: 'The White Man's Burden,' and the Philippine-American War: Theorizing Masculinist Ambivalence in Protest," *Gender and Society* 23 (2009): 244–70; Allison L. Sneider, *Suffragists in an Imperial Age: U.S. Expansion and the Woman Question, 1870–1929* (New York: Oxford University Press, 2008).

5. See, especially, William Appleman Williams, *Roots of the Modern American Empire: A Study of the Growth and Shaping of Social Consciousness in a Marketplace Society* (New York: Vintage Books, 1969); Walter LaFeber, *The New Empire: An Interpretation of American Expansion, 1860–1898* (Ithaca, NY: Cornell University Press, 1963); Thomas J. McCormick, *China Market: America's Quest for Informal Empire, 1893–1901* (Chicago: Ivan R. Dee, 1967); Carl P. Parrini and Martin J. Sklar, "New Thinking about the Market, 1896–1904: Some American Economists on Investment and the Theory of Surplus Capital," *Journal of Economic History* 43 (September 1983): 559–78; Paul Wolman, *Most Favored Nation: The Republican Revisionists and U.S. Tariff Policy, 1897–1912* (Chapel Hill: University of North Carolina Press, 1992).

6. Anti-imperialists abhorred the Republican Party's coercive economic nationalist imperial policies. See Marc-William Palen, "The Imperialism of Economic Nationalism, 1890–1913," *Diplomatic History* 39 (January 2015): 157–85; April Merleaux, *Sugar and Civilization: American Empire and the Cultural Politics of Sweetness* (Chapel Hill: University of North Carolina Press, 2015), 30–31; Michael Patrick Cullinane, *Liberty and American Anti-Imperialism 1898–1909* (London: Palgrave Macmillan, 2012), 109–10; Tompkins, *Anti-Imperialism in the United States*, 245–49.

7. Richard Huzzey, *Freedom Burning: Anti-Slavery and Empire in Victorian Britain* (Ithaca, NY: Cornell University Press, 2012), 108.

8. Michael Patrick Cullinane, "Transatlantic Dimensions of the American Anti-Imperialist Movement, 1899–1909," *Journal of Transatlantic Studies* 8 (2010): 301–14.

9. Leslie Butler, *Critical Americans: Victorian Intellectuals and Transatlantic Liberal Reform* (Chapel Hill: University of North Carolina Press, 2007), 243.

10. On American Anglophobia, see especially Jay Sexton, "Anglophobia in Nineteenth-Century Elections, Politics, and Diplomacy," in *America at the Ballot Box: Elections and Political History*, edited by Gareth Davies and Julian E. Zelizer (Philadelphia: University of Pennsylvania Press, 2015), 98–117; Stephen Tuffnell, "'Uncle Sam Is to Be Sacrificed': Anglophobia in Late Nineteenth-Century Politics and Culture," *American Nineteenth Century History* 12 (March 2011): 77–99; William C. Reuter, "The Anatomy of Political Anglophobia in the United States, 1865–1900," *Mid-America* 61 (April–July 1979): 117–32; Edward P. Crapol, *America for Americans: Economic Nationalism and Anglophobia, 1876–1896* (Westport, CT: Greenwood Press, 1973).

11. Richard Seymour, *American Insurgents: A Brief History of American Anti-Imperialism* (Chicago: Haymarket Books, 2012), xv. In comparison to the American side, there is a wealth of scholarship on the economic ideologies of British anti-imperialists. See P. J. Cain, "Capitalism, Aristocracy and Empire: Some 'Classical' Theories of Imperialism Revisited," *Journal of Imperial and Commonwealth History* 35 (March 2007): 25-47; Gregory Claeys, *Imperial Sceptics, 1850–1920* (Cambridge, U.K.: Cambridge University Press, 2010); Anthony Howe, *Free Trade and Liberal England, 1846–1946* (Oxford: Clarendon Press, 1997); Stephen Howe, *Anticolonialism in British Politics: The Left and the End of Empire, 1918–64* (Oxford: Oxford University Press, 1993); Bernard Porter, *Critics of Empire: British Radicals and the Imperial Challenge* (London: I. B. Tauris, 2007); Bernard Semmel, *The Liberal Ideal and the Demons of Empire* (Baltimore: Johns Hopkins University Press, 1993).

12. Stephen Howe, "New Empires, New Dilemmas—and Some Old Arguments," *Global Dialogue* 5 (Winter/Spring 2003), http://www.worlddialogue.org/content.php?id =216. Rare exceptions to this free-trade portrayal include Tom Terrill, *The Tariff, Politics, and American Foreign Policy, 1874–1901* (Westport, CT: Greenwood Press, 1973); Crapol, *America for Americans.*

13. Marc-William Palen, "Empire by Imitation? U.S. Economic Imperialism in a British World System," in *Oxford History of the Ends of Empire*, edited by Martin Thomas and Andrew Thompson (Oxford: Oxford University Press, 2018), doi:10.1093/ox-fordhb/9780198713197.013.12.

14. On the turn-of-the-century American Closed Door Empire, see Mary Speck, "Closed-Door Imperialism: The Politics of Cuban-U.S. Trade, 1902–1933," *Hispanic American Historical Review* 85 (August 2005): 449–84; Marc-William Palen, *The "Conspiracy" of Free Trade: The Anglo-American Struggle over Empire and Economic Globalisation, 1846-1896* (Cambridge: Cambridge University Press, 2016); Palen, "The Imperialism of Economic Nationalism"; Merleaux, *Sugar and Civilization.*

15. Marc-William Palen, "Adam Smith as Advocate of Empire, c. 1870–1932," *Historical Journal* 57 (March 2014): 179–98.

16. Some of the era's popular economic nationalist theorists, most notably the German American theorist Friedrich List (1789–1846), were quite explicit in their support of colonialism. See Mauro Boianovsky, "Friedrich List and the Economic Fate of Tropical Countries," *History of Political Economy* 45 (2013): 647–69; Onur Ulas Ince, "Friedrich List and the Imperial Origins of the National Economy," *New Political Economy* 21 (2016): 380–400; Palen, *The "Conspiracy" of Free Trade*, chapter 1.

17. Oliver MacDonagh, "The Anti-Imperialism of Free Trade," *Economic History Review* 14 (April 1962): 489–501.

18. Peter Cain, "Capitalism, War, and Internationalism in the Thought of Richard Cobden," *British Journal of International Studies* 5 (October 1979): 229–47; David Nicholls, "Richard Cobden and the International Peace Congress Movement, 1848–1853," *Journal of British Studies* 30 (October 1991): 351–76; Richard Francis Spall, "Free Trade, Foreign Relations, and the Anti-Corn-Law League," *International History Review* 10 (August 1988): 405–32; Anthony Howe and Simon Morgan, eds., *Rethinking Nineteenth-Century Liberalism: Richard Cobden Bicentenary Essays* (Aldershot, U.K.: Ashgate, 2006); R. A. Fletcher, "Cobden as Educator: The Free-Trade Internationalism of Eduard Bernstein, 1899–1914," *American Historical Review* 88 (June 1983): 561–78.

19. Marc-William Palen, "Free-Trade Ideology and Transatlantic Abolitionism: A Historiography," *Journal of the History of Economic Thought* 37 (June 2015): 291–304; Anthony Howe, "Free Trade and the International Order: The Anglo-American Tradition, 1846–1946," in *Anglo-American Attitudes: From Revolution to Partnership*, edited by Fred M. Leventhal and Roland Quinault (Aldershot, U.K.: Ashgate, 2000), 142–67; Stephen Meardon, "Richard Cobden's American Quandary: Negotiating Peace, Free Trade, and Anti-Slavery," in Howe and Morgan, *Rethinking Nineteenth-Century Liberalism*, 208–28; W. Caleb McDaniel, *The Problem of Democracy in the Age of Slavery: Garrisonian Abolitionists and Transatlantic Reform* (Baton Rouge: Louisiana State University Press, 2013).

20. Marc-William Palen, "Foreign Relations in the Gilded Age: A British Free-Trade Conspiracy?," *Diplomatic History* 37 (April 2013): 217–47; Palen, "Free-Trade Ideology and Transatlantic Abolitionism"; Palen, *The "Conspiracy" of Free Trade*.

21. Marc-William Palen, "The Great Civil War Lie," *New York Times*, June 5, 2013; Marc-William Palen, "The Civil War's Forgotten Transatlantic Tariff Debate and the Confederacy's Free Trade Diplomacy," *Journal of the Civil War Era* 3 (March 2013): 35–61; Palen, *The "Conspiracy" of Free Trade*, chapter 2.

22. Palen, *The "Conspiracy" of Free Trade*, chapter 1.

23. *League*, June 1867; *Free-Trader*, June 1868, 1; *Free-Trader*, January 1870, 125, 127; *Free-Trader*, March 1870, 168.

24. *Constitution of the American Free Trade League and List of Members* (1865), New York Public Library; *League*, June 1867; *Free-Trader*, June 1868, 1; *Free-Trader*, January 1870, 125, 127; *Free-Trader*, March 1870, 168; *Address of the Free Trade Association of London, to the American Free Trade League, New York* (London: P. S. King, 1866), 4; Howe, "Free Trade and the International Order," 145; "Appendix: Alphabetical List of U.S. Cobden Club Members," in Palen, *The "Conspiracy" of Free Trade*, http://admin.cambridge.org /academic/subjects/history/economic-history/conspiracy-free-trade-anglo-american -struggle-over-empire-and-economic-globalisation-18461896.

25. "In Times of Peace, etc.," *Free-Trader*, May 1870, 207; David Ames Wells, "The Creed of Free Trade," *Atlantic Monthly* (August 1875), 15; David Ames Wells, *Freer Trade Essential to Future National Prosperity and Development* (New York, 1882), 3–4; David Ames Wells, *Free Trade* (New York: M. B. Cary, 1884), 294; David Ames Wells, *A Primer on Tariff Reform* (London, 1885), 9.

26. *League*, September 1867, 40; Edward Atkinson to Henry Ward Beecher, June 25, 1867, carton 14, Atkinson Papers, Massachusetts Historical Society, Boston; Mahlon Sands, *The Free Trade League to Its Subscribers and the Public* (unidentified publisher, 1869); Charles DeBenedetti, *The Peace Reform in American History* (Bloomington: Indiana University Press, 1980), 63, 64; *Constitution of the American Free Trade League and List of Members* (1865).

27. On Fenian radicalism and U.S. foreign policy, see David Sim, *A Union Forever: The Irish Question and U.S. Foreign Relations in the Victorian Age* (Ithaca, NY: Cornell University Press, 2014).

28. Paul T. Phillips, *The Controversialist: An Intellectual Life of Goldwin Smith* (London: Praeger, 2002), 45–53; Christopher A. Kent, "Smith, Goldwin (1823–1910)," in *Oxford Dictionary of National Biography*, edited by H. C. G. Matthew and Brian Harrison (Oxford: Oxford University Press, 2004).

29. Craufurd D. W. Goodwin, *Canadian Economic Thought: The Political Economy of a Developing Nation 1814–1914* (Durham, NC: Duke University Press, 1961), 59–70.

30. *Memorial of the American Free Trade League to the Senate and House of Representatives*, February 1866, New York Public Library; Melville Egleston to David Wells, January 11, 1876, reel 4, microfilm 15, 662–9P, David Ames Wells Papers, Library of Congress, Washington, DC; *New Century*, December 1875, 3–6; *New Century*, February 1876, 53–54; Henry George, *Protection or Free Trade: An Examination of the Tariff Question with Especial Regard to the Interests of Labor* (New York: Doubleday, Page, 1886), 352–53.

31. Palen, *The "Conspiracy" of Free Trade*, chapters 6–7.

32. Andrew L. Slap, *The Doom of Reconstruction: The Liberal Republicans in the Civil War Era* (New York: Fordham University Press, 2006), 122.

33. R. R. Bowker, *Free Trade the Best Protection to American Industry* (New York: New York Free Trade Club, 1883), proof copy, Box 89, R. R. Bowker Papers, New York Public Library, New York City.

34. Palen, *The "Conspiracy" of Free Trade*, 250–52. On British free-trade imperialism in India and South America, see, for instance, Peter Harnetty, "The Imperialism of Free Trade: Lancashire, India, and the Cotton Supply Question, 1861–1865," *Journal of British Studies* 6 (November 1996): 70–96; John Gallagher and Ronald Robinson, "The Imperialism of Free Trade," *Economic History Review* 6 (1953): 1–15.

35. Patterson, *Toward a Warless World*, 74.

36. Harlen Eugene Makemson, "Images of Scandal: Political Cartooning in the 1884 Presidential Campaign," PhD diss., University of North Carolina at Chapel Hill, 2002, 145–46; Terrill, *Tariff, Politics, and American Foreign Policy*, 91; Patrick Cudmore, *Buchanan's Conspiracy, the Nicaragua Canal and Reciprocity* (New York: P. J. Kennedy, 1892); Patrick Cudmore, *Cleveland's Maladministration: Free Trade, Protection and Reciprocity* (New York: P. J. Kennedy, 1896); James Morris Morgan, *America's Egypt: Mr. Blaine's Foreign Policy* (New York: Hermann Bartsch, 1884).

37. *Nation* 40 (January 1, 1885): 8–9. See also Milton Plesur, *America's Outward Thrust: Approaches to Foreign Affairs, 1865–1890* (DeKalb: Northern Illinois University Press, 1971), 144–56; LaFeber, *New Empire*, 53; Murray Lee Carroll, "Open Door Imperialism in Africa: The United States and the Congo, 1876 to 1892," PhD diss., University of Connecticut, 1971.

38. U.S. Department of State, *Index to the Executive Documents of the House of Representatives for the First Session of the 49th Congress* (Washington, DC: Government Printing Office, 1885–86), 259.

39. Grover Cleveland, *The Public Papers of Grover Cleveland Twenty-Second President of the United States March 4, 1885 to March 4, 1889* (Washington, DC: Government Printing Office, 1889), 471; "Protocol of First Samoan Conference," June 25, 1887, in *Foreign Relations of the United States* (Washington, DC: Government Printing Office, 1890), 204–5; Henry C. Ide, "Our Interest in Samoa," *North American Review* 165 (August 1897), 155–58; Stuart Anderson, "'Pacific Destiny' and American Policy in Samoa, 1872–1899," *Hawaiian Journal of History* 12 (1978): 53–54.

40. Thomas J. Osborne, *Annexation Hawaii* (Waimanalo, HI: Island Style Press, 1998), 17–39; Allan Nevins, *Grover Cleveland: A Study in Courage* (New York: Dodd, Mead, 1933), 549–62.

41. Henry Cabot Lodge, "Our Blundering Foreign Policy," *Forum* 19 (March 1895), 15; Roosevelt to Lodge, December 27, 1895, in *Selections from the Correspondence of Theodore Roosevelt and Henry Cabot Lodge*, 2 vols. (New York: Charles Scribner's Sons, 1925), 1:203–5. See also Theodore Roosevelt to Alfred T. Mahan, December 13, 1897, in *Theodore Roosevelt Letters*, 8 vols., edited by Elting E. Morison (Cambridge, MA: Harvard University Press, 1951–54), 1:741.

42. Merleaux, *Sugar and Civilization*.

43. Erving Winslow to Herbert Welsh, December 7, 1901, Box 2, Herbert Welsh Papers, Special Collections Library, University of Michigan, Ann Arbor.

44. Harriet Hyman Alonso, *Peace as a Women's Issue: A History of the U.S. Movement for World Peace and Women's Rights* (Syracuse, NY: Syracuse University Press, 1993), 72. On the transimperial influence of free trade within the international women's peace movement, see Marc-William Palen, "British Free Trade and the International Feminist Vision for Peace, c. 1846–1946," in *Imagining Britain's Economic Future, c. 1800–1975: Trade, Consumerism and Global Markets*, edited by David Thackeray, Richard Toye, and Andrew Thompson (London: Palgrave Macmillan, 2018), 115–31.

45. U.S. Congress, House of Representatives, "Reciprocity with Cuba," *Hearings before the Committee on Ways and Means*, 57th Cong., 1st Sess. (Washington, DC: Government Printing Office, 1902), 144–45, 149, 91, 94–95. On the U.S. insular empire, see especially A. G. Hopkins, *American Empire: A Global History* (Princeton, NJ: Princeton University Press, 2018).

46. Speck, "Closed-Door Imperialism," 455–58.

47. Palen, "Imperialism of Economic Nationalism," 176–77.

48. Raul Rafael Ingles, *1908: The Way It Really Was* (Quezon City, Philippines: Diliman Univ. of the Philippines Press, 2008), 172; *El Renancimiento* (Manila), July 13, 1908, Garrison Family Papers, Box 178, Folder 15, Sophia Smith Collection, Smith College, Northampton, MA.

49. "Cobden on Land Value Tax," *Public* 1 (April 16, 1898), 13.

50. John M. Gates, "Philippine Guerrillas, American Anti-Imperialists, and the Election of 1900," *Pacific Historical Review* 46 (Feb. 1977), 54.

51. George quoted in Thomas Hudson McKee, ed., *Protection Echoes from the Capitol* (Washington, DC: McKee, 1888), 155; Henry George, *Protection or Free Trade* (New York: Henry George, 1886), 324; Elwood P. Lawrence, *Henry George in the British Isles* (East Lansing: Michigan State University Press, 1957), 83, 84; Louis F. Post, *The Prophet of San Francisco: Personal Memories and Interpretations of Henry George* (New York: Vanguard Press, 1930), 114–24; John L. Thomas, *Alternative America: Henry George, Edward Bellamy, Henry Demarest Lloyd and the Adversary Tradition* (Cambridge, MA: Harvard University Press, 1983), 320; Charles Albro Barker, *Henry George* (New York: Oxford University Press, 1955), 72–78, 142.

52. Henry George to Louis Post, March 31, April 2, 1891, reel 5, Henry George Papers, New York Public Library, New York City.

53. Henry George, *A Perplexed Philosopher* (New York: C. L. Webster, 1893), 73; Lawrence, *Henry George in the British Isles*; George J. Stigler, "Alfred Marshall's Lectures on Progress and Poverty," *Journal of Law and Economics* 12 (April 1969): 181–226; John D. Wood, "Transatlantic Land Reform: America and the Crofters' Revolt 1878–1888," *Scottish Historical Review* 63 (April 1984): 79–104; Peter D'A. Jones, "Henry George and British Socialism," *American Journal of Economics and Sociology* 47 (October 1988): 473–91; Bernard Newton, "The Impact of Henry George on British Economists I: The First Phase of Response, 1879–82. Leslie, Wicksteed and Hobson," *American Journal of Economics and Sociology* 30 (April 1971): 179–86; Bernard Newton, "The Impact of Henry George on British Economists II: The Second Phase of Response, 1883–84. Marshall, Toynbee

and Rae," *American Journal of Economics and Sociology* 30 (July 1971): 317–27; Bernard Newton, "The Impact of Henry George on British Economists III: The Third Phase of Response, 1885–1901. Rogers, Symes and McDonnell," *American Journal of Economics and Sociology* 31 (January 1972): 87–102.

54. Jane Cobden, *The Land Hunger: Life under Monopoly* (London: T. Fisher Unwin, 1913); Anthony Howe, "The 'Manchester School' and the Landlords: The Failure of Land Reform in Early Victorian Britain," in *The Land Question in Britain, 1750–1950*, edited by M. Cragoe and P. Readman (London: Palgrave Macmillan, 2010): 74–91; Antony Taylor, "Richard Cobden, J. E. Thorold Rogers and Henry George," in Cragoe and Readman, *The Land Question in Britain*, 146–66. On the radical activism of Cobden's daughters, see especially Sue Millar, "Middle Class Women and Public Politics in the Late Nineteenth and Early Twentieth Centuries: A Study of the Cobden Sisters," MA thesis, University of Sussex, 1985; Sarah Richardson, "'You Know Your Father's Heart': The Cobden Sisterhood and the Legacy of Richard Cobden," in Howe and Morgan, *Rethinking Nineteenth-Century Liberalism*, 229–46.

55. Hobson, in turn, had been influenced by the imperial theorist Gaylord Wilshire. See P. J. Cain, "Hobson, Wilshire, and the Capitalist Theory of Capitalist Imperialism," *History of Political Economy*, Fall 1985, 455–60. For Hobson and Cobdenism, see P. J. Cain, "J. A. Hobson, Cobdenism and the Radical Theory of Economic Imperialism, 1898–1914," *Economic History Review* 31 (November 1978): 565–84.

56. John M. Craig, "Lucia True Ames Mead: American Publicist for Peace and Internationalism," in *Women and American Foreign Policy: Lobbyists, Critics, and Insiders*, edited by Edward P. Crapol (Westport, CT: Greenwood Press, 1987), 67–90, 72–73.

57. *Report of the Fourth Annual Meeting of the New England Anti-Imperialist League* (Boston: New England Anti-Imperialist League, 1902), 8; "Imperialism: J. A. Hobson's New Book on Its Growth and Its Influence in British Politics," *New York Times*, November 15, 1902.

58. *Report of the Fifth Annual Meeting of the New England Anti-Imperialist League* (Boston: New England Anti-Imperialist League, 1903), 11; "Mr. Perris in America," *Advocate of Peace* 65 (January 1903): 9–10.

59. *Report of the Fifth Annual Meeting of the New England Anti-Imperialist League*, 5–7; *Report of the Eleventh Annual Meeting of the Anti-Imperialist League* (Boston: Anti-Imperialist League 1909), 34–35. The American sociologist and imperial theorist Thorstein Veblen, for example, reviewed Hobson's *Imperialism* quite favorably upon its publication and agreed with Hobson's central thesis. See Cain, "Capitalism, Aristocracy and Empire," 31–32.

60. J. A. Hobson, *The Fruits of American Protection* (New York: Cassell, 1906).

61. Joseph Fels, "Free Trade and the Single Tax vs. Imperialism: A Letter to Andrew Carnegie," December 1910, School of Cooperative Individualism, http://www.cooperative-individualism.org/fels-joseph_free-trade-and-the-single-tax-vs-imperialism-1910.htm.

62. "Public Opinion Force to End Great Wars, Mrs. Fels Declares," unknown newspaper, July 31, 1916, Folder 7, Box 5, Joseph and Mary Fels Papers, Historical Society of Philadelphia.

8. THE PERMEABLE SOUTH: IMPERIAL INTERACTIVITIES IN THE ISLAMIC PHILIPPINES, 1899–1930S

Oliver Charbonneau

"Example is contagious," José Rizal wrote about the desire for empire in an 1890 piece for *La Solidaridad*. "Perhaps the great American Republic, which has interest in the Pacific and does not share in the spoils of Africa may some day think of ultramarine possessions."[1] Rizal's prediction manifested less than a decade later, when the United States took possession of the Philippines from Spain. The Filipino nationalist correctly diagnosed the character of empire during a period of accelerated Euro-American territorial acquisition, when empires simultaneously competed with and drew from one another. Example *was* contagious, extending to shared governance strategies, inclusionary and exclusionary cultural codes, modes of violence, and extractive goals. An emergent body of literature on European empires has parsed the "mentalities, images, stereotypes, narratives, and ideologies" circulating through the late nineteenth- and early twentieth-century world in an effort to locate "reservoirs" of imperial knowledge production.[2] Although important theoretical groundwork is in place, countless sites of transfer and overlap remain underanalyzed. This is especially true in the case of U.S. imperialism, which has been obscured through popular amnesia, nationalist disavowal, and historiographic absence.

This essay approaches transimperial connection and exchange by focusing on their manifestations in the Islamic Philippines under U.S. rule. The Muslim South's American occupiers acquired incompletely colonized territories from the Spanish, who had struggled to control the dynamic maritime sultanates of Mindanao-Sulu for centuries.[3] After assuming sovereignty over the region, the

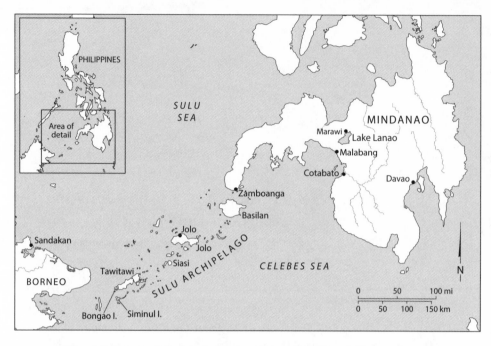

MAP 8.1. Mindanao and the Sulu Archipelago. Drawn by William L. Nelson.

American colonial administration in Manila partitioned it from the Christian North and designated it as the Moro Province, a militarized substate where U.S. Army officers doubled as civilian administrators. Colonial authorities believed the separation to be a necessity, citing the dangers posed by "semi-savage" Moros and questioning the ability of Filipino leaders to reform and integrate hostile Muslim populations into their nascent (and continuously postponed) nation-state.[4] After the end of military rule in 1914, the South saw its government bureaucracy undergo a process of Filipinization, which for most Muslims meant replacing one foreign interloper with another. Americans continued to guide policy in the region well into the 1930s, formally from Manila and informally through networks of white elites in communities like the port city of Zamboanga, in southern Mindanao (map 8.1). Throughout this series of colonial transitions Mindanao-Sulu remained a frontier zone in both American and Filipino imaginaries.[5]

While scholars of Southeast Asia have increasingly integrated the southern Philippines into their border-crossing histories, the literature on the U.S. colonial period has yet to move very far beyond contained studies of American-Moro-Filipino relations.[6] In this essay I explore how global, regional, and local interactions molded the colonial cultures of the Muslim South. The first section analyzes American rule in Mindanao-Sulu through its myriad linkages with other empires. Connectivity came ready-made to the U.S. regime in the form of Spanish colonial inheritances. Americans extended and deepened these connective webs through diverse exchanges with the Dutch, British, French, and German empires. Colonial agents also responded to the challenges of governing an Islamic population with its own global relationships by turning to the Ottoman Empire for guidance. The second section considers the preexisting networks Americans encountered in Mindanao-Sulu and how U.S. officials worked with, against, and around them. I argue that a range of transimperial intersections, operating well beyond the traditional power centers in Manila and Washington, shaped the colonial state in the southern Philippines.

Recent studies that situate U.S. history within global imperial currents inform this essay, helping to place it outside what Pierre-Yves Saunier calls "self-narratives of autonomous production."[7] This approach does not deny American power its own specificities but stipulates a reading of the colonial encounter that incorporates multiple zones of reciprocal connection involving "outside" actors. Studying the resultant cross-pollinations—with their adaptations, critiques, hybridities, and rejections—allows for a richer conceptualization of the period that bypasses national-exceptionalist and colonial-exceptionalist models. Heeding Tony Ballantyne and Antoinette Burton's call to move beyond "the metropole-colony binary that has organized so much writing on empires," I illustrate how colonial power was shaped and mediated by traffic between empires (Western and non-Western alike) and also through the surprising ability of specific regions and localities to assert themselves against broader prerogatives of control and reconfiguration. In doing so I recenter the imperial fringe of Mindanao-Sulu within heterogeneous webs of exchange and provide a window onto the contingent and coproduced qualities of U.S. imperial rule there.[8]

Inheritance and Exchange

The many borrowings of the American colonial state in the Islamic Philippines began with ethnographic and environmental knowledge acquired from Spain. Initially press coverage of the Spanish-American War emphasized a morally debased Spanish colonial culture at odds with the progressive outlook of the American republic. Whereas the Spanish authorities were irredeemably corrupted by their incestuous relationship with missionary Catholicism, Americans saw themselves as beyond such conflicts due to their elevated Protestant sensibilities.[9] Likewise American colonials believed their transformational visions for the people of the Philippine Archipelago would not be compromised and fragmented like the Spanish versions, which they viewed in racial terms as products of a corrupt Latinate culture. Rationalized colonial governance would replace the tyranny and inefficiency of the religious orders in managing underdeveloped lands, and the peoples of the archipelago would be uplifted from neglected squalor via modern sanitary technologies, secular education, and honest wage labor.[10] These strategies of differentiation did not survive the practical challenges of managing a colonial possession. Americans looked to Jesuit scientific production in reorganizing the Philippine Meteorological Service, recognizing the significant accomplishments of the religious order at their Manila Observatory. Elsewhere economic experts studied Spanish monetary policies to reduce the frictions of colonial transition. The state called upon Spanish elites in Manila and other cities to provide intelligence on the intrigues of Filipino *ilustrados*.[11] While public pronouncements on the Spanish continued to emphasize the "religious despotism and greed" of their colonial enterprise, the Americans in the Philippines were also learning from their predecessors.[12]

In the South, early negotiations over U.S. sovereignty took place throughout the summer of 1899. Brigadier General John Bates and Sultan Jamalul Kiram II of Sulu each relied on treaties the Tausūg Moro royals had made with the Spanish in the previous half-century. Bates and his staff paid close attention to material in previous treaties on the suppression of piracy, the purchase and sale of firearms, the exclusive use of the Spanish flag, the treatment of missionaries, matters of trade and taxation, and salaries for the sultan and other important Tausūg leaders. Bates also took notes on the 1851 agreement that stipulated the Spanish not interfere in Tausūg religion and customs.[13] In interviews with Kiram and leading *datus*, he sought a revised version of the 1878 treaty between Spain and the Sulu sultanate, wherein the Spanish assumed sovereignty over the islands of the archipelago. Elwell S. Otis, military governor of the Philippines, did not mince words, explaining, "The Kingly prerogatives of Spain, thus abridged by solemn concession, have descended to the United States, and conditions existing at the time of transfer should remain." Otis continued, saying the Moros were "entitled to enjoy identical privileges" to those they maintained under the Spanish "until abridged or modified by future mutual agreement."[14]

With limited information available from English-language sources, military officers posted in the South relied upon Spanish texts to interpret their surroundings. American authorities translated the Jesuit priest Francisco X. Baranera's *Compendio de la Historia de Filipinas* into English during the first year of occupation. The book contained long descriptions of the physical characteristics of the islands, including flora and fauna, mineral resources, and crop-growing strategies. More important for incoming administrators, Baranera's text was a blueprint for Spanish colonial rule, providing military garrison numbers by district, outlining efforts to establish a school system, and detailing commercial operations.[15] Other Spanish assessments of the Moros instructed Americans how to approach their new wards. A translated Jesuit account in the possession of John Pershing described the Moros as "very cunning characters, hypocritic, treacherous, suspicious, cowardly, not serviceable and beggarly beyond expression" and suggested they possessed "souls habituated towards crime." The text continued in this vein, mixing condemnatory proto-anthropological observation with more sedate data on physical geography and trade.[16] Many Americans stationed in Mindanao-Sulu inherited Spanish outlooks on fighting and governing Moro populations with little alteration.[17]

After the animosities of the Spanish-American War ebbed, U.S. officials praised their erstwhile adversaries. During his time as governor of the Moro Province, Tasker Bliss gave a ringing endorsement of the Spanish colonial legacy. He claimed that when the Americans came to the southern Philippines, they encountered "in operation a form of government and code of laws not ill adapted to the requirements of the people, which had been evolved by the intelligence and the experience of a long line of Spanish rulers during 300 years." The buildings, roads, and other infrastructural projects left behind by Spain demonstrated "skill," while the "heroic labors of Spanish priests who carried the Cross and its influence into the most remote regions of the province" were honorable.[18] Rather than dismissing them, Americans adopted and transformed the remnants of Spanish colonialism in the southern Philippines. While U.S. colonial agents believed they would pacify and transform the region in ways a decayed European monarchy could not, they were still eager to utilize the intellectual and physical byproducts of Spain's three centuries of engagement with Mindanao-Sulu. After its retreat from Asia at the close of the nineteenth century, the Spanish Empire lived on through what it transmitted to the United States.

Americans sought out more current knowledge on colonial governance among other European empires. The British, in particular, provided a familiar template from which to draw symbolic and practical lessons. Sharing historical, cultural, and economic linkages, many British and American elites bought into a conjoined sense of Anglo-Saxon mission in the colonized world, which they applied to everything from joint business ventures to globe-spanning moral reform movements.[19] A range of important figures in the shaping of Mindanao-Sulu saw British successes (and some failures) as a blueprint upon which to model their own colonial future, borrowing and refining where necessary. This extended to the highest levels of the colonial state. In order to better manage an Islamic population, the governor-general of the Philippines W. Cameron Forbes met repeatedly with the famed Lord Cromer at the Foreign Office in London and visited Egypt, where he weighed the merits of British irrigation projects and wage labor schemes. After climbing the Great Pyramid, attempting (unsuccessfully) to acquire an Arabian stallion for polo, and reflecting on the *Rubaiyat of Omar Khayyam* in idle moments, Forbes returned to the Philippines by way of the Suez Canal and Indian Ocean. Five months later he put the ideas he gathered abroad to work on an extended inspection trip to the Moro Province.[20] Charles Brent, the Episcopalian missionary bishop at the heart of cultural and religious life in the American Philippines, likewise visited Cromer, writing letters to officials in Zamboanga about how the military project in Mindanao was the talk of the colonial establishment in Cairo. Brent, who remained actively involved in education and state-building projects in the Muslim South until the end of his life, possessed an unflagging affinity for the British, believing that Americans could learn much about ruling subject populations from figures like Cromer, General Charles Gordon, and Foreign Secretary Lord Palmerston.[21]

The first governor of the Moro Province, Leonard Wood, took lessons in being colonial through travel. Alongside his aide Frank McCoy, Wood conducted a series of "pilgrimages" to European capitals in 1902, before visiting colonial possessions in North Africa and Asia the following year en route to the Philippines. McCoy took assiduous notes on the state of India, and his view that the civilizing project in the Raj would be "a question of centuries" anticipated later Republican opposition to Philippine independence. The group was especially dazzled during their ten-day inspection tour of the Dutch East Indies, drawing the conclusion that the civil service system used there could be replicated in the soon-to-be-formed Moro Province. McCoy was fascinated by the method the Dutch used to subdue (and sometimes kill) Malay subjects who had "run amok"—a problem that Americans used the adopted Spanish term *juramentado* to describe.[22] The Dutch model, considered to be the most austere and efficient of the Southeast Asian colonial states, impressed high-ranking Americans and regularly factored into their administrative considerations. In 1902 George Davis, military commander of the southern Philippines, advocated for a native army of Moros and Christian Filipinos under the command of officers drawn from a new class of American settler families modeled on the Dutch example. He also looked to the Dutch East Indies (and British India) for medical expertise in containing beriberi and cholera outbreaks.[23] Building up the town of Dansalan in 1908, the district governor of Lanao John McAuley Palmer also mimicked the Dutch, experimenting with the "enforced or directed" agricultural labor programs found on Java. A punishment-and-reward system for the conscripted Moros, he wrote to the provincial governor Tasker Bliss, would be "similar to the method employed by the Dutch to secure the loyalty of the native chiefs on Java."[24]

Transimperial influences likewise shaped the middle and lower tiers of the state apparatus. The "circuits of expert knowledge" Emily Rosenberg identifies as symptomatic of the late colonial period featured prominently in the Muslim South. The province worked hard to attract engineers, who brought "essential components of the civilizing mission" through their labor.[25] A junior engineer in Zamboanga named Manly typified the phenomenon of the border-crossing specialist. After graduating from the Indiana College of Agricultural and Mechanical Arts, he worked in Central America, South America, New Zealand, and Australia. On Mindanao, Manly directed the construction of roads, bridges, docks, and buildings. After departing the Philippines, he worked on sewage systems in Canton, for Standard Oil in Burma, and on the railway line through Kenya.[26]

Americans also prized the violent expertise of military men like Oscar Preuss, another global wanderer who served the Philippine Constabulary as a traveling expert on the elimination of banditry. Born in Germany, Preuss had a truly global résumé: enlistment in the German and Austrian armies; service in the Boxer Rebellion, German East Africa, and the Boer War; and stints in "various South and Central American revolutions."[27] After serving in the U.S. 3rd Cavalry, Preuss joined the Constabulary as lieutenant and earned a legendarily brutal reputation as a "ruthless" Moro killer. Preuss's field reports contained unblinking descriptions of the violence he and his men meted out. Confronted by superiors over rumors he had personally killed 250 Moros, Preuss bragged the number was in fact 265. His unit took to shaving the ends off their bullets to create dum-dums that "blew a hole in a man as large as a bucket."[28] Preuss left the Philippines in 1911 to serve under W. Morgan Shuster in the American gendarmerie in Persia before returning to the German Army and fighting on the Galician front during the First World War.[29]

Non-European imperial formations and actors also factored into the dynamics of colonial Moroland. In 1899 the U.S. ambassador to Turkey, Oscar Straus, convinced the Ottoman sultan Abdul Hamid II to draft a directive to the Muslims of the Philippine Islands "forbidding them to enter into any hostilities against the Americans, inasmuch as no interference with their religion would be allowed under American rule."[30] Nevertheless Moros fighting the U.S. Army in the early years of colonial occupation used the "Sultan of Stanboul" as a figure of protection, exaggerating their links to the Ottoman Empire as leverage in the hopes of intimidating their adversaries. Part of John Pershing's negotiating strategy in the 1902–3 campaigns to conquer the Lanao region included convincing recalcitrant datus of U.S. friendship with the Sublime Porte.[31] Participation in the *hajj* pilgrimage and the presence of Arab-speaking imams in Mindanao-Sulu meant that the Islamic world remained a vital cultural counterweight to Euro-American colonial modernity for many Moros.

Successive provincial governors denounced the influence of the "Arab priest" and worried about the radicalizing potential of the hajj. Missionary figures like Charles Brent conjured visions of the Islamic world as a "unified and sensitive organ" that was a "plague spot" in Europe, British India, and Southeast Asia. Brent called for a halt to "Arabian immigration" to Mindanao-Sulu, condemning Islamic interconnection as vociferously as he praised the phenomenon among Western empires. "A word in Europe to the Turk sets the wild Pathan tribes in Asia aflame," he warned his congregation in Manila.[32]

More enterprising colonial agents sought to harness Islam and direct it toward civilizational reconfiguration. In 1906 the superintendent of schools for the Moro Province, Charles Cameron, attempted to launch a "datu school" for the children of the Moro elite, recruiting an Arab teacher to combine religious instruction with the imperatives of the colonial state.[33] This approach crystallized in the multiyear attempt by the district governor of Zamboanga, John Finley, to transform Moro populations "through the instrumentality of modern Mohammedanism" as practiced in Ottoman lands. Between 1911 and 1914 Finley drafted petitions, traveled to Constantinople, and circumvented official channels to arrange for an Ottoman representative to be sent to the southern Philippines. In 1914 Sayyid Wajih al-Kilani, a religious scholar and official, toured Mindanao and Sulu and adopted the title "Shaykh al-Islam" of the Philippines. Under the tutelage of Wajih, Finley argued, Moros would learn to be "frugal, temperate, industrious, obedient to the laws, and respectful of the authorities." To lend legitimacy to his plan, the district governor cited British, French, and Dutch antecedents, contending that the integration of native customs had salutary effects on colonial rule and did not "endanger the maintenance of proper control by the home government."[34] Other American officials disagreed with this assessment, labeling Wajih a "Mohammedan propagandist" who stoked rumors of a coming holy war against Christendom. According to J. Franklin Bell, military commander of the Philippines, Finley's actions were "objectionable from a military point of view," and he quickly became persona non grata among his peers in government.[35] Authorities "obliged" Wajih to leave the Philippines within a few months, and Finley was transferred back to the United States, where he continued to advocate for closer ties between the Moros and the Ottoman Empire.[36]

The "good-will and fact finding" missions Wood and his coterie took in 1902–3 continued as a preferred mode of imperial learning into the later phases of American rule. In 1931 Governor General Dwight F. Davis toured French Indochina, Siam, British Malaya, and the Dutch East Indies, declaring in a speech that the "countries of the Far East" could profit from an "interchange of ideas." His forty-five-day trip covered six thousand miles through Southeast Asia. Davis found himself "continually . . . comparing things and places . . . [to] conditions as they exist in the Philippines." The party visited an impressive array of sites: banks, post offices, scientific stations, hospitals, farms, schools, museums, tin mines, automobile factories, and even opium plantations. This ambitious itinerary allowed Davis and accompanying officials to map out broad comparisons between the Philippines and other colonial regimes, as well as exchange political, technical, governmental, and cultural information with them.[37] After the trip the governor general sent a memorandum to the Department of War in Washington containing more pointed observations and critiques. The missive assessed European colonies in terms of their physical conditions, governmental systems, policies, personnel, revenues, expenditures, and commercial dispositions. It also reviewed the role of the native elite, the living conditions of the native peasantry, and the role and organization of the military in the colony. Davis dedicated the majority of the memorandum to the two colonial possessions with Muslim-majority populations, British Malaya and the Dutch East Indies, perhaps because of continued uncertainties over the fate of the Muslim South after decolonization.[38]

Intermediaries and Border-Crossings

Durable flows of cultural and economic exchange gave Mindanao-Sulu a permeable quality of its own, predating American rule and shaping the colonial state in unexpected ways. For centuries the sultanates of Sulu and Maguindanao—situated in the titular island chain in the Sulu Sea and along the western Mindanao littoral, respectively—proved remarkably resilient in maintaining their positions as small but dynamic polities in Island Southeast Asia. Ethnically subdivided yet linked through Islam and vigorous maritime commerce, the South's inhabitants chafed at the accelerating consolidation of Euro-American colonialism in the late nineteenth century.[39] This supraregional fluidity ran counter to American boundary-making initiatives that sought to monopolize and harness outside transmissions and entanglements. Faced with a host of practical obstacles to their demarcating agendas, colonial authorities looked toward hybridic interlocutors and ad hoc imperial coordination to shore up control of Mindanao-Sulu. The platonic ideal for imperial exchange remained studious, rigorously applied adaptations of European expertise. In practice, however, negotiating rule in porous spaces often meant pragmatic concessions to a region with its own entrenched linkages, as previously shown in American dealings with the Ottoman Empire.

Zamboanga, the provincial capital, maintained a cosmopolitan character throughout the American period. Adopted by the Spanish as their southern hub in 1635, for centuries the community remained the only real imperial foothold in western Mindanao. By the time U.S. forces arrived in 1899, it was home to a variety of peoples: Spanish military officials and traders; Christian Filipino descendants of *deportados* exiled from the North for political offenses; creole *Zamboanguenos*, who claimed both Filipino and Spanish identities; a Chinese merchant class; assorted Europeans; and, on the perimeters of the settlement, Samal Moros. Under American rule, military officers and their families represented the upper strata of colonial society, establishing racially segregated clubs, entertaining visiting dignitaries from other empires, and having their domestic needs met by native servants.[40] The white population also included small business owners, professionals, and even some aspiring frontiersmen who struck out for the Mindanaoan interior to establish plantations. European representatives of banking concerns, steamship lines, and trading companies also filtered through the Muslim South. In the 1930s, for instance, a Scottish banker named Ian McDougal represented the Charted Bank of India, Australia, and China and served as the British consul in Zamboanga. In his memoirs Philippine Scouts officer Charles Ivins recalls debating military issues with McDougal, golfing together, and attending parties featuring "white coated bare-footed Filipino boys" as servers. Among well-heeled Americans and Europeans in the provincial capital racial-civilizational kinship often trumped national competition.[41]

Outside of the rationalized spaces of central Zamboanga, officials relied on intermediary figures who acted as conduits between the colonial regime and the various Moro and Lumad groups. In the Sulu Archipelago, the Schuck family often filled this role. The patriarch, Herman Schuck, was a German trader-explorer based out of Singapore who developed a friendship with the sultan of Sulu in the 1860s. The Tausūg Moro leader liked Schuck enough to grant him land on the island of Jolo and in Sandakan Bay in North Borneo. The German used his new allotments to create his own Singapore-based trade network. Schuck moved opium, firearms, tobacco, and other goods from Singapore to Tawi-Tawi, exchanging them for slaves, which he in turn bartered on Jolo for mother-of-pearl shell. He served as an advisor to the sultan on the latter's previously discussed 1878 treaty with Spain, ran a large plantation on Jolo, and maintained links with German colonial enterprises in Southeast Asia. After he died of cholera in 1887, his five sons, one of whom was from a Tausūg wife, remained in the archipelago.[42]

The Schuck brothers—Edward, Charles, Herman, William, and Julius— solidified their positions in Tausūg society by marrying local women. It is difficult to overstate how frequently U.S. authorities turned to the Schucks. Few Americans had any knowledge of Sulu or its people, and the Schucks, bridging Westerners and natives, were ideal middlemen. They acted as interpreters, advisors, guides, amateur police detectives, militia leaders, and government officials. Edward Schuck served as translator during the Bates Treaty negotiations in 1899; Charles translated for Colonel Joseph Duncan during the 1906 expedition that ended in the Bud Dajo massacre; William was the deputy governor of Tawi-Tawi in the 1920s; and Julius was involved in government affairs on Jolo during the 1930s.[43]

The Chinese in Mindanao-Sulu, whose presence dated back centuries but had grown rapidly in the nineteenth century, often served state purposes. Many of them moneylenders or merchants, they existed in a space between the Americans, Filipinos, Moros, and Lumad groups. Although subject to racist tropes, the Chinese functioned as useful "others" for the authorities. Governor Bliss declared that the Chinese residents of the Moro Province were "hard at work improving and developing the country," reflecting the commonly held American view that the Chinese were more pliable than native populations.[44] On Jolo white residents turned to the merchant Ah Wah On for suit tailoring, new shoes, food, and "Moro curios."[45] In the Cotabato district, colonial officials relied heavily on a local leader of Chinese descent named Datu Piang. Born to a Chinese father and a Moro mother in 1846, Piang grew up in the court of the Maguindanao ruler Datu Uto and as an adult gained political power through collaboration with the Spanish.[46] Recognizing opportunity in a time of imperial transfer, he raised the American flag in Cotabato before U.S. Army troops arrived there.[47] Unlike more traditionally minded local strongmen in the southern Philippines, he understood that the integration of Southeast Asia into larger colonial trade regimes signaled the end of Maguindanao as a politically independent space. In an era of increased commercial regulation, Piang adapted to new realities better than most, leveraging the goodwill of U.S. military authorities (who viewed him as the ideal Moro) to expand his commercial holdings, all while exercising firm control of a regional despot. Piang's liminal origins and considerable natural abilities allowed him to negotiate the power dynamics of the Maguindanao elite as well as successive colonial regimes. He enjoyed a mutually beneficial relationship with the Americans until his death in 1933.[48]

Regional relationships also shaped the U.S. colonial state in Mindanao-Sulu, especially those with British North Borneo. Acquired through negotiations between British businessmen and the sultans of Brunei and Sulu, the territory received a royal charter in 1881, and the resulting British North Borneo Chartered Company attempted to develop it for the profit of its shareholders and the glory of the empire.[49] Viewing the resulting demarcations (rightly) as revenue-generation schemes by their leaders, the inhabitants of Sulu and North Borneo made a limited distinction between the territories. In the years following the Spanish-American War, the southern Philippines maintained closer links with Sandakan than they did with the North. On a practical level, this meant Zamboanga was a nodal point for commercial and political networks operating out of London and Singapore rather than Washington and Manila. Recognizing these important linkages, John Bates attempted to secure the services of the British academic Nicholas Belfield Dennys—then working for the North Borneo Company at Sandakan—during his treaty negotiations with Sultan Jamalul Kiram in 1899.[50] American military officials saw their own fortunes reflected in the British experiences on Borneo. The district governor of Sulu Hugh Scott felt Rajah James Brooke of Sarawak's efforts to reduce banditry and build a "substantial" government provided strong examples for the United States to emulate.[51] Not all Americans approved of British methods on the island, however. Visiting Sandakan in 1922, one administrator, John C. Early, sneered at the British, who lived off the "wages of shame" by legalizing and regulating vice. The British had failed in their paternal mission, he believed, by running the colony like a business (which, in effect, it was). This disavowal of the "uplift movement" caused a state of dissipation so acute that opium-addicted Chinese laborers fled to Sulu and Mindanao to escape their intolerable conditions.[52]

Despite their best efforts, Americans had a difficult time controlling traffic between the southern Philippines and Borneo. Authorities snuffed out trans-border slaving and smuggling rings only to have others reappear. Plans to regulate trade, migration, and vice foundered in the face of entrenched regional practices driven by kinship and commercial networks. Apart from the "constant ingress of Chinese from Borneo through the southern islands" that bothered officials such as John C. Early, population transfers also occurred during times of famine or epidemic. A variety of challenges confronted Americans, from responding to Sandakan brothel owners who petitioned for permission to operate in Zamboanga, to chasing, detaining, and deporting illegal migrants.[53]

E. L. Cook, a customs inspector in Jolo, found the smuggling of people and goods so vexatious that he submitted plans to Manila aimed at reorganizing the entire district. The situation never resolved itself under the Americans. Two decades later the government experimented with travel passes aimed at "minimizing the smuggling of aliens between the southern islands and the colonies near Mindanao, like Borneo and the East Indies."[54]

The unchecked movement of goods and peoples through the Sulu Sea led Americans to work directly with other empires. British and Dutch authorities already coordinated to limit the illicit trade of firearms and munitions between their respective spaces and were soon joined by their U.S. counterparts. The "enormous flows" of weapons traveling through the smuggling routes of Sulu troubled American military figures, ultimately leading to sustained campaigns to disarm the Moros.[55] Dialogues on intercolonial policing and surveillance began as early as 1899, when the head of the Philippine Commission, Jacob Gould Schurman, liaised with R. M. Little, the British resident at Labuan. After establishing a system of colonial policing in Sulu, the Americans there regularly swapped information and coordinated actions with the British Bornean possessions. The theft of ivory from a museum in Sandakan, for example, elicited the execution of searches on U.S.-controlled Siminul. In 1905 a Sulu-based outlaw named Pala raided a settlement in North Borneo, killing thirty-five before returning to Jolo. Signaling the severity of the crime, District Governor Hugh Scott received an official arrest and extradition request from the British government at Whitehall. Some 1,200 men from the U.S. Army, Philippine Scouts, and Moro Constabulary moved against Pala and his followers, killing nearly all of them in close-quarters fighting.[56] Similar incidents occurred in Dutch possessions. In 1909 seven Moros from the island of Manuk Manka in the Sulu Archipelago robbed and killed two planters on Sulawesi. Chased by a Dutch gunboat, they fled back to U.S. territory and disembarked before they could be captured. The Dutch contacted the Americans at Bongao, who took the attack seriously enough that they sent four companies of infantry from Jolo to aid in tracking the fugitives. The Dutch gunboat patrolled the waters while U.S. forces searched the island for the outlaws, and the suspects were soon apprehended.[57]

Pervasive Connections

Speaking before an assembled crowd at Baguio in 1932, John C. Early commemorated Leonard Wood and Charles Brent. Quoting Cecil Rhodes, he called the governor general and Episcopal missionary "gentleman adventurers," placing the career army officer and the moral reformer alongside colonial legends from both sides of the Atlantic. Early believed the British political officer John Nicholson, in particular, remained a "vivid personality" to the Pashtuns of the North-West Frontier, and he claimed Wood and Brent would similarly be "living personalities" in the hearts of Moros and Filipinos. Early's sentimental address bonded the grand figures of two empires within a unified moral history.[58] As evidenced, this romanticism emerged from numerous border-crossing linkages.

In constructing a colonial state in the Islamic Philippines, Americans consciously drew from other empires. Inherited Spanish infrastructure provided the foundations for development projects, and Jesuit ethnographies and regional histories informed views of the Moros. An aspirational desire to emulate and surpass the successes of the British Empire drove American colonial elites, while inspection tours of Dutch and French colonies inspired administrative and cultural policies in the Moro Province. Personnel with experience across empires alternately contributed to constructive and destructive state impulses. In turn, the imperial world took interest in the Muslim South. Annual reports from the Moro Province reached the commander of British forces in Lahore, the French ambassador to Spain, Lord Cromer, the British minister in Havana, Dutch officials on Java, a representative of Standard Oil in Batavia, a major in the German imperial army, members of the Panama Canal Commission, and an assortment of European and American academics and journalists.[59] Moro groups also looked afield, using pilgrimages and Ottoman pan-Islamism as spiritual and temporal bulwarks against U.S. colonial encroachment. Viewing the religious realm as a Trojan horse for civilizational reform, some Americans tried to co-opt Islam by utilizing foreign imams and importing emissaries from the Ottoman Empire. All of this took place amid a maritime environment with its own connections, forcing Americans to negotiate rule through intermediary figures and coordinate across borders that were often more notional than real to the region's inhabitants.

If territorial boundaries are "illusory means of keeping histories apart," imperial historiographies have added to this illusion by staying within the bounds of particular empires.[60] Though ostensibly the hinterland of America's Pacific possessions, the Muslim South was actually a site of pervasive connectivities linking it to the wider world through durable transregional networks. Mindanao-Sulu became sequestered only through narrow interpretations of empire that served the historiographic imperatives of the nation-state. Mapping the American period, then, requires multiscalar and multidirectional methodologies that track interactions across localities, provinces, nations, and empires.[61] The occupiers of the southern Philippines wrestled with the heterogeneous and overlapping social geographies of the region, while also actively constructing reciprocal avenues for transfer with other empires. These dense relational webs and their "uneven pulses" shaped how Americans, Moros, Filipinos, Europeans, and a variety of other groups positioned themselves relative to one another.[62] Studying the Islamic Philippines from the outside in uncovers the coproduced character of the U.S. Empire in the early twentieth century, while viewing it from the inside out illustrates how preestablished regional connections shaped a colonial state. By relocating an erstwhile periphery, these approaches reveal the composite character of American rule and the societies Americans ruled over in the Pacific.

NOTES

1. José Rizal, "Filipinas Dentro De Cien Años—IV," *La Solidaridad* 18 (January 31, 1890): 48.

2. Christoph Kamissek and Jonas Kreienbaum, "An Imperial Cloud? Conceptualising Interimperial Connections and Transimperial Knowledge," *Journal of Modern European History* 14, no. 2 (2016): 167. Literature on European empires has steered scholarship on transimperial interactivities in new directions. See Volker Barth and Roland Cvetkovski, eds., *Imperial Co-operation and Transfer, 1870–1930: Empires and Encounters* (New York: Bloomsbury, 2015); Heinz-Gerhard Haupt and Jürgen Kocka, eds., *Comparative and Transnational History: Central European Approaches and New Perspectives* (New York: Berghahn Books, 2009).

3. Jeremy Beckett, "The Datus of the Rio Grande de Cotabato under Colonial Rule," *Asian Studies* 15 (1977): 46–64; Samuel K. Tan, *Sulu under American Military Rule, 1899–1913* (Quezon City: University of the Philippines Press, 1968). The relationship between commerce and mobility figures heavily into regional histories of Sulu and western Mindanao. See James Francis Warren, *The Sulu Zone: The Dynamics of External Trade, Slavery, and Ethnicity in the Transformation of a Southeast-Asian Maritime State* (Singapore: National University of Singapore Press, 2007); James Francis Warren, *Pirates, Prostitutes, and Pullers: Explorations in the Ethno- and Social History of Southeast Asia* (Crawley: University of Western Australia Press, 2008).

4. The problematic and reductive construction of "Moro" identity first by Spanish and then U.S. colonial administrators is given the space it deserves in Michael C. Hawkins, *Making Moros: Imperial Historicism and American Military Rule in the Philippines' Muslim South* (DeKalb: Northern Illinois University Press, 2013), 3–53.

5. Patricio Abinales, *Making Mindanao: Cotabato and Davao in the Formation of the Philippine Nation-State* (Quezon City, Philippines: Ateneo de Manila University Press, 2000), 61–65; Oliver Charbonneau, "Civilizational Imperatives: American Colonial Culture in the Philippines, 1899–1942," PhD diss., University of Western Ontario, 417–23; Carl N. Taylor, "Powder Keg in Mindanao," *Today Magazine*, March 7, 1936.

6. Two important exceptions venture into comparative and transimperial territory: Donna J. Amoroso, "Inheriting the 'Moro Problem': Muslim Authority and Colonial Rule in British Malaya and the Philippines," in *The American Colonial State in the Philippines: Global*

Perspectives, edited by Julian Go and Anne L. Foster (Durham, NC: Duke University Press, 2003), 118–47; Karine V. Walther, *Sacred Interests: The United States and the Islamic World, 1821–1921* (Chapel Hill: University of North Carolina Press, 2015), 157–240. The standard account of the Moro Province and the Department of Mindanao and Sulu remains Peter G. Gowing, *Mandate in Moroland: The American Government of Muslim Filipinos, 1899–1920* (Quezon City, Philippines: New Day, 1983).

7. Pierre-Yves Saunier, *Transnational History* (New York: Palgrave Macmillan, 2013), 7; Michael Adas, "From Settler Colony to Global Hegemon: Integrating the Exceptionalist Narrative of the American Experience into World History," *American Historical Review* 106, no. 5 (2001): 1692–720; Julian Go, *Patterns of Empire: The British and American Empires, 1688 to the Present* (Cambridge, U.K.: Cambridge University Press, 2011); Anne L. Foster, *Projections of Power: The United States and Europe in Colonial Southeast Asia, 1919–1941* (Durham, NC: Duke University Press, 2010); Frank Schumacher, "The United States: Empire as a Way of Life?," in *The Age of Empires*, edited by Robert Aldrich (London: Thames and Hudson, 2007), 278–303; Ian Tyrrell, *Reforming the World: The Creation of America's Moral Empire* (Princeton, NJ: Princeton University Press, 2010).

8. Tony Ballantyne and Antoinette Burton, "Empires and the Reach of the Global," in *A World Connecting: 1870–1945*, edited by Emily Rosenberg (Cambridge, MA: Harvard University Press, 2012), 296.

9. Susan K. Harris, *God's Arbiters: Americans and the Philippines, 1898–1902* (Oxford: Oxford University Press, 2011), 3–37.

10. Kristin L. Hoganson, *Fighting for American Manhood: How Gender Politics Provoked the Spanish-American and Philippine-American Wars* (New Haven, CT: Yale University Press, 1998), 15–42; Greg Bankoff, "The Science of Nature and the Nature of Science in the Spanish and American Philippines," in *Cultivating the Colonies: Colonial States and Their Environmental Legacies*, edited by Christina Folke Ax et al. (Columbus: Ohio University Press, 2011), 78–108.

11. Aitor Anduaga, "Spanish Jesuits in the Philippines: Geophysical Research and Synergies between Science, Education and Trade, 1865–1898," *Annals of Science* 71, no. 4 (2014): 519–21; Bankoff, "The Science of Nature," 88–91; Allan E. S. Lumba, "Imperial Standards: Colonial Currencies, Racial Capacities, and Economic Knowledge during the Philippine-American War," *Diplomatic History* 39, no. 4 (2015): 603–28; Alfred W. McCoy, *Policing America's Empire: The United States, the Philippines, and the Rise of the Surveillance State* (Madison: University of Wisconsin Press, 2009), 59–125.

12. John Foreman, "Spain and the Philippine Islands," *Contemporary Review* 74 (1898): 32–33.

13. Memorandum I, 1899, Folder 9, Box 2, John C. Bates Papers, U.S. Army Heritage and Education Center, Carlisle, PA (henceforth USAHEC).

14. Elwell Otis to John Bates, July 3, 1899, Folder 1, Box 2, John C. Bates Papers, USAHEC.

15. Francisco X. Baranera, *Compendio de la Historia de Filipinas* (Manila: Establecimiento Tipo-Litografico de M. Perez, 1884), 120–21.

16. Untitled Spanish history of the southern Philippines, Box 319, John J. Pershing Papers, Manuscript Division, Library of Congress, Washington, DC (henceforth LOC-MD).

17. "Wearing the Khaki: Diary of a High Private," 1901–2, Box 1, Walter L. Cutter Papers, USAHEC; John Finley to John Pershing, January 1, 1910, Box 320, John J. Pershing Papers, LOC-MD; Memorandum on Policy for the Province of Sulu, September 8, 1934, Folder 4, Box 30, Joseph Ralston Hayden Papers, Bentley Historical Library, University of Michigan, Ann Arbor (henceforth BHL).

18. Speech, February 1907, Folder 5, Box 43, Tasker Bliss Collection, USAHEC.

19. Paul A. Kramer, "Empires, Exceptions, and Anglo-Saxons: Race and Rule between the British and United States Empires, 1880–1910," *Journal of American History* 88, no. 4 (2002): 1326; Frank Schumacher, "The American Way of Empire: National Tradition and Transatlantic Adaptation in America's Search for Imperial Identity, 1898–1910," *GHI Bulletin* 31 (2002): 42; Ian Tyrrell, "The Regulation of Alcohol and Other Drugs in a Colonial Context: United States Policy towards the Philippines, c. 1898–1910," *Contemporary Drug Problems* 35 (2008): 539–69.

20. Patrick M. Kirkwood, "'Lord Cromer's Shadow': Political Anglo-Saxonism and the Egyptian Protectorate as a Model in the American Philippines," *Journal of World History* 27, no. 1 (2016): 1–26; Carnes Lord, *Proconsuls: Delegated Political-Military Leadership from Rome to America Today* (Cambridge, U.K.: Cambridge University Press, 2012), 79; Journal of W. Cameron Forbes, vol. 3, January 1909, W. Cameron Forbes Papers, LOC-MD.

21. Charles Brent to Frank McCoy, April 17, 1905, Folder 1, Box 11, Frank Ross McCoy Papers, LOC-MD; "Bishop Brent at Zamboanga," *Hartford (CT) Courant*, January 15, 1913; Charles Henry Brent, *The Inspiration of Responsibility and Other Papers* (New York: Longmans, Green, 1915), 161–64.

22. Andrew J. Bacevich, *Diplomat in Khaki: Major General Frank Ross McCoy and American Foreign Policy, 1898–1949* (Lawrence: University Press of Kansas, 1989), 22–27; Frank McCoy to Margaret McCoy, September 3, 1903, Folder 2, Box 15, Hermann Hagedorn Papers, LOC-MD.

23. George W. Davis, *Annual Report of Major General George W. Davis, United States Army, Commanding Division of the Philippines, from October 1, 1902 to July 26, 1903* (Manila: N.p., 1903), 12–110.

24. John McAuley Palmer to Tasker Bliss, January 12, 1908, Folder 11, Box 1, John McAuley Palmer Papers, LOC-MD.

25. Emily Rosenberg, "Transnational Currents in a Shrinking World," in Rosenberg, *A World Connecting*, 919–20; Michael Adas, *Dominance by Design: Technological Imperatives in America's Civilizing Mission* (Cambridge, MA: Belknap Press of Harvard University Press, 2007), 150.

26. "Address to be Delivered by Major General Frank R. McCoy at Graduation Exercises, New Mexico College of Agricultural and Mechanical Arts," May 23, 1933, Box 82, Frank Ross McCoy Papers, LOC-MD.

27. "Lieutenant Preuss Wounded in Action," Box 1, Sterling Loop Larrabee Papers, USAHEC; Vic Hurley, *Jungle Patrol: The Story of the Philippine Constabulary* (New York: E. P. Dutton, 1938), 286–87; John Pershing, *My Life before the World War, 1860–1917: A Memoir*, edited by John T. Greenwood (Lexington: University Press of Kentucky, 2013), 572; Robert Fulton, *Moroland: The History of Uncle Sam and the Moros, 1899–1920* (Bend, OR: Tumalo Creek Press, 2009), 407–9.

28. Hurley, *Jungle Patrol*, 287; "Official Reports relating to Punitive Expedition to Lake Numungan, "1911, Folder 2, Box 2, Sterling Loop Larrabee Papers, USAHEC; "The Horseman's Album: A Tribute to Sterling Loop Larrabee, Master of the Old Dominion Foxhounds," January 1935, Folder 3, Box 2, Sterling Loop Larrabee Papers, USAHEC.

29. "Shuster's Gendarmerie in Persia," August 1912, Folder 2, Box 2, Sterling Loop Larrabee Papers, USAHEC; Pershing, *My Life before the World War*, 573.

30. John Finley, "The Mohammedan Problem in the Philippines," *Journal of Race Development* 5, no. 4 (1915): 357–58.

31. "Conversation with Datu Gundar, Datu Dumiar, Datu Ali, and Datu Acoti," June 21, 1902, Box 319, John J. Pershing Papers, LOC-MD.

32. Leonard Wood and Tasker Bliss, *Annual Report Department of Mindanao—From July 1, 1905 to June 30, 1906* (Manila: Bureau of Printing, 1906), 9; "Sermon by Charles Brent Preached at the American Cathedral in Manila," December 22, 1912, Box 42, Burton Norvell Harrison Family Papers, LOC-MD.

33. "Prospectus of the Proposed Datu School to Be Established in Zamboanga," September 24, 1906, Box 320, John J. Pershing Papers, LOC-MD.

34. "A Review of the Moro Petition, Its Origin, Scope and Purpose, and How Its Object May Be Realized in Aid of the American System of Control," 1912, Folder 1, Box 1, John P. Finley Papers, USAHEC; Joshua Gedacht, "Holy War, Progress, and 'Modern Mohammedans' in Colonial Southeast Asia," *Muslim World* 105, no. 4 (2015): 459.

35. Frank Carpenter to Francis Burton Harrison, February 8, 1914, Box 41, Burton Norvell Harrison Family Papers, LOC-MD; J. Franklin Bell to Francis Burton Harrison, February 11, 1914, Box 41, Burton Norvell Harrison Family Papers, LOC-MD.

36. Wajih took his role seriously and in 1915 traveled to the United States to petition President Wilson to allow him to return to the Philippines. His persistence vexed officials in the Philippines, although the affair resolved itself in an unspectacular manner in May 1916, when Wajih fell ill and died in a sanatorium in Richmond, Virginia. Governor Frank Carpenter, of the newly formed Department of Mindanao and Sulu, called his death "timely." For a full account of the Shaykh al-Islam of the Philippines, see William G. Clarence-Smith, "Wajih al-Kilani, Shaykh al-Islam of the Philippines and Notable of Nazareth, 1913–1916," in *Nazareth History and Cultural Heritage: Proceedings of the 2nd International Conference, Nazareth, July 2–5, 2012*, edited by Mahmoud Yazbak et al. (Nazareth, Israel: Municipality of Nazareth Academic Publications, 2013), 172–92.

37. "Speech by Dwight F. Davis at Manila Hotel," April 14, 1931, File 18865–55, Box 916, General Classified Files 1898–1945 (1914–45 Segment), Record Group 350.3—Entry 5, National Archives and Records Administration, College Park, MD (henceforth NARA-CP).

38. Dwight F. Davis to Patrick J. Hurley, File 18865–55, Box 916, General Classified Files 1898–1945 (1914–45 Segment), RG 350.3—Entry 5, NARA-CP; Anne L. Foster, *Projections of Power: The United States and Europe in Southeast Asia, 1919–1939* (Durham, NC: Duke University Press, 2010), 39–41.

39. James Francis Warren, "The Sulu Zone, the World Capitalist Economy and the Historical Imagination: Problematizing Global-Local Interconnections and Interdepen-

dencies," *Southeast Asian Studies* 35, no. 2 (1997): 177–83; Eric Tagliacozzo, *Secret Trades, Porous Borders: Smuggling and States along a Southeast Asian Frontier, 1865–1915* (New Haven, CT: Yale University Press, 2005), 307–9.

40. Domingo M. Non, "Moro Piracy during the Spanish Period and Its Impact," *Southeast Asian Studies* 30, no. 4 (1993): 401–10; Charbonneau, "Civilizational Imperatives," 268–83.

41. "The Monkeys Have No Tails in Zamboanga," unpublished memoirs of Charles Ivins, Box 1, Charles Ivins Papers, USAHEC.

42. Volker Schult, "Sulu and Germany in the Late Nineteenth Century," *Philippine Studies* 48, no. 1 (2000): 80–99. For a more detailed account of Herman Schuck's life, see Michael Schuck Montemayor, *Captain Herman Leopold Schuck: The Saga of a German Sea Captain in 19th-Century Sulu-Sulawesi Seas* (Honolulu: University of Hawai'i Press, 2006).

43. "Report by John Bates on Trip to Jolo," August 21, 1899, Folder 1, Box 2, John Bates Papers, USAHEC; "Proceedings of a Board of Officers Convened at Jolo," December 13, 1903, Folder 6, Box 55, Hugh Lenox Scott Papers, LOC-MD; "Report of Engagement with the Enemy on Bud Dajo, Island of Jolo," March 10, 1906, Folder 6, Box 217, Leonard Wood Papers, LOC-MD; James Fugate to Henry L. Stimson, September 1, 1928, Folder 28, Box 29, Joseph Ralston Hayden Papers, BHL; James Fugate to Joseph Hayden, December 28, 1933, Folder 29, Box 29, Joseph Ralston Hayden Papers, BHL.

44. Tasker Bliss, *The Annual Report of the Governor of the Moro Province—for the Fiscal Year Ended June 30, 1907* (Manila: Bureau of Printing, 1907), 23.

45. *Programme of the Jolo Agricultural and Industrial Fair* (Jolo, Philippines: R. B. Hayes Printer, 1906), 10.

46. Patricio Abinales, "From *Orang Besar* to Colonial Big Man: Datu Piang of Cotabato and the American Colonial State," in *Lives at the Margin: Biography of Filipinos Obscure, Ordinary, and Heroic*, edited by Alfred W. McCoy (Quezon City: Ateneo de Manila University Press, 2000), 200; Thomas M. McKenna, *Muslim Rulers and Rebels: Everyday Politics and Armed Separatism in the Southern Philippines* (Berkeley: University of California Press, 1998), 91–92.

47. John Bates to 8th Army Chief of Staff, December 17, 1899, Folder 13, Box 2, John Bates Papers, USAHEC.

48. Abinales, "From *Orang Besar* to Colonial Big Man," 208

49. Amity Doolittle, "Colliding Discourses: Western Land Laws and Native Customary Rights in North Borneo, 1881–1918," *Journal of Southeast Asian Studies* 34, no. 1 (2003): 99–100; Nicholas Tarling, "Further Notes on the Historiography of British Borneo," *Borneo Research Bulletin* 36 (2005): 213–28.

50. Vic Hurley, *The Swish of the Kris* (New York: E. P. Dutton, 1936), 79–80; John Bates to Adjutant General, August 21, 1899, Folder 1, Box 2, John Bates Papers, USAHEC.

51. "Killing of Moros," *Washington Post*, March 20, 1906.

52. "Reminiscences of John C. Early," 1920s, Box 1, John C. Early Papers, BHL.

53. John C. Early to Dwight F. Davis, December 20, 1930, Folder 29, Box 28, Joseph Ralston Hayden Papers, BHL; Otama to William Kobbé, February 27, 1901, Folder 7, Box 3, William August Kobbé Papers, USAHEC.

54. E. L. Cook to W. Morgan Shuster, August 11, 1906, Folder 66, Box 15, Tasker Bliss Collection, USAHEC; "Passes for Moros," August 29, 1926, Folder 11, Box 30, Joseph Ralston Hayden Papers, BHL.

55. Tagliacozzo, *Secret Trades*, 308–10.

56. R. M. Little to U.S. Navy Commander, August 23, 1899, Folder 2, Box 1, John Bates Papers, USAHEC; Kramer, "Empires, Exceptions, and Anglo-Saxons," 1352; George Duncan to Adjutant General, November 1, 1902, Folder 3, Box 55, Hugh Lenox Scott Papers, LOC-MD; "Report from Leonard Wood to Military Secretary on 3rd Sulu Expedition," May 22, 1905, Folder 2, Box 11, Frank Ross McCoy Papers, LOC-MD; Fulton, *Moroland*, 242–44.

57. John Pershing, *Annual Report of Brigadier General John J. Pershing, U.S. Army, Governor of the Moro Province, for the Year Ending August 31, 1910* (Zamboanga, Philippines: Mindanao Herald, 1910), 19–20.

58. "Gentlemen Adventurers," speech given at Baguio, February 1932, Box 1, John Early Papers, BHL.

59. "Mailing List for Annual Reports of the Governor—Moro Province," Folder 4, Box 217, Leonard Wood Papers, LOC-MD.

60. Prasenjit Duara, "Transnationalism and the Challenge to National Histories," in *Rethinking American History in a Global Age*, edited by Thomas Bender (Berkeley: University of California Press, 2002), 43.

61. Kamissek and Kreienbaum, "The Imperial Cloud," 180–81; Durba Ghosh, "Another Set of Imperial Turns?," *American Historical Review* 117 (June 2012): 778–79.

62. Shane Ewen, "Lost in Translation? Mapping, Molding, and Managing the Transnational Municipal Moment," in *Another Global City: Historical Explorations into the Transnational Municipal Moment, 1850–2000*, edited by Pierre-Yves Saunier and Shane Ewen (New York: Palgrave Macmillan, 2008), 174.

PART IV. LIVING TRANSIMPERIALLY

9. AFRICAN AMERICAN MIGRATION AND THE CLIMATIC LANGUAGE OF ANGLOPHONE SETTLER COLONIALISM

Ikuko Asaka

In 1830 leaders from northern free black communities convened in Philadelphia in response to the founding of the Wilberforce colony, a settlement established by black migrants who had fled to Upper Canada from Cincinnati's deteriorating political environment.[1] The Philadelphia meeting offered blessings and pledges of material support to the settlement and kicked off the black convention movement, an annual conference series in which delegates discussed abolitionist strategies and the social and political conditions of northern African Americans. By 1832, however, the wisdom of free African Americans' migration to Canada had already been called into question. When the convention learned that the Upper Canada House of Assembly had passed antiblack resolutions in reaction to the Wilberforce colony, it "turned its attention more to the elevation of our people in this, our native home," although the convention "did not wholly abandon the subject."[2]

Even as Upper Canada lost much of its appeal as a practical way to advance the lives of northern African Americans, it took on symbolic significance. Upper Canada served the convention in its fight against a bane of northern black Americans: the American Colonization Society (ACS), which promoted the removal of free and freed African Americans to the colony of Liberia in West Africa. In 1833 the convention called Upper Canada "a region of country possessing all the advantages of a healthy and salubrious climate, fertile soil, and equitable laws." This contrasted favorably with "the desolate regions of Africa," where emigrants scorched by the "rays of a meridian sun" would "be compelled to sacrifice their lives in the insalubrious climate of Liberia, provided for them by the American Colonization Society."[3] This statement was emblematic of the general trend among northern African Americans to compare Canada and Liberia in climatic terms. The simultaneous claim of African Americans' compatibility with Canada's environment and their unfitness for Liberia's pervaded northern black discourse on the Wilberforce colony. Support of the colony and opposition to Liberia went hand in hand in an effort to rebut the biological foundations of the Liberian colonization scheme—the belief that Africa offered a climate naturally suitable for African Americans.

Northern black Americans' strategic invocation of the Wilberforce colony came in response to essentialist arguments made by supporters of Liberia who denied the compatibility of the black body with Canada's climate and, by implication, with any northern clime. Advocates for removal to Liberia denounced migration to Canada as unnatural and claimed that their project adhered to the natural law of black fitness for the tropics. Biological assertions about black people's unfitness for Canada also appeared in British advocacy of Liberian colonization. Such assumptions about climate and habitation gave legitimacy to the project to remove free African Americans from U.S. northern states and Canada; they also undergirded ongoing white settler colonialism in the British and U.S. empires.

Behind the opposition to the Wilberforce colony lay presumptions of the inevitability of white settler dominance in North America. When supporters of the ACS justified Liberian colonization with climatic arguments, they commonly lumped Canada and the United States as a site for unceasing and inevitable white expansion and domination unfavorable to free blacks' social and political advancement. Thomas Hodgkin, a British physician with a humanitarian bent, added concern for Indigenous peoples to the mix, maintaining that black migration to Canada, which he opposed on biological grounds, would further encroach on the already diminished Native land in the province. Although Hodgkin's desire to protect Native populations differentiated him from U.S. supporters of Liberian colonization, he too viewed white control over Indigenous land and peoples as destined. Importantly, both British and U.S. advocates of Liberia understood black freedom within a transimperial geographic framework. They collectively developed an image of a white settler Anglophone North America in which free African Americans figured as a deviant population.

Examining how these settler colonial dynamics unfolded in British and U.S. discourse on Liberia adds to a growing body of work that foregrounds connections and parallels between settler colonial formations in the United States and the British Empire.[4] According to Zoë Laidlaw, scholars of British imperial history have been "extending their discussion of settlers beyond the formal limits of Britain's nineteenth-century empire." Laidlaw's own work analyzes how Hodgkin's support for Liberia formed a constitutive part of his criticism of the empire's white settler colonies. She demonstrates that Hodgkin championed Liberia—a "non-British settler society" ostensibly established for antislavery and "civilising" purposes—as a model for more benign "settler-Indigenous relations" in British settler colonies. Laidlaw characterizes the African settler society as a site where "seemingly disconnected places and topics" converged.[5] Her work compels us to recognize "the benefits of placing the post-revolutionary United States in the same frame as the British Empire" so as to understand the broad intellectual framework of British humanitarian attitudes toward settler colonialism.[6]

Bronwen Everill likewise shows the value of placing U.S. and British African colonization efforts in the same frame. She compares and connects the development of Liberia and the British colony of Sierra Leone, arguing that they both demonstrated the imperialistic nature of British and U.S. humanitarian interventions driven by nonwhite settlers and metropolitan antislavery allies. Such interventions, she notes, led to the disruption of "local economies, power structures, ideologies, and religions in much the same way that settlers in Australia or North America overcame the aboriginal peoples."[7] Highlighting the parallels between Anglo-American white and nonwhite settler colonies, her work situates the interconnected formation of Liberia and Sierra Leone within broader studies of British and U.S. settler colonialism and points to the transimperial nature of the antislavery politics that combined emancipation and relocation.

This essay offers another example of such transimperial dynamics in Britain and the United States. Discourses surrounding the Wilberforce colony lay bare white Britons' and Americans' interlocking pursuit of white settler dominance and building of Liberia as a place of black freedom. Furthermore, in both Britain and the United States, the language of climate justified a racialized geography that divided a white North America and a black Africa, with the important exception of South Africa, which British discourse considered a temperate climate.[8] Because climatic essentialism was a biological language, it gave form to a geographic view that traversed Canada and the United States. Faced with such an encompassing system of categorization, African American leaders in the U.S. Northeast felt compelled to highlight black successes in Canada, not only to refute colonizationists' opposition to the Wilberforce colony but also to secure their positions at home.

The Wilberforce colony was a product of white animosity against the rising number of black newcomers in Ohio. The historian Nikki Taylor details how black migration into the state spurred a series of laws designed to deter the arrival of formerly enslaved refugees and free black people. In 1804 Ohio passed a law that required all African Americans to register themselves. It levied fees on every person registered, including children. The law also provided that anyone who settled after June 1, 1804, produce a certificate of freedom. Three years later another act to inhibit black settlement passed. This time, all African Americans settling in Ohio were ordered to obtain a certificate of settlement by posting a $500 bond. These laws were not enforced for decades, but an increase of black arrivals between 1800 and 1830 led to a movement to revive the 1807 statute. During those three decades the number of black Ohioans grew from 9,568 to 376,673, the majority of whom settled in the state's urban areas. Reacting to an enlarged African American population, white inhabitants of Cincinnati, which saw its black population increase by 400 percent between 1820 and 1829, called for the enforcement of the 1807 law. The ominous development led to a meeting of the city's black residents to elect two representatives to survey a site in Upper Canada for a colony.[9]

According to Taylor, black Ohioans responded by moving to Upper Canada to realize their aspirations of becoming landowning settlers. Their representatives met with the lieutenant governor of Upper Canada, General John Colbourne, and reportedly received these affirming words: "Tell the Republicans on your side of the line that we Royalists do not know men by their color. Should you come to us you will be entitled to all the privileges of the rest of His Majesty's subjects." The agents arranged a contract to purchase a tract of land from the Canada Company, the royal chartered company established to promote the colonial development of the province. Subsequently black residents left the city in the summer of 1829 for a new colony located in Biddulph Township, a secluded community surrounded by thick forests. Ensuing recruiting efforts brought in settlers from other northern cities, and by 1832 there were thirty-two families in the new settlement, which was named after the British abolitionist William Wilberforce.[10]

The Wilberforce colony rankled white colonists in its vicinity. In no time, local residents submitted petitions to the provincial parliament to "prohibit the general influx of colored population from entering their limits."[11] In response, the House of Assembly passed a series of resolutions, one of which read, "The sudden introduction of a mass of Black Population, likely to continue without limitation, is a matter so dangerous to the peace and comfort of the inhabitants, that it now becomes necessary to prevent or check, by some prudent restrictions, this threatened evil."[12]

The resolutions fused the colonial settlers' antiblack sentiment and their discontent with metropolitan and oligarchical dominance over provincial affairs. The assembly viewed the Canada Company's sale of land as a disregard of white settlers' welfare by the metropolitan government and colonial elites who had ties to the company. The assembly members charged that "the Canada Company seems not to have duly reflected on the danger in which it involves the peace and happiness of the people." "The act of Imperial Parliament, constituting this Company," they declared, "marks the subject of these resolutions, as one of the many evils which must result from Legislation, by the Imperial parliament in matters of the internal concerns of this Province."[13]

From the Canada Company's standpoint, the Wilberforce settlers provided readily available labor for the cultivation of land and for the construction of a railroad. Some of the residents were contracted to work on six and a quarter miles of the stretch of rail line running from "the district of London to the village of Goderich, a distance of about forty miles."[14] But the company's inducement of black migrants impressed the colonists as a glaring example of the overarching reach of metropolitan and oligarchical powers. Such frustrations soon exploded in the Rebellion of 1837, in which opponents of the Family Compact took up arms.

News of the assembly's denouncement of the black migrants quickly reached the United States, leading ACS supporters to propagate the view that the Canadian frontier had joined the new state of Ohio as off-limits to free blacks. Calling the migrants "unwelcome intruders," the *African Repository*, the official organ of the ACS, characterized Upper Canada as equally adverse as Ohio to black residence. Because of the province's comparable racial hierarchy, the paper opined, it "never expected any beneficial results, from the attempt of the coloured people in Ohio, to settle themselves in Canada."[15] Black exclusion was not limited to the United States; it was par for the course in British North America as well.

John Russwurm, an African American convert to the cause of Liberian colonization, put forth a racial geography of the Atlantic world in which Canada and the United States, unlike Liberia, signified denial of equal status to black people. Russwurm, one of the founding editors of the first African American newspaper, the *Freedom's Journal*, did an about-face on his position on Liberia in early 1829 and later that year left for the colony to become superintendent of Liberian schools and editor of the colony's first newspaper, the *Liberian Herald*.[16] Upon hearing of Upper Canada's antiblack resolutions, he wrote in the *Herald* that the Wilberforce migrants proved "ignorant" of the "prejudices" about which "the Resolutions of the Legislature of Upper Canada speak volumes." The doctrine of black exclusion operated across borders, making the two Anglophone North American settler societies into a whites-only space. This white North America, in his geographic view, racially contrasted with a black Africa: "It requires no prophetic eye to foretell that to them and their posterity, there is no abiding place on the other side of the Atlantic."[17]

After being reprinted in the *African Repository*, Russwurm's editorial reached a wider audience of colonization supporters in the United States. Concurring with Russwurm, the New York State Colonization Society called the migration to Upper Canada "unfortunate and injudicious." It drew a parallel between the province and the United States, classifying both as inimical to free African Americans. "These poor people," it concluded, "must there be under the same unfavorable circumstances, in regard to their advancement and improvement, as they were in the United States."[18] Neither the United States nor the British colony offered equitable or favorable prospects to free blacks.

The bleak outlook accompanied imagery of unstoppable white expansion. Henry Clay, a founder of the ACS who later became its president, rhetorically asked where free blacks should go when "the South casts them out, the North has no place for them, the West pushes them onward, Canada repels them." Should they start moving further west "toward the setting sun?" The answer was no, for "the tide of population would ere long push them into the Pacific." With the unceasing expansion that would soon reach the Pacific, "in Africa alone can they escape the ruinous rivalry of the white man, for there the white men dare not follow them." Clay's remark revealed two things: his recognition that black persecution traversed North America's Anglophone white settler societies and his belief in the integral role that Liberian colonization should play in the establishment of a white North America.[19]

Supporters of whites-only settler societies worked to naturalize their visions through the racialized concept of black tropical fitness. This ideology had played a major role in British discourse on the black Loyalists' relocation to Sierra Leone in the aftermath of the American Revolution.[20] By the 1830s references to climatic fitness had spread from discussions of Sierra Leone to discussions of nearby Liberia. Therefore, when the Wilberforce colony entered the conversation, the ACS quickly turned to the familiar language of climate. Even before the migrants had lived in the province for a full year, the *African Repository* jumped to the conclusion that "neither the Government, the people, nor the climate of Canada, are favorable to their wishes." The paper saw no need to collect empirical evidence, for it believed that the black body's inherent unfitness for cold climates had already been proven true by the black Loyalists who had moved from Nova Scotia to Sierra Leone. Failing to acknowledge the role of inequitable land distribution in driving the Loyalists from Nova Scotia, the *African Repository* ascribed their departure solely to climatic reasons: "It ought to be remembered, that the coloured people who joined the English in the Revolutionary War, and had lands assigned to them in Nova Scotia, entreated the British Government, to remove them from that frosty region, to Sierra Leone, and that a compliance with that request alone, probably saved them from destruction."[21]

George Washington Parke Custis, an avid supporter of the ACS, likewise employed climatic language when he joined in the chorus of objections to black migration to Canada. Much like Clay, he juxtaposed a black Africa and a white Anglophone North America, envisioning white Americans' destined monopoly on Indigenous land:

> Some say, colonize in Canada. Is that the region, Sir, for the children of the sun, who are barely comfortable at a temperature of 98 of Farenheit [sic]? The idea is ridiculous—absurd. Others say, establish colonies of free colored people in the far West. I say no. We want all the West for ourselves.—"Westward the star of empire takes its way," and soon our own citizens will tread the shores of the Pacific. By oceans alone, are we to be bound. No, Sir; let us return the children of Africa under their own blazing vertical sun; the climate best adapted to their nature and habits.[22]

Custis's remarks exhibited the degree to which Liberian colonization served white settler colonial interests by claiming the North American West only for whites. He drew on biological language to make black exclusion seem both humanitarian and inevitable. In resorting to such language, he promoted a geographic outlook that transcended national distinctions. According to this line of thinking, social and political differences between Britain's Canadian colony and the United States held little meaning because racial biology outweighed nationally distinct factors in the explanation of a group's relationship to a place.

African Americans in the U.S. North were well aware of the racially essentialist grounding of Liberian colonization advocacy. This was manifest at a meeting of "the colored citizens of Boston," convened in early 1831 "for the purpose of expressing their sentiments in a remonstrance against the doings of the [Massachusetts] State Colonization Society." In protesting against "the plan of dragging us to Africa," the participants rebutted the colonizationist assertion that "the climate will be more congenial to our health" with evidence of debilitation among the migrants: "What better proof do we want of its salubrity, than to know that of the numerous bodies who have embarked [in Liberia], a large portion of them have immediately fallen victims, on their arrival, to the pestilence usual to that place?"[23]

The Boston meeting also brought to light African Americans' awareness of the white settler impulse underlying the Liberian colonization project. The black Bostonians objected to "one of the leaders of the newly formed Society [the Massachusetts State Colonization Society]" who "argued that in case a colony was formed for the blacks in the United States, they would in a short time be removed, as has been the case with the poor Indians." They protested against this outlook "on the ground of there being sufficient land in the United States, on which a colony might be established that would better meet the wishes of the colored people."[24]

Black residents of Trenton, New Jersey, expressed similar sentiments. They enumerated the main arguments peddled by the ACS, which included climatic essentialism and black exclusion from settler expansion in the western territories and states, and they called the organization their enemy because of those objectionable positions. In addition to negative characterizations of African Americans, disregard of their American identity, and opposition to their education, "opposition to our having a part of the West appointed to us" and "false statements in relation to the health of the colony at Liberia" made the ACS "our greatest foe."[25] Since slaveholders were seizing the Southwest for themselves, the areas of colonial settlement they desired access to were those in the Northwest.

The Wilberforce colony became politically significant in this larger context. African Americans were cognizant that Liberian colonizationists' opposition to the colony served to buttress their claim that Africa was the natural home of free African Americans. In rebuttal, black northerners publicly expressed their support of the Wilberforce colony in climatic terms at anticolonization meetings. At "a respectable meeting of Afric-Americans" in Columbia, Pennsylvania, convened "with a view of taking into consideration the novel scheme of the American Colonization Society," the attendees referred to the Canadian settlement in their protest of the African scheme. In addition to citing cultural and linguistic affinity with Canada, they explained their "support [for] the colony at Canada" in terms of "the climate being healthier, better adapted to our constitutions."[26]

Similar juxtapositions of Africa and Canada suffused anticolonization meetings in other parts of the North. Black residents in Brooklyn espoused "Upper Canada; a place far better adapted to our constitutions, our habits, and our morals" than Liberia.[27] Their counterparts in Rochester, New York, contrasted Africa and Upper Canada in similar fashion: "We never will remove to Africa; but should any of our brethren wish to emigrate, we would recommend Canada as a country far more congenial to our constitutions."[28] And in Harrisburg, Pennsylvania, an anticolonization meeting resolved, "That we will support the Colony in Canada, the climate being healthy and the rights of our brethren secured."[29]

The Wilberforce colony thus became a locus through which questions of race and belonging unfolded in the United States. Opponents and supporters of Liberian colonization weighed in on the settlement by way of presenting their views on African Americans' place in the expanding settler republic.

The U.S. supporters of Liberian colonization were not the only ones who rejected the Wilberforce colony as senseless and unnatural. Thomas Hodgkin, the English physician, jumped into the fray. His support of Liberia was conjoined with his disapproval of the Canadian settlement. He framed his opposition in biological language and characterized Canada as a white settler society out of bounds to black residence. His defense of black exclusion, however, proved slightly different from that of white Americans. Hodgkin's backing of Liberia stemmed from a combination of two strands of British humanitarianism: older antislavery commitments and the emergent concern about anti-Indigenous violence in the empire's new white settler colonies.[30]

In regard to the first issue, Liberia offered him a means to precipitate gradual abolition of U.S. slavery and the abolition of the Atlantic slave trade by promoting "legitimate commerce."[31] This antislavery impulse intersected with another concern of British abolitionists during this time: the future of the emancipated people in the British Caribbean. These people came into the picture when Hodgkin established a London-based organization to promote the colonization of Liberia. Because British abolitionists proved unreceptive to the ACS, Hodgkin felt the need to set up a base independent of the ACS: the British African Colonization Society. This organization, founded in July 1833, sought to build British-led settlements at Cape Mount (in present-day northwestern Liberia), with the attendant goal of repressing the Atlantic and African slave trade through British merchants' "co-operation, to introduce a mutual and beneficial commerce." The settlements' residents would come from local Indigenous people, "a few individuals from Liberia," and emancipated people from the British Caribbean. The promotion of British commerce and the introduction of Caribbean emancipated people made this endeavor "more exclusively British": "It turns its attention to our own colonies, and opens a field of promising and laudable enterprise to some of their emancipated slaves."[32]

With regard to the issue of settler colonial violence, Hodgkin agreed with U.S. opponents of the Wilberforce colony that white settler colonists would inevitably oppress blacks in Upper Canada. He warned that "this or any other colony of Blacks, either within or closely-adjoining territories already in the occupation of Whites," would surely fail because "the colonists [would] necessarily have to compete with the Whites, and at the same time to contend with the violent and general prejudice against themselves," as was plainly displayed by "the Authorities of Canada."[33]

But Hodgkin's view of settler colonial relations departed from that of his American colleagues in one respect: his interest in Indigenous protection. Such an attitude reflected the rise of humanitarian interest that accompanied the historical "proliferation of new encounters between emigrant Britons and Indigenous peoples between 1820 and 1860" in Britain's white settler colonies in North America, Oceania, and South Africa.[34] Faced with the new settler frontiers in which abuse, violence, and dispossession ran rampant, the government appointed a Select Committee on Aborigines to survey white-Indigenous relations in Britain's expanding settler empire and to devise a proper strategy. Hodgkin arranged witnesses and evidential material for the committee and went on to found the Aborigines Protection Society with some of the members of the select committee to ensure that the government implemented the committee's policy recommendations.[35]

Hodgkin's objection to black migration to Canada was part of his effort to restrain the rapacious dispossession of Indigenous people in British settler colonies. This did not mean that he contested colonization itself. He saw colonial expansion as inevitable and aimed only for regulation and reform. He urged imperial intervention to rein in avaricious settlers, regulate land grabs, and train and educate Indigenous groups in British social, legal, and political customs as a tool for self-protection within the colonial system.[36] As Laidlaw rightly notes, the "attempt to protect or elevate the uncivilized" involved "the removal (even if temporary and voluntary) of children for education in Britain, the conversion of heathens to Christianity and the inherently destructive process of 'civilising' societies."[37] In short, Hodgkin never acknowledged the right of Indigenous peoples to exist as autonomous, sovereign entities.

Although white settlers were responsible for Indigenous dispossession in both the British and U.S. settler empires, Hodgkin focused his ire on black settlement in frontier regions in Upper Canada and the United States. He predicted that "in proportion as it [black settlement] succeeds, it must tend to accelerate the extinction of another race, the yet more unfortunate victims of European and American policy—I mean that of the North-American Indians." The humanitarian physician expressed his "heartfelt regret, that . . . nothing effectual should be undertaken for that interesting but most-injured Race, once the sole possessors of that vast territory now appropriated by the United States."[38] In this statement, Hodgkin cast his opposition to the Wilberforce colony as a means to a righteous end: reducing the erosion of Indigenous land. Instead of calling for a halt to white expansion, Hodgkin opposed free blacks' settlement in North America and advocated for their relocation to Africa.

Biological essentialism buttressed such racial mapping. Hodgkin's leading objection to the Wilberforce colony was climatic incongruity. "In the first place," he wrote, "the climate presents an insuperable physiological objection to the settlement, as a Negro colony. . . . The attempt to colonize the African race in the North appears to me to be in evident opposition to the indications of nature; and to be very much like attempting to substitute the palm-trees of the same continent for the pines on the mountains of Norway."[39]

Hodgkin drew on "the valuable researches of Dr. Prichard, in support of the assertion, that a population of African Race is not calculated to be permanent in the latitude of the Wilberforce Settlement."[40] James Cowles Prichard, a physician and ethnologist, was one of the founding members of the Aborigines Protection Society. A believer in monogenesis, Prichard maintained that Indigenous peoples, originating from the same species as Europeans, had the capacity of civilizational advancement equal to Westerners.[41] But his monogenetic belief also held that different races had various climatic compatibilities. Such an idea, as contemporaries pointed out, closely resembled the polygenetic notion of "the peculiar fitness of different races of men to inhabit different climates." An adherent of distinct racial origins noted comparability between Prichard's theory and polygenism: "The Caucasian he [Prichard] pronounces best suited to temperate, and the African to torrid regions. He even confesses, that by an interchange of climate, planting the former under a tropical, and the latter under a northern sky, the health of each is materially injured."[42]

Indeed Prichard wrote in his treatise *Researches into the Physical History of Mankind* that "the diseases to which both kinds of people are subject in the climate appropriated to the other, is the impediment which had prevented large colonies of whites from forming themselves and multiplying in tropical Africa, and of Negroes in the North." However, his monogenetic theory on how "the varieties of mankind likewise are in a degree suited to certain climates" differed from its polygenetic counterpart in that the former explained the variations without denying common ancestry of the races. That is, Prichard argued that each race's peculiar suitability resulted from its long-term adaptation to "particular local situations." He called this process "local adaptation," a process that "appears to have been accomplished by the original modification of a genus into a variety of species."[43]

Hodgkin's monogenetic strand of climatic essentialism did ideological work commensurate with Custis's enlistment of determinist theories. Hodgkin distinguished the West African coast and Anglophone settler societies into two separate geographic categories along a black-white axis. In a letter to the 1840 World Anti-Slavery Convention—a meeting organized in London by the leading British abolitionist society, the British and Foreign Anti-Slavery Society—he contrasted the "colonization of American colored people" with the efforts of "Europeans to emigrate to America, South Africa, or New Zealand." The latter regions were considered temperate, while "the coast of Africa" was by nature a black destination, "where, had I a colored skin myself to enable me to endure the scorching, yet enriching influence of the sun, together with sufficient ambition for the enterprise, I would seek the *magnum imperium ubi virtus enitescere posset* [the great government where a man's valor could shine]."[44]

Hodgkin's demurral to the Wilberforce colony was precipitated by the visit of Nathaniel Paul, an African American pastor who had moved from Albany, New York, to the Canadian settlement in 1830. Sent by the colony's board of managers, Paul took a four-year tour in England, from 1832 to 1836, to collect donations for the newly established settlement. His call for support of the Wilberforce colony coincided with an upswing in British opposition to Liberian colonization. His campaign solidified anti-Liberian sentiment already pervasive among British abolitionists, thanks to the transatlantic flow of American abolitionist newspapers, and impressed on Elliott Cresson, an ACS agent sent to Britain in 1831 to muster British support for the society, that "success of [Cresson's] agency depended on the ability of the ACS to undermine the Canadian Colony's credibility with British humanitarians."[45] It was against this backdrop that Hodgkin, along with Cresson, established the British African Colonization Society to discredit Canadian migration and shore up the cause of African colonization.[46]

From Hodgkin's point of view, African Americans' preference of the Wilberforce colony over Liberia seemed illogical. In his mind, Liberia could become what the Canadian settlement was advertised to be: "a place of retreat or refuge for those Blacks who wish to remove from the pains and penalties to which prejudice subjects them in the United States." "In granting this merit to the colony of Wilberforce," he continued, "it may very fairly be urged, that Liberia possesses the same advantages."[47]

Hodgkin did not understand that African Americans' support of the Wilberforce colony was inseparably tied to their antipathy toward the limiting racial ideas underlying Liberian colonization. Neither have scholars of black abolitionism fully discussed this aspect of black support of the Wilberforce colony. Much has been said about the importance of the Canadian settlement as a means to demonstrate African Americans' capacities for U.S. citizenship. In Robert Levine's words, Paul presented the Wilberforce colony "as a voluntary black community near the borders of the U.S. (wholly unlike the comparatively involuntary colony of Liberia) that would demonstrate blacks' capabilities of becoming productive citizens in the U.S."[48] But proof of civic virtue was not the only value African Americans attached to the Wilberforce colony. The repeated emphasis on the environmental advantage of Canadian migration testified to an urgently felt need to combat the racial determinism lying at the core of Liberian colonization. The Wilberforce colony served as a means to prove African Americans' fitness for life in the U.S. Northeast and in settler frontiers on both sides of the U.S.-Canadian line.

To that end, black northerners criticized Hodgkin's pro-Liberia stance, painting a positive picture of black life in Canada. They charged that, if given a choice, any black person would choose Canada over Africa as their new abode. In its critique of Hodgkin's letter to the World Anti-Slavery Convention, New York's *Colored American* invoked the *Saluda* incident, in which some passengers on the Liberia-bound ship (all of them had been freed on condition of colonization to Liberia) chose to migrate to Canada "with their own choice" when an occasion arose.[49] The transatlantic voyage began as a pro-colonization propagandist enterprise but served the opposite cause in the end. Samuel Wilkeson, a judge from Buffalo, New York, arranged for African Americans to navigate the *Saluda* with a view to "affording them an opportunity of showing their capacity for the management of their own affairs." With an advance of $3,000 granted by the ACS, Wilkeson executed the project. The ship sailed from New York to Liberia after stopping at Norfolk, Virginia, to pick up more migrants.[50] After departing from Norfolk, the *Saluda*, suffering a leak, anchored at Philadelphia for repairs. During the stop some of the manumitted passengers "bade farewell to the *Saluda*, and changed their course for this British asylum, where they now are 'contented and happy' alike beyond the power of the cruel monster, slavery, and the pestiferous, gangrenous, murderous influence of colonizationism, and man slaying missionaries."[51] Black opponents of colonization cited this incident to refute Hodgkin, claiming that it represented "one of the many instances that would occur, if the same opportunity was offered."[52]

Despite the initial enthusiasm, the Wilberforce colony eventually disbanded following internal feuds.[53] After the dissolution, Irish migrants moved to the area in the late 1840s, overwhelming the already shrunken black population. These settlers went to great lengths to expel the remaining black residents, resorting to acts of intimidation and demanding that the Canada Company not sell any more land to blacks. Eventually the Irish took over the Wilberforce settlement altogether by purchasing the property and appropriating its buildings.[54]

On the other side of the Atlantic, Hodgkin's appeal at the World Anti-Slavery Convention fell on deaf ears. Paul's mission in England had played an essential role in consolidating the British rejection of Liberian colonization.[55] In dismay, in late 1834 Hodgkin wrote to Cresson that the British African Colonization Society had become defunct because of waning interest among its members.[56] The plan of building settlements at Cape Mount evaporated as inquiries about land received no replies from Liberia.[57]

The rejection of Liberian colonization by British abolitionists did not mean that they were above climatic essentialism. In the coming decades the British and Foreign Anti-Slavery Society labored to remove self-emancipated people living in Canada to the British Caribbean plantations with help from the ideological authority of biological determinism. American supporters of Liberian colonization continued to work within the same racial paradigm. The notion of black tropicality became so deeply entrenched in U.S. popular and political discourse that it went on to define the contours of Republican debates on emancipation during the Civil War.[58]

Correspondingly, challenging and negotiating this ideology came to constitute a main strand of black politics in both Canada and the United States. Recourse to national specificity—emphasizing the distinction between a slaveholding republic and a free monarchy, for instance—still held political appeal and enjoyed abolitionist currency, but free African Americans also fought a mode of dominance that transcended the nation in its significance and operation. Faced with biological language, they pressed for political rights and social inclusion as they insisted on their capacity to thrive in the "temperate" settler societies of North America.

NOTES

1. *Constitution of the American Society of Free Persons of Colour, for Improving Their Condition in the United States; for Purchasing Lands; and for the Establishment of a Settlement in Upper Canada, also The Proceedings of the Convention, with Their Address to the Free People of Colour in the United States* (Philadelphia: J. W. Allen, 1831), 9, in *Minutes of the Proceedings of the National Negro Conventions, 1830–1864*, edited by Howard Bell (New York: Arno Press and New York Times, 1969).

2. *Minutes and Proceedings of the Second Annual Convention, for the Improvement of the Free People of Color in These United States, held by adjournments in the city of Philadelphia, from the 4th to the 13th of June inclusive, 1832* (Philadelphia: Published by order of the convention, 1832), 17, 18, 20, in *Minutes of the Proceedings of the National Negro Conventions*.

3. *Minutes and Proceedings of the Third Annual Convention*, 23, in *Minutes of the Proceedings of the National Negro Conventions*.

4. James Belich, *Replenishing the Earth: The Settler Revolution and the Rise of the Anglo-World, 1783–1939* (Oxford: Oxford University Press, 2009); Lisa Ford, *Settler Sovereignty: Jurisdiction and Indigenous People in America and Australia, 1788–1836* (Cambridge, MA: Harvard University Press, 2011); Marilyn Lake and Henry Reynolds, *Drawing the Global Colour Line: White Men's Countries and the International Challenge of Racial Equality* (Cambridge, U.K.: Cambridge University Press, 2008).

5. Zoë Laidlaw, "Breaking Britannia's Bounds? Law, Settlers, and Space in Britain's Imperial Historiography," *Historical Journal* 55, no. 3 (2012): 817.

6. Zoë Laidlaw, "Slavery, Settlers and Indigenous Dispossession: Britain's Empire through the Lens of Liberia," *Journal of Colonialism and Colonial History* 13, no. 1 (Spring 2012), doi:10.1353/cch.2012.0005. See also Zoë Laidlaw, "'Justice to India—Prosperity to England—Freedom to the Slave!' Humanitarian and Moral Reform Campaigns on India, Aborigines and American Slavery," *Journal of the Royal Asiatic Society of Great Britain and Ireland* 22, no. 2 (2012): 300.

7. Bronwen Everill, *Abolition and Empire in Sierra Leone and Liberia* (Houndmills, U.K.: Palgrave Macmillan, 2013), 178.

8. On European views on South Africa, see Brett M. Bennett, "Naturalising Australian Trees in South Africa: Climate, Exotics and Experimentation," *Journal of Southern African Studies* 37, no. 2 (2011): 265–80; John Edwin Mason, *Social Death and Resurrection: Slavery and Emancipation in South Africa* (Charlottesville: University of Virginia Press, 2003), 124–25.

9. Nikki M. Taylor, *Frontiers of Freedom: Cincinnati's Black Community, 1802–1868* (Athens: Ohio University Press, 2005), 21, 28, 32–33, 51, 58, 61.

10. Taylor, *Frontiers of Freedom*, 61, 67.

11. *Minutes and Proceedings of the Second Annual Convention, for the Improvement of the Free People of Color in These United States*, 17.

12. "Colony of Coloured People in Canada," *African Repository and Colonial Journal* 6, no. 1 (March 1830): 28.

13. "Colony of Coloured People in Canada," 28.

14. *Report from the Select Committee on the Extinction of Slavery throughout the British Dominions; with the Minutes of Evidence, and General Index* (London: J. Haddon, 1833), 216.

15. "Colony of Coloured People in Canada," 27.

16. Winston James, *The Struggles of John Brown Russwurm: The Life and Writings of a Pan-Africanist Pioneer, 1799–1851* (New York: New York University Press, 2010).

17. Quoted from editorial remarks in *Liberia Herald*, February 1830; "Liberia Herald," *African Repository and Colonial Journal* 7, no. 1 (March 1831): 26.

18. New York State Colonization Society, *African Colonization: Proceedings of the New York State Colonization Society, on Its Second Anniversary; Together with an Address to the Public, from the Managers Thereof* (Albany, NY: Webster and Skinners, 1831), 19.

19. "We Deem the Intrinsic Merit of Mr. Clay's Address," *African Repository, and Colonial Journal* 6, no. 1 (March 1830): 26.

20. Ikuko Asaka, *Tropical Freedom: Climate, Settler Colonialism and Black Exclusion in the Age of Emancipation* (Durham, NC: Duke University Press, 2017).

21. "Colony of Coloured People in Canada," 27–28.

22. American Colonization Society, *The Sixteenth Annual Report of the American Society for Colonizing the Free People of Colour of the United States with an Appendix* (Washington, DC: James C. Dunn, 1833), xvii.

23. William Lloyd Garrison, *Thoughts on African Colonization: Or an Impartial Exhibition of the Doctrines, Principles and Purposes of the American Colonization Society, together with the Resolutions, Addresses and Remonstrances of the Free People of Color, Part II* (Boston: Garrison and Knapp, 1832), 17–19.

24. Garrison, *Thoughts on African Colonization*, 20.

25. Nathaniel Paul, *Reply to Mr. Joseph Phillips' Enquiry respecting "the Light in which the Operations of the American Colonization Society Are Viewed by the Free People of Colour in the United States"* (London: J. Messeder, 1832), 4.

26. Garrison, *Thoughts on African Colonization*, 31–33.

27. Garrison, *Thoughts on African Colonization*, 26.

28. Garrison, *Thoughts on African Colonization*, 43.

29. Garrison, *Thoughts on African Colonization*, 42.

30. Alan Lester and Fae Dussart, *Colonization and the Origins of Humanitarian Governance: Protecting Aborigines across the Nineteenth-Century British Empire* (Cambridge, U.K.: Cambridge University Press, 2014), 14.

31. Quoted in Laidlaw, "Slavery, Settlers and Indigenous Dispossession."

32. "Dr. Hodgkin's Remarks on the African Colonization Society," *African Repository and Colonial Journal* 10, no. 10 (December 1834): 309–10. On the British African Colonization Society, see also Laidlaw, "'Justice to India,'" 310; Laidlaw, "Slavery, Settlers and Indigenous Dispossession"; R. J. M. Blackett, "Anglo-American Opposition to Liberian Colonization, 1831–1833," *Historian* 41, no. 2 (February 1979): 292; Amalie M. Kass and Edward H. Kass, *Perfecting the World: The Life and Times of Dr. Thomas Hodgkin, 1798–1866* (Boston: Harcourt Brace Jovanovich, 1988), 234.

33. Thomas Hodgkin, *An Inquiry into the Merits of the American Colonization Society: And a Reply to the Charges Brought against It, with an Account of the British African Colonization Society* (London: J. and A. Arch, 1833), 18.

34. Lester and Dussart, *Colonization and the Origins of Humanitarian Governance*, 23.

35. Michael D. Blackstock, "Trust Us: A Case Study in Colonial Social Relations Based on Documents Prepared by the Aborigines Protection Society, 1836–1912," in *With Good Intentions: Euro-Canadian and Aboriginal Relations in Colonial Canada*, edited by Celia Haig-Brown and David A. Nock (Vancouver: University of British Columbia Press, 2006), 51–71, 58; James Heartfield, *The Aborigines' Protection Society: Humanitarian Imperialism in Australia, New Zealand, Fiji, Canada, South Africa, and the Congo, 1836–1909* (New York: Columbia University Press, 2011), 7–10; Kass and Kass, *Perfecting the World*, 270–71.

36. Zoë Laidlaw, "Heathens, Slaves and Aborigines: Thomas Hodgkin's Critique of Missions and Anti-slavery," *History Workshop Journal* 64 (Autumn 2007): 143; Laidlaw, "Slavery, Settlers and Indigenous Dispossession"; Laidlaw, "'Justice to India,'" 303; Patrick Bratlinger, *Dark Vanishings: Discourse on the Extinction of Primitive Races, 1800–1930* (Ithaca, NY: Cornell University Press, 2003), 93; Heartfield, *The Aborigines' Protection Society*, 43.

37. Zoë Laidlaw, "Indigenous Interlocutors: Networks of Imperial Protest and Humanitarianism in the Mid-Nineteenth Century," in *Indigenous Networks: Mobility, Connections and Exchange*, edited by Jane Carey and Jane Lydon (New York: Routledge, 2014), 117.

38. Hodgkin, *An Inquiry into the Merits of the American Colonization Society*, 19.

39. Hodgkin, *An Inquiry into the Merits of the American Colonization Society*, 18.

40. Hodgkin, *An Inquiry into the Merits of the American Colonization Society*, 19.

41. See Michael T. Bravo, "Ethnological Encounters," in *Cultures of Natural History*, edited by N. Jardine, J. A. Secord, and E. C. Spary (Cambridge, U.K.: Cambridge University Press, 1996), 340; Laidlaw, "Heathens, Slaves and Aborigines," 137; Heartfield, *The Aborigines' Protection Society*, 26; Kass and Kass, *Perfecting the World*, 260.

42. Charles Caldwell, *Thoughts on the Original Unity of the Human Race* (New York: E. Bliss, 1830), 15.

43. James Cowles Prichard, *Researches into the Physical History of Mankind*, vol. 2, 2nd edition (London: John and Arthur Arch, 1826), 571, 574, 575.

44. "Interesting Letter," *New York Observer and Chronicle*, October 24, 1840.

45. Blackett, "Anglo-American Opposition," 284, 278. See also R. J. M. Blackett, *Building an Antislavery Wall: Black Americans in the Atlantic Abolitionist Movement, 1830- 1860* (Baton Rouge: Louisiana State University Press, 1983).

46. Blackett, "Anglo-American Opposition," 292.

47. Hodgkin, *An Inquiry into the Merits of the American Colonization Society*, 18.

48. Robert S. Levine, "Fifth of July: Nathaniel Paul and the Construction of Black Nationalism," in *Genius in Bondage: Literature of the Early Black Atlantic*, edited by Vincent Carretta and Philip Gould (Lexington: University Press of Kentucky, 2001), 242–60, 251.

49. "Thomas Hodgkin and Colonization," *Colored American*, October 31, 1840.

50. Colonization Society of the City of New York, *Seventh Annual Report of the Colonization Society of the City of New York* (New York: Mercein and Post's Press, 1839), 12.

51. "Letter from H. Wilson to J. Leavitt," *Colored American*, September 19, 1840.

52. "Thomas Hodgkin and Colonization."

53. By the middle of 1832 a grave rift had emerged between the colony's board of managers, led by Austin Steward and Israel Lewis, who was accused of embezzling the funds he collected during his fund-raising agency.

54. Taylor, *Frontiers of Freedom*, 78–79.

55. Laidlaw, "Heathens, Slaves and Aborigines," 153.

56. Blackett, "Anglo-American Opposition," 292.

57. Kass and Kass, *Perfecting the World*, 238.

58. See Asaka, *Tropical Freedom*.

10. ENTANGLED IN EMPIRES: BRITISH ANTILLEAN MIGRATIONS IN THE WORLD OF THE PANAMA CANAL

Julie Greene

British Antilleans of African descent migrated by the tens of thousands from their home islands during the early twentieth century for jobs on the Panama Canal construction project as dynamiters, diggers, blacksmith helpers, laundresses, railroad workers, and similar occupations. Their travels took them from the world of sugar plantations to a highly regimented and industrialized construction project, and from the British Empire to territory controlled by the United States. In this way Afro-Caribbeans became entangled in new landscapes of empire as well as work discipline regimes. As they traveled, these mobile imperial subjects drew upon resources developed in British colonies such as Jamaica, Barbados, and Antigua to navigate work and life under U.S. rule in Panama; they also developed new strategies that leveraged their unique position of circulating within two empires.

Focusing on cosmopolitan migrants as they journeyed across the Americas provides an opportunity to explore the transimperial realm from the bottom up. In reading between the lines of scant primary sources to determine how these migrants felt about the empires with which they contended or how lessons learned in one shaped approaches to another, we should keep in mind that they were moving not just from one empire to another but also across distinctive social and economic landscapes and work regimes created by those empires. Imperial politics did not always figure largely in the consciousness of these workers, but a sense of British subjecthood profoundly affected strategies of resistance to U.S. rule. And adaptations to work on British colonial sugar plantations likewise shaped strategies in the more bureaucratic industrial regime of the Panama Canal Zone.

To explore such dynamics, this essay draws on testimonies written for a 1963 competition. The Isthmian Historical Society solicited submissions for the "best true story of life and work" during the construction of the Panama Canal. The competition was open only to non-U.S. employees, and it particularly encouraged submissions from British Caribbean men. The Society received 113 entries. All but two were from men, and nearly all were written by West Indians. They ranged greatly in length and level of detail: some were mere fragments, a few sentences long, while others were five or six pages in length. The entries evoked powerful, harrowing portraits of deadly disease, fatal or crippling accidents, and systemic racism. They constitute the best first-person accounts by Afro-Caribbean canal workers during the early twentieth century.[1]

Most of the testimonies say little or nothing about the islands from whence canal workers came. In several cases we are not even able to determine their origin. Most often, like the canal workforce more generally, they hailed from Barbados or Jamaica. Others traveled from Antigua, Martinique, St. Vincent, Grenada, St. Lucia, Dominica, Trinidad, Honduras, Nicaragua, Colombia, and the Republic of Panama. They told stories of leaving their homes in Barbados and Jamaica, of working hard as diggers, dynamiters, or blacksmith helpers. They spoke of premature dynamite explosions, avalanches, and train accidents. The men writing these testimonies were now older, some nearing death or coping with deafness or loss of sight. Even as they looked back with pride and astonishment at the work they had done forty-odd years earlier, they also recalled dramatic accidents and hardships. To broaden our understanding of these workers' lives, I connect their testimonies to personnel records of canal employees held at the St. Louis National Personnel Records Center. These make it possible to trace shifting occupations over the years, workers' problems with the U.S. government, and, as the decades wore on, their struggles with disability, old age, and death. Together with Colonial Office Records from the National Archives of the United Kingdom and records from the Jamaican National Archives, these sources provide insight into the life strategies of ordinary workers as they tangled with the British and American empires.

Empire and the Land Left Behind

Albert Peters, a young carpenter from the city of Nassau in the Bahamas, sat reading the paper one day: "I saw where they were digging a canal from ocean to ocean on the Isthmus of Panama and needed thousands of men." It was the summer of 1906. Peters was twenty-one years old. He talked over the news with two friends. "We were all eager for some adventure and experience." His parents opposed the idea, warning that he would confront yellow fever and malaria, "but I told them I and my pals are just going to see for ourselves."[2]

Albert Peters's words provide a rare glimpse into the thinking of a young man who made the journey to Panama. Although he mentions the allure of adventure, structural considerations also prompted labor mobility. Across the British Caribbean colonies, a small white planter-merchant class controlled virtually all access to power, and Afro-Caribbeans worked long, hard days of agricultural labor with wages so low that starvation often proved a very real danger. Most workers' connection to the British Empire came indirectly, via their labor within the dominant plantation economy. Most islands historically focused on sugar production, and most also confronted economic crisis in the late nineteenth century as a result of competition from sugar beet producers in Europe and changing British tariff policies. Exports fell, causing even more economic distress for working men and women. As estates went bankrupt, some islands abandoned export-oriented sugar production; diversification often became the key to economic survival. Comparing conditions in Jamaica and Barbados, the two main sources of migrant labor to Panama, reveals different responses to the crisis of the late nineteenth century, as well as the ways these responses shaped migration patterns.

The Morant Bay Rebellion of 1865 demonstrated ex-slaves' determination to fight for true equality in Jamaica, but the colonial government brutally crushed that uprising. In the decades that followed, a slowly increasing number of peasants came to own a bit of land and, typically, combined that with work on someone's estate to bring cash into their household. Afro-Jamaicans' landholdings were small and the quality of their land often inferior. Needing some cash for taxes and duties, farmers could not survive solely on subsistence agriculture. Some peasants, unable to own the land they worked, managed to squat on Crown land or lease a bit of acreage. A few achieved a degree of financial prosperity, enough that we might consider them part of the black middle class, but the vast majority lived lives of insecurity. When they needed more cash than they could earn, they faced an exploitative credit system organized by shopkeepers. Those who had to lease land faced the uncertainly of not knowing from one year to another whether their contracts would be continued. The sugar crisis of the late nineteenth century made life even more precarious: work on estates became more sporadic, and the full-time agricultural laborers who purchased small farmers' produce lost purchasing power as their wages were slashed. Increased banana and logwood production, as the economy diversified, reduced small-scale farmers' access to land.[3]

Compared to other Caribbean islands, Jamaica had a relatively robust black middle class. In addition to relatively prosperous small farmers, professionals (teachers and constables, for example), and shopkeepers, there was a significant class of artisans: blacksmiths, carpenters, masons, bricklayers, painters, tailors, hatters, and shoemakers. Jamaica's black middle class lost income during the late nineteenth century due to Jamaica's broader economic crisis as well as increased competition from cheap imported goods. Yet the vast majority of black Jamaicans who worked as landless agricultural laborers fared worse, since they possessed no financial cushion in times of need.[4] The urban trades became more attractive to those who could secure a foothold, because the decline of sugar and the rise of banana production decreased the need for agricultural labor. Gradually urban populations expanded and with them the number of artisans, professionals, and small shopkeepers. The number of higglers (petty traders) also increased, providing a source of income for urban women in particular.[5]

In all these ways, conditions in Jamaica differed from those in Barbados, the other island that sent the most laborers to Panama. If anything, the plantation system in Barbados proved crueler. Black Barbadians were more completely entrapped in landless agricultural labor. The plantation elite in Barbados strenuously resisted selling any land to laborers, preferring to maintain an agricultural proletariat with few options. There were no Crown lands upon which laborers might squat, as in Jamaica. Indeed, according to the historian Hilary Beckles, the government and planters collaborated in overappraising the value of land in order to keep it out of the hands of black Barbadians. The typical Barbadian thus rented a small chattel house and a quarter acre of land for growing some food but relied primarily upon cash wages earned by laboring on a neighboring sugar estate. Only a precious few people escaped their fate as landless laborers, which not only constrained the amount of surplus income available to the black population as a whole but also suppressed the development of a robust professional or artisanal class. Similar conditions characterized Antigua and St. Kitts, where, as in Barbados, sugar production dominated the economy into the twentieth century and employed most of the black population.[6]

The sugar crisis hit Barbados as it did Jamaica, but with a different consequence. Estates that were put on the market were typically purchased by resident merchants, leading to the creation of a new merchant-planter elite, and rather than diversify, as in Jamaica, Barbadian planters further impoverished their laborers to make ends meet. Poverty had long been a favored form of discipline, with planters believing that laborers would become idle as soon as they had enough food to eat. But when economic crisis hit in the late nineteenth century and lasted well into the twentieth, planters cut wages by some 20 percent, thereby pushing the workers below starvation level. Mortality rates and malnutrition rose, and when disease hit (such as typhoid and dysentery after the 1898 hurricane), the laboring classes suffered mightily. Reports circulated of starvation across the countryside, and food scavenging became common. With the high population density on the island (highest in the West Indies) and no available land on which to take refuge, laborers had few options. Sporadic outbreaks of protest occurred. Workers engaged repeatedly in potato raids during the 1880s and 1890s, cane fires occurred daily, and broader riots and social unrest became endemic.[7]

If Barbados and Jamaica thus represented two divergent histories of economic transformation resulting from the sugar crisis, the other islands that supplied workers for the Panama Canal fell somewhere between the two. Most, like Jamaica, experienced a strengthening of the peasant class. But as economic crisis hit the British Caribbean, life became more challenging for black workers, adding to the appeal of migration as a means of escape. From the days of enslavement onward, internal migration and emigration had been key strategies for islanders locked into poverty and backbreaking labor, and colonial governments had encouraged this to varying degrees.[8] Since emancipation, some Barbadians had migrated from rural to urban areas of the island, particularly during times of economic crisis, and they emigrated to British Guiana and Trinidad as well to seek the higher wages offered there. Jamaicans likewise emigrated in small numbers throughout the nineteenth century, with 1,500 to 2,000 traveling to the Isthmus of Panama to help build the first transcontinental railroad in the 1850s. In the 1880s Jamaicans provided the French with a major source of labor during their doomed effort to build a canal across Panama, and a smaller number of Jamaicans traveled to Costa Rica for railroad construction jobs. In 1888, when the French canal project failed, thousands of Jamaicans stranded on the isthmus relied upon the Jamaican government for repatriation, at great expense to the latter.[9] The massive emigration also caused acute labor shortages for Jamaican planters. Consequently the Jamaican government passed laws to prevent further exoduses on this scale. Most significantly Law 23, passed in 1902, allowed the government to require that an exit permit be purchased for 25 shillings.[10]

Thus when the United States in 1903 began planning its own canal construction project—and locating a source of labor loomed large—it immediately had to contend with the priorities of the British Empire. U.S. officials found negotiating difficult with many of the British colonial governments. Although U.S. officials promised the Jamaican government that its men would be treated well—

even offering to hire Jamaicans as foremen so they would not have to work under Americans—colonial officials refused to allow a recruiting station on the island and adhered to its law requiring an exit permit. Other islands, including St. Kitts, Antigua, Montserrat, and Grenada, likewise refused to allow recruiting agents in their domains. R. E. Wood, the recruiting agent for the U.S. government, observed to his dismay that recruiters were forced to "wander from island to island, picking up men here and there, like discredited fugitives."[11]

These circumstances made Barbados an especially important source for labor. Its colonial government was agreeable to labor recruitment, and the island had a surplus of English-speaking laborers whom U.S. recruiters considered polite, obedient, and orderly. As early as 1893 the Barbadian colonial government had begun to consider sponsored emigration schemes as a safety valve that could help their impoverished laborers. After U.S. officials presented a sample labor contract, Barbadian government officials agreed to allow a recruiting station on the island. Established in 1905, within a year or two the office was sending several ships a week to Panama. Laborers made a mass exodus from the estates, creating a remarkable sight as they marched across the island to Bridgetown. People began to speak of a fever for traveling to Panama. To many, if not all, of the men who signed contracts for Panama, the attraction was certainly a desire to throw off the yoke of impoverishment, exploitation, and backbreaking work on plantations. Planters expressed dismay at the large number of laborers heading to the recruiting office. Police struggled to maintain order as thousands showed up at a time. One man heading with other laborers to Bridgetown had shouted to a gang of sugar workers, "Why you don't hit de manager in de head, and come along wid we!"[12]

As word of the job opportunities spread across the Caribbean, workers traveled to Bridgetown from other islands in hopes of securing a contract and passage to Panama. Gradually many Barbadians who could not win a contract, including women and children, began looking for money to pay their own way to Panama. Such strategies make it difficult to determine with precision how many workers from Barbados ultimately traveled to work on the canal. Bonham Richardson estimates that twenty thousand (male) contract laborers traveled from Barbados to Panama, and as many as forty thousand more men and women traveled without a labor contract, a remarkable number considering that Barbados's population at the time was only some 180,000 people. The Panama movement constituted the largest emigration in Barbadian history. Those who stayed in Barbados used the new labor scarcity to bargain for higher wages, but planters resisted this by hiring women to do work previously assigned to men. As Richardson has demonstrated, Barbadians in Panama sent home remittances (nearly 546,000 pounds) and returned home with money that allowed a significant number of people to purchase land. In these ways, "Panama fever" exerted a seismic impact on the Barbadian society.[13]

Transimperial labor recruiting proved more difficult in the case of Jamaica. The Jamaican government would not allow its citizens to become contract laborers for the canal unless the United States agreed to pay insurance for each individual. Chief Engineer John Wallace refused, worried that paying an insurance fee would constitute labor trafficking. Unable to reach agreement, the Jamaican government held to its 25 shilling requirement for emigrants. Despite these obstacles, Jamaicans headed to Panama in large numbers, as many as eighty thousand making their way there. The Jamaican author Herbert G. de Lisser alluded to challenges faced by the migrants who traveled alongside him to Panama in 1910: "For weeks and months before they left their homes they had been thinking of this voyage and preparing for it. They had saved a little money, but most likely had found it was not enough; so the household gods were sacrificed, the chairs and tables, perhaps even the bed, had to be sold before the necessary sum could be made up to pay for the passage and to lodge in the Treasury the 25s. demanded by the Government for repatriation purposes." The financial requirement ensured that those who departed Jamaica possessed somewhat more access to money than did men and women from other islands. Consequently the profile of the typical Jamaican who headed to Panama was quite distinctive: few were landless laborers; most were artisans, small shopkeepers, and peasants who owned some land. As a result, when Jamaicans arrived in Panama, they were more likely to acquire jobs as craftsmen, foremen, teachers, or policemen. The many who returned to Jamaica after construction ended often displayed their wealth conspicuously. Jamaicans writing up their memories decades later recalled how the men returning from Panama often flashed gold teeth as well as a gold watch and chain.[14]

By the end of the canal construction era, some 150,000 to 200,000 people had traveled to the Canal Zone from the islands of the Caribbean. Many traveled on their own from across the Caribbean; others made the trip to Bridgetown and signed a labor contract with the U.S. government. However they journeyed, they sold belongings and packed bags for an uncomfortable journey across the sea to Panama. Harrigan Austin was among the first to depart for Panama, leaving Bridgetown in October 1905 for a "hazardous trip, of thirteen days of bad weather, bad accommodation in general with sparing meals on a Crowded Ship, we were all more or less hungry." Mary Couloote left her home in Castries, St. Lucia, traveling on the ship *La Plata* along with a sister. They stopped in Jamaica and then headed across the Gulf of Mexico. When a heavy storm hit, crew members ordered everyone downstairs. Sailors working up top had chains around their waist. "When we reach colon," she said, they called everyone's name but "5 men where [sic] missing." Undoubtedly relieved to be in Panama, Couloote headed to Pedro Miguel to join her mother and brother.[15]

The migrants climbing aboard ships to Panama were typically quite young men and women, in their late teens and early twenties. They had grown up in a culture where emigration was an important life strategy; most had known relatives or family friends who left their home islands for work across the Caribbean and Central America, if not farther afield. A sense of cosmopolitanism was in the air they breathed. And they undoubtedly found some pleasure in fleeing the hard lives ahead of them, mired in colonial exploitation, racism, and impoverishment as landless laborers in Barbados or St. Lucia or as peasants struggling to make ends meet in Jamaica.

John Altyman Richards explained the appeal of Panama in his competition entry: "Many years ago while still yet a young man in Jamaica I was intrigued by the Canal Construction done in this beautiful tropical country. I discussed the possibilities of working in a different country and of learning a strange language with my relatives; as soon as permission was granted I partook for Panama in 1914." Like other migrants across time and place, Richards had surveyed his current life and determined that Panama beckoned as an improvement. There were good Yankee jobs building the canal. Migrants could make enough money to open a business or buy some land upon their return. As de Lisser wrote, "The West Indian peasant dreams of Panama as the country where fortune awaits him, and where a few months of effort will bring a golden reward."[16] The same held true for those who traveled to Panama not for canal jobs but to create their own businesses; thus E. W. Martineau, for example, left his home in Grenada, equipped with aerated water equipment, to set up shop as a soda factory.[17]

Hopes for economic opportunity certainly pushed migrants like these to the Canal Zone as they sought to escape the extreme poverty on their home islands. Yet in addition Afro-Caribbeans had ample reason to feel let down by the British Crown. The racist and undemocratic structures of colonialism, the oppression exerted by the planter elite, and the devastation caused by economic crisis all suggested their denial of rights as British subjects. Furthermore, on these islands the enslavement of men and women was not too distant a memory. One Jamaican recalled his days as a young boy in the 1870s, when many formerly enslaved men were still alive. Every August 1 the town of Negril would gather at the Presbyterian Chapel to sing hymns and hear a sermon about life under slavery. Then some of the freedmen would climb up on the stage to tell stories of their lives. Afterward everyone would adjourn outside for a feast, drinks, and dancing to celebrate emancipation.[18]

In this environment, with enslavement a close memory and landlessness offering little beyond toil and impoverishment, the planter elite strenuously promoted a cult of the British Empire and the monarchy as a glue that might hold society together. As Brian Moore and Michele Johnson have explained, the lower classes were "encouraged to remember they were part of a mighty whole, at the centre of which was a power so distant yet so omnipotent and worthy that only displays of adoration were deemed appropriate."[19] Planters celebrated love and loyalty to the mother country and the queen as central to respectability and civilization. Although one should not exaggerate the degree to which imperial and monarchic fervor pervaded the lower classes of the islands, it is clear that Afro-Caribbeans shared in the pride of British culture, education, and language. Furthermore, they had their own reasons for royalist Anglophilia: historians have observed that Afro-Caribbeans linked the emancipation of slaves to Queen Victoria. Great sadness pervaded the islands when she died in 1901. Upon her death Victoria Day was changed to Empire Day, and efforts to inculcate in children a pride in British imperialism and a strong connection to the mother country grew even more robust.[20]

The ships steaming toward the Isthmus of Panama, then, brought young emigrants carrying wide-ranging ideas and loyalties in addition to their bags and deck chairs. As they entered the Canal Zone, with its harsh industrial discipline, Caribbeans' loyalties to monarch and empire would become entangled with new strategies they developed to resist exploitation at the hands of American officials.

Confronting the Industrial Empire of the United States

The United States created a regimented, disciplined, authoritarian, impersonal, and industrialized operation in the Panama Canal Zone. Government officials, engineers, surveyors, and medical personnel hustled to begin work as soon as the ink had dried on the Hay-Bunau-Varilla Treaty that gave the United States permanent and complete control over the vast swath of land, the Panama Canal Zone, that cut through the heart of the young Republic of Panama. In the early years of 1904 and 1905, red tape and mosquito-borne diseases befuddled U.S. officials, but by 1906 a vast industrial society had blossomed across the Zone. The United States developed the ability to carry more than thirty thousand people to and from the worksite each day by train and carry away the spoils of digging; it built showcase towns for the thousands of white American employees and family members, complete with essential trappings of home, and much more rustic housing for Afro-Caribbeans and Europeans; it constructed police headquarters, prisons, hospitals, health clinics, and vast machine shops that serviced steam shovels and other equipment. The harshness Caribbean migrants confronted in the Canal Zone undoubtedly made them look anew at the British emphasis on royalism and imperial belonging on their home islands.

In the eyes of U.S. officials, the tens of thousands of men from Barbados, Jamaica, Grenada, St. Lucia, and other islands were essential tools of the production process to be managed and disciplined as efficiently as possible. They had settled upon Caribbeans as their major source of labor for many reasons, chief among them the perception that Antilleans were "harmless and law-abiding," childlike, and easily controlled. That Jamaican laborers had worked well, overall, during the 1880s French construction effort, and that they spoke English, was an added benefit.[21]

Yet these essential tools of production were young, exhausted men who found conditions in the new industrial empire extremely difficult. Harrigan Austin described a difficult trip from his home island of Barbados: thirteen days on rough seas, a crowded ship, and very little food. He was only eighteen years old. He and the others arrived hungry, and as they disembarked they saw piles of brown sugar: "And the whole crowd of us like ants fed ourselves on that sugar without questioning any one, and no one said any thing to us either." The officials sent Austin to a tent camp and assigned him a cot. He arrived with experience as a carpenter and his own tools, so he landed a good job repairing quarters. Nonetheless he found the work to be harrowing. West Indians worked often in the rain. If it rained so hard that they had to stop, their pay was cut. The food was so bad they could barely eat it. They bathed and washed their clothes in the same river used by horses and cattle. They succumbed to malaria, and when they took quinine to fight disease, some went deaf from its effects. Too many men Austin knew died from disease, railroad accidents, or premature dynamite explosions, and the doctors and nurses lacked the training to restore good health to so many sufferers—especially in the early years. Occasionally men tried to heal themselves when sick, going into the bush to try a homemade remedy, but if caught they "would be brutalized and some time carried to jail." Remembered Austin, "Life was some sort of semi slavery, and there was none to appeal to, for we were strangers and actually compelled to accept what we got . . . and the bosses or policemen or other officials right or wrong could be always winning the game."[22]

In some ways their situation—the feeling of "semi slavery," as Austin put it—must have felt familiar to Caribbeans accustomed to British colonialism and the stranglehold over the economy by the planter elite. In both old and new worlds, white men ruled over them like slave drivers. Eric Walrond, the Trinidadian author who wrote so eloquently of Panama, portrayed a West Indian mother in the Canal Zone scolding her aimless son in his short story "Panama Gold": You must work, she declared, because otherwise where will I get any food? She admonished him to accept the authority of his foreman, using the Jamaican patois term for a white man in authority and rooted originally in slave relations: "Boy yo' bes' mek up yo' min' an' get under de heel o' de backra."[23] As in Barbados and Jamaica, workers found that organized mass protests were difficult or impossible to achieve. The new stranglehold they faced stemmed from the infinite authority of U.S. officials, who could deport or imprison anyone deemed troublesome or unproductive. Officials also maintained a vast surplus of Caribbean workers and made a point of bringing workers from diverse islands and from Spain, Italy, and Greece in order to manage and control them more easily. Together these conditions forced workers either to accommodate themselves to the harsh regime or develop hidden forms of resistance.

Officials' reliance on a vast surplus provides one indication that Afro-Caribbeans asserted themselves when they could. In the earliest, most chaotic and disease-ridden days of construction, the first and final act of rebellion for some workers involved a lesson learned back on their home islands, when slaves fled into the hills or plantation workers feigned illness to avoid work: many simply jumped back onto a ship and fled for home. In later years the typical work pace was so intense that workers routinely stayed away from the job, particularly on rainy days or when they had earned enough money to get by for a while. Some workers went beyond taking a break for a day or two to slip away to their home island for a visit. The engineer D. D. Gaillard, who oversaw the work on Culebra Cut, noted that he had to keep a workforce of fourteen thousand men in order to ensure that at least ten thousand would show up on any given day.[24]

Workers also resisted by eluding the control and surveillance of U.S. authorities, and again they surely drew upon strategies developed after emancipation to elude colonial control. Dissatisfaction with the quality and price of food in government cafeterias generated a mass exodus out of government housing. Rent outside the U.S.-controlled Zone, in Panama City or Colon, was terribly high, yet most Antillean workers preferred either moving to those cities or making a home for themselves in the Panamanian bush. And although officials quickly responded by ending the requirement that employees purchase meal tickets, the number of residents in government housing never rebounded. Living on their own meant they could cook for themselves, and it also meant freedom from much of the government's surveillance and harsh discipline, including roundups and possible imprisonment for skipping a day of work.[25]

U.S. officials tended to see Caribbean workers as a homogeneous group, but in fact they followed very different paths in Panama. Because Jamaicans had to pay an emigration tax to go to Panama, and because a larger independent peasantry and black middle class existed on that island, those in the Canal Zone were often more skilled, more likely to possess some resources, and more likely to receive plum jobs as teachers, policemen, foremen, or skilled workers. As a result, Jamaicans were often feared or distrusted by other Antilleans. Other Caribbean workers saw them as most likely to support and enforce the U.S. government's authoritarian regime. Over time the occupational landscape of the Antillean community in the Canal Zone grew more complex as U.S. officials, seeking to save money, began training Caribbeans to do skilled work that had previously been carried out by white U.S. workers. Although still generally referred to as "helpers," kept on the lower-status silver payroll rather than the gold roll (which was reserved for white U.S. workers), and paid far less than white men, these skilled Caribbean workers received training and became carpenters, machinists, plumbers, railroad conductors, firemen, brakemen, and switchmen. Widening job opportunities improved life for many silver employees: their pay increased, their work became easier than that of diggers and dynamiters, and their greater access to resources afforded them more freedom from U.S. government surveillance.[26]

As workers adjusted to the Americans' regime on the Isthmus of Panama, as they confronted racism, harsh discipline, extremely difficult and dangerous working conditions, widespread disease, poor food, and uncomfortable or exploitative housing, they found they had little recourse. It was dangerous at worst and often futile at best to complain to a supervisor or foreman. Silver employees had no union to represent them. George Washington Goethals, chief engineer of the construction project from 1907 to 1914, opened his office every Sunday morning to any resident or employee who had a grievance and hired one full-time inspector to investigate problems and suggest potential remedies. The records of that inspector demonstrate that complaints were indeed investigated, but they also show that most grievances were filed by white U.S. men and women, not silver roll workers. Considering the demographics of the Zone, and that the number of Afro-Caribbeans far overwhelmed the number of white U.S. citizens (somewhere above thirty thousand for the former vs. fewer than five thousand for the latter), Goethals's grievance system could hardly have been sufficient.[27]

The other recourse for Caribbeans, and one that made a greater impact on their daily lives, kept them entangled in the British Empire even as they toiled for the Americans. Although the United States dominated the Zone, diplomatic representatives from the British Empire watched over and reported on the conditions facing tens of thousands of subjects. The colonial governments of each Caribbean island—from Martinique and Haiti to Barbados, St. Lucia, Grenada, and Jamaica—played a role as well. But the most intense observation and most powerful interventions were provided by the British Consul's Office. Claude Mallet, the man in charge, had a full-time job representing the subjects of his queen.

Mallet had lived in Panama since 1879, when his father began serving as British consul. He served on the consulate staff for the next forty years, becoming consul himself in 1903 and minister to Panama and Costa Rica in 1914. Some Antilleans wrote directly to London for help, or to inform the diplomatic corps of an injustice, but most relied on Consul Mallet. They informed him of problems ranging from poor food to unsatisfactory housing, mean or racist foremen, bad job assignments, undeserved incarceration, and bad treatment by Panamanian police.[28]

Mallet often found Caribbeans' grievances annoying. That he regarded West Indians as harshly as any white American can be seen in his response to riots on a United Fruit Company (UFCO) plantation in Limon, Costa Rica, in 1910. Migrants from St. Kitts demanded to be repatriated after many of their group had fallen ill and some had died, while UFCO did little or nothing to help. Mallet deemed their protest "preposterous." He bragged that he had handled many strikes during the French and now the American phases of construction: "What I have always done has been to get the employer to do what is just towards the men and then tell them in unmistakable language to work, and if they do not work they will starve, and that if they disturb public order the government counts upon enough force to keep the peace, and their acts be upon their own heads if they suffer in consequence of defying armed forces."[29]

Mallet himself was a transimperial actor, of course, a representative of emerging Anglo-American cooperation and collaboration in the Caribbean and beyond during the early twentieth century. And unfortunately for laborers, he saw the Americans as a vast improvement on the French construction project and felt little sympathy for British colonial subjects. In 1906 Mallet wrote to the governor of the Canal Zone, "The conditions of the labouring man in the Canal Zone, as regards his treatment, are better to-day than they have ever been within my recollection." That same year, when President Theodore Roosevelt visited the isthmus and inquired of Mallet how the West Indians were doing, the British consul admitted he had not personally inspected the housing or food provided to laborers: "[But] since the negro is quick to bring a grievance to the attention of the Consul . . . [and] at the present time, they were so few and trivial I generally found upon investigation that they had no foundation and therefore was convinced the labourers must be well treated and well cared for by the Commission."[30]

Conditions undoubtedly were better than they had been during the French construction era, but that they were nonetheless problematic is also beyond debate. J. Keir Hardie, a British Socialist member of Parliament, wrote the Colonial Office after hearing complaints about treatment of West Indians: "Surprise is expressed among American officials at the non-interference of the British government." Hardie had no doubt that conditions would improve if the British intervened. British Colonial Office officials required Mallet to report on the matter. Privately they noted they had been right not to promote Mallet to a higher position, suggesting that they, like Hardie, saw him as too sympathetic to U.S. officials' way of handling laborers.[31]

When laborers pushed Consul Mallet to provide help, they often emphasized their rights as subjects of the Crown. One man wrote Mallet to ask him to help a friend who had been unjustly imprisoned in Panama. "Sir I am not his Counsil But I am an English subject also I has a great knowledge of this Law I know what you can do from what you cant Therefor I ask you to take a Part of that young man life as I do remember the Laws of England." When Mallet refused to help, many laborers pleaded to their diplomatic representatives in England. One man wrote for help after an accident required amputation of his leg and he had received neither compensation nor even a wooden leg from the U.S government: "I know that my Mother Court will not forsake these few lines."[32]

In the end, the problem lay not just with Mallet: British officials generally seem to have shared his willingness to see racism in the Canal Zone as inevitable and, perhaps, justified. In 1910 Caribbeans in the Zone reacted with horror when a white U.S. citizen killed a West Indian and then was acquitted despite strong evidence against him. The American, Louis Dennison, shot his victim in the heart with no provocation. Mallet noted that West Indians were very upset and believed that the case showed "that a white American can kill a negro with impunity in the Canal Zone." Mallet confessed, "There is certainly good grounds for that belief, and I agree . . . that it is unlikely a jury composed of Canal employees will ever convict a white American and a fellow employee for the murder of a negro." Dennison had even confessed to the crime, saying, "I have only killed a nigger, don't be too hard on me boys." A. Mitchell Innes, a British official based in Washington, DC, reflected on the incident: "All those who are accustomed to dealing with the evidence of coloured people know how hard it is to obtain from them a consistent, truthful, unvarnished tale, and unless the witnesses have concocted a story beforehand, irreconcilable discrepancies arise which are fatal to the case of the prosecution." A handwritten note added to this one, by someone in the London office of Foreign Secretary Edward Grey, stressed that Dennison was undoubtedly guilty, yet since the writer believed West Indians could not be trusted he saw no way to remedy the situation.[33]

Many observed that Afro-Caribbeans, when in a pinch, stressed their rights as subjects of the British Empire. William J. Karner, who served briefly as acting chief engineer in the early days of construction, commented on his dislike of the Jamaican laborers: "They are sort of an I.D.W.W. class (I don't want to work unless driven to it). As British subjects, they think they are close to royalty and quite superior to white laborers from the U.S." When ordered too curtly by a foreman to do something, he related, "the laborer would straighten himself up and say, 'I wish you to understand, sir, that I am a British subject, and if we cannot arrange this matter amicably we will talk to our Consul about it.'" Labor supervisors like Karner undoubtedly found it difficult, amid their assumptions of racial and national superiority over Caribbean laborers, that they had to contend with self-assertion, a fluency with the English language, and even perhaps the backing of the British Empire when seeking to order their workers about.[34]

In the end, it is difficult to judge how dearly Caribbeans held the British Crown in their hearts and minds. The writer Eric Walrond wrote in the 1930s that West Indians possessed too much admiration for the English, suggesting that he at least observed a true affection and pride in their British citizenship. But at the very least it is clear that Caribbean workers leveraged their position as British subjects against the Americans when it served their purpose. In his short story "Panama Gold," Walrond explores this theme through a character who returns to Barbados after having lost a leg working on the Canal. The man, Mr. Poyer, brags that his status as a British subject forced the canal authorities to pay him damages. Poyer threatened action if he were not paid: "I'll sick de British bulldog on all yo' Omericans!" He added, "I let dem understand quick enough dat I wuz a Englishman and not a bleddy American nigger! A' Englishman . . . And dat dey couldn't do as dey bleddy well please wit' a subject o' de King!"[35]

Reena Goldthree's research on the British West Indies Regiment during World War I also supports the notion that British citizenship became particularly important to the migrants working on the Panama Canal. Caribbean migrants on the isthmus—or their children—were some of the first and most enthusiastic to sign up for military service, and ultimately more than 2,000 of the regiment's 15,600 soldiers came from Panama. It seems likely that the intensity of West Indians' patriotism resulted from their experiences under U.S.

imperial rule. In that context, stressing their loyalty to a rival empire proved useful—so useful that a Flag Day fund-raiser in 1915 saw crowds of "loyal Britishers" parading down the streets of Bocas del Toro, Panama. Women and girls sold Union Jack pins and raised hundreds of dollars in Panamanian silver for the British war cause.[36]

West Indian migrants remained entangled with both the American and British empires throughout their time in the Canal Zone, and often beyond it as well. Upon completion of the canal construction project, when many towns of the Zone were shut down, with forced relocations so the flooding of Gatun Lake could take place, most employees were let go. Years of chaos and uncertainty followed, as tens of thousands of workers had to find new jobs in Panama or, in many cases, return to their home islands or settle into new lives in other parts of Central or South America, the Caribbean, or the United States.[37] This complex transition required careful collaboration between American and British officials, who worked alongside UFCO representatives and colonial governments on the home islands to find the best places to send laid-off employees. The transimperial negotiations that characterized the entire construction project continued long after the grand opening of the canal.

Conclusion

Caribbean laborers in the Panama Canal Zone lived difficult and dangerous lives and had few resources to fall back on for help. The racism and discrimination they experienced in the Canal Zone must have seemed reminiscent in many ways of dynamics they had known in Jamaica, Barbados, and other islands. Some felt they had replaced one "backra" with another, and they responded to their American foremen as they had to overseers on the plantation at home: they struggled to improve their lives by their own accord. Shifting back and forth between the British and American empires, Afro-Caribbeans developed strategies where they could, moving out of government housing, refusing government food, changing jobs, or taking time off. Yet moving across imperial boundaries opened up a new strategy for resistance: playing one empire against another. This began, to a degree, with the decision to leave for Panama, a choice that played out against episodic loyalty to the British Empire. Once they joined the massive, regimented workforce of the Canal Zone, however, Caribbean workers' identities as British subjects took on much greater significance. From their vantage point in Panama, Caribbean workers found ways to deploy the British Empire, and their status as its subjects, as a resource—which in turn fueled their resistance. They found tactics developed in coping with one empire helped them create limited space for independence in another. Along the way Caribbeans' work for the United States fostered their claims on and attachment to the British Empire.

NOTES

1. "Isthmian Historical Society Competition for the Best True Stories of Life and Work on the Isthmus of Panama during the Construction of the Panama Canal," Panama Collection of the Canal Zone Library-Museum, Box 25, Folders 3–4, Manuscript Division, Library of Congress, Washington, DC. The testimonies are also available online at the University of Florida George A. Smathers Libraries, http://ufdc.ufl.edu/AA00016037 /00001. The author heartily thanks Jay Sexton and Kristin Hoganson for their excellent editing, and James Maffie and Diana Paton for their advice on the manuscript.

2. Albert Peters, "Isthmian Historical Society Competition," http://ufdc.ufl.edu /AA00016037/00001, accessed September 2, 2017.

3. On the aftermath of Morant Bay, see Brian L. Moore and Michele A. Johnson, *Neither Led nor Driven: Contesting British Cultural Imperialism in Jamaica, 1865–1920* (Mona, Jamaica: University of West Indies Press, 2004). On class structure and landholding, see Patrick Bryan, *The Jamaican People, 1880–1902: Race, Class, and Social Control* (Mona, Jamaica: University of West Indies Press, 2012), 8–9, 132–33.

4. Bryan, *The Jamaican People*, 218–27.

5. David C. Wong, "A Theory of Petty Trading: The Jamaican Higgler," *Economic Journal* 106 (March 1996): 507–18; Bryan, *The Jamaican People*, 133.

6. Bonham Richardson, *Panama Money in Barbados, 1900–1920* (Knoxville: University of Tennessee Press, 2004), 53–57. On similar conditions in Antigua and St. Kitts, see Robert Cassá, "The Economic Development of the Caribbean from 1880 to 1930," in *General History of the Caribbean*, vol. 5: *The Caribbean in the Twentieth Century*, edited by Bridget Brereton (New York: UNESCO and Macmillan, 2004), 7–41, 10–11.

7. Henderson Carter, *Labour Pains: Resistance and Protest in Barbados, 1838–1904* (Kingston, Jamaica: Ian Randle, 2012); Hilary Beckles, *Great House Rules: Landless Emancipation and Workers' Protest in Barbados, 1838–1938* (Kingston, Jamaica: Ian Randle, 2004); Aviston D. Downes, "Barbados, 1880–1914: A Socio-Cultural History," PhD diss., York University, 2004, 41–48; Bonham C. Richardson, "Depression Riots and the Calling of the 1897 West India Royal Commission." *New West Indian Guide* 66, nos. 3–4 (1992): 169–91.

8. For an overview of Caribbean migrations, see Bonham Richardson, "The Migration Experience," in Brereton, *General History of the Caribbean*, 5:434–64.

9. Gisela Eisner, *Jamaica, 1830–1930: A Study in Economic Growth* (Manchester, U.K.: Manchester University Press, 1961), 147–49.

10. Eisner, *Jamaica*, 150.

11. See Julie Greene, *The Canal Builders: Making America's Empire at the Panama Canal* (New York: Penguin Press, 2009), 51; R. E. Wood to John Stevens, October 22, 1906, Isthmian Canal Commission Records, 2-E-1, "Labor Recruiting." Record Group 185, U.S. National Archives and Records Administration, College Park, Maryland.

12. Quoted in Richardson, *Panama Money in Barbados*, 106; from *Debates LC*, July 16, 1907, 85–87.

13. The estimates for how many Barbadians headed to Panama come from Richardson, "The Migration Experience," 441. See also Downes, "Barbados," 54. For the full story of Panama money's impact on Barbados, see Richardson, *Panama Money in Barbados*. The amount of remittance money comes from Hilary Beckles, *History of Barbados: From Amerindian Settlement to Nation-State* (Cambridge, U.K.: Cambridge University Press, 1990), 145.

14. Notes of meetings held on December 6 and 12, 1904, Colonial Secretariat Records, 1B/5/76/3/152 Emigrants Protection Law, Jamaican National Archives, Kingston; Herbert G. de Lisser, *In Jamaica and Cuba* (Kingston, Jamaica: Gleaner, 1910), 154–55, http://ufdc.ufl.edu/UF00080939. The figure of eighty thousand Jamaicans migrating to Panama is from Richardson, "The Migration Experience," 441. On memories of returning Jamaicans displaying their wealth, see, for example, the entries of Rev. R. A. L. Knight, Kingston, and H. R. Milliner, Falmouth, in the Jamaican Memories Collection, Competition held by the Jamaican Gleaner, 1959, Jamaican National Archives, Kingston.

15. Testimonies by Harrigan Austin and Mary Couloote are in the Isthmian Historical Society Competition, http://ufdc.ufl.edu/AA00016037/00010. Information that Austin came from Barbados is in the Isthmian Canal Commission Silver Roll Personnel Records, National Personnel Records Center, St. Louis, Missouri. For the figure of 150,000 to 200,000 Caribbeans traveling to Panama, see Michael Conniff, *Black Labor on the White Canal: Panama, 1904–1981* (Pittsburgh, PA: University of Pittsburgh Press, 1985), 25–29.

16. De Lisser, *In Jamaica and Cuba*, 154.

17. Martineau submission to the Isthmian Historical Society Competition.

18. Daniel B. Tait, born 1874, Jamaican Memories Collection.

19. Moore and Johnson, *Neither Led nor Driven*, 281.

20. Moore and Johnson, *Neither Led nor Driven*, 293–97.

21. *Hearings before the Committee on Interstate and Foreign Commerce of the House of Representatives, on the Isthmian Canal* (Washington, DC: Government Printing Office, 1906), 1:53; John Stevens to Theodore Shonts, December 14, 1905, Isthmian Canal Commission Records, 2-E-1, U.S. National Archives and Records Administration, College Park, Maryland.

22. Information on Harrigan Austin's experiences comes from his submission to the Isthmian Historical Society Competition and from the Personnel Records (Silver Roll) of the Isthmian Canal Commission, National Personnel Records Center.

23. Eric Walrond quotation is from his story "Panama Gold" in *Tropic Death* (New York: Collier Books, 1954), 103. For a useful discussion of Walrond, see James Davis, *Eric Walrond: A Life in the Harlem Renaissance and the Transatlantic Caribbean* (New York: Columbia University Press, 2015), particularly chapter 5.

24. Greene, *The Canal Builders*, 146–47.

25. For more on this, see Greene, *The Canal Builders*, chapter 3.

26. The silver and gold payroll system became central to the U.S. effort to segregate and discipline its workforce. For more on this aspect of U.S. labor management, see Greene, *The Canal Builders*.

27. The work of T. B. Miskimon, Goethals's inspector, can be traced by examining his personal papers: to cite just one example, see T. B. Miskimon to Goethals, April 25, 1907, Folder 1, T. B. Miskimon Papers, MS 86–5, Special Collections, Ablah Library, Wichita State University, Wichita, Kansas.

28. Mallet's role can be traced by examining correspondence in the Foreign Office Records of the U.K. National Archives. For background information on Mallet, see Matthew Parker, *Panama Fever: The Epic Story of the Building of the Panama Canal* (New York: Anchor Books, 2007).

29. Claude Mallet to Consul Cox, December 8, 1910, Foreign Office 371/944, U.K. National Archives, London.

30. Mallet to Governor Magoon, January 17, 1906, Foreign Office 371/101, General Correspondence of the Foreign Office; Mallet to Sir, November 19, 1906, Foreign Office 288/98, both from U.K. National Archives, London. For more on Mallet's career (and a more positive interpretation of it), see Parker, *Panama Fever*.

31. J. Keir Hardie to Colonel Seely, Colonial Office, November 24, 1908, Foreign Office Records, 271/494; see also the handwritten note on Mallet's letter to Sir, November 19, 1906, Foreign Office 288/98, both from U.K. National Archives.

32. No author to Mallet, September 26, 1914, Foreign Office 288/160, Miscellaneous Consul Records, U.K. National Archives; Jacob Marsh to Foreign Secretary of State, United Kingdom, January 7, 1911, FO 371/1176, U.K. National Archives. For other examples of Caribbean workers appealing to their rights as British subjects, see Greene, *The Canal Builders*, e.g., 264.

33. Claude Mallet to Sir Edward Grey, May 6, 1910; H. O. Chalkley, Vice-Consul, to C. C. Mallet, May 3, 1910; and A. Innes to Grey, October 21, 1910; all FO 371/943, U.K. National Archives.

34. William J. Karner, *More Recollections* (Boston: T. Todd, 1921), 41.

35. Walrond, *Tropic Death*, 42; Davis, *Eric Walrond*, 163.

36. See Reena Goldthree, "'A Greater Enterprise than the Panama Canal': Migrant Labor and Military Recruitment in the World War I–Era Circum-Caribbean," in the special issue on empire, edited by Julie Greene and Leon Fink, *Labor: Studies in Working-Class History of the Americas*, 13 (3–4), December 2016, 57–82, especially 58–59.

37. On the number of workers employed during the construction decade, see Conniff, *Black Labor on the White Canal*. On the vast project to dismantle historic towns of Panama as construction of the canal wrapped up, see Marixa Lasso, *Erased: The Untold Story of the Panama Canal* (Cambridge, MA: Harvard University Press, 2019).

11. WORLD WAR II AND THE PROMISE OF NORMALCY: OVERLAPPING EMPIRES AND EVERYDAY LIVES IN THE PHILIPPINES

Genevieve Clutario

Filipinos found themselves firmly wedged between two imperial powers when World War II reached the Philippines in December 1941. Immediately after the bombing of Pearl Harbor, Japanese forces destroyed the U.S. Air Force Station at Clark Field. Under the command of General Douglas MacArthur, the United States Army Forces Far East, which combined the U.S. military with the Philippine Army, left Manila to combat Japanese soldiers in Bataan and Corregidor. In late December, Manileños experienced, not for the first time, a military invasion in the name of "liberation." Much as U.S. forces had once contended that they were fighting to liberate the Philippines from Spanish tyranny, Japanese occupiers promised to free Filipinos from an oppressive U.S. colonial regime. Just as in the Philippine-American War that began in 1899, violence again ravaged the archipelago, resulting in thousands of deaths, destruction of homes, and devastated land.[1] When U.S. forces returned to the Philippines in late 1944, civilians were once more caught in the crossfire, with an estimated 100,000 to 200,000 deaths.[2]

Although many Filipinos had demanded an end to U.S. sovereignty during the U.S. colonial era, the Japanese occupation was not the endgame that Filipinos had envisaged. For many Filipinos, U.S. rule in the Philippines came to seem the lesser of two evils. When the U.S. military retreated from the Philippines in May 1942, underground radio shows and renegade print propaganda promised Filipino listeners that a return to American colonialism would eventually lead Filipinos to freedom. This goal could be achieved only by expelling Japanese forces. In pursuit of that aim, Filipinos had to resist all things Japanese. Keenly aware of the hardships endured by the Filipino people, the anti-Japanese resistance played up the appeal of normalcy, invoking a nostalgic vision of life before World War II under U.S. rule.[3]

Having established their power in the Philippines the same way the Americans had—by force of arms—Japanese officials embarked on a public relations campaign to counter Filipino resistance. In response to claims that life had been better under U.S. rule, the new Japanese military government initiated a propaganda campaign that deployed rhetoric of a happy and normal life. Japan's "Co-Prosperity" ideology promised Filipinos that freedom from forty years of U.S. colonial oppression would lead to a better quality of life, with bountiful food, clean clothing, and housing for all.[4] The new normal of a more prosperous life would manifest only under a Pan-Asian alliance, led by Japan. Yet even as the Japanese aspired to make a clean and decisive break from U.S. power, capital, commodities, and culture, Japanese occupiers occasionally accommodated the sense that normality for Filipinos meant adherence to past practice.[5] Try as they might to lay the groundwork for a new vision of Japanese dominance, they could not completely expunge all traces of the American Empire from the Philippines. Though nominally in control, Japanese imperial forces navigated a landscape in which the U.S. occupation was still, in many ways, part of everyday life.

Japanese imperial expansion ignited sudden and terrifying changes that rippled through all modes of Philippine life. The personal written accounts of Filipino women and girls grappled with the disruptions of war and living between empires through a framework of normalcy. Helen Mendoza, a teenager in Iloilo in 1941, later remembered the war as the rupture of routines and accepted norms of everyday life, provoking an "unusual calling for unusual adaptation."[6] She recalled how daily schedules at school and home shifted to accommodate new customs like enforced blackouts and air raid drills. In Manila, Pacita Pestaño-Jacinto also witnessed the Pacific War's disruption of daily life and struggled to "go on as usual" when "life was no longer normal."[7] Flora Gimenez's romantic relationship was abruptly put on hold when her sweetheart, Gim, a Filipino ROTC officer, was called to report to a U.S. military base. In a February 3, 1945, diary entry, Lydia Gutierrez, a fourteen-year-old from Manila, reflected that normalcy under war had come to mean "the same half-boring, half-scary life."[8] Such attention to abrupt swings between terror and routine raise questions: Why did normalcy figure so largely in women's accounts of the war and Japanese occupation? How did the transition from one imperial regime to another affect their daily lives?[9] What did it mean to live transimperial lives—in this case, lives that played out under overlapping and competing imperial regimes? What did gendered notions of normalcy imply in a country long subject to imperial rule?[10]

Although women are all too often regarded as peripheral to imperial histories, this essay makes the case for the importance of women's perspectives. To dwell with women's perspectives is to foreground everyday life in a time of violent imperial transitions between the United States and Japan during World War II. Their experiences and points of view are often obscured by histories that focus on masculinity, diplomacy, territory, and policymaking. Too often, civilian experiences of precarity are obfuscated in statist histories that focus solely on casualties on battlefields. Focusing on Filipinas' wartime narratives can help us understand the larger range of ways in which gendered colonial subjects have inhabited a war. By placing women's everyday lives at the heart of war, this essay can help us think anew life under overlapping empires. These overlaps appeared not only in political structures and bureaucracies but also in the creation of what was to become the new normal. Women played a central role in trying to preserve normalcy in a time of precarity, with consequences not only for their own well-being and that of their families and neighbors but also for political positioning.[11]

Sources that focus on women's experiences of World War II, including Filipino women's diaries, memoirs, and letters as well as newspaper articles, provide valuable insights into transimperial lives under the duress of war.[12] This essay depends largely on women's written accounts, focusing particularly on writings by Helen Mendoza, Pacita Pestaño-Jacinto, and Flora Gimenez. These women represent different geographies of the mainly Christian areas of the archipelago. Their writing provides insights into how the war impacted both urban spaces like Manila and rural provinces in the Visayan region. For example, food scarcity and food policies, as each of their testimonies shows, developed differently along geographic lines. But along with revealing regional differences, these women also reveal commonalities. All these women had grown up under the U.S. regime, in areas in which the colonial state had a significant presence. The local schools, which they attended, aimed to Americanize their pupils. Their consequent ability to write in English is just one manifestation of American colonialism in their every day life.[13] These Filipino women's access to colonial-state-run education also helped cement their status as middle- and upper-class women. Though critical of the U.S. presence prior to 1941, these authors had also fared relatively well under U.S. rule.

Writings on women and by women such as Mendoza, Pestaño-Jacinto, and Gimenez reveal the amount of attention that middle- and upper-class women devoted to maintaining normalcy during the war. These sources pay acute attention to the "stuff" of everyday life during World War II, including dress, house and home, and food. These writings also provide insights into the politics of normalcy by showing ways in which normalcy both real and imagined was associated with the remainders of both Spanish and U.S. imperial life. References to normalcy reveal how vestiges of previous empires collided and sometimes existed alongside Japanese imperial occupation.[14] While historical periodization of colonial rule might suggest a decisive changeover between regimes, descriptions of everyday life offer an alternative view, underscoring the temporal layering of multiple empires.[15] While references to transimperial histories might bring to mind histories of border-crossers, such histories can also be found in particular places, among people who navigated different imperial presences in the course of daily life.

War's Threat to U.S. Colonial Normalcy

Japanese imperial interest in the Philippines and Southeast Asia had been growing since the turn of the twentieth century. Competition and conflict between the United States and Japan over Philippine markets and resources became more acute during the 1930s. The United States tried to carefully maneuver around its promise of Philippine independence, granting a ten-year transition period (the Commonwealth period) and maintaining its own economic and political hold on the archipelago and its people. Japan's expansion across Asia and the Pacific and the fact that the Philippines was a U.S. colony made the Philippines a prime target for Japanese aggression. In Cebu, an island in the central Visayan region, Flora Gimenez recalled, the "air was rife with rumors of war [and] America's presence in the country was an invitation to an invasion by Japan."[16] The demand that soldiers on reserve call in for active duty and the army's urgent call for Filipino civilians to serve seemed to give credence to the rumors. Even before the panic the bombing of Pearl Harbor produced, awareness of the possibility of being caught between two empires existed, causing a slow and steady increase in anxiety.

News outlets addressed the possibility of war and what this would mean for Filipino civilians. In July 1941 *Graphic*, a popular Manila-based magazine, published an issue with Filipino women dressed in khakis and the title "Dressed for Evacuation" emblazoned across the cover. The magazine asked women, "How will you be dressed come evacuation time? How will you bundle yourself off with neatness and dispatch to safety? Call us a pessimist, if you will, but it is not too early to start growing gray hairs over these and a multitude of other questions."[17] While the question of dress for war at first glance might seem like an unimportant and even frivolous concern, the article's focus on women's sartorial choices gets at the kinds of minute details civilians would consider if war in fact came to the Philippines.

Promoting the purchase of an outfit made from American khaki, the article suggested transforming women's wear so that it could help women survive a pending war. The article insisted that a woman civilian might need a coat to be as "tough as the elements," as evacuation would entail leaving the shelter of home. She would also benefit from wearing pants with utility pockets and a cap that could serve as a bag, to hold rations such as canned foods, presumably imported from the United States.[18] Even prior to Japan's initial military attack, Filipinas felt caught between two empires. They prepared for the invasion of the Japanese Empire by adopting and adapting American military wear. Fearing the prospect of evacuation in advance of a Japanese invasion, they sought protection in the fabric of a familiar empire, the United States.

The sense of imperial overlaps played out as rumors intensified and the probability of war increased. Growing numbers of civilians began to evacuate urban centers, including Manila, Iloilo, and Cebu City. According to Gimenez, "tension was palpable in Cebu City" and houses were "disgorging themselves of their occupants," who sought to escape the "devastation of a war they [were] sure was coming."[19] Although still under U.S. rule, Filipino civilians upended their lives in anticipation of a Japanese attack. Evacuees brought with them what they could: pots, pans, clothing, and foodstuffs that would not spoil. Mendoza described how she and her family were constantly relocating, from Iloilo to various small mountain towns and villages. Her memoir describes predicaments from life on the move that she found unusual, such as bathing in rivers (keeping her clothes on for modesty), not having a toilet, and sleeping without mosquito nets. The shifts were rapid and drastic, "but," Mendoza asserted, "we adapted."[20] Her poignant statement about this experience conveys her sense that women and girls had to be independent and resilient under the precarious situations that war produced.

In December 1941 the Japanese Air Force bombed Manila and Clark Air Field Base. Japanese ground troops made their first landings at the most northern and southern points of Luzon island. Not only did Japanese forces expel American occupiers, but they also claimed the places Americans had left.[21] Manila architecture of the U.S. colonial period, called "America's triumph" by the colonial governor William Howard Taft, had been designed to embody American culture and power. Edifices and neighborhoods, particularly the large American concrete homes in Pasay and Parañaque, enclaves of Manila, reinforced racial, social, and, class hierarchies.[22] After Manila was declared an open city, U.S. colonial officials evacuated and the Japanese military arrested the remaining American civilians, placing many in internment camps.[23]

Almost immediately, Japanese high-ranking military officials moved into U.S. colonial government buildings and grand American homes. In her diary, Pacita Pestaño-Jacinto, a middle-class housewife, documented rumors of Japanese "generals and the highest in command . . . liv[ing] like princes" after seizing all "enemy" properties. She cynically commented, "They [sank] contentedly into upholstered chairs, gorging themselves on good food."[24] Prior to the war, American colonizers had inserted themselves into daily life through the physical presence of grand houses that demonstrated their authority across the colonial landscape. Filipino civilians like Pestaño-Jacinto noted how changes in power manifested not only in terms of military force and policy changes but also in the Japanese colonial takeover of American spaces that had come to be accepted as symbols of power in colonial everyday life, particularly in the capital city of Manila. Pestaño-Jacinto's cynical reaction to Japanese colonial officials' ability to live in relative comfort, while many Filipinos faced displacement after witnessing the destruction of their cities and neighborhoods, reveals the resentment felt by civilians dislocated by war. In a follow-up diary entry, she expressed her contempt for Japanese dominance over the Philippines. She noted that "pan-Asianism" urged "every true Filipino to forget the harmful culture that thirty years of oppression under the yoke of the white people ha[d] forced on us." While not necessarily disagreeing with this sentiment of "Asia for Asiatics," she nevertheless took issue with Japanese imperial control, writing, "Yes, but why must Japan be the Master Asiatic?"[25]

Despite her own resentments of American occupation, Pestaño-Jacinto had been able to live a relatively comfortable life as a middle-class wife of a medical doctor. With the coming of Japanese occupation, her life dramatically changed. She wrote, "Although business tried to go on as usual, life was no longer normal. The atmosphere of war had gripped us." She lamented that she could not easily return to ordinary routines or the life she had become accustomed to with the loss of her home and garden that she and her husband had purchased as newlyweds just prior to the war.[26] Here Pestaño-Jacinto's resentment reflects the dissonance wrought by the war. The occupiers were living a lush life, while the reality of war for Pestaño-Jacinto and many other Filipinos was one of deprivation and displacement.

Food and Transimperial Economies of the Everyday

From the moment Japan began its battle for the Philippines in 1941 until the war's end in 1945, the threat of being caught in the crossfire between the United States Army Forces Far East and the Japanese military induced fear and panic. Filipinos would live with this anxiety throughout the occupation. In urban centers like Manila, looters raided warehouses and stores.[27] Among the coveted items taken were foodstuffs. As a result, many households and individuals keenly felt the impetus to hoard canned meat, rice, and sugar.[28] Pestaño-Jacinto immediately inventoried her household's food supplies and sent out a household servant for more canned goods, candles, matches, and extra cots.[29] The threat of the coming Japanese was felt at the everyday level of sustenance and needs. To maintain normalcy, Pestaño-Jacinto hoarded food with the hope that she could continue to provide meals for her family as well as prepare familiar American-influenced dishes. The panic over the lack of imported canned meats and vegetables was widespread. Anxieties about food were central in women's accounts of Japanese occupation in the Philippines.

Pestaño-Jacinto was right to worry that the Japanese presence would profoundly affect her family's access to food. Plans for Japanese imperial expansion sought to reorganize the economy of the Philippines to transfer profits from the United States to Japan.[30] Economic transformations would ideally offer the resources that Japan needed to win the war and effectively cut off economic ties between Southeast Asia and enemy Western imperial regimes like the United States.[31] The Japanese military government passed strict economic regulations and sanctions that prohibited U.S.-Philippine import and export relations. These sanctions particularly affected the availability of food.

As part of its economic restructuring, the Japanese military administration introduced a new paper currency. Women described the difficulties of using the currency in everyday life. By the end of the war, it took 500 notes to equal the purchasing power of one peso. Lydia Gutierrez's diary described women bringing bushels of notes to the market in order to purchase just one week's food provisions.[32] The currency deflated in value so quickly that Manila residents began to refer to it as "Mickey Mouse money." Thus Manileños mockingly referred to the currency of the Japanese Empire with an American popular cultural reference.[33] By comparing Japanese currency to play money, Filipino civilians underscored that the new Japanese war notes had no value.

Middle-class Filipinos' resentment toward the Japanese occupation reflected the dramatic shift in their standard of living. In the years leading up to the war, middle-class civil servants directly benefited from U.S. education and the colonial state's establishment of civil servant jobs for Filipinos. Women who attended university began to participate in new forms of white-collar jobs, such as pharmacy and secretarial work. They witnessed their buying power "soar."[34] Even as Filipinos still worked for independence from the United States prior to World War II, many longed for the economic comfort of the previous colonial regime and became increasingly antagonistic toward Japanese control as their quality of life declined.[35] Inflation and the lack of resources led to severe challenges to daily survival.[36]

In the face of Filipino skepticism about the new Japanese regime, the new military government introduced a "Co-Prosperity" propaganda campaign that aimed to sever the Philippines from the United States. This campaign had three components. First, as Japanese economic sanctions suggest, Co-Prosperity emphasized the necessity for Filipinos to become independent of American products and cultural forms. Second, the Co-prosperity campaign bolstered local production of agricultural products, aiming to make the Philippines agriculturally self-sustaining. Third, Japanese propaganda portrayed life under Japanese rule as more prosperous than under that of their American counterparts.

The Japanese Propaganda Corps, a branch of the Japanese military administration, played a central part in promoting Japanese pan-Asian rhetoric. Media regulated and funded by the Propaganda Corps widely circulated the benefits of the Japanese imperial regime over Western empires. Corps-funded media tried to break Filipino-American alliances and win over Filipinos, as Japan had done in Indonesia, Burma, and Malaysia. Japanese government agencies funneled money to publish heavily curated and censored journals, which promised co-prosperity between Japanese and Filipino peoples. In the midst of military violence between Japanese and Filipino American allied forces, the Japanese government hoped to reduce opposition by persuading Filipinos to "resume normal lives."[37] Despite visions of pan-Asian collaboration, the disruption of Filipino life made many wary and distrustful of the new colonial authority. After military confrontations between U.S. and Japanese armed forces shut down production and commerce, many Filipino men and women refused to return to work. Others joined guerrilla movements and continued to battle against the Japanese military and protest the new imperial state.[38] Japanese propaganda campaigns promoting "normalcy" attempted to assuage Filipino resistance.

Although "normal" life before the war would have meant life under U.S. colonial rule with dependence on U.S. imports, Japanese propaganda promoted a new normalcy that would encourage Filipinos to return to mundane routines but not consume U.S. goods. The Co-Prosperity campaign emphasized that

Japanese authority brought even more prosperity and encouraged Filipinos to abandon skeptical appraisals of and resistance to Japanese rule. The Japanese colonial regime thus created a new normal which insisted that Filipinos would experience greater prosperity under Japanese authority. A Japanese colonial state would provide better resources for everyday life than the displaced U.S. colonial regime.

In fact Japanese propaganda denied the existence of any social or economic problems incited by war, using the image of happy and prosperous Filipino women. Propagandists understood the gendered impact of war and relied on images of women to promote the Japanese ideology of co-prosperity.[39] Publications like the *Tribune* and *Shin Seiki*: *Bagong Araw, A New Era*, a pictorial magazine with articles written in English, Tagalog, and Japanese, depicted women as the gauge of normalcy. Newspapers and magazines consistently circulated images of abundance in food and other necessities alongside smiling women.[40] One issue of *Shin Seiki* published an image of an elderly Filipino woman receiving rice emblazoned with the script "Sapat na Bigas Ukol Sa Lahat," with the English translation appearing at the bottom of the page: "Enough Rice for All." Another photo spread exhibited middle-class women as the embodiment of an idealized normalcy. The spread, entitled "Women at Work," showed women in a variety of occupations, including a *tindera*, or storekeeper. Behind her are shelves filled with canned foods. Japanese propagandists who circulated this image recognized that canned goods were staples of everyday life, particularly for middle-class households. But this image makes no reference to the ways that inflation and limited access to everyday necessities shaped the majority of Filipinos' lives during World War II.[41] It also overlooks the imperial connotations of canned goods. In the photo, the young Filipino woman, dressed in a clean fashionable dress with her hair perfectly coiffed, smilingly hands a small girl a box of Purico shortening. Japanese propagandists no doubt regarded Purico as a local brand produced by the Philippine Manufacturing Corporation. Purico, however, was originally an American-owned coconut refinery.[42] The image thus unwittingly associated the prosperity of Japanese rule with the availability of American manufactured or imported goods.

Women's diaries and memoirs revealed the ineffectiveness of Japanese food campaigns. While Japanese rhetoric advocated a new and better normal, Filipino women who had to carry on with daily routines in the context of war could not escape the difference between Japanese propaganda and the difficulties they faced daily. For middle-class women, the food crisis was as much about the unavailability of certain coveted imported American foods as it was about the shortage of food in general. Pestaño-Jacinto outright accused papers of "evad[ing] the issue" in their refusal to recognize the conditions that necessitated rationing.[43] On the ground, stores and markets carried fewer and fewer of the goods considered staples. A few months into Japanese occupation, Lourdes Montinola expressed her panic while watching "important items . . . [disappear] from grocery stores. There was no butter, no refined sugar, no fresh milk; there was a lack of most canned goods."[44] Similarly Pestaño-Jacinto noted in her diary, "Milk, canned or powdered, has gone the way of all imported commodities."[45]

The anxiety over the lack of imported American foodstuffs reflects the deep reach of U.S. Empire into food practices before the war. U.S. education officials had taken great pains to educate young girls in "sanitary" food preparation and encourage so-called better nutrition. At the same time, cookbooks that promoted American recipes and palates circulated among mostly middle-class Filipina consumers.[46] It is important to note that not all Filipinos could afford imported foodstuffs, and therefore imported goods came to symbolize higher social and class status. Thus civilians, especially among the middle class, regarded these economic strictures as the denial of staples considered essential to good and healthy living during the American colonial period. The disappearance of these goods also threatened the symbols of middle-class status in Filipino society.[47] For elite and middle-class Filipinos, normalcy implied food habits that had been shaped by U.S. colonialism.

Even as Japanese occupation progressed, urban middle-class women, like Pestaño-Jacinto, continued to long for food from the U.S. colonial era. The war's numerous disruptions to food supplies changed what was to be expected of day-to-day living, creating a new normal. These conditions engendered a range of reactions and coping strategies that reflected gender and class positions. Pestaño-Jacinto's status and life during the American colonial period had been largely defined by her position as a middle-class housewife. This status had enabled her to consume "modern" household goods and food.[48] She lamented that food had become "so colorless, so prosaic" under Japanese rule. She longed for the food of the American colonial period, what she called "real bread" as well as muffins, waffles and bacon, cakes, asparagus tips, peas, macaroni, and liver spread.[49] The "real" bread and other baked goods would have required imported flour made from wheat. The other products she so longingly catalogued were also American imports. She disclosed in her diary that she and other housewives hoarded these coveted food items. On special occasions, like her daughter's baptism, Pestaño-Jacinto took from her limited supply and made dishes introduced in the American colonial period that continued to represent desirability and status, like stuffed turkey and chicken salad. She declared, "I want to put the menu on record. . . . I want to remember good food when it can no longer be had."[50] Despite living under Japanese occupation, middle-class Filipino women such as Pestaño-Jacinto created a normalcy from the vestiges of U.S. Empire. In this account, baptism, a Catholic ceremony and a signifier of Spanish colonial rule, came together with an American-influenced menu. Overlapping empires manifested in a celebration for a newborn daughter who faced an uncertain future under a new imperial regime.

In women's accounts of the war, holidays and festivities were portrayed as a break from the new normal of both tedium and violence.[51] Montinola recalled celebrating her mother and father's silver wedding anniversary in November 1944 and how she "opened a can of treasured Wesson oil to make real mayonnaise" to put in a chicken salad.[52] The routines of holidays under U.S. Empire became a means to enact a sense of normalcy. For Montinola and her family, creating that desired normalcy meant conjuring the minutiae of everyday life prior to World War II. Whether or not she was conscious of the product's and recipe's U.S. colonial roots, Montinola's use of these food items nevertheless provided a reprieve from the stress of war. The strong sense of nostalgia for the seemingly banal objects of the U.S. colonial period presents a certain irony. Montinola couches her desire for freedom from Japanese tyranny as a desire for the materials of another colonial past. The items that evoked happier times and a past normal life were in fact vestiges of an American colonial regime. That these items continued to exist and produce such powerful feelings illustrates the ways in which U.S. colonial power lingered even during the Japanese occupation.

While nostalgia for American food products pervaded practices in everyday urban life, Filipinos in rural provinces confronted different challenges to everyday food practices. As some migrated from urban areas to provincial towns, they improvised food practices utilizing local resources and networks. Staying in Palompon, a small coastal Visayan town, the Gimenezes had access to local seafood, such as small fish and krill. Gim Gimenez earned a living by selling *guinamus*, salted and fermented krill, made with local food preservation techniques that long predated canned meats.

While Flora Gimenez praised her husband for his entrepreneurial spirit, she also relied on her own resourcefulness and connections with other women to generate income during the war. From the sale of guinamus Gimenez could purchase more expensive products, like rice and pork, which she used to make and sell delicacies derived from the Spanish colonial period. She depended on her mother-in-law's labor-intensive recipe for chorizos that she sold door-to-door.[53] Gimenez innovated Spanish-influenced recipes with local food sources in order to assemble a new food economy and increase her household income.

The Gimenezes were able to hire two helpers to assist them in both business and household work. With the extra help, Gimenez expanded her business. She targeted local wealthy women, who played mahjong to pass the time during the malaise of the war, as potential patrons, after noticing that they lacked variety during their daily *merienda* (afternoon snacks). Hoping to capitalize on the desire for food variety during a time of scarcity, Gimenez began making and selling empanadas. Much in the same way that Japan could not completely eliminate traces of U.S. colonialism, almost fifty years of U.S. control had not eradicated Spanish colonial influences. The layering of empires appeared in Filipinas' adaptations of food practices and tastes. The comfort offered by Spanish-inflected empanadas and chorizos enhanced the comfort offered by social networks—revealed by family recipes and friendships among women—to help civilians cope with the duress of war.

Across the archipelago, war made the production and consumption of food increasingly difficult. Levels of starvation and famine varied across the Philippines. For example, in Luzon and the Visayan region, restrictions on U.S. imports like wheat flour necessitated the use of a locally sourced substitute, cassava flour. Cassava, a root vegetable that the Spanish Empire imported from Mexico to the Philippines via the Manila Galleon, once again became a food staple throughout the archipelago. Like *kamote* (sweet potato), also indigenous to Mexico, cassava could be planted and easily foraged.[54] While food practices during the American colonial period created a food economy that rendered cassava and kamote less valuable and desirable than American imported vegetables, the reality of scarcity spurred Filipino civilians to return to older colonial products.[55]

Japanese administrators also promoted the revitalization of local agriculture, with indigenous crops as well as those crop varieties introduced by the Spanish and Americans prior to World War II. Food shortages and the conditions of war prompted colonial authorities to demand Filipino farmers in Luzon and the Visayas to resume work on the land. The Ministry of Agriculture's food campaigns in agricultural rural areas encouraged the growing of food crops, namely cassava, kamote, soy, corn, and rice.[56] However, the damage caused by the war and continued battles between guerrilla forces and the Japanese Imperial Army made it difficult for farmers to comply with new policies.[57]

As food shortages persisted, Japanese officials homed in on domestic life, targeting Filipino women. They emphasized the importance of utilizing locally produced food. Although Japanese-controlled newspapers denied widespread food shortages and starvation, they strongly encouraged the use of cassava.[58] Articles directed toward women readers provided new recipes with cassava as the main ingredient, such as cassava cake and cassava pudding.[59] Cassava desserts and the use of canned fruits in Filipino treats embodied the layering of Japanese, U.S., and Spanish cultural and economic forces. The shifts in food economies left an indelible mark on Filipino cuisine and tastes and show the far reaches of colonial conflicts in Filipino lives.[60] Today in the Philippines and the Filipino diaspora, for example, cassava is a coveted ingredient used in celebratory delicacies like cassava cakes.[61]

Conclusion

Although histories of war and competing empires have focused on spectacular events, attempts to establish control and power in the Philippines relied heavily on controlling perceived norms and normalcy. Understanding the power of the fantasy of "normalcy" in the day-to-day, Japanese colonial authorities in the war-torn Philippines promised a return to life as usual, if not a life better than before. Even as they strove for a clean and decisive break from U.S. power, capital, commodities, and culture, Japanese military authorities went to great lengths to frame war as the introduction of a new and greater normal. The images they produced of accessible and abundant food and healthy, clean, and smiling Filipinos attempted to secure Filipinos' trust in a new colonial regime. Yet the distance between Japanese propaganda and lived experience as articulated by middle-class Filipino women was profound. Writing the history of the everyday through personal archives reframes triumphalist narratives of war, policy changes, and the imperial state as a history of precarity, fear, and uncertainty. These difficult conditions were felt acutely by women. Japan's failure to actually create a new and better normal for Filipinos forced ordinary women to pursue a range of survival strategies.

Tracing middle-class Filipinas' efforts to achieve normalcy reveals the extent to which they navigated imperial overlaps. Instead of experiencing a clean break, they were surrounded by residue from previous imperial regimes, whether in housing, clothing, or food. The layering of imperial power in the context of war structured norms and normalization. Having introduced new forms of precarity, the Japanese military government inadvertently enhanced attachments to prior colonial regimes. Even Filipinos who ardently wanted national independence came to see elements of past occupations as far preferable to the Japanese colonial present and promised future. Firsthand knowledge of multiple imperial regimes enabled Filipinos to assess one in relation to others, to the detriment of Japanese efforts to win hearts and minds.

As Filipina civilians' pursuit of normalcy in a time of war suggests, the Philippines provides a critical case to think about the application of the concept of transimperialism in one geographic location. Their pursuit of normalcy provides insights into how empires overlap in particular places and how imperial legacies shaped daily lives long after the formal cession of imperial power. Just as *transimperialism* can help us grasp the history of changing imperial policies, institutions, and bureaucracies across different imperial spatial regimes, it can also help us understand the consequences and lived experiences that followed from imperial overlaps and transitions in a particular place. For Filipinos during World War II, that meant living with the decisions of the Japanese military administration and the long legacies of the United States and the Spanish who came before.

NOTES

1. Denise Cruz and Rey Ileto's work underscores that World War II was in fact the third modern war in the Philippines: first was the Philippine Revolution, then the Philippine-American War, and then World War II. See Denise Cruz, introduction to Yay Panlilio, *The Crucible: An Autobiography by Colonel Yay, Filipina American Guerrilla* (New Brunswick, NJ: Rutgers University Press, 2009), ix–xxviii; Reynaldo Clemena Ileto, "Philippine Wars and the Politics of Memory," *positions: east asia cultures critique* 13, no. 1 (2005): 215–35.

2. For more on a general history of World War II and the Philippines, see Teodoro A. Agoncillo, *The Fateful Years: Japan's Adventure in the Philippines, 1941–45*, vols. 1–2 (Quezon City: University of the Philippines Press, 2001); John W. Dower, *War without Mercy: Race and Power in the Pacific War* (New York: Pantheon Books, 1993).

3. Pacita Pestaño-Jacinto, *Living with the Enemy* (Pasig City, Philippines: Anvil, 1999), 2.

4. Motoe Terami-Wada, "The Japanese Propaganda Corps in the Philippines," *Philippine Studies* 38, no. 3 (third quarter 1990): 279–300.

5. For an intellectual history of Japanese ideologies of pan-Asianism, see Sven Matthiessen, *Japanese Pan-Asianism and the Philippines from the Late Nineteenth Century to the End of World War II: Going to the Philippines Is Like Coming Home?* (Boston: Brill, 2015); Vicente L. Rafael, "Anticipating Nationhood: Collaboration and Rumor in the Japanese Occupation of Manila," *Diaspora: A Journal of Transnational Studies* 1, no. 1 (1991): 67–82.

6. Helen Mendoza, *Memories of the War Years: A Teenage Girl's Life in the Philippines under Japanese Rule* (Quezon City, Philippines: Pantas, 2016).

7. Pestaño-Jacinto, *Living with the Enemy*, 2.

8. Lydia C. Gutierrez, "Liberation Diary: The Longest Wait," *Sunday Times Magazine*, April 23, 1967, *Philippine Diary Project*, http://philippinediaryproject.com/category/diary -of-lydia-c-gutierrez/.

9. Eiichiro Azuma, *Between Two Empires: Race, History, and Transnationalism in Japanese America* (Oxford: Oxford University Press, 2005). Historians Rey Ileto and Resil Mojares are critical of dominant nationalist histories that frame World War II in the Philippines as a story of allied Filipino-American forces battling against the tyranny of Japanese imperialism. The joint struggle thus rallied together Filipinos in patriotic fervor for the shared goal of Philippine national independence. The narrative of Filipino-American alliance framed the period of Japanese occupation as an aberration from the linear progression of modernization and nation-making. In other words, World War II was a time of the abnormal, an extreme deviation of normal conditions. A return to normal could be achieved only through the joint efforts of Filipinos and Americans to defeat and expel Japanese forces. Ileto, "Philippine Wars and the Politics of Memory"; Resil B. Mojares, "The Formation of Filipino Nationality under US Colonial Rule," *Philippine Quarterly of Culture and Society* 34, no. 1 (2006): 11–32.

10. Veena Das discusses the "mutual absorption of the violent and the ordinary" and argues that in recognizing that there is violence in the everyday we also come to an understanding that the "event" is "always attached to the ordinary." This is a useful framework to explain civilian experiences of war as encompassing both spectacular "events" of warfare and what becomes the everyday of war. Veena Das, *Life and Words: Violence and the Descent into the Ordinary* (Berkeley: University of California Press, 2007), 7.

11. Michael Warner addresses the normal and normality as a "regime of normal" in *The Trouble with Normal: Sex, Politics, and the Ethics of Queer Life* (New York: Free Press, 1999). See also Canguilhem Georges, *The Normal and the Pathological* (New York: Zone Books, 1991); Judith Halberstam, *In a Queer Time and Place: Transgender Bodies, Subcultural Lives* (New York: New York University Press, 2005); Rosemarie Garland Thomson, ed., *Freakery: Cultural Spectacles of the Extraordinary Body* (New York: New York University Press, 1996).

12. Antoinette Burton makes a compelling case for centering women's writing and writings about women in studies of empire. Antoinette M. Burton, *Dwelling in the Archive: Women Writing House, Home, and History in Late Colonial India* (Oxford: Oxford University Press, 2003).

13. For more on the American colonial period and the impact of English education on the making of Filipino women writers and an English canon, see Denise Cruz, *Transpacific Femininities: The Making of the Modern Filipina* (Durham, NC: Duke University Press, 2012).

14. On imperial residues, see Ann Laura Stoler, "Imperial Debris: Reflections on Ruins and Ruination." *Cultural Anthropology* 23, no. 2 (2008): 191–219.

15. Here I borrow from cultural critics such as Ju Yon Kim and Henri Lefebvre who argue for analyzing the depths of the mundane as repetitive behaviors, everyday enactments, and everyday life. Ju Yon Kim, *The Racial Mundane: Asian American Performance and the Embodied Everyday* (New York: New York University Press, 2015), 8–9; Henri Lefebvre, *Critique of Everyday Life* (London: Verso, 1991), 2:196.

16. Maceda, *Bride of War*, 33.

17. "Dressing for Evacuation," *Graphic*, July 10, 1941, n.p.

18. Helen Mendoza recounts meticulously curating what was necessary for evacuation and the amount she could carry herself. She packed three sets of clothes, two pairs of socks, a pair of slippers, and an extra pair of rubber shoes (*Memories of the War Years*, 29).

19. Maceda, *Bride of War*, 33.

20. Mendoza, *Memories of the War Years*, 31.

21. Pestaño-Jacinto, *Living with the Enemy*, 11.

22. Kiyoko Yamaguchi, "The New 'American' Houses in the Colonial Philippines and the Rise of the Urban Filipino Elite," *Philippine Studies* 54, no. 3 (2006): 418.

23. Frances B. Cogan, *Captured: The Japanese Internment of American Civilians in the Philippines, 1941–1945* (Athens: University of Georgia Press, 2012).

24. Pestaño-Jacinto, *Living with the Enemy*, 114.

25. Pestaño-Jacinto, *Living with the Enemy*, 21.

26. Pestaño-Jacinto, *Living with the Enemy*, 2–4.

27. Daniel F. Doeppers, *Feeding Manila in Peace and War, 1850–1945* (Madison: University of Wisconsin Press, 2016), 308–9; Pestaño-Jacinto, *Living with the Enemy*, 11.

28. Agoncillo, *The Fateful Years*, 2:518; Pestaño-Jacinto, *Living with the Enemy*, 7.

29. Pestaño-Jacinto, *Living with the Enemy*, 7.

30. The Philippines was part of what Japan deemed "Area A," along with British Malaya, Dutch East Indies, and Borneo. For more on the Japanese imperial expansion in the Philippines and across Southeast Asia, see Theodore Friend, *The Blue-Eyed Enemy: Japan against the West in Java and Luzon, 1942–1945* (Princeton, NJ: Princeton University Press, 2014); Benito Justo Legarda, *Occupation: The Later Years* (Quezon City, Philippines: De La Salle University–Manila, 2007); Setsuho Ikehata and Ricardo Trota Jose, eds., *The Philippines under Japan: Occupation Policy and Reaction* (Quezon City, Philippines: Ateneo de Manila University Press, 1999); Terami-Wada, "The Japanese Propaganda Corps in the Philippines."

31. Agoncillo, *The Fateful Years*, 2:517.

32. Gutierrez, "Liberation Diary," February 3, 1945; Lourdes R. Montinola, *Breaking the Silence: A War Memoir* (Diliman, Quezon City: University of the Philippines Press, 1996), 47.

33. Ricardo T. José, "War and Violence, History and Memory: The Philippine Experience of the Second World War," *Asian Journal of Social Science* 29, no. 3 (2001): 457–70.

34. Ian Brown, "The Philippine Economy during the World Depression of the 1930s," *Philippine Studies* 40, no. 3 (third quarter, 1992): 385.

35. For more on economic conditions of the 1930s, growing labor unrest, and persistent communist movements that resisted both the U.S. and Japanese regimes, see Benedict J. Kerkvliet, *The Huk Rebellion: A Study of Peasant Revolt in the Philippines* (Lanham, MD: Rowman and Littlefield, 2002); Vina A. Lanzona, *Amazons of the Huk Rebellion: Gender, Sex, and Revolution in the Philippines* (Madison: University of Wisconsin Press, 2009).

36. Doeppers, *Feeding Manila in Peace and War*, 308.

37. Terami-Wada, "The Japanese Propaganda Corps in the Philippines," 281.

38. Lanzona, *Amazons of the Huk Rebellion*.

39. Japanese colonial occupation strategies also took up this idea of the gift of freedom throughout its campaign in colonized Southeast Asia. In the Philippines they promised freedom from the tyranny of the West and solidarity in a pan-Asian movement.

40. *Shin Seiki: Bagong Araw, A New Era* (Manila, Philippines, 1942–43).

41. Doeppers, *Feeding Manila*, 333.

42. For more on food politics, colonial hygiene, and hydrogenated oils, see Dawn Bohulano Mabalon, "As American as Jackrabbit Adobo: Cooking, Eating, and Becoming Filipina/o American before World War II," in *Eating Asian America: A Food Studies Reader* (New York: New York University Press, 2013), 147–76.

43. Pestaño-Jacinto, *Living with the Enemy*, 113.

44. Montinola, *Breaking the Silence*, 37. Additionally, the depletion of rice from local markets pushed the military administration to regulate rice, and other products like soap and medicine. For more on the rice shortage in Manila, see Doeppers, *Feeding Manila*, 307–32.

45. Pestaño-Jacinto, *Living with the Enemy*, 137.

46. Megan Elias, "The Palate of Power: Americans, Food and the Philippines after the Spanish-American War," *Material Culture* Vol. 46, No. 1, Special Issue (2014): 44–57.

47. For more on food politics during the U.S. colonial period, see Doreen G. Fernandez, "Culture Ingested: Notes on the Indigenization of Philippine Food," *Philippine Studies* 36, no. 2 (1988): 219–32; René Alexander Orquiza Jr., "Lechon with Heinz, Lea & Perrins with Adobo: The American Relationship with Filipino Food, 1898–1946," in *Eating Asian America: A Food Studies Reader*, edited by Robert Ji-Song Ku, Martin F. Manalansan IV, and Anita Mannur (New York: New York University Press, 2013), 177–85; Felice Prudente Santa Maria, *The Governor-General's Kitchen: Philippine Culinary Vignettes and Period Recipes: 1521–1935* (Pasig City, Philippines: Anvil, 2006).

48. Raquel A.G. Reyes, "Modernizing the Manileña: Technologies of Conspicuous Consumption for the Well-to-do Woman, circa 1880s–1930s," *Modern Asian Studies* 46, no. 1 (2012): 193–220.

49. Pestaño-Jacinto, *Living with the Enemy*, 206.

50. Pestaño-Jacinto, *Living with the Enemy*, 71–72. Montinola's memoir expressed similar rituals around food from the American colonial era (*Breaking the Silence*, 49).

51. Mendoza, *Memories of the War Years*, 64; Pestaño-Jacinto, *Living with the Enemy*, 25.

52. Montinola, *Breaking the Silence*, 49.

53. Maceda, *Bride of War*, 88.

54. Even prior to the war, the Commonwealth government encouraged civilians to plant kamote in preparation for the war. Doeppers, *Feeding Manila in Peace and War*, 321–23.

55. Mendoza, *Memories of the War Years*, 32; Agoncillo, *The Fateful Years*, 2:556.

56. In addition to planting root crops, the Ministry of Agriculture also planned to produce and harvest grains in the provinces surrounding Manila, such as Isabella, Cagayan, Nueva Ecija, Bulucan, and Cavite. Francis K. Danquah, "Japan's Food Farming Policies in Wartime Southeast Asia: The Philippine Example, 1942–1944," *Agricultural History* 64, no. 3 (1990): 64.

57. Danquah, "Japan's Food Farming Policies in Wartime Southeast Asia."

58. The problem of inflation was further exacerbated by an already deficient food supply, brought on by natural disasters between 1938 and 1941.

59. "Re-discovering the Cassava, Camote's Forgotten Cousin," *Tribune*, March 22, 1942, 5.

60. For more on colonial and wartime legacies affecting Filipino cuisine and food cultures, see Gilda Cordero-Fernando, ed., *Culinary Culture of the Philippines* (Manila: Bancom Audiovision, 1976); Doreen Fernandez, *Palayok: Philippine Food through Time, on Site, in the Pot* (Manila: Bookmark, 2006); Doreen Fernandez, *Tikim: Essays on Philippine Food and Culture* (Manila: Anvil, 1994), 62, 223; Doreen Fernandez, *Kinilaw: A Philippine Cuisine of Freshness* (Manila: Bookmark, 1991).

61. Fernandez, *Tikim.*

PART V.　RESISTANCE ACROSS EMPIRES

12. FIGHTING JOHN BULL AND UNCLE SAM: SOUTH ASIAN REVOLUTIONARIES CONFRONT THE MODERN STATE

Moon-Ho Jung

Born in 1884 to a literary caste (Kayastha) and a father in the colonial bureaucracy, Har Dayal's intellectual gifts placed him on a fast track to a career in civil service, but his anticolonial radicalism made him instead a target of the British imperial security state. After earning his bachelor's and master's degrees in India, he left in 1905 to study at Oxford University on a scholarship sponsored by the colonial government of India. Although his academic achievements momentarily eclipsed his political activities, the British government's Investigation Department had grown concerned enough to file a report in 1904 stating that "a sense of revolt had taken deep root in his mind and had even permeated strongly a select circle of his friends." Dayal engaged in formal historical studies at Oxford and informal political studies with fellow colonized subjects in England. His outrage against the British Empire compelled him, as he put it, to "resign" his scholarship in 1907, a year before he was expected to graduate with high honors. The British colonial educational system, he would write the following year back in India, was "one huge octopus which is *sucking out the moral life-blood of the nation.*" Hounded by British undercover agents and repressive laws, Dayal left India in less than a year, returning to England and then finding a home briefly in the radical world of Paris. He edited a revolutionary newspaper there, *Bande Mataram*, for South Asians everywhere, especially back home in India.[1]

Dayal soon sought refuge across the Atlantic, to recover from ill health and to regenerate his political philosophy and revolutionary organizing. Having grown tired of the socialist orthodoxy pervading the exiled left in Paris, he embarked in 1910 for Martinique, a French colony in the Caribbean. Dayal led an ascetic life on the tropical island, evidently determined to bequeath a new religion to the world modeled on Buddha's life. His mission took him to the libraries of Harvard University by way of the Danish Virgin Islands, the U.S. colony of Puerto Rico, and New York City. A couple months in Cambridge were apparently long enough. Hearing that there were thousands of South Asian laborers on the Pacific Coast who might be organized in the struggle for the liberation of the Indian subcontinent, Dayal made his trek westward in the spring of 1911. The United States, he wrote then, was an "ethical sanitarium, where eternal sunshine prevails, and the wrecks of other climes are wrought into beautiful specimens of restored humanity." His love affair with America would be short-lived, but he was ready to make the Bay Area home, at least for a while. After a short trip to Hawai'i, where he read Karl Marx and became friends with Japanese residents, he received a temporary appointment as a lecturer of Indian philosophy at Stanford University. In California, Dayal began writing and lecturing again on the British Empire and revolutionary politics. He was ready to move back into the spotlight.[2]

Both the U.S. program of intelligence and surveillance, which had emerged from the campaign to consolidate colonial rule in the Philippines, and the British system, which had originated in the colonial administration of India, took notice. By January 1913 William C. Hopkinson, in charge of monitoring South Asians for the Canadian government since 1909, had established a transimperial network of state officials and paid informants to keep track of "seditious" activities in the Bay Area. The British consul general, whose government had urged Canadian authorities to dispatch Hopkinson, provided him with names of South Asian college students willing to provide information on Dayal. Hopkinson also made contact with U.S. officials at the immigration station on Angel Island and in the Department of Justice, all of whom promised cooperation and support in his investigation of "Hindu agitators." He attended Dayal's public lectures, which were featured regularly in local radical circles, trying to gather criminal evidence to pass on to his American colleagues. Like Stanford administrators who pressured Dayal to resign his academic post, Hopkinson was dismayed by Dayal's unflinching radicalism and adoring leftist audiences. "Of all the Indian agitators who have visited the States and of all those whom I have a knowledge," he reported, "I am led to believe that Har Dayal is the most dangerous."[3]

Dayal's intrepid rhetoric and anticolonial politics—and false reports of his close association with Emma Goldman, the most prominent anarchist in the

United States—drove U.S. and British officials to intensify their surveillance of Dayal and his comrades. In January 1914 Samuel W. Backus, the head of the immigration station on Angel Island, requested from Commissioner General of Immigration Anthony W. Caminetti an arrest warrant. Time was of the essence. "The reason this subject is presented at this time is that from information received," Backus explained, "he has been in the United States nearly three years; and if the Bureau shall be of the opinion that he comes within the excluded classes, he may be arrested before the statute of limitation operates and then his case can be considered at leisure." Caminetti complied immediately, securing a warrant for Dayal's arrest on February 10, 1914. "That the said alien is a member of the excluded classes in that he was an anarchist or person who believed in or advocated the overthrow by force or violence of the Government of the United States, or of all government, or of all forms of law," the warrant read, "or the assassination of public officials, at the time of his entry into the United States."[4]

The U.S. bureaucrats' plan to deport Dayal backfired. Their failure to locate the exact date of Dayal's landing in New York—February 9, 1911—led them to miss the statutory three-year window by a single day, a fateful mistake that they tried to cover up by investigating whether Dayal had subsequently left and reentered the United States. Not only did Dayal pounce on that error, but he fought back, loudly. News of his arrest, which took place at the conclusion of a socialist meeting in San Francisco's Bohemian Hall on March 25, 1914, stunned local South Asians, two hundred of whom accompanied Dayal as he was taken away to Angel Island for questioning the following morning. In his interview with an immigrant inspector, Dayal refused to renounce or apologize for his political beliefs and anticolonial activities. "As a general rule I believe that tyrannical government[s] should be over-thrown by mass uprisings," he replied at one point, "but this does not mean that I must condemn the assassination of public officials in all lands, in all ages, and under all circumstances, as a principle." He presented himself as an intellectual, denying that he was an anarchist three years earlier but admitting his later espousal of what could be called "philosophical anarchism." "I will never enter a country by denying my convictions," Dayal shot back. After posting a $1,000 bond, he returned to San Francisco and proceeded directly to the Industrial Workers of the World Hall to deliver a lecture titled "The Problem of Unemployment."[5]

Dayal's confrontation with U.S. immigration authorities revealed the deep and vast colonial roots of modern state power. Propelled by global demands for migrant labor and a repressive colonial security state at home, South Asian workers and activists moved to all corners of the world, including the Pacific Coast of North America, where they forged an anticolonial movement in the opening decades of the twentieth century that reverberated across oceans and continents. But, as Dayal discovered, the U.S. state was becoming intimately wedded to the British Empire, literally fighting on the same side during World War I, in a wider project to erect and protect imperial borders and racial hierarchies and to silence and criminalize revolutionary ideas and revolutionary peoples. As waves of "foreigners" appeared to threaten the "domestic" order of things, the U.S. state increasingly recognized and mobilized against revolutionary movements that critiqued and transgressed those borders and hierarchies. The outbreak of World War I, in turn, unleashed transpacific visions of anticolonial revolution, visions that appeared to solidify and magnify racial and radical alliances emerging out of the U.S.-occupied Philippines and all across colonized Asia. The U.S. state's repression of South Asians mobilizing against the British Empire ultimately exposed and created the racial and colonial edifice of the modern state, which became indispensable to preserving white supremacy and empire and to extending U.S. claims to power across the Pacific.

Mobilizing against British and U.S. Empires

Virtually blocked from entering Canada and the United States by 1910 through immigration statutes and their expansive enforcement, South Asian migrants came face to face with British and U.S. government officials driven to control their movements. On November 4, 1910, nineteen South Asians left Manila for Seattle, where immigration authorities summarily rejected them for being "likely to become a public charge" and, in the case of four individuals, believers "in the practice of polygamy." Herbert W. Meyers, an attorney representing the migrants, appealed the decisions, arguing that his clients were able-bodied workers and that they had been admitted legally into the United States in the Philippines. "This country of ours has been heralded as the hope of the downtrodden," he pleaded, "but if we go out of our way to exclude men who have *once been rightfully admitted* in the country and who, under the law, should really not be rejected, we will soon find we have made a serious mistake." Meyers added that Taraknath Das, "a college graduate and a writer of some repute," vowed to post bond that "these men will not become public charges" and to employ fifteen of them immediately. As they strove to gain entry into Seattle, these migrants exploited the contradictions of empire. The U.S. government could not claim jurisdiction over the Philippines and, as Meyers put it, over his clients' "journey from one section of our country to another."[6]

U.S. immigration authorities, in effect, concluded that they could do both. Ellis DeBruler, the commissioner of immigration in Seattle, affirmed the decisions, stressing the dangers of allowing "an open gateway to the mainland of the United States," thereby flooding the market for "common labor." White workers, he continued, would not stand by idly, "and one of the ways in which these men would all finally become public charges would be the fact that the American laborers would drive them from the fields and the camps and then they would be for us to feed and not only to feed, but to protect from violence which would ultimately ensue." Commissioner General of Immigration Daniel J. Keefe sustained DeBruler's views, ruling that the migrants were not being denied entry but being deported from the United States. "While ordinarily it is doubtless assumed that aliens admitted to so distant a part of the 'United States' as the Philippines intend to remain there, where climatic and economic conditions are very different from on the mainland . . . ," he stated, "the matter takes on another aspect when viewed retrospectively in determining whether aliens who have not remained in the islands, but have attempted to move into a part of the country where conditions are dissimilar, are subject to deportation." Keefe allowed two migrants who had resided in the Philippines for longer than three years to land in Seattle, but all of the others were to be deported to Hong Kong, "where they embarked originally for the Philippines."[7]

These particular migrants would find a reprieve from the deportation orders, but their legal appeals unwittingly reinforced U.S. imperial ambitions in the Philippines. In March 1911 Secretary of Commerce and Labor Charles Nagel overruled the judgment of immigration officials. "No doubt deportation could be ordered and could be made effective," he reasoned, "but I can not bring myself to believe that such a course would be a fair enforcement of the law." Motivated less by a sense of fairness than by the conviction that entry decisions rendered by War Department officials in the Philippines should stand, at least in the absence of legislation authorizing his department to conduct another round of independent inspections, Nagel sided with the migrants. By asserting the legality of his colleagues' decisions in the Philippines, Nagel's conclusion sanctified the U.S. state's claims to sovereignty in the Philippines at a moment of heightened imperial insecurities. Rumors of another Philippine revolution, in alliance with Japan, swirled in the Philippines, driving the U.S. security state to monitor an ever growing number of potential revolutionaries. In June 1911 a Philippine Constabulary agent submitted a report on an Indian peddler in Manila, "an intelligent man" who was leaving soon for Japan and China before returning to India. He concluded that the man was "an Indian political agitator." "He is a slick individual anyhow and I believe he could stand some close watching," the agent suggested. In 1911 the state authority to monitor an "agitator" in Manila and to admit South Asian migrants from Manila into Seattle helped to make the Philippines a part of the "United States."[8]

The state surveillance of anticolonial revolutionaries expanded apace in North America. By the time Har Dayal set off on his speaking tour of the Pacific Coast in 1913, Hopkinson's surveillance network extended to every stop along the way. On June 9, 1913, Hopkinson rushed a telegram to a U.S. immigration commissioner in Canada to ask for assistance. "Har Dayal, notorious Hindu revolutionist and anarchist, delivering course of lectures in Oregon and Washington; was in Astoria third instant," he wrote. "Would it be possible for any officers of your service to attend his lectures and take notes?" The commissioner requested that his boss, the commissioner general in Washington, DC, send agents "to attend the lectures given by this man, with a view to determining whether he comes within any of the excluded classes." Commissioner General Anthony Caminetti responded instantly. Through an informant Hopkinson also learned that Guru Dutt Kumar—who had been active in organizing and publicizing revolutionary work against the British Empire in Victoria, Vancouver, and Seattle—had recently left for Manila, where he hoped to establish a base to "supervise the work near China, Hong-Kong, Shanghai" and "to export to South America, Mexico, Chili [sic], Peru and Brazil." "Information I have received is to the effect that Kumar was going to the P.I. with a view to encourage Hindu immigration into the United States," Hopkinson wrote.[9]

Hopkinson's reports reinforced U.S. immigration officials' resolve to curb South Asian migrations from the unincorporated Philippines to the incorporated United States. Since 1912 Hopkinson had framed the Philippines as the weak link in the regulation of U.S. borders, an opening through which revolutionary ideas and revolutionary peoples could enter. In June 1913, three months into Woodrow Wilson's presidency, his appointees formalized a new approach. Commissioner General of Immigration Caminetti and Secretary of Labor William B. Wilson authorized immigration officers "to reject aliens coming from insular possessions unless it should appear that at the time of entry they were not members of the excluded classes or persons 'likely to become a public charge.'" In contrast to his predecessor, Secretary Wilson was willing to appropriate the authority to reconsider decisions made by U.S. officials in the Philippines. As much as the U.S. state had an investment in claiming the Philippines as a part of the "United States," it had a deeper commitment to demarcating a clear boundary between the metropole (or the U.S. nation) and its colonies (or the U.S. Empire). The decision to amend U.S. immigration regulations followed the reasoning of Supreme Court Justice Edward Douglass White, who in 1901 argued, "Whilst in an international sense Porto Rico was not a foreign country, since it was subject to the sovereignty of and was owned by the United States, it was foreign to the United States in a domestic sense, because the island had not been incorporated into the United States, but was merely appurtenant thereto as a possession."[10]

South Asians from the unincorporated U.S. possession of the Philippines would be "deported," not denied entry, but that legal distinction did nothing but underscore their subjection to the British and U.S. empires. In September 1913, when more than seventy of two hundred South Asians arriving from Manila received deportation orders in Seattle for "likely to become a public charge" and then appealed those orders in court, the local federal judge refused to grant them writs of habeas corpus. Immigration and deportation matters, he argued, rested with the executive branch, beyond the reach of judicial review. The deportation orders infuriated South Asians across North America. At a mass meeting in Vancouver, British Columbia, Rajah Singh articulated that collective rage by calling for vengeance. "All Hindustani, Mohomedans [sic], Sikhs should speak up for your rights, and I have to say this, that when these Canadians, Australians and New Zealanders do not allow us to enter into their country, why should we not drive them from India?" he exclaimed. "We should take those steps and we could start a struggle and exclude those people from our India, and I have great hope with our friends and our people that this work can be done." There was no question that "their country" now included the United States. "Hindustani Brothers, for what reason are we being deported?" asked another speaker, who had tried in vain to enter the United States with his family. He proposed to raise money to assist the deportees in Seattle and "to force the Indian Government to recognize our status." Attendees pledged $24,000.[11]

When Dayal began publishing *Ghadar* ("revolt" in Urdu) in November 1913, his unrelenting rebuke of empire and unremitting calls for collective action articulated and resonated with South Asian migrants' frustrations and aspirations. "It is fifty-six years since the Rebellion of 1857," he wrote, "now it is urgently necessary to have another." Dayal presented extensive reports on the many crimes committed by the British in India and the British criminalization of political activities, a combination of which, he argued, demanded concerted and direct action. In December 1913 *Ghadar* commemorated the attempted assassination of Lord Hardinge, the viceroy of India, one year earlier. "The echoes of that bomb have spread all over the world," Dayal argued, "for the newspapers in far distant countries published articles (about the incident) and asked what is wrong with the government of India that such a terroristic group has appeared." And he spelled out the future course of history. "Similarly, all events clearly indicate that the rain storm of 'revolt' is about to burst on India soon," he predicted, "which sweeping away the debris of (the ruins of) centuries will establish a republic." For an audience trying to make sense of their migrations and persecutions, Dayal's words provided direction and resolution. "It becomes immediately the duty of every patriot who reads this paper to become a soldier of the Rebellion," he implored, "to join the regiment of the Rebellion; to pre-pare for the Rebellion; to see visions of the Rebellion; to wait impatiently for the day of the Rebellion." Copies of *Ghadar* soon circulated in North America, India, East and Southeast Asia, Africa, and everywhere South Asians resided.[12]

Immigration Laws and the U.S. Security State

By January 1914 U.S. immigration authorities were on high alert for South Asian migrants' revolutionary activities. Commissioner Backus, head of the San Francisco office, provided a comprehensive report on "Hindu colonies" in the United States, highlighting the locations where Dayal and many other individuals engaged in anticolonial politics. He expressed particular concern over college students, or those claiming to be students to gain admission into the United States, "whose primary purposes are to foment and foster a revolu-tionary movement in India, to prepare and distribute circulars and pamphlets inciting their countrymen to such a revolution, to prepare and train leaders for the uprising, and to collect funds for the promotion of their plans." Those congregated at the University of California, Berkeley, Backus noted, went so far as to conduct "rifle and revolver practice" nearby. They also supported *Ghadar*, which he described as "highly revolutionary in character" and "suppressed by the British Government in India." In addition to editing the newspaper, Backus reported, Dayal was delivering "periodical addresses at various points on the Pacific Coast under the same auspices wherefrom such agitators as Emma Goldman secure their support." He hoped soon to gather evidence of Dayal's "apparently anarchistic advocacies" to initiate deportation proceedings. Backus vowed to commit his office "to scrutinize with the greatest care all Hindu ap-plications for admission in order that we may bring the fullest strength of the immigration laws against those who may be coming to join in the movement referred to."[13]

Dayal and his supporters struck back because they realized the intimate links between British and U.S. governments. In January 1914 Dayal wrote a letter to Charles H. Reily, a U.S. immigrant inspector stationed in Astoria, Oregon, to convey that he was, in Reily's paraphrasing, "aware of the plot of the British government and the United States Immigration Service to 'kidnap him' because of his activities in behalf of the Hindu Nationalist party." Unless Reily replied personally to suspend the plot, Dayal threatened to divulge it to a San Francisco newspaper and to report to Reily's superiors that he had received improper subsidies from the British government. Although Reily dismissed Dayal's letter, he could not so easily disregard a long series of threats from local residents. "At various times since June, 1913, at which time inquiry concerning these Hindus was first directed, I have been approached by Hindus who have warned me if any effort was made to find either Har Dayal or R[am] Chandra [another Ghadar leader] they would personally see that I was 'blown up,' or 'pushed off the dock at night,' or my family molested," Reily reported. "It was explained to me that the work of Har Dayal, and the interests of the Hindu Nationalist party were of such importance that rather than permit any interferance [sic] with their plans they would cheerfully dispose of me in some manner." "As evidence of their proficiency in the art of 'blowing people up,'" he added, "I was assured that most of the members of the Hindu nationalist party were also 'i.w.w.'s.'"[14]

As the revolutionary movement against the British Empire mobilized increasingly against the U.S. state, U.S. immigration officials redoubled their efforts to secure the United States from South Asian revolutionaries. At the end of January 1914 Commissioner Backus decided that it was time to arrest Dayal since he "ha[d] been connected with alleged revolutionary movements in this vicinity for some time" and "may be considered anarchistic." "This office has no definite information as to the exact period of his arrival," he admitted, "but it is believed that evidence can be obtained showing his presence in London, Paris and Martinique within three years, from which his movements can be traced to the United States." As Backus's request moved up the chain of command, Dayal arrived in Washington, DC, to appear before the congressional Committee on Immigration and Naturalization. He wished to voice his opposition to an immigration bill prohibiting Asian laborers. Commissioner General Caminetti secretly informed Representative John L. Burnett, chair of the committee, of Dayal's impending arrest warrant so that "it may be possible to illicit [sic] some testimony from him which otherwise would not come to light." Dayal did not testify before the committee, but he evidently stopped by Caminetti's office to protest that Asians were categorized "with all idiots, imbeciles, feeble-minded persons, and so forth" in the bill. In his testimony before the committee, Caminetti conveyed Dayal's objection, identifying Dayal only as "a cultured man and a graduate of Oxford University," and suggested revising the bill's language to deflect criticisms from "some people of that race."[15]

Besides recounting his conversation with Dayal, who might have said a lot more in person, Caminetti lobbied fervently for a more stringent immigration law and a more forceful administrative state. Discretionary and emergency measures, such as the examination of aliens arriving from the Philippines, he insisted, were not enough. "We have not been able to exclude, under the present conditions of the law," he stated, "more than 50 per cent." Like Chinese immigration before it, "Hindu immigration" had grown "stealthily" over the years, to number twenty thousand to thirty thousand, according to Caminetti, far in excess of the official figure on legal entrants (6,656). "The question is, shall we allow this experience we have had on the Pacific coast to be repeated with the Hindu before we take action," he asked, "or shall we profit by the experience of the past and meet the question now?" In addition to a new immigration law, Caminetti appealed for greater resources from Congress to build "patrolling facilities on both borders and on the extensive coasts, east, south, west, and on the Great Lakes," and to improve "water patrol particularly in the Northwest," all in an effort "to protect ourselves from people who desire to come in surreptitiously." In his letter to Congress, Secretary of Labor Wilson transmitted the same message, arguing that indirect "expedients and makeshifts . . . to prevent a large and ever-increasing influx of laborers of that race, who to all intents and purposes are 'coolies' in the same sense that Chinese were regarded," now required explicit legislation and "direct methods."[16]

As one of the most outspoken and visible anticolonial activists in the United States, Dayal came to represent the growing rift between the U.S. state and South Asian communities. With an arrest warrant dated February 10, 1914, based on the premise that he had arrived in "an unknown port, subsequent to the 26th day of February 1911," U.S. immigration authorities arrested Dayal in March 1914 after his return to California. "For many months I have been spied upon by British secret service operatives," he informed local newspapers, "but have gone about my affairs openly and have not tuned my statements or modulated my declarations because of their presence." He condemned the Wilson administration for "licking the boots of England" and for demonstrating its "despicable pro-British subservience" by arresting him. "This is a political question and not an ordinary immigration case," he asserted. His case revealed the emerging alliance between Britain and the United States around race and empire. "It is simply ridiculous to think that I am being prosecuted in the United States and in the twentieth century because of my ideas," Dayal said. "I have broken no laws, and I have not advocated breaking of any laws. The only overt act I have committed is advocating the overthrow of the British in India by an armed revolt." He exuded confidence. "I am not afraid of any Government," he wrote in *Ghadar*. "If I am turned out of this country I can make preparations for the Ghadr in any other country."[17]

Dayal mounted a challenge that placed U.S. officials on the defensive. "The Government of Great Britain has had no part in the matter nor has it either directly or indirectly requested either the arrest or the deportation of the alien," Caminetti announced in a statement to deny Dayal's accusations. Dayal's attorney, in the meantime, stressed in his brief that his client's articles and speeches were "incorrectly and most unfavorably translated . . . to give violent and anarchistic significance." "Mr. Dayal has never advocated terrorism," he explained, "but only a national rebellion." At bottom, what Dayal might or might not have stated did not matter legally, his attorney argued, since he "had actually and continuously been a resident of the United States of America" for longer than three years. Dayal conveyed the same message directly to Caminetti. Within two days of Dayal's arrest, the acting commissioner of immigration at Ellis Island certified that Dayal had indeed arrived in New York from San Juan, Puerto Rico, on February 9, 1911, three years plus one day before the arrest warrant was issued. That he had sailed from an unincorporated U.S. possession might have served as a bone of contention if the date of arrival had been even a day later—Dayal's attorney could have argued that he had landed in the United States when he set foot on Puerto Rico on February 3, 1911—but, as it was, U.S. officials knew they had missed the legal window of opportunity by one day.[18]

Even with his legal argument in hand, Dayal could not ignore the power of the modern state to legitimize and consolidate race and empire. At the same time that Dayal was arrested in San Francisco in March 1914, Gurdit Singh chartered the *Komagata Maru* in Hong Kong to transport nearly four hundred South Asians to Canada, in defiance of Canadian immigration restrictions. At stopovers in Shanghai, Moji, and Yokohama, those affiliated with the Ghadar movement delivered fiery speeches against the British Empire and circulated copies of *Ghadar* to passengers. The arrival of the *Komagata Maru* in British Columbia in May precipitated a standoff between South Asian migrants and Canadian officials that reverberated around the world. Refused entry and receiving deportation orders, the passengers lived nearly two months aboard the vessel in Vancouver's harbor, with their once hopeful outlooks and daily living conditions deteriorating week by week. The fate of the *Komagata Maru* consumed the attention of Canadian, British, and U.S. authorities and South Asian communities, as it came to symbolize the legitimacy of the state to restrict immigration and to suppress revolutionary movements. "The Hindusthanees, subjected to eternal hunger and maltreatment of every sort in their native land," Taraknath Das wrote, "want to be recognized as human beings and have equal rights to come to Canada or any other place in the World just as others have the right to come to India." The impasse concluded in July with a Canadian naval cruiser forcibly escorting the *Komagata Maru* west toward the Pacific.[19]

In contrast to the drama unfolding in Vancouver's harbor, Dayal's stay in the United States ended on an anticlimactic note. In early April 1914 he sent a telegram to the Department of State to offer a concession. "Considering all circumstances we have decided to discontinue publication in this country of Hindu Nationalist anti-British paper and other similar propaganda here," he related. "No necessity now of persecuting educated political refugees." Commissioner Backus, in the meantime, was investigating rumors that Dayal had traveled outside of the United States after his initial entry. Dayal probably sensed that the U.S. government was not going to allow the facts of his case to impede his deportation. At the end of April, Backus demanded that Dayal appear before him for further examination, but no one knew his whereabouts. A short time later Backus learned from "an authentic source" that Dayal had left for Switzerland, a turn of events that drove him to seek revenge. Backus wanted to collect the $1,000 bond. His superiors disagreed. "At the time the bond was taken it had not been shown, nor has it since been established," the commissioner general stated, "that the three-year period had not expired—indeed, it seemed quite clear that it had at the time the proceedings were instituted." The Department of Labor canceled the bond. But the Bureau of Immigration refused to withdraw the arrest warrant in case of Dayal's return because "some advantage might result from not having absolutely closed the previous proceedings."[20]

Even as Dayal evaded U.S. authorities, his departure pointed to the growing authority of the modern state to secure nation and empire from racialized and radicalized subjects. Amid his confrontation with the Bureau of Immigration, eleven individuals in Delhi faced charges that they had conspired with one another and with others, including Dayal, to murder public officials. During their trial in May 1914, the prosecuting attorney reportedly "read an effusion of Hardyal's [sic] which was a mixture of religion and anarchy." He also read passages from *Ghadar* "to show the revolutionary trend of the publication." The U.S. consul in Bombay, in turn, requested from British officials information on Dayal's "alleged anarchistic activities" and on all "suspected or known to be anarchists" leaving India for the United States. The prosecution and deportation of itinerant anarchists, presumed to signify and include anticolonial revolutionaries, seemingly demanded transimperial and interstate collaboration. In July 1914, in Geneva, Dayal explained why he had decided to leave the United States. "I understood that my presence in the country was undesirable, as I was carrying on an active anti-British propaganda among the Hindus on the Pacific Coast, and certain unfounded charges have been preferred by the English Government against me with reference to incidents in India," he informed U.S. officials. "I hope that the U.S. government will not needlessly molest my poor and ignorant compatriots who live in the United States and cherish dreams of the freedom of their country." As Dayal knew from his own experience, that wish would not be granted.[21]

John Bull, Uncle Sam, and Bhagwan Singh

Bhagwan Singh, a fellow Ghadar leader, learned firsthand the global reach of the Anglo-American alliance that would haunt and stifle revolutionary politics in the opening decades of the twentieth century. According to British police and intelligence reports, Singh left India around 1909 for the British Federated Malay States "on account of having got into trouble through taking away a married woman." A religious leader (*granthi*) by training, Singh worked at a *gurdwara* (a Sikh place of worship) until he came into a quarrel with local Sikhs for "preaching sedition." He moved to Hong Kong in 1910 and secured a post at another gurdwara. His tenure in that British colony proved even more scandalous. "Bhagwan Singh had got himself into bad odour by consorting with loose Chinese women, which is a serious religious offence from the Sikh point of view," a British police officer reported, "and his preaching, although it could not at that time be proved to be actually seditious, was certainly directed against the British Government, and encouraged a considerable amount of loose talk." In May 1913 Singh departed for British Columbia, where he "openly preached sedition." He was deported in November 1913 for having given false statements when entering Canada. He sailed back across the Pacific to Japan and, in the spring of 1914, greeted the *Komagata Maru* as it stopped over on its way to Vancouver. The British embassy in Tokyo related that Singh "sold a pistol to the leader of the expedition, Gurdit Singh . . . and made speeches of extreme violence to those on board."[22]

Singh's transpacific movements and connections unnerved British and U.S. officials. In Japan he lived with Muhammed Barakatullah, who had been a professor of Hindi-Urdu languages at the University of Tokyo and editor of *Islamic Fraternity*, a pan-Islamic newspaper banned in India. By the time Singh arrived in Japan, Barakatullah's anti-British politics had already led to the loss of his teaching position and the Japanese government's suppression of his newspaper. Barakatullah and Singh decided to devote their energies to the Ghadar Party in the United States, taking over leadership positions in San Francisco just as Dayal fled to Switzerland. When war broke out between Britain and Germany, Barakatullah and Singh toured with Ram Chandra up and down the Pacific

Coast to urge Ghadarites to incite a revolution in India. Singh himself left San Francisco in October 1914, traveling under a false name, and landed in Manila the following month on a journey that he hoped would lead back to India. In an interview published in the *Manila Daily Bulletin* in March 1915, Singh explained how state repression—rather than disputes with fellow Sikhs or his sexual escapades—had forced him to move repeatedly:

> For three years I officiated as a priest among my people in Hongkong. . . . I mingled among the Indian soldiers garrisoned there and preached revolution to them. They were all opposed to British oppression and gave me their assurance that they were ready to fight for their country when the time came. . . . The British authorities finally became suspicious. They were afraid of my influence. A false charge was brought against me and I was place[d] under arrest. Their case against me, however, was so flimsy that they were obliged to order my release. Then I went to Canada and British Columbia. I began there as a teacher among the Indians in that country and when the British learned of my mission, I was ordered deported to Hongkong. I knew what would happen to me if I was taken back there, so I succeeded in escaping from the steamer in Japan. I was in Yokohama when the Yamagata [*sic*] Maru stopped there with the Indian[s] bound for Canada, who were afterwards deported to India, and I went aboard and delivered a lecture to them. Finally a secret service man who was sent to watch me told me that the British authorities were after me and advised me to go away. I then went to the United States and was working among my people there when the war broke out.

Reproduced, shared, and filed by U.S. agents in Manila, Singh's interview illustrated both the apparent necessity and the perpetual futility of state surveillance. British authorities could never quite contain his movements or his ideas.[23]

To U.S. authorities grappling with anticolonial revolutionaries of their own in the Philippines, Singh's arrival in Manila generated anxiety and insecurity. In January 1915, unable to find a non-British ship to India, Singh left Manila to try to reach the Dutch East Indies by way of the southern islands of the Philippines. Suspecting that Singh was up to no good, an Englishman working as a U.S. customs inspector in the Sulu archipelago arrested him for attempting to incite an insurrection among the Moros. Singh was eventually transferred to Zamboanga, on the island of Mindanao, where U.S. authorities interrogated him. After a short time, an agent of the Philippine Constabulary and the customs office in Zamboanga reported, "I found out that he had not been talking, or had he in any way or manner had any connection with the moros [*sic*]." In his statement, though, Singh embraced revolution. "My business is to get all of my countrymen to assist in the general uprising which is about to take place (probably next month) in India against the English Government," he said. "It was for this purpose that I have visited the United States, Canada, and Mexico and am now here in the Philippines." Claiming that German agents had promised him at least a million rifles, Singh avowed that, once back in Punjab, he would command "an army of three or four hundred thousand men." He was not alone, he said, for there were anticolonial organizers like him "in all parts of the world wherever any of our people live."[24]

Released after being deemed "not a serious menace to public order though perhaps somewhat unbalanced mentally," Singh decided to test the bounds of political freedom in the Philippines. When he returned to Manila, he frankly informed the governor general, "I am working for the revolution in India." He also recounted his personal story to the *Manila Daily Bulletin* and declared, "The revolution has already begun." British authorities had heard enough. In May 1915 the U.S. consul in Hong Kong related to the governor general's office in Manila that British colonial authorities had approached him several times about Singh. The consul recommended strongly that Singh "be deported to Hongkong or Singapore and the authorities notified at the time of his deportation and the vessel by which he will arrive at either place." The Philippine Constabulary investigated the matter and concluded that there were "no grounds upon which to base legal proceedings against this Indian." When British officials demanded again a few months later that "Indian agitators in Manila" be deported to Hong Kong, U.S. authorities refused politely. But they also had Manila's secret agents warn the "agitators" that the government "could not permit any activity on the part of the Indians residing in these Islands looking to the creation of disturbances in a neighboring colony, and that further activity on their part would result in immediate steps being taken to rid the Islands of them." The U.S. colonial government, with agents at "every meeting of the Indians in Manila," pledged to monitor revolutionary activities in the Philippines.[25]

Singh, for his part, continued to evade British and U.S. authorities to advance his work against the British Empire. In June 1915 he left Manila for Japan and reportedly established communications with German agents in Shanghai. Four months later he and a compatriot traveled to Tientsin (Tianjin), "where they were nearly captured by the British." By June 1916, according to information gathered by British officials and shared with U.S. officials, Singh was back in San Francisco, having "concealed his traces so skil[l]fully that it ha[d] not been possible to ascertain by what vessel he arrived." He quickly sailed to

Panama, traveling under the alias B. Pritam, and thence to Cuba, from which he was forced to leave because of a physical ailment (trachoma). Singh returned to Panama, staying at "a hotel and restaurant of more or less bad repute and which used to be a resort for Germans." "Pritam while in Panama formed secret meetings with the East Indians and collected funds for the purpose of starting a revolution to free India from British rules [sic]," the U.S. minister reported. Nearly all four hundred East Indians in Panama "promised to support the movement." The British minister to Panama, the U.S. minister noted, actively sought to have Singh deported, accusing him of being a Turk and pressuring the government of Panama to apply its immigration laws against "members of the Turkish race and certain other races." Given fourteen days "to prove he was not a Turk or leave Panama," Singh headed back to San Francisco.[26]

Singh's movements—and the Ghadar movement—led to the expansion of the U.S. security state across the Americas. In the wake of Singh's forced departure and local protests against it, U.S. authorities in Panama maintained a "practically complete list of East Indians resident on the Isthmus of Panama in the vicinity of the Canal Zone," prioritizing "all members of the Ghadr (or Gadar) Party" and keeping the "leaders of these men" under "observation, and any information received . . . transmitted to the American Minister to Panama." Claiming authority over the Panama Canal Zone translated into monitoring South Asian revolutionaries. The U.S. government's surveillance of the Ghadar movement also intensified in San Francisco. As Singh assumed control of *Ghadar* headquarters in the opening months of 1917, after an acrimonious struggle with Ram Chandra, U.S. officials decided that the moment to strike had arrived. The United States was about to enter World War I, in alliance with the British Empire, an act that the attorney general feared might drive Ghadar leaders to seek refuge elsewhere. In April 1917 he instructed U.S. Attorney John W. Preston of San Francisco to carry out immediate arrests in the "Hindoo revolution matter." "Advise arrest in advance declaration War since fear escape Ram Chandra," he explained in a telegram. Feeling besieged, Singh decided to flee to Mexico before it was too late. Contesting the British Empire meant contending with the U.S. Empire and its security apparatus.[27]

Once the United States entered World War I, various agents and agencies of the U.S. state bolstered and coordinated their efforts to suppress revolutionary movements. On April 18, 1917, U.S. immigration authorities in Naco, Arizona, detained Singh for appearing "very suspicious." At first he reportedly claimed that "he was an English Jew by the name of William James" on his way to visit his white "sweetheart." Assuming Singh to be connected with the "Indian Revolution movement," the immigrant inspector immediately contacted the Bureau of Investigation, the forerunner to the Federal Bureau of Investigation. When examined by a Bureau agent and the immigrant inspector the next day, Singh explained that he was planning to "preach" to "my people" in Mexico about "their duties as Hindus, about nationalism." Pressed by the agent if that meant "to teach your countrymen to raise up in arms against the English Government in India," Singh replied: "We are not allowed to speak anything in India; so we are getting new ideas in this country and so we are teaching them to our people so that they will not be behind." Not satisfied, the agent asked repeatedly if Singh was, in fact, "a revolutionist against the British Government in India." "If the English are going to oppress my people in India I am against them. . . I want to see India enjoy freedom and happiness like other countries," Singh responded. "If this is a crime, then let me be a criminal."[28]

The U.S. state indeed deemed Singh a criminal, issuing a warrant for his arrest, a turn of events that expanded and sharpened Singh's critique of empire. In July 1917, as he and dozens of fellow South Asian revolutionaries awaited trial for violating U.S. neutrality laws, Singh wrote a piercing column on U.S. claims to be fighting for "the protection of democracy." "If America has entered [World War I] with the purpose of emancipating small nations then what need is there for a revolution, for she will liberate all," he posed. "The question is, but will she fulfill her purpose?" Long before the Paris Peace Conference, Singh knew the answer. Having "never dreamt of endeavouring to secure the emancipation of smaller nations," he argued, the United States offered no hope, for "the cause of the evil existing in India to-day is the friendship of America and England." The contradiction between empire and democracy was too stark to ignore. "When a nation . . . keeps in subjection the Philippines and Porto Rico," he observed, "then her claim appears a matter of astonishment to the whole world." As Singh penned those words, U.S. Attorney Preston was busy compiling his writings to prosecute him. That was the state of affairs South Asian revolutionaries faced in the United States and around the world. By daring to confront the colonial roots and colonial objectives of the modern states flying the Union Jack and the Stars and Stripes, they bore the brunt of state repression.[29]

NOTES

1. Emily C. Brown, *Har Dayal: Hindu Revolutionary and Rationalist* (Tucson: University of Arizona Press, 1975), 9–81, quotes from 18 and 57.

2. Brown, *Har Dayal*, 81–126, quote from 86; P. A. Baker to Commissioner-General of Immigration, April 3, 1914; W. A. Clark, Academic Secretary, Stanford University, to A. Caminetti, April 21, 1914; File 53572/92–92A, Records of the Immigration and Natural-

ization Service (INS), Record Group (RG) 85, National Archives and Records Administration, Washington, DC (hereafter NARA).

3. Alfred W. McCoy, *Policing America's Empire: The United States, the Philippines, and the Rise of the Surveillance State* (Madison: University of Wisconsin Press, 2009); Brown, *Har Dayal*, 111–12, 131–33, Hopkinson quote on 133; Joan M. Jensen, *Passage from India: Asian Indian Immigrants in North America* (New Haven, CT: Yale University Press, 1988), 163–64.

4. A. Caminetti to Immigration Service, Seattle and Portland, June 12, 1913 (telegram); Wm. C. Hopkinson to John L. Zurbrick, August 2, 1913; Samuel W. Backus to Commissioner-General of Immigration, January 30, 1914; J. B. Densmore, Acting Secretary of Labor, to Samuel W. Backus, February 10, 1914; File 53572/92–92A, INS, RG 85, NARA.

5. Har Dayal to A. Caminetti, March 29, 1914 (telegram); Charles Sferlazzo, Attorney for Har Dayal, "Defendant's Brief, In the Matter of the arrest of Har Dayal, alleged anarchist arrested under the authority of Departmental Warrant dated February 10th, 1914," n.d.; Samuel Backus to Commissioner-General of Immigration, April 24, 1914; Hearing on Har Dayal by F. H. Ainsworth on Angel Island, March 26, 1914; File 53572/92–92A, INS, RG 85, NARA; *San Francisco Chronicle*, March 27, 1914.

6. Ellis DeBruler to Commissioner-General of Immigration, January 11, 1911; Herbert W. Meyers, "Aliens' Brief," in the Matter of the Arrest of Arjan Singh et al., February 28, 1911; File 53154/2–2A, INS, RG 85, NARA.

7. Ellis DeBruler to Commissioner-General of Immigration, January 11, 1911; Daniel J. Keefe, "Memorandum for the Acting Secretary," January 27, 1911; File 53154/2–2A, INS, RG 85, NARA.

8. Charles Nagel, "Memorandum," March 7, 1911, File 53154/2–2A, INS, RG 85, NARA; Agent 30 to Colonel, June 27, 1911, Harry H. Bandholtz Papers, Bentley Historical Library, University of Michigan.

9. Seema Sohi, *Echoes of Mutiny: Race, Surveillance, and Indian Anticolonialism in North America* (New York: Oxford University Press, 2014), 84–91, 126; John H. Clark to Commissioner-General of Immigration, June 10, 1913 [including Hopkinson's telegram]; A. Caminetti to Immigration Service, Seattle and Portland, June 12, 1913; Wm. C. Hopkinson to John H. Clark, September 9, 1913; G. D. Kumar to "My dear Dass," July 8, 1913 (copy); Tarak[nath Das] to "My dear Harnam," August 13, 1913 (copy); File 53572/92–92A, INS, RG 85, NARA.

10. Sohi, *Echoes of Mutiny*, 124–26; Amy Kaplan, *The Anarchy of Empire in the Making of U.S. Culture* (Cambridge, MA: Harvard University Press, 2002), 2; *Downes v. Bidwell*, 182 U.S. 244.

11. Sohi, *Echoes of Mutiny*, 124–25; "Report of Proceedings at Meeting of Hindus, Held in O'Brien Hall, Vancouver, B.C., on September 29, 1913. With Reference to 73 Hindus, held by United States Immigration Authorities at Seattle, Wash.," File 52903/110-C, INS, RG 85, NARA. Seven of the two hundred were rejected ostensibly for medical reasons (hookworm), while seventy-three were ordered deported for "likely to become a public charge."

12. Translations of *Ghadar* by Har Dayal in his immigration file, File 53572/92–92A, INS, RG 85, NARA; F. C. Isemonger and J. Slattery, *An Account of the Ghadr Conspiracy*

(*1913–1915*) (1919; Berkeley: Folklore Institute, 1998), 20. The issues, not all of which were dated, are from March 3, 1914, December 9 and 23, 1913.

13. Samuel W. Backus to Commissioner-General of Immigration, January 23, 1914, File 52903/110-D, INS, RG 85, NARA.

14. Charles H. Reily to Acting Inspector in Charge, Portland, Oregon, January 14, 1914, File 53572/92–92A, INS, RG 85, NARA.

15. Samuel W. Backus to Commissioner-General of Immigration, January 30, 1914; *Washington Post*, February 10, 1914; A. Caminetti to John L. Burnett, February 7, 1914; File 53572/92–92A, INS, RG 85, NARA; Brown, *Har Dayal*, 154; 63rd Congress, 2nd Session, *Hearings before the Committee on Immigration . . . Relative to Restriction of Immigration of Hindu Laborers*, Part 2 (Washington, DC: Government Printing Office, 1914), 85–86.

16. 63rd Congress, 2nd Session, *Hearings before the Committee on Immigration . . . Relative to Restriction of Immigration of Hindu Laborers*, Part 1 (Washington, DC: Government Printing Office, 1914), 45–46, 48, 50; 63rd Congress, 2nd Session, *Hearings before the Committee on Immigration . . . Relative to Restriction of Immigration of Hindu Laborers*, Part 4 (Washington, DC: Government Printing Office, 1914), 141.

17. J. B. Densmore, Acting Secretary of Labor, to Samuel W. Backus, February 10, 1914; *San Francisco Chronicle*, March 29, 1914; *San Francisco Bulletin*, March 27, 1914; *San Francisco Examiner*, March 28, 1914; File 53572/92–92A, INS, RG 85, NARA; "Har Dayal on His Arrest," *Ghadar*, March 31, 1914, translated copy in Box 1, Neutrality Case Files, Records of the U.S. District Attorney, RG 118, National Archives, San Bruno, California (hereafter NASB).

18. A. Caminetti, Memorandum, April 4, 1914; Charles Sferlazzo, Attorney for Har Dayal, "Defendant's Brief, In the Matter of the arrest of Har Dayal, alleged anarchist arrested under the authority of Departmental Warrant dated February 10th, 1914," n.d.; Har Dayal to A. Caminetti, March 29, 1914 (telegram); Acting Commissioner, Ellis Island, to Commissioner of Immigration, Angel Island Station, Certificate of Admission of Alien, March 27, 1914; Acting Commissioner P. A. Baker to Commissioner-General of Immigration, April 3, 1914; File 53572/92–92A, INS, RG 85, NARA.

19. Sohi, *Echoes of Mutiny*, 134–44; Tapan K. Mukherjee, *Taraknath Das: Life and Letters of a Revolutionary in Exile* (Calcutta: National Council of Education, Jadavpur University, 1998), 57. For a fuller account, see Hugh Johnston, *The Voyage of the Komagata Maru: The Sikh Challenge to Canada's Colour Bar* (Delhi: Oxford University Press, 1979); Renisa Mawani, *Across Oceans of Law: The Komagata Maru and Jurisdiction in the Time of Empire* (Durham, NC: Duke University Press, 2018).

20. Robert Lansing, Counselor, Department of State, to Secretary of Labor, April 7, 1914 (quoting Dayal's telegram dated April 4, 1914); Backus to Immigration Bureau, Washington, DC, April 1, 1914 (telegram); Samuel W. Backus to United States Fidelity and Guaranty Co., April 28, May 6, 1914; Charles Sferlazzo to Samuel W. Backus, May 2, 1914; Borland and Johns to Samuel W. Backus, May 4, 1914; Samuel W. Backus to Commissioner-General of Immigration, May 11, June 20, 1914; W. J. P., Department of Labor, "Memo. For Mr. Larned," May 26, 1914; Acting Secretary to Commissioner of Immigration, Angel Island Station, June 13, 1914; Commissioner-General to Commissioner of Immigration, San Francisco, June 29, 1914; File 53572/92–92A, INS, RG 85, NARA.

21. *Times of India*, May 27, 1914; Henry D. Baker to Secretary of State, May 27, 1914; Har Dayal to "Sir," July 13, 1914; File 53572/92–92A, INS, RG 85, NARA; *Sedition Committee Report 1918* (1918; Calcutta: New Age Publishers Private Limited, 1973), 143–46.

22. C. McI. Messer, Captain, Superintendent of Police, May 17, 1915; British Embassy, Tokyo, "Bhagwan Singh's Antecedents" (confidential), June 11, 1915; Box 10, Neutrality Case Files, RG 118, NASB.

23. Sohi, *Echoes of Mutiny*, 50; "Bhagwan Singh" [no author and no date, but most likely written by British agents for Preston]; John W. Green, Chief, Secret Service Bureau, Department of Police, City of Manila, to F. N. Berry, Acting Secretary to the Governor-General, May 4, 1917; Box 10, Neutrality Case Files, RG 118, NASB.

24. John W. Green to F. N. Berry, May 4, 1917, Box 10; Mr. Blanford, "Documents from Manila," August 2, 1917 (including full copies of Singh's statement, as reported by the Customs Secret Service Agent, Zamboanga, February 13, 1915, and the agent's report, March 1, 1915), Box 7; J. S. Robertson, Custom Secret Service Agent and Philippine Constabulary Agent, Zamboanga, to Chief Custom Secret Service, "Narrative Report, for February 1915," March 1, 1915, Box 2; Perry L. Machlan, Customs Secret Service Agent, Jolo, to Chief, Customs Secret Service, February 13, 1915, Box 2; Neutrality Case Files, RG 118, NASB.

25. F. W. Carpenter, Governor of Mindanao and Sulu, to Executive Secretary, March 25, 1915; John W. Green to F. N. Berry, May 4, 1917; George E. Anderson to Executive Secretary, May 24, 1915; S. Ferguson, Acting Executive Secretary, to George E. Anderson, August 9, 1915; Herman Hall, Chief of Constabulary, to Executive Secretary, June 3, 1915; Box 10, Neutrality Case Files, RG 118, NASB.

26. Notes on defendants, n.d., 30–33, Box 4; Wm. Jennings Price, American Minister, to Secretary of State (confidential), October 30, 1917, Box 1 (and Box 12); American Legation, Panama, "Confidential Memorandum No. 124," to Colonel Commanding, Panama Canal Department, November 12, 1917, Box 12; Neutrality Case Files, RG 118, NASB.

27. Captain, C.A.C., Intelligence Officer, Panama Canal Department, to Chief, Military Intelligence Branch, Washington, DC, March 19, 1918; Gregory to US Attorney, San Francisco, April 6, 1917; Box 2, Neutrality Case Files, RG 118, NASB; Sohi, *Echoes of Mutiny*, 171.

28. A. A. Hopkins, "In Re: Bhagwan Singh (Hindu) Fugitive," Warren, Arizona, April 22, 1917, Box 7, Neutrality Case Files, RG 118, NASB.

29. "Extract from Yugantar of Bhagwan Singh," July 1917, Box 4, Neutrality Case Files, RG 118, NASB.

13. INDIGENOUS CHILD REMOVAL AND TRANSIMPERIAL INDIGENOUS WOMEN'S ACTIVISM ACROSS SETTLER COLONIAL NATIONS IN THE LATE TWENTIETH CENTURY

Margaret D. Jacobs

In the 1970s Mollie Dyer, an Australian Indigenous community organizer, was working for the Aboriginal Legal Service in Fitzroy, an inner-city neighborhood of Melbourne.[1] She provided representation for Indigenous defendants in court, offered general welfare advice, and assisted with the running of a hostel for Indigenous people recently released from jail and for the temporarily homeless. Mollie was deeply dismayed to become acquainted with hundreds of Indigenous children who had been removed from their families and then put in child welfare institutions or fostered or adopted out to non-Aboriginal families.[2]

At nearly the same time, eight thousand miles across the Pacific Ocean, Maxine Robbins, a member of the Yakama Indian Nation, was serving as a social worker with the Washington State Department of Social and Health Services. As she carried out her work, Maxine became deeply pained to learn that every year the state removed about thirty-five Yakama children from their families, took them off the reservation, and placed them with non-Indian foster or adoptive families.[3] Maxine and Mollie each agonized over why so many of their communities' children were living apart from their families. Over the ensuing decades each woman helped bring attention to and address an Indigenous child welfare crisis within their communities and their nations.

In the late 1970s Mollie and Maxine's lives became intertwined. On an overseas study tour, Mollie ended up staying with Maxine. The two women became fast friends, and they learned from one another that the Indigenous child welfare crises they had witnessed firsthand reflected not just a local problem within their own communities but a phenomenon that extended across settler colonial nations. The United States, Canada, and Australia had been removing Indigenous children from their families and communities for nearly a hundred years as a strategy of empire, of dispossessing Indigenous peoples and laying claim to their lands. By the 1960s Indigenous children were dramatically over-represented in the child welfare systems of these three former British colonies. This was not a mere coincidence. All three settler colonial nations had studied one another's management of Indigenous peoples.[4]

But transimperial networks across settler colonial nations did not just pro-duce similar ways of managing and controlling Indigenous peoples; they also grew from and fostered Indigenous activism. Maxine and Mollie developed their own transimperial network; they gathered knowledge and strength from one another as they confronted policies and practices that threatened to de-stroy Indigenous families and extinguish Indigenous communities altogether. This network grew out of Indigenous women's grassroots community work to reclaim the care of Indigenous children by Indigenous families and communi-ties. This essay follows the transimperial jetstreams of Mollie and Maxine in the 1970s as they discovered the ubiquity of Indigenous child removal, befriended one another, and worked in concert to reverse the flow of Indigenous children out of their communities. By tracking their movements across settler colonial empires, I demonstrate how transimperial sensibilities shaped Indigenous women's movements for self-determination in the late twentieth century.

Settler Colonial Nations as Empires

Both North America and Australia had been colonized by the British Empire. In contrast to British colonies such as India, these colonies were characterized by large-scale settlement. The incoming population displaced the local Indig-enous inhabitants from their land and replaced them with families subject to the British Crown. As the United States gained independence and Canada and Australia federated, they continued to interact with Indigenous peoples as set-tler colonial powers, operating under what the historian Patrick Wolfe has la-beled "the logic of elimination." Whereas other types of colonial systems sought to harness the local population for labor, settler colonial authorities prized the acquisition of land and thus sought to dispossess Indigenous people, forcibly moving or even eliminating them.[5]

Indigenous child removal constituted a key means by which settler colo-nial powers undermined Indigenous communities. From the late nineteenth century to World War II, Australian, Canadian, and American officials all engaged in the practice of separating Indigenous children from their families and communities, often forcibly, and shipping them to segregated institutions far from their homes, where authorities ostensibly sought to assimilate them into the mainstream. Institutions did not prepare their Indigenous wards to be fully equal citizens, however, but to be "useful" landless laborers who would fill low-wage, mostly unskilled occupations on the margins of settler colonial economies. In short, child removal constituted an aggressive attempt to eliminate Indigenous peoples through assimilation.[6]

Indigenous Family Survival under the Logic of Elimination

Mollie and Maxine came of age in the mid-twentieth century at a time when Indigenous families were reeling from generations of child removal. Mollie was born in 1927, when Australian state policies of "protection" were in full force. Her family, in fact, experienced child removal firsthand. Police had summarily removed Mollie's mother, Margaret Tucker, and her aunt May from Cumeroogunga, the Aboriginal mission on the Murray River that separated New South Wales from Victoria, despite the vehement resistance of Tucker's mother. Officials placed Margaret and May, ages thirteen and eleven, at the Cootamundra Girls Home in New South Wales to be trained as domestic servants and placed in white households, their Aboriginality destined for obliteration.[7]

Margaret Tucker resisted this plan, however, and became an activist. In the 1930s she served as a vice president of the newly formed Australian Aborigines' League of Victoria, which sponsored a Day of Mourning on Australia Day 1938, the sesquicentenary of Australia's founding.[8] After World War II Tucker served on the executive board of a new multiracial national organization called the Council for Aboriginal Rights and was later active in the Federal Council for Aboriginal Advancement, which led a successful campaign for a 1967 national referendum that eliminated a racially discriminatory clause from the Constitution and for the first time provided for the counting of Aboriginal people in the nation's census.[9] In 1979 Tucker published her autobiography, *If Everyone Cared*, which highlighted her removal from her family and helped to launch a movement to investigate the Stolen Generations in the 1990s.

Mollie Dyer inherited her mother's activist bent. She came of age among a new generation of Indigenous activists who increasingly sought greater self-determination in the 1960s and 1970s.[10] They influenced the federal government to fund a number of new agencies, including the Aboriginal Health Service and Aboriginal Legal Service, where Mollie worked for five years.[11] Like her mother, Mollie dedicated her activism to stopping child removal. She told a reporter in 1979 that "all her life she remember[ed] seeing Aboriginal mothers fretting for children who had been removed from their care."[12] She also learned and practiced Aboriginal women's ways of caring for extended kin and other children in need. She began fostering Aboriginal children alongside her own six children beginning in 1959, eventually taking in twenty-five foster children.[13] Jenny Munro, an Aboriginal activist in Victoria, called this the "grandmother law coming out in Mollie without her even realising." Munro explained, "Every child that presented, they were hers. It didn't matter whose child they were. She looked after them. . . . Didn't even know it then, but we were articulating it—the old law, the old way, the old system. The extended family. The way we looked after our own family was the way that we would survive."[14]

Maxine was about the same age as Mollie. Maxine's father had been a tribal policeman who had built a home in 1910 on the Yakama reservation. He was reportedly the first Yakama man to marry a white woman; the couple reportedly experienced rejection from both of their families.[15] Although her father and grandparents would have experienced great pressure to assimilate, Maxine came of age at a time when the United States began to question and retreat, temporarily, from its aggressive assimilation policy and forcible removal of Indigenous children to boarding schools. Indigenous activists and their allies protested the federal government's heavy-handed policies in the 1920s, leading to the appointment of one such white ally, John Collier, as commissioner of Indian Affairs under Franklin Delano Roosevelt's administration. In the 1930s Collier promoted greater Indian self-government, shuttered many of the boarding schools, and emphasized day-school education with a more Indian-centered curriculum. Still, Indian communities were so hard hit by the Great Depression that many Indian families sent their children voluntarily to boarding schools, to ensure that the children would have adequate food, clothing, and shelter.[16] As in Australia, extended family was a key feature of Indigenous survival. Maxine, in fact, was raised by her great-grandmother during at least part of her childhood.[17]

As a young adult, Maxine experienced changes wrought by World War II and a federal Indian policy shift toward "termination" and "relocation" in the 1950s. During the war, many Indigenous Americans served in the armed forces; others relocated to urban areas. After the war Congress rejected Collier's tentative steps toward Indigenous self-determination and instead sought to terminate the federal government's unique trust relationship with tribal nations. Congress also promoted the urban relocation of Indians in a renewed attempt to assimilate Indian people and to eradicate Indigeneity. As part of this urban migration, Maxine and her brother had moved away from Yakama. Her brother became a research engineer with Boeing Aircraft Company, while Maxine attained a master's degree in social work at the University of Washington. Before returning to Yakama, Maxine had served as director of the National Social Workers Associate Program for the Indian Health Service, training social workers to work in Indigenous communities in Arizona, New Mexico, South Dakota, and Alaska. She also sought to increase the numbers of Indigenous social workers through the Association of American Indian Social Workers.[18] In recognition of her work on behalf of Indian families and communities, the National Association of Social Workers named Maxine the Social Worker of the Year in 1980.[19]

Indigenous Women Reclaiming the Care of Children in the Era of Self-Determination

Both Maxine and Mollie found themselves on the front lines of an Indigenous child welfare crisis in their communities. After her stint with the Indian Health Service, Maxine had worked in the Yakima County office of the state Department of Social and Health Services in Washington from 1964 to 1974. There she witnessed with alarm the removal of many children from her tribe and their placement in non-Indian foster homes and adoptive families. The Washington Public Health Service assigned Maxine to work with the Yakama tribe from 1974 to 1980. She applied for and received a grant of nearly $170,000 from a program of the Department of Health, Education, and Welfare for a three-year demonstration project, Project Ku-nak-we-sha, or "the caring place," a reception center for children housed in the home her father had built in 1910 and which she purchased with her own funds.[20] The program aimed to return children to their homes by providing counseling and services to their parents. "The home works to maintain and strengthen the Indian family," Mollie would later observe. "According to an Indian Health Service worker, the home works in a quiet way to advocate the return of jurisdiction over children to the tribe."[21] Authorities removed no Yakama children from the reservation in 1975, when Maxine's program had been in operation only one year, whereas prior to that they had removed about thirty-five children a year.[22]

What Maxine experienced and addressed at Yakama was part of a national trend in the post–World War II era to promote the adoption of Indian children by non-Indian families. Authorities had grown disenchanted with the boarding schools, now seeing them as an economic crutch that sustained Indian dependency and fostered a distinctive Indian identity. At the same time, Congress sought to turn responsibility for Indian child welfare over to the states, as part of the termination sensibility of the era. Social workers from the state and Bureau of Indian Affairs (BIA) continued to engage in child removal. Now, however, they promoted the placement of removed children within white families rather than in institutions. From 1958 to 1967 the BIA contracted with the Child Welfare League of America to run the Indian Adoption Project (IAP), which developed "a permanent inter-state plan for the placement of Indian children requiring adoption" and stipulated that these children were "to be placed primarily in non-Indian adoptive homes . . . in the eastern area." The Adoption Resource Exchange of North America, a program of the Child Welfare League, absorbed the IAP in 1968 and ran it until 1978. The combined IAP and Adoption Resource Exchange avidly promoted the increased removal and adoption of Indian children, both through their own program and through state social service agencies.[23]

American promoters of adoption characterized it as win-win for all involved: as a means to save Indian children and to provide children to couples who wanted to adopt. Social workers routinely portrayed Indigenous communities and families as hopelessly dysfunctional; they called Indian children "forgotten children" who faced a "dead end" if they remained in their families and communities but had a "chance" if they were adopted.[24] Promoters even portrayed Indigenous adoption as a means to heal racial divisions and inequalities. During a 1977 set of congressional hearings on Indian child welfare, one white woman submitted a statement in support of continued adoptions, concluding, "We *cannot* point with pride to the results of government policies during the past 150 years; in fact we should be ashamed of the way Indians have been treated. It seems to me that this present-day trend towards person-to-person assistance should be encouraged, not frustrated."[25]

Indigenous people, by contrast, saw the adoptive placement of their children as an all-out assault on their families and communities. During congressional hearings in the 1970s, Indigenous women testified to the intense pressures they experienced to put their infants up for adoption. They also related how social workers routinely removed their children because they were in the care of extended family members or were living in poverty, not because of true neglect or abuse. The Association on American Indian Affairs (AAIA) provided evidence of legal abuses of Indian families, and tribal social service workers detailed the unequal funding for tribal versus state foster care programs.[26]

As the testimony before Congress on Indian child welfare suggests, Maxine was part of a larger movement among Indigenous peoples to develop programs within their own communities to reclaim the care of children. The AAIA had become involved, accidentally, in Indian child welfare in 1968. While working with the Devils Lake (now Spirit Lake) Sioux on Fort Totten, North Dakota, on other issues, the AAIA learned that a number of Indian families were battling North Dakota state authorities who sought to remove their children. The AAIA arranged for a delegation of five outspoken Indian mothers, accompanied by the tribal chair, to travel to New York for a press conference and to Washington, DC, for lobbying efforts. The AAIA condemned the state actions as "child snatching" and charged that the "forcible removal of Indian youngsters without due process of law . . . has reached epidemic proportions." The AAIA distributed a fact sheet noting that out of 1,100 Devils Lake Sioux Indians under twenty-one years of age living on the Fort Totten reservation, 275, or 25 percent, had been separated from their families.[27] In response, President Lyndon Johnson ordered an inquiry into the allegations, and North Dakota temporarily suspended its harsh policies and practices.[28] Subsequently the AAIA collected data on Indian children from BIA regional offices and hundreds of state and private agencies, finding that an average of 25 to 35 percent of Indian children had been removed from their families and tribal communities and that Indian children were vastly overrepresented in the child welfare system.[29] The AAIA started an Indian Family Defense legal program and devoted an attorney on staff to helping these families reclaim their children.[30]

The AAIA held a one-day Indian Child Welfare and Family Services Conference at the ritzy Biltmore Hotel in New York City in 1974 to strategize about the Indian child welfare crisis. About twenty people attended the conference, including AAIA staff members, national Indian leaders, local Indian activists, child psychiatrists, legal experts, and journalists. There were only two women in attendance, Maxine and Judge Justine Wise Polier, a white woman who was there as a substitute for a young attorney named Hillary Rodham specializing in child advocacy.[31] The AAIA invited Maxine because her "caring place" program had gained a national reputation, coming to serve as a model for many other Indian tribes and urban Indian groups.[32]

Attendees despaired that an Indian child welfare crisis imperiled Indian communities. If Indian families and communities lost generations of children who never learned their tribal practices and customs, over time Indian communities would cease to exist. Building on her personal and professional experience, Maxine ruminated on the breakdown of traditional caring. She asserted, "These are the things that we have lost, the tradition of families—extended families . . . being the agent that socializes the children and raises them. This has broken down." She and other conference attendees linked the removal of Indian children in their time to the federal government's earlier programs of boarding school education for Indian children. Many children who attended the schools suffered abuse and trauma and never learned from their parents, extended family, or community how to take care of children. Conference attendees agreed that the ongoing removal of Indian children in the postwar era represented both a consequence of earlier removals and its latest manifestation.

Maxine and others at the conference sought solutions to this Indian child welfare crisis. Maxine promoted the reclamation or adaptation of extended family traditions: "Certainly the most critical issue is: How can we at the reservation level begin to provide for some kind of tribal institutions that will do the work that the generations did in the past? I'm not at all certain, of course, that we can go back and recreate what was. I'm not sure that it is desirable if we could. There have been too many changes. Certainly, the concept is still there, and I think we should attempt to support it at the tribal level."[33]

Maxine and other attendees also came to the conclusion that comprehensive federal legislation was needed to help keep Indian children within Indian communities. The AAIA soon approached the chairman of the Senate Select Committee on Indian Affairs, James Abourezk of South Dakota, who committed to holding hearings on the issue later that year.[34] Following the 1974 hearings, the AAIA embarked on the task of writing the Indian Child Welfare Act.[35] At the same time the AAIA began to publish *Indian Family Defense*, a small newsletter that championed the association's legislative work and publicized its legal defense cases of Indian families who were working to get their children back. This small publication reached well beyond U.S. borders and served as the catalyst that brought Mollie and Maxine together.

In Melbourne, Mollie got a copy of *Indian Family Defense*. The striking parallels with the situation of Aboriginal children in Australia prompted her to write an impassioned letter to the editor, Steven Unger, who published it in the July 1976 issue. "In Australia a similar situation exists," she wrote. "It has generally been assumed that the Aboriginal parents are not capable of caring adequately for their little ones so the children have been fostered out to white families, and in some cases even adopted without the consent of their mothers." In many cases these children "'have become 'lost' to us," Mollie lamented.[36]

As Maxine was developing Project Ku-Nak-We-Sha in Washington State, Mollie was working with the Aboriginal Legal Service in Melbourne. She became deeply concerned with the number of Aboriginal juvenile offenders she encountered who had been in the child welfare system. She demanded a formal state inquiry into the rates of Indigenous child removal in her home state of Victoria. Researchers discovered that Aboriginal children in Victoria were placed in foster care or adoptive homes at twenty-six times the rate of non-

Aboriginal children.[37] Activists and scholars uncovered similar high levels of removal in other Australian states.

The scope of the problem alarmed Mollie. She and other activists sought to understand why state authorities were removing so many Aboriginal children. In some cases, police officers were apprehending children based on some well-defined conditions of neglect: the child was found begging, wandering, abandoned, or sleeping in a public place, for example. In other cases, however, the widespread removal of Aboriginal children seemed to be based on vague and value-laden standards: "not sufficiently provided for"; "is under unfit guardianship"; "is *likely* to lapse into violence or crime"; and "is exposed to moral danger."[38] In many cases, Mollie charged, child welfare officials were removing children without true evidence of neglect or abuse (just as in the United States), simply because they deemed Aboriginal families to be too permissive or too impoverished or because they disapproved of the longtime practice of Indigenous communities having extended family members care for children.[39]

Mollie and many other activists learned that authorities now saw adoption as the most effective means of assimilating Indigenous children. The Native Affairs commissioner for Western Australia, S. G. Middleton, declared in 1955, for example, "[Adoption] is the shortest cut to complete assimilation I know. What speedier way can there be?"[40] With this aim in mind, social workers put intense pressure on Indigenous mothers to give up their children for adoption at birth or shortly thereafter, as they did in the United States. One nineteen-year-old Aboriginal mother, Jennifer Thomas, alleged that while she was ill and recuperating in the hospital in 1978, she had handed over her one-year-old son Richard to two women for temporary care. The women did not return him. A year later Thomas still had not heard from the women or regained Richard. Mollie got involved in the case and made allegations of baby stealing, which led to a police investigation. Police traced Richard to Brisbane and eventually returned him to his mother.[41]

Mollie and other activists also documented the widespread informal removal of Aboriginal children by "well meaning people" and their informal placement with foster families. Some non-Aboriginal people simply took children "for a holiday" and never returned them. "When parents request[ed] the return of their children, some [could not] be traced," Mollie noted. She added, "Some of these children have even been taken Interstate and may never again be seen by their families."[42]

Mollie's charge was not the hyperbole of an activist with a political agenda. From 1962 to 1974 the Harold Blair Aboriginal Children's Project brought seventy to eighty Indigenous children each year from the North, primarily

Queensland, to spend their holidays with white urban families in Victoria. All told the Blair Project placed over two thousand children with white urban families.[43] This led directly to the adoption of Aboriginal children—sometimes formally but often informally. The Frith family of Victoria, for example, hosted Charity Carbine, an Aboriginal girl for a holiday in 1964. "'We very quickly grew to love her and before the holiday was over we wanted to adopt her,'" Mrs. Frith told a reporter. The Friths claimed that Charity was an orphan, a common and usually false justification for removal and adoption that ignored the importance of extended family relationships. Authorities flew Charity from Woorabinda in Central Queensland, where she had lived the first nine years of her life, to live with the Friths.[44]

Just as in the United States, the adoption of Indigenous children by white families became popular in the 1960s. Mrs. Pettit, cofounder of the Harold Blair Project, noted, "The publicity given to the problems of aboriginals today and the people—the academics and intellectuals—who are fighting for them, have made adoptions of aboriginal children—not only babies—the 'in' thing."[45] This interest, in both Australia and the United States, may have been intensified by the decreasing numbers of white babies who were available for adoption.[46] Officials told the Miller family of Bondi in New South Wales that they would have to wait years to adopt a baby in Australia. However, when they were in Queensland, they "approached the Native Affairs Department and within two months the department had found [a twenty-one-month-old Aboriginal girl] and turned the adoption papers over to the State Children's Department."[47]

This desire to adopt Aboriginal children rested too on configurations of Indigenous communities and families as hopelessly dysfunctional and their children as unwanted, abandoned, and neglected, just as in the United States. "No one in the world needs more help now than these little aboriginal children," Mrs. Frith said in the process of adopting Charity.[48] Another adoptive couple declared, "We thought we should do something to help children no one else wanted."[49] News stories on adoption, with titles such as "From Lean-to to Luxury" and "The Aboriginal Cinderella," focused on the material aspects of what adoptive families could offer. A Queensland couple became foster parents to a five-year-old Aboriginal girl in order to "give her a loving home background, a wardrobe of pretty clothes—and an education to fit her to compete for a worthwhile job in later life."[50]

White Australians heralded adoption as ushering in a new age of racial reconciliation and progress, just as Americans did. When dozens of white families responded positively to an advertisement for 150 Aboriginal children in the 1950s in New South Wales, a reporter concluded, "The warm-hearted response to the plight of these children seems to illustrate that point that the color bar does not exist in Australia. It seems that in helping our aboriginals we have helped ourselves."[51] Such pronouncements fit with the new liberal era that prevailed in the postwar era.

To Mollie and other Indigenous activists, however, adoption represented just the latest manifestation of a longtime policy of destroying Indigenous families. "If one makes a cross study of a section of Aboriginal families," Mollie asserted, "it would soon become apparent that 'decimation' is the only appropriately descriptive word which sums up the results of one hundred years of European policy on Aboriginal families." Further, she added, "the lack of a sensitized policy on the part of housing, health, education and welfare authorities has resulted in nothing short of a total break-up, social dislocation and alienation of Aboriginal people."[52] She traced what was happening in the 1970s back a century to the policies that her family had experienced firsthand. Now, however, authorities focused on placing removed Aboriginal children in foster care or for adoption with non-Aboriginal families instead of institutionalizing them.

Transimperial Indigenous Women's Activism

Mollie's letter to the editor of *Indian Family Defense* launched a transimperial activist network. After ardently but unsuccessfully seeking financial support from the Victorian state government for her work, she sought out alliances with North American activists. In 1976 she won an Aboriginal Overseas Study Award from the Australian government in order to study responses to the Indigenous child welfare crises in North America.[53] She had learned that Indigenous children in Canada also experienced unprecedented rates of removal and that many Canadian provinces were promoting adoption, as in Saskatchewan's Adopt Indian Metis, or AIM, program. Canadian provincial governments were even placing Canadian Indigenous children in white families across the border in the United States. Transimperial networks of bureaucratic authorities who managed Indigenous children had in fact become much more robust since World War II.[54]

Mollie began her transpacific tour by visiting child welfare organizations and tribal groups in Ontario. Then she flew to Saskatchewan, where she attended a three-week course "designed by Indians for Indians" on Indigenous child welfare at the new Saskatchewan Indian Federated College in Prince Albert. At first other participants in the course were suspicious of Mollie and asked her to speak about her background and her purpose. After she explained herself, a man in the audience "came to the platform and suggested that the students give a sister they never knew they had a warm Indian welcome."[55] Each day during lunch, Mollie recalled, "we would discuss and compare what was happening in our communities."[56] Through her travels, Indigenous activists were becoming aware that what they considered to be a problem limited to their settler colonial nations actually transcended borders.

From Saskachewan, Mollie flew to Washington, DC, and then journeyed to New York City, where she met with various non-Indian authorities who offered her the official position on Indian child welfare.[57] Then she met Steven Unger and his colleague, the attorney Bert Hirsch from the AAIA. They discussed Indian perspectives on the child welfare crisis with her while taking her on a whirlwind tour of the city.

Unger had arranged for the rest of Mollie's trip to "visit reservations where the programs were largely managed and controlled by Indian people."[58] From New York City she traveled to Mississippi, Arizona, Michigan, Ohio, and Illinois, visiting various agencies concerned with either Indian or black children in care.[59] Finally she flew to Washington State, where she stayed with Maxine Robbins. "After my long journey, it was here, at the end of it, that I would find the program that I had been searching for," wrote Mollie. "I felt comfortable with [Maxine] right from the start. She was about my age. . . . She was like our own elders who, with patience and perseverance, constantly chipped away at problems and made consistent gains until they achieved the final result."[60] This friendship would prove crucial to building a border-crossing network that would bolster each woman's efforts to reclaim the care of Indigenous children.

Mollie was inspired by her trip to North America, particularly her time with Maxine. Soon after she returned home to Melbourne she convened a group of Aboriginal child care workers to tell them about her experiences and to push for their newly established organization to model itself on Maxine's Ku-Nak-We-Sha. Mollie's group began by changing its name from the Aboriginal Child *Placement* Agency to the Aboriginal Child *Care* Agency (ACCA). This name change signified a shift away from accepting Indigenous child removal and placement outside their families as the norm. Mollie told a group of workers in the Department of Aboriginal Affairs that "the Government wanted her to set up a child *placement* agency." A child *care* agency, by contrast, "emphasizes the retention of the Aboriginal child within his family."[61] And then, using her notes from Maxine, Mollie and a colleague drew up a "sophisticated submission" to the Victorian government for funds, which, to Mollie's great anger, rejected her, for the second time.[62]

Soon Mollie sought to activate the new border-crossing Indigenous network to accelerate change in Australia. She arranged for Maxine to attend a conference for

Australia's celebration of Children's Week in October 1978, at which Indigenous child welfare was a major topic. While there Maxine questioned Australian government authorities as to why there were no provisions made for Aboriginal people to attend or speak at the conference. They told her the conference was to educate whites, but she "countered this by saying that this education should come from Australian Aborigines rather than a Native American Indian." As a result, conference organizers welcomed Aboriginal people to attend their meeting in Morwell, a small city in eastern Victoria, where they "turned up in force." At the meeting, according to Mollie, "Maxine's skill rose like cream to the top. She had Aborigines join in their own afternoon workshops. She put everyone in a circle . . . [and] would draw out the quiet folk to have their say. . . . She asked each Aborigine to talk about the struggles they had experienced in a community dominated by white culture."[63] Maxine helped Mollie get the attention and respect of government administrators.

Maxine stayed on for two weeks after the conference to strategize with the staff of ACCA and meet with government officials. After she met with the federal government's coordinator of Aboriginal Legal Services, she and Mollie received an invitation from the minister for Aboriginal affairs in Canberra, during which Maxine "described the opposition of Indians to adoption as the same as Aborigines." She "stressed the importance that funding for ACCA not be placed under any [state] government agency." Through Maxine's visit, Mollie gained increasing access to and support from government agencies; in fact the Office of Child Care for the state of Victoria made its first substantial grant to ACCA shortly after Maxine returned home.[64]

During the same time, Indigenous activists and their allies in the United States were making their final push for the Indian Child Welfare Act (ICWA) of 1978.[65] This act enabled tribal courts to take unprecedented jurisdiction over most child welfare matters involving Indian children, even children who lived off the reservation. The act also required the highest possible level of proof of neglect or abuse before an Indian child could be removed. It created a hierarchy of placement for a removed Indian child. Ideally a child would be placed first with a member of his or her extended family, or, second, with other members of the child's tribe, or, third, with another Indian family. The act contained a number of provisions for services to Indian families—through Indian tribes and organizations—that would prevent Indian children from being removed. And it called for a study of the remaining Indian boarding schools, with the objective of finally closing them or turning over their control to Indian tribes.[66]

Mollie and other Australian activists took inspiration from the passage of ICWA. Building on the success of her 1978 conference as well as the act's passage, in April 1979 Mollie organized a seminar that she named after the title of her mother's autobiography, *If Everyone Cared*, and built in funds to bring back Maxine as well as Steve Unger from the AAIA.[67] At the close of the seminar, the Aboriginal delegates passed a resolution calling for "all states to enact Aboriginal child welfare legislation (similar to the Indian Child Welfare Act USA)."[68] Eventually, although they did not succeed in enacting a national law, Australian Aboriginal activists negotiated with states to recognize an Aboriginal Child Placement Principle, modeled on parts of ICWA.[69] The collaboration of two resourceful and committed Indigenous women across the borders of two settler colonial states had helped Indigenous people reclaim the care of their children.

Mollie and Maxine's serendipitous meeting, transpacific friendship, and activist network provide several key insights into our understandings of transimperial histories of settler colonial nations in the postwar era. First, their critiques of Indigenous child removal, their activism to stop it, and their framing of the issue as a transimperial phenomenon represent significant interventions into common rhetoric in both the United States and Australia that framed child removal as a benevolent policy. Without recognizing Indigenous child removal as a transimperial phenomenon, settler colonial national discourse has often framed the separation of Indigenous children from their families and their placement in white adoptive homes as a gesture of humanitarianism, as based solely on "the best interests of the child." By showing local, regional, and national practices to be part of a larger settler colonial politics, Indigenous activists challenged this insidious liberal narrative.

Second, Maxine and Mollie's friendship and activism recenters Indigenous women working at the grassroots in late twentieth-century Indigenous movements for self-determination across different imperial formations. Recent scholarship on Indigenous activism has often overlooked the crucial roles that Indigenous women played in these movements. Maxine and Mollie's intertwined lives demonstrate the significance of Indigenous grassroots women activists who, as Mollie put it in reference to Maxine, "with patience and perseverance, constantly chipped away at problems and made consistent gains until they achieved the final result."[70]

Third, Maxine and Mollie's story helps us to reposition Indigenous women within *women's* social movements in the late twentieth century. Mollie and Maxine were just two of hundreds, if not thousands, of Indigenous women activists who articulated their own brand of feminism. In Redfern, a neighborhood in Sydney that was home to many urban Indigenous people, a dynamic group of Indigenous women "decided that their children and those of other poor families should have breakfast in their stomachs to give them a fair chance of getting through the day when they went to school. Then they saw the pressing need to keep the little children off the streets, help the working mothers, give them a place to meet and learn about their Aboriginal culture and heritage." They established a preschool for Aboriginal children and by 1979 had obtained funds to buy a building for their preschool and a hostel for Aboriginal women.[71] Many Indigenous women in the United States engaged in similar forms of community activism aimed at empowering women and children.[72]

Mollie and Maxine's efforts demonstrate the unique style of Indigenous women's activism. They were both engaged in the work of caring for future generations, what feminist scholars have deemed social reproduction or carework. To white feminists in the 1970s, caring for children and looking after family consigned women to a shrunken domain, but to Indigenous women it was critical to their efforts to survive, reclaim their cultures, define their destinies, and assert Indigenous sovereignty. Mollie and Maxine acted on an Indigenous feminist ideal centered around Indigenous women's esteemed caring roles that implicitly critiqued white feminism. Indeed the very title of Mollie's autobiography, *Room for One More*, offers an Indigenous alternative to the Virginia Woolf book and concept of *a room of one's own* that became so prized by white feminists in the 1970s and 1980s. For Mollie and Maxine, emancipation was never an individual matter, and it did not require the abnegation of caring. No wonder, then, that Mollie titled her seminar after her mother's book, *If Everyone Cared*. This evocative title called upon non-Indigenous people to learn and care about the shameful histories of child removal that Indigenous peoples had experienced and honored the significant care work that Indigenous women had long carried out in their communities. Through their cross-border connections, Maxine and Mollie developed a wider Indigenous feminism; they shared more with one another as Indigenous women struggling against forms of colonial power than they did with white women within their own borders.

Finally, Maxine and Mollie's collaborations shed light on how perhaps the most marginalized victims of transimperial settler colonial projects of Indigenous child removal could also seize upon the transimperial nature of Indigenous experience in the late twentieth century to forge a powerful network to challenge child removal within their own communities as well as at the state and national levels. The exchange of transimperial strategies of rule among officials—especially involving intervention in Indigenous families—could be devastating to Indigenous peoples in settler colonial nations. Conversely, however, the circulation of strategies of family reclamation among Indigenous women across the borders of settler colonial states also offered a means to counteract transimperial tyrannies. Mollie and Maxine's friendship exposed and challenged the late twentieth-century forms of eliminationist logic. The crises they identified and worked assiduously to reverse, however, are still going strong in settler colonial nations.[73] The recovery of their history is therefore all the more pressing.

NOTES

1. There is no universally agreed-upon term for the descendants of the original inhabitants of Australia and North America. One overarching term that I use in this essay is *Indigenous*. Where possible I will use the tribal or group designation preferred by Indigenous people.

2. While it is standard to use surnames to refer to individuals in academic essays, I intentionally use Mollie Dyer's and Maxine Robbins's first names. This is not meant as a sign of disrespect but as a means of bringing readers into close association with the two women and into the world of their intimate friendship. Brenda Nicholls, "Award for Services to Aborigines," *Courier*, Ballarat, Victoria, June 23, 1979, news clipping, Box 67, Folder 1, Association on American Indian Affairs Records, 1851–2010, Public Policy Papers, Department of Rare Books and Manuscripts, Princeton University Library, Princeton, New Jersey (hereafter AAIA papers).

3. Jerry Bergsman, "Indian Family Program Wins Honor for Founder," *Seattle Times*, March 22, 1980, Box 67, Folder 1, AAIA papers. The Yakama tribe began to spell their name "Yakama" in the mid-1990s to more closely approximate its correct pronunciation. Place-names in Washington have retained the earlier spelling, "Yakima." See Yakama Nation History, Yakama Nation, http://www.yakamanation-nsn.gov/history3.php, accessed September 1, 2017.

4. In the pre–World War II era, there is just a little evidence of direct communication about child removal as a strategy of empire. For example, Canada sent an emissary to the United States in 1879 to look into its industrial schools as a model for Indian residential schools. See Andrew Woolford, *This Benevolent Experiment: Indigenous Boarding Schools, Genocide, and Redress in Canada and the United States* (Lincoln: University of Nebraska Press, 2015), 68. More often, however, it was international transimperial networks among missionaries, reformers, and academics that contributed to similar strategies of rule. For example, white women in the Woman's Christian Temperance Union participated in a worldwide movement, where they exchanged ideas about the "protection" of "dependent peoples" of the world. See Ian Tyrrell, *Woman's World, Woman's Empire: The Woman's Christian Temperance Union in International Perspective, 1880–1930* (Chapel Hill: University of North Carolina Press, 1991). For the transimperial circulation of other racial ideas, see Tony Ballantyne, "Race and the Webs of Empire: Aryanism from India to the Pacific," *Journal of Colonialism and Colonial History* 2, no. 3 (2001), online; Henry Reynolds and Marilyn Lake, *Drawing the Global Colour Line: White Men's Countries and the International Challenge of Racial Equality* (Cambridge, U.K.: Cambridge University Press, 2008).

5. Patrick Wolfe, "Land, Labor, and Difference: Elementary Structures of Race," *American Historical Review* 106, no. 3 (June 2001): 866–905; Daiva Stasiulis and Nira

Yuval-Davis, eds., *Unsettling Settler Societies: Articulations of Gender, Race, Ethnicity and Class* (London: Sage, 1995); Lorenzo Veracini, *Settler Colonialism: A Theoretical Overview* (London: Palgrave, 2010).

6. David Wallace Adams, *Education for Extinction: American Indians and the Boarding School Experience, 1875–1928* (Lawrence: University Press of Kansas, 1995); John S. Milloy, *A National Crime: The Canadian Government and the Residential School System, 1879 to 1986* (Winnipeg: University of Manitoba Press, 1999); J. R. Miller, *Shingwauk's Vision: A History of Native Residential Schools* (Toronto: University of Toronto Press, 1996); Woolford, *This Benevolent Experiment*; Anna Haebich, *Broken Circles: Fragmenting Indigenous Families, 1800–2000* (Fremantle, WA: Fremantle Arts Centre Press, 2000).

7. Margaret Tucker, *If Everyone Cared* (Melbourne: Grosvenor Books, 1977), 88–96.

8. Mollie Dyer, *Room for One More* (East Melbourne, Victoria: Aboriginal Affairs, Victoria, 2003), 9–21; Bain Attwood, *Rights for Aborigines* (Crows Nest, NSW, Australia: Allen and Unwin, 2003), 31–35, 54–78.

9. Dyer, *Room for One More*, 40–41, 54, 65; Attwood, *Rights for Aborigines*, 131–60.

10. Dyer, *Room for One More*, 65–68; Attwood, *Rights for Aborigines*, 307–49.

11. Letter from Dyer to Unger, May 20, 1977, Box 66, Folder 7, AAIA papers.

12. Nicholls, "Award for Services to Aborigines."

13. Letter from Mollie Dyer to American Indian Law Center at UNM, October 29, 1975; letter from B. V. Brown, Office of Australian Consulate-General, to Steven Unger, July 22, 1976, both in Box 66, Folder 7, AAIA papers.

14. Quoted in Linda Briskman, *The Black Grapevine: Aboriginal Activism and the Stolen Generations* (Leichhardt, NSW, Australia: Federation Press, 2003), 27–28.

15. Dyer, *Room for One More*, 117.

16. Lawrence C. Kelley, *The Assault on Assimilation: John Collier and the Origins of Indian Policy Reform* (Albuquerque: University of New Mexico Press, 1983); Kenneth R. Philp, *John Collier's Crusade for Indian Reform, 1920–1954* (Tucson: University of Arizona Press, 1977).

17. Proceedings, Indian Child Welfare and Family Services Conference, AAIA, January 20 [26], 1974, p. 6, Biltmore Hotel, New York, 207, Box 365, Folder 4, AAIA papers [hereafter Biltmore Conference Proceedings].

18. Dyer, *Room for One More*, 117; Mollie Dyer, "Yakima" section, 3, "Programs and Places Visited during My Recent Aboriginal Overseas Study Grant Tour through Canada and United States, 20 June 1976 to 17 November 1976," Report, Australian Institute of Aboriginal and Torres Strait Islander Studies, Canberra, Australia (hereafter "Yakima, Overseas Study Grant Tour Report").

19. Bergsman, "Indian Family Program Wins Honor for Founder."

20. Dyer, *Room for One More*, 117–18; Dyer, "Yakima, Overseas Study Grant Tour Report," 5.

21. Dyer, "Yakima, Overseas Study Grant Tour Report," 6.

22. Dyer, *Room for One More*, 117–18; Bergsman, "Indian Family Program Wins Honor for Founder"; "From the Office of Child Development," *Yakima Nation Review* 4, no. 7 (August 11, 1975): 1.

23. Arnold Lyslo, "The Indian Adoption Project, 1958–1967," Report, April 1, 1968, Box 17, Folder 4, Child Welfare League of America papers, University of Minnesota Library Special Collections, Minneapolis.

24. Arnold Lyslo, "The Indian Adoption Project: An Appeal to Catholic Agencies to Participate," *Catholic Charities Review* 48, no. 5 (May 1964): 13.

25. Letter from Mrs. Winifred Kromholtz to Senator Warren Magnuson, *Indian Child Welfare Act of 1977*, Hearing before the U.S. Senate Select Committee on Indian Affairs, 95th Congress, First Session on S. 1214, August 4, 1977 (Washington, DC: Government Printing Office, 1977) (hereafter ICWA *Congressional Hearings*, 1977), 493.

26. Congress held three sets of hearings on Indian child welfare. The first, in 1974, provides the most extensive testimony from Indigenous people. See U.S. Senate, *Hearings before the Subcommittee on Indian Affairs of the Committee on Interior and Insular Affairs*, 93rd Congress, 2nd Session, on "Problems that American Indian Families Face in Raising their Children and How these Problems are Affected by Federal Action of Inaction," April 8 and 9, 1974 (Washington, DC: Government Printing Office, 1975) (hereafter, *Indian Child Welfare Congressional Hearings*, 1974). See also ICWA *Congressional Hearings*, 1977; U.S. House of Representatives, *Hearings before the Subcommittee on Indian Affairs and Public Lands of the Committee on Interior and Insular Affairs*, 95th Congress, 2nd Session, S. 1214, February 9 and March 9, 1978 (Washington, DC: Government Printing Office, 1981) (hereafter ICWA *Congressional Hearings*, 1978).

27. List of Devil's Lake Delegation at AAIA press conference, July 16, 1968; telegram from William Byler to 100 media representatives, July 11, 1968; AAIA press release and fact sheet, July 12, 1968, all in Box 77, Folder 7, AAIA papers.

28. Video of Bertram Hirsch presentation on ICWA to Alaska Native group on Kodiak Island, July 18, 1989, in possession of the author. For the BIA response, see Report from Claire Jerdone, October 21, 1968, and related correspondence, Box 2, Folder: General Program Admin., January–December 1968, Miscellaneous Subject Files, 1929–68, Division of Social Services, Records of the Bureau of Indian Affairs, Record Group 75, National Archives and Records Administration, Washington, DC.

29. Video of Bertram Hirsch and letter from Hirsch [to state agencies], n.d. [1968], seeking information on numbers of Indian children in foster care or placed for adoption, Box 77, Folder 7, AAIA papers. In the mid-1970s, under contract from the American Indian Policy Review Commission, established by Congress, the AAIA conducted a comprehensive survey of Indian child placements in nineteen states. These statistics were included in Appendix G, "Indian Child Welfare Statistical Survey," July 1976, in ICWA *Congressional Hearing*, 1977.

30. "American Indian Family Defense Project: A Three Year Program," n.d. (c. 1972); "Report on Great Plains Family Defense Project," May 1, 1972–January 2, 1973; "Indian Family Defense Legal Services Program," Proposal to the Lilly Endowment, n.d. (ca. 1975), "Indian Child Welfare Reform First Report," March 1976–June 1976, all in Box 365, Folder 1, AAIA papers.

31. Biltmore conference participants (partial list), Biltmore Conference Proceedings, 1974.

32. Pat Bellanger, an activist in Minneapolis, mentioned in the 1978 Congressional Hearings that she had visited Ku-Nak-We-Sha and was impressed with how it worked. See ICWA *Congressional Hearings*, 1978, 132.

33. Biltmore Conference Proceedings, 1974, 6.

34. Interview with Bert Hirsch by Margaret D. Jacobs, September 23 30, 2011; Video of Bertram Hirsch.

35. Steven Unger, "The Indian Child Welfare Act of 1978: A Case Study," PhD diss., University of Southern California, 2004, 215. *Indian Family Defense* is available in the AAIA papers.

36. Letter to the Editor from Mollie Dyer, *Indian Family Defense*, no. 5 (July 1976): 7–8.

37. Gabrielle Schneeman, "A Pilot Study Exploring and Where Possible Describing the Position of a Sample of Aboriginal Wards of the State of Victoria Known to Be in Residential Care at the Time of the Study, in regard to Their Background, Present Situation and Expected Future," November 28, 1978, 7, Box 66, Folder 8, AAIA papers.

38. Research Study by Christine Watson, Department of Aboriginal Affairs, Canberra, "Aboriginal Children and the Care of the State in Victoria," November 1976, 7, included in Box 66, Folder 7, AAIA papers.

39. Dyer quoted in Schneeman, "A Pilot Study," 23.

40. Quoted in "Opportunity Opening Up for Native Children," *Daily News* (Perth, Australia), March 5, 1955, Scrapbook: "Aboriginal Children, 1965, 1966, 1967, Box 21/2 Scrapbooks, Vols. 19–21, Council for Aboriginal Rights papers, MS 12913, State Library of Victoria, Melbourne, Australia (hereafter CAR papers).

41. Tonie Blackie, "Missing Richard Returns Home," *Age*, September 5, 1978, 1. In another article, Thomas is identified as Jeannette, not Jennifer. See Lindsay Murdoch, "Countdown for a Happy Reunion," *Age*, September 6, 1978, 3.

42. "Aboriginal Child Care Agency History and First Six Months' Operation," November 15, 1978, 15, 16; "Aboriginal Child Care Agency History and First Twelve Months' Operation," November 15, 1978, Appendix F, both in Box 66, Folder 7, AAIA papers.

43. "Harold Blair Talks on Assimilation of Aborigines," April 13, 1966, *Leader Budget*, Northcote, Victoria, Scrapbook: "Aboriginal Children, 1965, 1966, 1967," Box 21/2 Scrapbooks, Vols. 19–21, CAR papers; Anna Haebich, *Spinning the Dream: Assimilation in Australia, 1950–1970* (Fremantle, Western Australia: Fremantle Press, 2008), 368–69.

44. "The New Arrival," *The Sun*, Melbourne, April 1, 1966, Scrapbook: "Aboriginal Children, 1965, 1966, 1967," Box 21/2 Scrapbooks, Vols. 19–21, CAR papers.

45. Claudia Wright, "'My Son Is No Symbol,'" *Herald* (Melbourne), April 22, 1967; Scrapbook: "Aboriginal Children, 1965, 1966, 1967," Box 21/2 Scrapbooks, Vols. 19–21, CAR papers.

46. Ellen Herman, *Kinship by Design: A History of Adoption in the Modern United States* (Chicago: University of Chicago Press, 2008), 197; H. Philip Hepworth, *Foster Care and Adoption in Canada* (Ottawa, Ontario: Canadian Council on Social Development, 1980), 1, 19–28; Marian Quartly, Shurlee Swain, and Denise Cuthbert, *The Market in Babies: Stories of Australian Adoption* (Clayton, Victoria, Australia: Monash University Press, 2013), 3.

47. "They Adopt Their Family 'At Home,'" *Daily Telegraph* (Sydney), July 29, 1963; Box 16/3 Press Cuttings, Children, CAR papers.

48. "The New Arrival."

49. "Family Adopts Aborigines," *Advertiser* (Adelaide), September 20, 1962, Box 14/8 Children, 1960–62, Press Cuttings, CAR papers.

50. Isabel Carter, "The Aboriginal Cinderella," *Woman's Day* (Sydney), September 8, 1958 and "Joyce Wakes to a Glittering World: From Lean-to to Luxury," no publication, August 16, 1958, Box 13/5, Press Cuttings, Children 1952–58; Erica Parker, "Rosy Life for Young Aboriginal," *Telegraph* (Brisbane), September 4, 1962, Box 14/8 Children, 1960–62, Press Cuttings, CAR papers.

51. Fay Patience, "It's Not the Color That Counts," *Woman's Weekly* (Melbourne), April 2, 1956, Box 13/5, Press Cuttings, Children 1952–58, CAR papers.

52. "Aboriginal Child Care Agency History and First Six Months' Operation," November 15, 1978, 3, Box 66, Folder 7, AAIA papers.

53. Dyer, *Room for One More*, 118.

54. Hepworth, *Foster Care and Adoption in Canada*; Department of Welfare, Province of Saskatchewan, "Adopt Indian-Metis Project," Report 1967–69, 4, 5, File 8.6.23, Folder 1, Department of Social Services, R-1655, Saskatchewan Archives Board, Regina; Margaret D. Jacobs, *A Generation Removed: The Fostering and Adoption of Indigenous Children in the Postwar World* (Lincoln: University of Nebraska Press, 2014), 169–210.

55. Dyer, *Room for One More*, 97–99, quotes from 98, 99.

56. Dyer, *Room for One More*, 99.

57. "Indian Adoption Project," April 1960, a seven-page document describing the project, probably written by Arnold Lyslo, 2, 1, Box 17, Folder 3, Child Welfare League of America papers.

58. Dyer, *Room for One More*, 100–101, quotes from 101.

59. Dyer, *Room for One More*, 101–3, 113–17.

60. Dyer, *Room for One More*, 118.

61. Sue Ingram, "Children's Services for Indigenous Peoples," description of meeting of Robbins and Dyer with Department of Aboriginal Affairs, 16, November 1977, Australian Institute of Aboriginal and Torres Strait Islander Studies.

62. Dyer, *Room for One More*, 119–21.

63. Dyer, *Room for One More*, 121–22.

64. Dyer, *Room for One More*, 121–22; "Aboriginal Child Care Agency History and First Six Months' Operation," November 15, 1978, inside cover, Box 66, Folder 7, AAIA papers.

65. Unger, "The Indian Child Welfare Act of 1978," 303–34; interview with Bert Hirsch by Margaret D. Jacobs, September 23, 2011.

66. *Indian Child Welfare Act of 1978*, U.S. Code, vol. 25 (1978), http://www.tribal -institute.org/lists/chapter21_icwa.htm, accessed September 1, 2017.

67. Dyer, *Room for One More*, 131; letter from Dyer to Unger, February 12, 1979, and Unger to Dyer, February 23, 1979, Box 67, Folder 1, AAIA papers.

68. Steven Unger to William Byler, April 30, 1979, Box 67, Folder 1, AAIA papers.

69. Briskman, *Black Grapevine*, 84, 110; Andrew Armitage, *Comparing the Policy of Aboriginal Assimilation—Australia, Canada, and New Zealand* (Vancouver: University of British Columbia Press, 1995), 54–55, 65–67.

70. Dyer, *Room for One More*, 118. For recent scholarship on Indigenous movements, see Bradley Shreve, *Red Power Rising: The National Indian Youth Council and the Origins of Native Activism* (Norman: University of Oklahoma Press, 2011); Daniel Cobb, *Native Activism in Cold War America: The Struggle for Sovereignty* (Lawrence: University Press of Kansas, 2008); Ravi de Costa, *A Higher Authority: Indigenous Transnationalism and Australia* (Sydney: University of New South Wales Press, 2006); Charles Wilkinson, *Blood Struggle: The Rise of Modern Indian Nations* (New York: Norton, 2005); Paul Chaat Smith and Robert Allen Warrior, *Like a Hurricane: The Indian Movement from Alcatraz to Wounded Knee* (New York: New Press, 1996).

71. Barbara Rowlands, "Caring for Kids Ended in Triumph," *Aboriginal News* 3, no. 7 (1979): 6–8; quote 6.

72. Julie Davis, *Survival Schools: The American Indian Movement and Community Education in the Twin Cities* (Minneapolis: University of Minnesota Press, 2013); Brenda Child, *Holding Our World Together: Ojibwe Women and the Survival of Community* (New York: Penguin, 2012); Jacobs, *A Generation Removed*, 97–124.

73. In the United States, American Indian children make up just 0.9 percent of the population of American children but 2.7 percent of those in foster care. See Alicia Summers, *Disproportionality Rates for Children of Color in Foster Care (FY 2014)* Technical Assistance Bulletin (Reno, NV: National Council of Juvenile and Family Court Judges, August 2016), 3, http://www.ncjfcj.org/sites/default/files/NCJFCJ%202014%20 Disproportionality%20TAB%20Final.pdf. In Canada Indigenous children make up only 7 percent of the population but represent 48 percent of all children in foster care. See Pam Palmater, "From Foster Care to Missing or Murdered: Canada's Other Tragic Pipeline," *Macleans*, April 12, 2017, available at http://www.macleans.ca/news/canada/from -foster-care-to-missing-or-murdered-canadas-other-tragic-pipeline/.

Bibliography

Abinales, Patricio. "From *Orang Besar* to Colonial Big Man: Datu Piang of Cotabato and the American Colonial State." In *Lives at the Margin: Biography of Filipinos Obscure, Ordinary, and Heroic,* edited by Alfred W. McCoy, 193–228. Quezon City, Philippines: Ateneo de Manila University Press, 2000.

Abinales, Patricio. *Making Mindanao: Cotabato and Davao in the Formation of the Philippine Nation-State.* Quezon City, Philippines: Ateneo de Manila University Press, 2000.

Abinales, Patricio. "Progressive Machine Conflict in Early Twentieth-Century U.S. Politics and Colonial State Building in the Philippines." In *The American Colonial State in the Philippines: Global Perspectives,* edited by Julian Go and Anne L. Foster, 148–81. Durham, NC: Duke University Press, 2003.

Adams, David Wallace. *Education for Extinction: American Indians and the Boarding School Experience, 1875–1928.* Lawrence: University Press of Kansas, 1995.

Adas, Michael. *Dominance by Design: Technological Imperatives and America's Civilizing Mission.* Cambridge, MA: Belknap Press of Harvard University Press, 2006.

Adas, Michael. "From Settler Colony to Global Hegemon: Integrating the Exceptionalist Narrative of the American Experience into World History." *American Historical Review* 106, no. 5 (2001): 1692–720.

Agoncillo, Teodoro A. *The Fateful Years: Japan's Adventure in the Philippines, 1941–45.* 2 vols. 2nd ed. Quezon City: University of the Philippines Press, 2001.

Agstner, Rudolf. *Austria (-Hungary) and Its Consulates in the United States of America since 1820: "Our Nationals Settling Here Count by the Millions Now."* Zurich: LIT Verlag, 2012.

Akami, Tomoko. "Imperial Politics, Intercolonialism, and the Shaping of Global Governing Norms: Public Health Expert Networks in Asia and the League of Nations Health Organization, 1908–1937." *Journal of Global History* 12, no. 1 (2017): 4–25.

Akami, Tomoko. "A Quest to Be Global: The League of Nations Health Organization and Inter-colonial Regional Governing Agendas of the Far Eastern Association of Tropical Health, 1910–1925." *International History Review* 38, no. 1 (2016): 1–23.

Ali, Tariq Omar. *A Local History of Global Capital: Jute and Peasant Life in the Bengal Delta.* Princeton, NJ: Princeton University Press, 2018.

Alonso, Harriet Hyman. *Peace as a Women's Issue: A History of the U.S. Movement for World Peace and Women's Rights.* Syracuse, NY: Syracuse University Press, 1993.

Amador, José. *Medicine and Nation Building in the Americas, 1890–1940.* Nashville, TN: Vanderbilt University Press, 2015.

Amoroso, Donna J. "Inheriting the 'Moro Problem': Muslim Authority and Colonial Rule in British Malaya and the Philippines." In *The American Colonial State in the Philippines: Global Perspectives*, edited by Julian Go and Anne L. Foster, 118–47. Durham, NC: Duke University Press, 2003.

Andersen, Casper. *British Engineers and Africa, 1875–1914.* London: Pickering and Chatto, 2011.

Anderson, Stuart. "'Pacific Destiny' and American Policy in Samoa, 1872–1899." *Hawaiian Journal of History* 12 (1978): 45–60.

Anderson, Stuart. *Race and Rapprochement: Anglo-Saxonism and Anglo-American Relations, 1895–1904.* Rutherford, NJ: Fairleigh Dickinson University Press, 1981.

Anderson, Warwick. "The Colonial Medicine of Settler States: Comparing Histories of Indigenous Health." *Health and History: Journal of the Australian and New Zealand Society for the History of Medicine* 9, no. 2 (2007): 144–54.

Anderson, Warwick. *Colonial Pathologies: American Tropical Medicine, Race, and Hygiene in the Philippines.* Durham, NC: Duke University Press, 2006.

Anderson, Warwick, and Hans Pols. "Scientific Patriotism: Medical Science and National Self-Fashioning in Southeast Asia." In *Endless Empire: Spain's Retreat, Europe's Eclipse, America's Decline*, edited by Alfred W. McCoy, Josep Fradera, and Stephen Jacobson, 265–72. Madison: University of Wisconsin Press, 2012.

Andrews, Naomi. "'The Universal Alliance of All Peoples': Romantic Socialists, the Human Family, and the Defense of Empire during the July Monarchy, 1830–1848." *French Historical Studies* 34, no. 3 (2011): 473–502.

Anduaga, Aitor. "Spanish Jesuits in the Philippines: Geophysical Research and Synergies between Science, Education and Trade, 1865–1898." *Annals of Science* 71, no. 4 (2014): 497–521.

Armitage, Andrew. *Comparing the Policy of Aboriginal Assimilation—Australia, Canada, and New Zealand.* Vancouver: University of British Columbia Press, 1995.

Armitage, David, and Alison Bashford, eds. *Pacific Histories: Ocean, Land, People.* London: Palgrave Macmillan, 2014.

Asaka, Ikuko. *Tropical Freedom: Climate, Settler Colonialism, and Black Exclusion in the Age of Emancipation.* Durham, NC: Duke University Press, 2017.

Aso, Michitake. "Patriotic Hygiene: Tracing New Places of Knowledge Production about Malaria in Vietnam, 1919–1975." *Journal of Southeast Asian Studies* 44, no. 3 (2013): 423–43.

Attwood, Bain. *Rights for Aborigines.* Crows Nest, NSW, Australia: Allen and Unwin, 2003.

Azuma, Eiichiro. *Between Two Empires: Race, History, and Transnationalism in Japanese America.* New York: Oxford University Press, 2005.

Bacevich, Andrew J. *Diplomat in Khaki: Major General Frank Ross McCoy and American Foreign Policy, 1898–1949.* Lawrence: University Press of Kansas, 1989.

Bailyn, Bernard. *Atlantic History: Concept and Contours.* Cambridge, MA: Harvard University Press, 2005.

Ballantyne, Tony. "Race and the Webs of Empire: Aryanism from India to the Pacific." *Journal of Colonialism and Colonial History* 2, no. 3 (2001), https://muse.jhu.edu/.

Ballantyne, Tony, and Antoinette Burton. "Empires and the Reach of the Global." In *A World Connecting, 1870–1945,* edited by Emily Rosenberg, 285–431. Cambridge, MA: Belknap Press of Harvard University Press, 2012.

Balogh, Brian. *A Government Out of Sight: The Mystery of National Authority in Nineteenth-Century America.* Cambridge, U.K.: Cambridge University Press, 2009.

Banerjee, Sukanya. "Who, or What, Is Victorian? Ecology, Indigo, and the Transimperial." *Victorian Studies* 58, no. 2 (2016): 213–23.

Bankoff, Greg. "The Science of Nature and the Nature of Science in the Spanish and American Philippines." In *Cultivating the Colonies: Colonial States and Their Environmental Legacies,* edited by Christina Folke Ax et al., 78–108. Columbus: Ohio University Press, 2011.

Baptist, Edward. *The Half Has Never Been Told: Slavery and the Making of American Capitalism.* New York: Basic Books, 2014.

Barker, Charles Albro. *Henry George.* New York: Oxford University Press, 1955.

Barr-Mele, Patrick. *Reforming Chile: Cultural Politics, Nationalism, and the Rise of the Middle Class.* Chapel Hill: University of North Carolina Press, 2001.

Barth, Volker, and Roland Cvetkovski, eds. *Imperial Co-operation and Transfer, 1870–1930: Empires and Encounters.* New York: Bloomsbury, 2015.

Basch, Linda, Nina Glick Schiller, and Cristina Szanton Blanc. *Nations Unbound: Transnational Projects, Postcolonial Predicaments, and Deterritorialized Nation-States.* Langhorne, PA: Gordon and Breach, 1994.

Bassi, Ernesto. *An Aqueous Territory: Sailor Geographies and New Granada's Transimperial Greater Caribbean World.* Durham, NC: Duke University Press, 2016.

Bayly, C. A., Sven Beckert, Matthew Connelly, Isabel Hofmeyr, Wendy Kozol, and Patricia Seed. "AHR Conversation: On Transnational History." *American Historical Review* 111, no. 5 (December 2006): 1441–64.

Beattie, Donald. "Sons of Temperance: Pioneers in Total Abstinence and 'Constitutional' Prohibition." PhD diss., Boston University, 1966.

Becker, William H. *The Dynamic of Business-Government Relations: Industry and Exports, 1893–1921.* Chicago: University of Chicago Press, 1982.

Beckert, Sven. *Empire of Cotton: A Global History.* New York: Knopf, 2014.

Beckert, Sven, and Seth Rockman, eds. *Slavery's Capitalism: A New History of American Economic Development.* Philadelphia: University of Pennsylvania Press, 2016.

Beckett, Jeremy. "The Datus of the Rio Grande de Cotabato under Colonial Rule." *Asian Studies* 15 (1977): 46–64.

Beckles, Hilary. *Great House Rules: Landless Emancipation and Workers' Protest in Barbados, 1838–1938.* Kingston, Jamaica: Ian Randle, 2004.

Beckles, Hilary. *History of Barbados: From Amerindian Settlement to Nation-State.* Cambridge, U.K.: Cambridge University Press, 1990.

Behrent, Michael C. "Foucault and Technology." *History and Technology* 29, no. 1 (2013): 54–104.

Beisner, Robert L. *Twelve against Empire: The Anti-Imperialists, 1898–1900.* New York: McGraw-Hill, 1968.

Belich, James. *Replenishing the Earth: The Settler Revolution and the Rise of the Anglo-World, 1783–1939.* Oxford: Oxford University Press, 2009.

Bell, Duncan. *Empire and the Future of World Order, 1860–1900.* Princeton, NJ: Princeton University Press, 2007.

Bell, Duncan. *The Idea of Greater Britain: Empire and the Future of World Order, 1860–1900.* Cambridge, U.K.: Cambridge University Press, 2009.

Belolavek, John M. *Broken Glass: Caleb Cushing and the Shattering of the Union.* Kent, OH: Kent State University Press, 2005.

Bender, Daniel E. *The Animal Game: Searching for Wildness at the American Zoo.* Cambridge, MA: Harvard University Press, 2016.

Bender, Daniel E., and Jana K. Lipman, eds. *Making the Empire Work: Labor and United States Imperialism.* New York: New York University Press, 2015.

Bender, Jill. *The 1857 Indian Uprising and the British Empire.* Cambridge, U.K.: Cambridge University Press, 2016.

Bender, Thomas. *A Nation among Nations: America's Place in World History.* New York: Hill and Wang, 2006.

Bennett, Brett M. "Naturalising Australian Trees in South Africa: Climate, Exotics and Experimentation." *Journal of Southern African Studies* 37, no. 2 (2011): 265–80.

Berguño, Jorge. "Las Shetland del Sur: El ciclo lobero." *Boletín Antártico Chileno* 12, no. 2 (1993): 5–13.

Berridge, Virginia. *Opium and the People: Opiate Use and Drug Control Policy in Nineteenth and Early Twentieth Century England.* London: Free Association Books, 1999.

Bertrand, Romain, Jean-Louis Briquet, and Peter Pels. "Introduction: Towards a Historical Ethnography of Voting." In *The Hidden History of the Secret Ballot,* edited by Romain Bertrand, Jean-Louis Briquet, and Peter Pels, 1–15. Bloomington: Indiana University Press, 2007.

Bestor, Theodore C. "How Sushi Went Global." *Foreign Policy,* no. 121 (2000): 54–63.

Birn, Anne-Emanuelle, and Theodore M. Brown, eds. *Comrades in Health: U.S. Health Internationalists, Abroad and at Home.* New Brunswick, NJ: Rutgers University Press, 2013.

Blackett, R. J. M. "Anglo-American Opposition to Liberian Colonization, 1831–1833." *Historian* 41, no. 2 (1979): 276–94.

Blackett, R. J. M. *Building an Antislavery Wall: Black Americans in the Atlantic Abolitionist Movement, 1830–1860.* Baton Rouge: Louisiana State University Press, 1983.

Blackstock, Michael D. "Trust Us: A Case Study in Colonial Social Relations Based on Documents Prepared by the Aborigines Protection Society, 1836–1912." In *With Good Intentions: Euro-Canadian and Aboriginal Relations in Colonial Canada,* edited by Celia Haig-Brown and David A. Nock, 51–71. Vancouver: University of British Columbia Press, 2006.

Bockstoce, John R. *Furs and Frontiers in the Far North.* New Haven, CT: Yale University Press, 2009.

Boehringer, Gill H. "Black American Anti-Imperialist Fighters in the Philippine American War." *Black Agenda Report*, September, 15, 2009. https://blackagendareport.com /content/black-american-anti-imperialist-fighters-philippine-american-war.

Boianovsky, Mauro. "Friedrich List and the Economic Fate of Tropical Countries." *History of Political Economy* 45, no. 4 (2013): 647–91.

Bose, Sugata. *A Hundred Horizons: The Indian Ocean in the Age of Global Empire*. Cambridge, MA: Harvard University Press, 2006.

Boxer, C. R. *The Dutch Seaborne Empire: 1600–1800*. New York: Knopf, 1965.

Bratlinger, Patrick. *Dark Vanishings: Discourse on the Extinction of Primitive Races, 1800–1930*. Ithaca, NY: Cornell University Press, 2003.

Bravo, Michael T. "Ethnological Encounters." In *Cultures of Natural History*, edited by Nicholas Jardine, James A. Secord, and E. C. Spary, 338–57. Cambridge, U.K.: Cambridge University Press, 1996.

Brent, Peter. "The Australian Ballot: Not the Secret Ballot." *Australian Journal of Political Science* 41, no. 1 (2006): 39–50.

Bridge, Carl, and Kent Fedorowich, eds. *The British World: Diaspora, Culture and Identity*. London: Routledge, 2003.

Briggs, Laura. *Reproducing Empire: Race, Sex, Science, and U.S. Imperialism in Puerto Rico*. Berkeley: University of California Press, 2002.

Briggs, Laura, Gladys McCormick, and J. T. Way. "Transnationalism: A Category of Analysis." *American Quarterly* 60 no. 3 (September 2008): 625–48.

Briskman, Linda. *The Black Grapevine: Aboriginal Activism and the Stolen Generations*. Leichhardt, NSW, Australia: Federation Press, 2003.

Britton, John A. *Cables, Crises, and the Press: The Geopolitics of the New International Information System in the Americas, 1866–1903*. Albuquerque: University of New Mexico Press, 2014.

Brody, David. "Building Empire: Architecture and American Imperialism in the Philippines." *Journal of Asian American Studies* 4, no. 2 (2001): 123–45.

Brown, Charles. *Agents of Manifest Destiny: The Lives and Times of the Filibusters*. Chapel Hill: University of North Carolina Press, 1980.

Brown, Emily C. *Har Dayal: Hindu Revolutionary and Rationalist*. Tucson: University of Arizona Press, 1975.

Brown, Ian. "The Philippine Economy during the World Depression of the 1930s." *Philippine Studies* 40, no. 3 (1992): 381–87.

Brunner-Hauser, Sylva. *Pionier für eine menschlichere Zukunft: Dr. med. Wilhelm Joos, Nationalrat 1821–1900*. Schaffhausen, Germany: Meili, 1983.

Bryan, Patrick. *The Jamaican People, 1880–1902: Race, Class, and Social Control*. Mona, Jamaica: University of West Indies Press, 2012.

Buenker, John D. "Sovereign Individuals and Organic Networks: Political Culture in Conflict during the Progressive Era." *American Quarterly* 40, no. 2 (1988): 187–204.

Burk, Kathleen. *Old World, New World: Great Britain and America from the Beginning*. New York: Atlantic Monthly Press, 2008.

Burns, Bradford. *Patriarch and Folk: The Emergence of Nicaragua, 1798–1858*. Cambridge, MA: Harvard University Press, 1991.

Burton, Antoinette M. *Dwelling in the Archive: Women Writing House, Home, and History in Late Colonial India*. Oxford: Oxford University Press, 2003.

Busch, Briton Cooper. *The War against the Seals: A History of the North American Seal Fishery*. Montreal: McGill-Queens University Press, 1985.

Butler, Leslie. *Critical Americans: Victorian Intellectuals and Transatlantic Liberal Reform*. Chapel Hill: University of North Carolina Press, 2007.

Byrd, Brandon. "To Start Something to Help These People: African American Women and the Occupation of Haiti, 1915–1934." *Journal of Haitian Studies* 21, no. 2 (2015): 127–53.

Cain, P. J. "Capitalism, Aristocracy and Empire: Some 'Classical' Theories of Imperialism Revisited." *Journal of Imperial and Commonwealth History* 35, no. 1 (2007): 25–47.

Cain, Peter. "Capitalism, War, and Internationalism in the Thought of Richard Cobden." *British Journal of International Studies* 5, no. 3 (1979): 229–47.

Cain, P. J. "Hobson, Wilshire, and the Capitalist Theory of Capitalist Imperialism." *History of Political Economy* 17, no. 3 (1985): 455–60.

Cain, P. J. "J. A. Hobson, Cobdenism and the Radical Theory of Economic Imperialism, 1898–1914." *Economic History Review* 31, no. 4 (1978): 565–84.

Campbell, Tracy. "Machine Politics, Police Corruption, and the Persistence of Vote Fraud: The Case of Louisville, Kentucky, Election of 1905." *Journal of Policy History* 15, no. 3 (2003): 269–300.

Capozzola, Christopher. "Legacies for Citizenship: Pinpointing Americans during and after World War I." *Diplomatic History* 38, no. 4 (2014): 713–26.

Cardon, Nathan, and Simon Jackson. "Everyday Empires: Trans-Imperial Circulations in a Multi-disciplinary Perspective—Origins, Inspirations, Ways Forward." *Blog, Past and Present*, May 5, 2017. http://pastandpresent.org.uk/everyday-empries-trans-imperial -circulations-multi-disciplinary-perspective-origins-inspirations-ways-forward/.

Carr, Albert. *The World and William Walker*. New York: Harper and Row, 1963.

Carroll, Murray Lee. "Open Door Imperialism in Africa: The United States and the Congo, 1876 to 1892." PhD diss., University of Connecticut, 1971.

Carter, Henderson. *Labour Pains: Resistance and Protest in Barbados, 1838–1904*. Kingston, Jamaica: Ian Randle, 2012.

Cassá, Robert. "The Economic Development of the Caribbean from 1880 to 1930." In *General History of the Caribbean*, Vol. 5: *The Caribbean in the Twentieth Century*, edited by Bridget Brereton, 7–41. New York: UNESCO and Macmillan, 2004.

Chang, Kornel. *Pacific Connections: The Making of the U.S.-Canadian Borderlands*. Berkeley: University of California Press, 2012.

Charbonneau, Oliver. "Civilizational Imperatives: American Colonial Culture in the Philippines, 1899–1942." PhD diss., University of Western Ontario, 2016.

Chaudhuri, K. N. "The Unity and Disunity of Indian Ocean History from the Rise of Islam to 1750: The Outline of a Theory and Historical Discourse." *Journal of World History* 4, no. 1 (1994): 1–21.

Child, Brenda. *Holding Our World Together: Ojibwe Women and the Survival of Community*. New York: Viking, 2012.

Cioc, Mark. *The Game of Conservation: International Treaties to Protect the World's Migratory Animals*. Athens: Ohio University Press, 2009.

Claeys, Gregory. *Imperial Sceptics: British Critics of Empire, 1850–1920*. Cambridge, U.K.: Cambridge University Press, 2010.

Clarence-Smith, William G. "Wajih al-Kilani, Shaykh al-Islam of the Philippines and Notable of Nazareth, 1913–1916." In *Nazareth History and Cultural Heritage: Proceedings of the 2nd International Conference, Nazareth, July 2–5, 2012*, edited by Mahmoud Yazbak et al., 172–92. Nazareth, Israel: Municipality of Nazareth Academic Publications, 2013.

Cobb, Daniel. *Native Activism in Cold War America: The Struggle for Sovereignty*. Lawrence: University Press of Kansas, 2008.

Cogan, Frances B. *Captured: The Japanese Internment of American Civilians in the Philippines, 1941–1945*. Athens: University of Georgia Press, 2012.

Cohen, Andrew Wender. "Smuggling, Globalization, and America's Outward State, 1870–1909." *Journal of American History* 97, no. 2 (2010): 371–98.

Colby, Barnard L. *For Oil and Buggy Whips: Whaling Captains of New London County*. Mystic, CT: Mystic Seaport Museum, 1990.

Conniff, Michael. *Black Labor on the White Canal: Panama, 1904–1981*. Pittsburgh, PA: University of Pittsburgh Press, 1985.

Conrad, Sebastian. *Globalisation and the Nation in Imperial Germany*. Cambridge, U.K.: Cambridge University Press, 2010.

Conroy-Krutz, Emily. *Christian Imperialism: Converting the World in the Early American Republic*. Ithaca, NY: Cornell University Press, 2015.

Cooke, Adam. "'An Unpardonable Bit of Folly and Impertinence': Charles Francis Adams Jr., American Anti-Imperialists, and the Philippines." *New England Quarterly* 83, no. 2 (2010): 313–38.

Cooper, Dana. *Informal Ambassadors: American Women, Transatlantic Marriages, and Anglo-American Relations, 1865–1945*. Kent, OH: Kent State University Press, 2014.

Cordero-Fernando, Gilda, ed. *Culinary Culture of the Philippines*. Manila: Bancom Audio-vision, 1976.

Courtwright, David T. *Dark Paradise: A History of Opiate Addiction in America*. Cambridge, MA: Harvard University Press, 2001.

Craig, John M. "Lucia True Ames Mead: American Publicist for Peace and Internationalism." In *Women and American Foreign Policy: Lobbyists, Critics, and Insiders*, edited by Edward P. Crapol, 67–90. Westport, CT: Greenwood Press, 1987.

Craig, Raymond. *Cartographic Mexico: A History of State Fixations and Fugitive Landscapes*. Durham, NC: Duke University Press, 2004.

Crapol, Edward P. *America for Americans: Economic Nationalism and Anglophobia, 1876–1896*. Westport, CT: Greenwood Press, 1973.

Cromwell, Jesse. "More than Slaves and Sugar: Recent Historiography of the Trans-imperial Caribbean and Its Sinew Populations." *History Compass* 12, no. 10 (2014): 770–83.

Cronin, B. P. *Technology, Industrial Conflict, and the Development of Technical Education in 19th-Century England*. Aldershot, U.K.: Ashgate, 2001.

Crook, Malcolm. "Reforming Voting Practices in a Global Age: The Making and Remaking of the Modern Secret Ballot in Britain, France and the United States, c. 1600–1950." *Past and Present* 212, no. 1 (2011): 199–237.

Crowley, John. "The Secret Ballot in the American Age of Reform." In *The Hidden History of the Secret Ballot*, edited by Romain Bertrand, Jean Louis Briquet, and Peter Pels, 43–68. Bloomington: Indiana University Press, 2006.

Cruz, Denise. Introduction to *The Crucible: An Autobiography by Colonel Yay, Filipina American Guerrilla*, edited by Denise Cruz, ix–xxviii. New Brunswick, NJ: Rutgers University Press, 2009.

Cruz, Denise. *Transpacific Femininities: The Making of the Modern Filipina*. Durham, NC: Duke University Press, 2012.

Cudmore, Patrick. *Buchanan's Conspiracy, the Nicaragua Canal and Reciprocity*. New York: P. J. Kennedy, 1892.

Cudmore, Patrick. *Cleveland's Maladministration: Free Trade, Protection and Reciprocity*. New York: P. J. Kennedy, 1896.

Cullather, Nick. "Damming Afghanistan: Modernization in a Buffer State." *Journal of American History* 89, no. 2 (2002): 512–37.

Cullinane, Michael Patrick. *Liberty and American Anti-Imperialism 1898–1909*. London: Palgrave Macmillan, 2012.

Cullinane, Michael Patrick. "Transatlantic Dimensions of the American Anti-Imperialist Movement, 1899–1909." *Journal of Transatlantic Studies* 8, no. 4 (2010): 301–14.

Curless, Gareth, Stacey Hynd, Temilola Alanamu, and Katherine Roscoe. "Networks in Imperial History." *Journal of World History* 26, no. 4 (2015): 705–32.

Cushman, Greg. *Guano and the Opening of the Pacific World*. New York: Cambridge University Press, 2013.

Daly, M. W. *Empire on the Nile: The Anglo-Egyptian Sudan, 1898–1934*. Cambridge, U.K.: Cambridge University Press, 1986.

Danquah, Francis K. "Japan's Food Farming Policies in Wartime Southeast Asia: The Philippine Example, 1942–1944." *Agricultural History* 64, no. 3 (1990): 60–80.

Darwin, John. *After Tamerlane: The Global History of Empire since 1405*. New York: Bloomsbury, 2007.

Darwin, John. *The Empire Project: The Rise and Fall of the British World-System, 1830–1970*. Cambridge, U.K.: Cambridge University Press, 2009.

Darwin, John. *Unfinished Empire: The Global Expansion of Britain*. London: Penguin, 2012.

Das, Veena. *Life and Words: Violence and the Descent into the Ordinary*. Berkeley: University of California Press, 2007.

Daughton, J. P. "Behind the Imperial Curtain: International Humanitarian Efforts and the Critique of French Colonialism in the Interwar Years." *French Historical Studies* 34, no. 3 (2011): 503–28.

Davis, James. *Eric Walrond: A Life in the Harlem Renaissance and the Transatlantic Caribbean*. New York: Columbia University Press, 2015.

Davis, Janet M. *The Circus Age: Culture and Society under the American Big Top*. Chapel Hill: University of North Carolina Press, 2002.

Davis, Julie. *Survival Schools: The American Indian Movement and Community Education in the Twin Cities*. Minneapolis: University of Minnesota Press, 2013.

Davis, Lance E., Robert E. Gallman, and Karin Gleiter. *In Pursuit of Leviathan: Technology, Institutions, Productivity, and Profits in American Whaling, 1816–1906*. Chicago: University of Chicago Press, 1997.

DeBenedetti, Charles. *The Peace Reform in American History*. Bloomington: Indiana University Press, 1980.

De Costa, Ravi. *A Higher Authority: Indigenous Transnationalism and Australia*. Sydney: University of New South Wales Press, 2006.

De Goey, Ferry. *Consuls and the Institutions of Global Capitalism, 1783–1914*. London: Pickering and Chatto, 2014.

Delmendo, Sharon. *The Star-Entangled Banner: One Hundred Years of America in the Philippines*. New Brunswick, NJ: Rutgers University Press, 2004.

De Visser, Marinus Willem. "Levensbericht van Willem Pieter Groeneveldt." *Jaarboek van de Maatschappij der Nederlandse Kunde, 1916* (1916). *Digitale bibliotheek voor de Nederlandse letteren*. http://www.dbnl.org/tekst/_jaa003191601_01/_jaa003191601_01_0016.php.

Dickinson, Anthony B. "Early Nineteenth-Century Sealing on the Falkland Islands: Attempts to Develop a Regulated Industry, 1820–1834." *Northern Mariner/Le Marin du Nord* 4, no. 3 (1994): 39–49.

Dickinson, Anthony B. "Southern Hemisphere Fur Sealing from Atlantic Canada." *American Neptune* 49, no. 4 (1989): 278–90.

Doeppers, Daniel F. *Feeding Manila in Peace and War, 1850–1945*. Madison: University of Wisconsin Press, 2016.

Doolittle, Amity. "Colliding Discourses: Western Land Laws and Native Customary Rights in North Borneo, 1881–1918." *Journal of Southeast Asian Studies* 34, no. 1 (2003): 97–126.

Dorsey, Kurkpatrick. *The Dawn of Conservation Diplomacy: U.S.-Canadian Wildlife Protection Treaties in the Progressive Era*. Seattle: University of Washington Press, 1998.

Dower, John W. *War without Mercy: Race and Power in the Pacific War*. New York: Pantheon Books, 1993.

Downes, Aviston D. "Barbados, 1880–1914: A Socio-Cultural History." PhD diss., York University, 2004.

Drayton, Richard. *The Masks of Empire: The World History underneath Modern Empires and Nations, c. 1500 to the Present*. London: Palgrave, 2017.

Drayton, Richard. *Nature's Government: Science, Imperial Britain, and the "Improvement" of the World*. New Haven, CT: Yale University Press, 2000.

Duara, Prasenjit. "Transnationalism and the Challenge to National Histories." In *Rethinking American History in a Global Age*, edited by Thomas Bender, 25–46. Berkeley: University of California Press, 2002.

Dyer, Mollie. *Room for One More*. East Melbourne, Victoria, Australia: Aboriginal Affairs Victoria, 2003.

Edmonds, Penelope. "'I Followed England round the World': The Rise of Trans-Imperial Anglo-Saxon Exceptionalism and the Spatial Narratives of Nineteenth-Century British Settler Colonies of the Pacific Rim." In *Re-Orienting Whiteness*, edited by K. Ellinghaus, J. Carey, and L. Boucher, 99–115. New York: Palgrave Macmillan, 2009.

Edney, Matthew. *Mapping an Empire: The Geographical Construction of British India, 1765–1843.* Chicago: University of Chicago Press, 1997.

Edwards, Penny. "Bitter Pills: Colonialism, Medicine and Nationalism in Burma, 1870–1940." *Journal of Burma Studies* 14, no. 1 (2010): 21–58.

Efford, Alison Clark. *German Immigrants, Race, and Citizenship in the Civil War.* Cambridge, U.K.: Cambridge University Press, 2013.

Eisner, Gisela. *Jamaica, 1830–1930: A Study in Economic Growth.* Manchester, U.K.: Manchester University Press, 1961.

Elias, Megan. "The Palate of Power: Americans, Food and the Philippines after the Spanish-American War." *Material Culture* 46, no. 1 (2014): 44–57.

Evans, Eldon Cobb. "A History of the Australian Ballot System in the United States." PhD diss., University of Chicago, 1917.

Everill, Bronwen. *Abolition and Empire in Sierra Leone and Liberia.* Houndmills, U.K.: Palgrave Macmillan, 2013.

Ewen, Shane. "Lost in Translation? Mapping, Molding, and Managing the Transnational Municipal Moment." In *Another Global City: Historical Explorations into the Transnational Municipal Moment, 1850–2000,* edited by Pierre-Yves Saunier and Shane Ewen, 173–84. New York: Palgrave Macmillan, 2008.

Ewing, Adam. *The Age of Garvey: How a Jamaican Activist Created a Mass Movement and Changed Global Black Politics.* Princeton, NJ: Princeton University Press, 2014.

Fernandez, Doreen G. "Culture Ingested: Notes on the Indigenization of Philippine Food." *Philippine Studies* 36, no. 2 (1988): 219–32.

Fernandez, Doreen. *Kinilaw: A Philippine Cuisine of Freshness.* Manila: Bookmark, 1991.

Fernandez, Doreen. *Palayok: Philippine Food through Time, on Site, in the Pot.* Manila: Bookmark, 2006.

Fernandez, Doreen. *Tikim: Essays on Philippine Food and Culture.* Manila: Anvil, 1994.

Findlay, Eileen. *Imposing Decency: The Politics of Sexuality and Race in Puerto Rico, 1870–1920.* Durham, NC: Duke University Press, 1999.

Fitzpatrick, Matthew. *Liberal Imperialism in Germany: Expansionism and Nationalism, 1848–1884.* New York: Berghahn, 2008.

Fletcher, R. A. "Cobden as Educator: The Free-Trade Internationalism of Eduard Bernstein, 1899–1914." *American Historical Review* 88, no. 3 (1983): 561–78.

Foner, Eric, ed. *Our Lincoln: New Perspectives on Lincoln and His World.* New York: Norton, 2008.

Ford, Lisa. *Settler Sovereignty: Jurisdiction and Indigenous People in America and Australia, 1788–1836.* Cambridge, MA: Harvard University Press, 2011.

Forth, Aidan, and Jonas Kreienbaum. "A Shared Malady: Concentration Camps in the British, Spanish, American and German Empires." *Journal of Modern European History* 14, no. 2 (2016): 245–67.

Foster, Anne L. "Models for Governing: Opium and Colonial Policies in Southeast Asia, 1898–1910." In *The American Colonial State in the Philippines: Global Perspectives,* edited by Julian Go and Anne L. Foster, 92–117. Durham, NC: Duke University Press, 2003.

Foster, Anne L. "Opium, the United States and the Civilizing Mission in Colonial Southeast Asia." *Social History of Alcohol and Drugs* 24, no. 1 (2010): 6–19.

Foster, Anne L. "Prohibition as Superiority: Policing Opium in South-East Asia, 1898–1925." *International History Review* 22, no. 2 (2000): 253–73.

Foster, Anne L. *Projections of Power: The United States and Europe in Colonial Southeast Asia, 1919–1941.* Durham, NC: Duke University Press, 2010.

Fredman, L. E. *The Australian Ballot: The Story of an American Reform.* East Lansing: Michigan State University Press, 1968.

Freidel, Frank. "Dissent in the Spanish-American War and the Philippine Insurrection." *Proceedings of the Massachusetts Historical Society* 81 (1960): 167–84.

Friend, Theodore. *The Blue-Eyed Enemy: Japan against the West in Java and Luzon, 1942–1945.* Princeton, NJ: Princeton University Press, 2014.

Fulton, Robert. *Moroland: The History of Uncle Sam and the Moros, 1899–1920.* Bend, OR: Tumalo Creek Press, 2009.

Gallagher, John, and Ronald Robinson. "The Imperialism of Free Trade." *Economic History Review* 6, no. 1 (1953): 1–15.

Gandy, Matthew. "The Bacteriological City and Its Discontents." *Historical Geography* 34 (2006): 14–25.

Gann, L. H., and Peter Duigan. *The Rulers of British Africa, 1870–1914.* Stanford, CA: Stanford University Press, 1978.

Gates, John M. "Philippine Guerillas, American Anti-Imperialists, and the Election of 1900." *Pacific Historical Review* 46, no. 1 (1977): 51–64.

Gedacht, Joshua. "Holy War, Progress, and 'Modern Mohammedans' in Colonial Southeast Asia." *Muslim World* 105, no. 4 (2015): 446–71.

Gelatt, T., R. Ream, and D. Johnson. "Northern Fur Seal: *Callorhinus ursinus*." IUCN Red List of Threatened Species 2015: e.T3590A45224953. https://www.iucnredlist.org /species/3590/45224953.

Gerwarth, Robert, and Erez Manela, eds. *Empires at War: 1911–1923.* Oxford: Oxford University Press, 2014.

Geyer, Alejandro Bolaños. *William Walker: The Gray-Eyed Man of Destiny.* 5 vols. Lake Saint Louis, MO: printed by the author, 1988–91.

Ghosh, Durba. "Another Set of Imperial Turns?" *American Historical Review* 117, no. 3 (2012): 772–93.

Ghosh, Durba, and Dane Kennedy, eds. *Decentring Empire: Britain, India, and the Transcolonial World.* Hyderabad, India: Orient Longman, 2006.

Gilmartin, David. "Towards a Global History of Voting: Sovereignty, the Diffusion of Ideas, and the Enchanted Individual." *Religions* 3, no. 2 (2012): 407–23.

Gilroy, Paul. *The Black Atlantic: Modernity and Double Consciousness.* Cambridge, MA: Harvard University Press, 1995.

Go, Julian. *American Empire and the Politics of Meaning: Elite Political Cultures in the Philippines and Puerto Rico during U.S. Colonialism.* Durham, NC: Duke University Press, 2008.

Go, Julian. "Anti-Imperialism in the U.S. Territories after 1898." In *Empire's Twin: U.S. Anti-Imperialism from the Founding Era to the Age of Terror,* edited by Ian Tyrrell and Jay Sexton, 79–96. Ithaca, NY: Cornell University Press, 2015.

Go, Julian. *Patterns of Empire: The British and American Empires, 1688 to the Present.* New York: Cambridge University Press, 2011.

Go, Julian. "The Provinciality of American Empire: 'Liberal Exceptionalism' and U.S. Colonial Rule." *Comparative Studies in Society and History* 49, no. 1 (2007): 74–108.

Go, Julian, and Anne L. Foster, eds. *The American Colonial State in the Philippines: Global Perspectives.* Durham, NC: Duke University Press, 2003.

Gobat, Michel. *Empire by Invitation: William Walker and Manifest Destiny in Central America.* Cambridge, MA: Harvard University Press, 2018.

Goldthree, Reena. "'A Greater Enterprise than the Panama Canal': Migrant Labor and Military Recruitment in the World War I–Era Circum-Caribbean." *Labor: Studies in Working-Class History of the Americas* 13, nos. 3–4 (2016): 57–82.

González de Reufels, Delia. *Siedler und Filibuster in Sonora: Eine mexikanische Region im Interesse ausländischer Abenteurer und Mächte (1821–1860).* Cologne, Germany: Böhlau Verlag, 2003.

Goodwin, Craufurd D. W. *Canadian Economic Thought: The Political Economy of a Developing Nation 1814–1914.* Durham, NC: Duke University Press, 1961.

Gosse, Van. "'As a Nation the English Are Our Friends': The Emergence of African American Politics in the British Atlantic World, 1772–1861." *American Historical Review* 113, no. 4 (2008): 1003–28.

Gowing, Peter G. *Mandate in Moroland: The American Government of Muslim Filipinos, 1899–1920.* Quezon City, Philippines: New Day, 1968.

Grandin, Greg. *The Empire of Necessity: Slavery, Freedom, and Deception in the New World.* New York: Metropolitan Books, 2014.

Graves, John William. "Negro Disfranchisement in Arkansas." *Arkansas Historical Quarterly* 26, no. 3 (1967): 199–225.

Greenberg, Amy. *Manifest Manhood and the Antebellum American Empire.* Cambridge, U.K.: Cambridge University Press, 2005.

Greene, Julie. *The Canal Builders: Making America's Empire at the Panama Canal.* New York: Penguin Press, 2009.

Greene, Julie. "The Wages of Empire: Capitalism, Expansion, and Working-Class Formation." In *Making the Empire Work: Labor and United States Imperialism,* edited by Daniel E. Bender and Jana K. Lipman, 35–58. New York: New York University Press, 2015.

Guettel, Jens-Uwe. *German Expansionism, Imperial Liberalism, and the United States, 1776–1945.* New York: Cambridge University Press, 2012.

Gunston, Henry. "The Planning and Construction of the Uganda Railway." *Transactions of the Newcomen Society* 74, no. 1 (2014): 45–71.

Guridy, Frank Andre. *Forging Diaspora: Afro-Cubans and African Americans in a World of Empire and Jim Crow.* Chapel Hill: University of North Carolina Press, 2010.

Haebich, Anna. *Broken Circles: Fragmenting Indigenous Families, 1800–2000.* Fremantle, Western Australia: Fremantle Arts Centre Press, 2000.

Haebich, Anna. *Spinning the Dream: Assimilation in Australia, 1950–1970.* Fremantle, Western Australia: Fremantle Press, 2008.

Hafner, Klaus, ed. *Grossherzog Leopold von Baden: 1790–1852.* Karlsruhe, Germany: Badischen Landesbibliothek, 1990.

Haines, Michael. "The Population of the United States, 1790–1920." In *The Cambridge Economic History of the United States.* Vol. 2: *The Long Nineteenth Century,* edited by

Stanley Engerman and Robert Gallman, 143–205. Cambridge, U.K.: Cambridge University Press, 2000.

Halberstam, Judith. *In a Queer Time and Place: Transgender Bodies, Subcultural Lives*. New York: New York University Press, 2005.

Hämäläinen, Pekka. *The Comanche Empire*. New Haven, CT: Yale University Press, 2008.

Harcourt, Freda. *Flagships of Imperialism: The P&O Company and the Politics of Empire from Its Origins to 1867*. Manchester, U.K.: Manchester University Press, 2006.

Harnetty, Peter. "The Imperialism of Free Trade: Lancashire, India, and the Cotton Supply Question, 1861–1865." *Journal of British Studies* 6, no. 1 (1996): 70–96.

Harrington, Fred H. "The Anti-Imperialist Movement in the United States, 1898–1900." *Mississippi Valley Historical Review* 22, no. 2 (1935): 211–30.

Harris, Susan K. *God's Arbiters: Americans and the Philippines, 1898–1902*. Oxford: Oxford University Press, 2011.

Harrison, Mark. *Contagion: How Commerce Has Spread Disease*. New Haven, CT: Yale University Press, 2012.

Hatfield, Shelley Bowen. *Chasing Shadows: Indians along the United States–Mexico Border 1876–1911*. Albuquerque: University of New Mexico Press, 1998.

Haupt, Heinz-Gerhard, and Jürgen Kocka, eds. *Comparative and Transnational History: Central European Approaches and New Perspectives*. New York: Berghahn Books, 2009.

Hawkins, Michael C. *Making Moros: Imperial Historicism and American Military Rule in the Philippines' Muslim South*. DeKalb: Northern Illinois University Press, 2013.

Headrick, Daniel R. *The Invisible Weapon: Telecommunications and International Politics, 1851–1945*. New York: Oxford University Press, 1991.

Headrick, Daniel R. *The Tentacles of Progress: Technology Transfer in the Age of Imperialism, 1850–1940*. New York: Oxford University Press, 1988.

Headrick, Daniel R. "The Tools of Imperialism: Technology and the Expansion of European Colonial Empires in the Nineteenth Century." *Journal of Modern History* 51, no. 2 (1979): 231–63.

Heartfield, James. *The Aborigines' Protection Society: Humanitarian Imperialism in Australia, New Zealand, Fiji, Canada, South Africa, and the Congo, 1836–1909*. New York: Columbia University Press, 2011.

Heckelman, Jac. "The Effect of the Secret Ballot on Voter Turnout Rates." *Public Choice* 82, nos. 1–2 (1995): 107–24.

Hepworth, H. Philip. *Foster Care and Adoption in Canada*. Ottawa: Canadian Council on Social Development, 1980.

Herman, Ellen. *Kinship by Design: A History of Adoption in the Modern United States*. Chicago: University of Chicago Press, 2008.

Herrera C., Miguel Angel. *Bongos, bogas, vapores y marinos: Historia de los "marineros" del río San Juan, 1849–1855*. Managua: Centro Nicaragüense de Escritores, 1999.

Herring, George. *From Colony to Superpower: U.S. Foreign Relations since 1776*. New York: Oxford University Press, 2008.

Hesselink, Liesbeth. *Healers on the Colonial Market: Native Doctors and Midwives in the Dutch East Indies*. Leiden, Netherlands: KITLV Press, 2011.

Hillemand, Bernard, and Alain Ségal. "Les six dernières conferences sanitaires internationales 1892 à 1926: Prémices de l'Organisation Mondiale de la Santé (O.M.S.)."
Histoire des sciences médicales 48, no. 1 (2014): 131–38.

Hobson, J. A. *Imperialism: A Study*. New York: James Pott, 1902.

Hochschild, Adam. *King Leopold's Ghost: A Story of Greed, Terror, and Heroism in Colonial
Africa*. Boston: Houghton Mifflin, 1998.

Hoerder, Dirk. "Migrations and Belongings." In *A World Connecting, 1870–1945*, edited by
Emily S. Rosenberg, 435–589. Cambridge, MA: Belknap Press of Harvard University
Press, 2012.

Hoganson, Kristin L. "'As Badly Off as the Filipinos': U.S. Women's Suffragists and the
Imperial Issue at the Turn of the Twentieth Century." *Journal of Women's History* 13,
no. 2 (2001): 9–33.

Hoganson, Kristin L. *Consumers' Imperium: The Global Production of American Domesticity,
1865–1920*. Chapel Hill: University of North Carolina Press, 2007.

Hoganson, Kristin L. *Fighting for American Manhood: How Gender Politics Provoked the
Spanish-American and Philippine-American Wars*. New Haven, CT: Yale University
Press, 1998.

Hoganson, Kristin L. "Meat in the Middle: Converging Borderlands in the U.S. Midwest,
1865–1900." *Journal of American History* 98, no. 4 (2012): 1025–51.

Hoganson, Kristin L. "Struggles for Place and Space: Kickapoo Traces from the Midwest
to Mexico." In *Transnational Indians in the North American West*, edited by Clarissa
Confer, Andrae Marak, and Laura Tuennerman, 210–25. College Station: Texas A&M
University Press, 2015.

Hogendorn, Jan S. "Economic Initiative and African Cash Farming." In *Colonialism in
Africa, 1870–1960*, edited by L. H. Gann and Peter Duigan, 4:283–328. Cambridge,
U.K.: Cambridge University Press, 1975.

Hogue, Michael. *Métis and the Medicine Line: Creating a Border and Dividing a People*.
Chapel Hill: University of North Carolina Press, 2015.

Hopkins, A. G. *American Empire: A Global History*. Princeton, NJ: Princeton University
Press, 2018.

Hopkins, A. G. "The United States, 1783–1861: Britain's Honorary Dominion?" *Britain
and the World* 4, no. 2 (2011): 232–46.

Hopkins, John H. *A History of Political Parties in the United States*. New York: G. P. Putnam's Sons, 1900.

Hotta, Eri. *Pan-Asianism and Japan's War 1931–1945*. New York: Palgrave Macmillan,
2007.

Howe, Anthony. "Free Trade and the International Order: The Anglo-American Tradition, 1846–1946." In *Anglo-American Attitudes: From Revolution to Partnership*, edited by
Fred M. Leventhal and Roland Quinault, 142–67. Aldershot, U.K.: Ashgate, 2000.

Howe, Anthony. *Free Trade and Liberal England, 1846–1946*. Oxford: Clarendon Press,
1997.

Howe, Anthony. "The 'Manchester School' and the Landlords: The Failure of Land Reform in Early Victorian Britain." In *The Land Question in Britain, 1750–1950*, edited by
M. Cragoe and P. Readman, 74–91. London: Palgrave Macmillan, 2010.

Howe, Anthony, and Simon Morgan, eds. *Rethinking Nineteenth-Century Liberalism: Richard Cobden Bicentenary Essays.* Aldershot, U.K.: Ashgate, 2006.

Howe, Stephen. *Anticolonialism in British Politics: The Left and the End of Empire, 1918–64.* Oxford: Oxford University Press, 1993.

Howe, Stephen. "New Empires, New Dilemmas—and Some Old Arguments." *Global Dialogue* 5, nos. 1–2 (2003): 1–13.

Hübner, Stefan. "Muscular Christianity and the Western Civilizing Mission: Elwood S. Brown, the YMCA, and the Idea of the Far Eastern Championship Games." *Diplomatic History* 39, no. 3 (2015): 532–57.

Hudson, Peter James. "On the History and Historiography of Banking in the Caribbean." *Small Axe* 18, no. 1 (March 2014): 22–37.

Hugill, Peter J. *Global Communications since 1844: Geopolitics and Technology.* Baltimore, MD: Johns Hopkins University Press, 1999.

Hunt, Lynn. *Writing History in the Global Era.* New York: Norton, 2014.

Hunt, Michael H. *Ideology and U.S. Foreign Policy.* New Haven, CT: Yale University Press, 1987.

Hurley, Vic. *Jungle Patrol: The Story of the Philippine Constabulary.* New York: E. P. Dutton, 1938.

Hurley, Vic. *The Swish of the Kris.* New York: E. P. Dutton, 1936.

Huzzey, Richard. *Freedom Burning: Anti-Slavery and Empire in Victorian Britain.* Ithaca, NY: Cornell University Press, 2012.

Hyde, Anne F. *Empires, Nations, and Families: A New History of the North American West, 1800–1860.* Lincoln: University of Nebraska Press, 2011.

Igler, David. *The Great Ocean: Pacific Worlds from Captain Cook to the Gold Rush.* Oxford: Oxford University Press, 2013.

Ikehata, Setsuho, and Ricardo Trota Jose, eds. *The Philippines under Japan: Occupation Policy and Reaction.* Quezon City, Philippines: Ateneo de Manila University Press, 1999.

Ileto, Reynaldo Clemena. "Philippine Wars and the Politics of Memory." *Positions: East Asia Cultures Critique* 13, no. 1 (2005): 215–34.

Ince, Onur Ulas. "Friedrich List and the Imperial Origins of the National Economy." *New Political Economy* 21, no. 4 (2016): 380–400.

Ingles, Raul Rafael. *1908: The Way It Really Was: Historical Journal for the UP Centennial, 1908–2008.* Diliman, Quezon City: University of the Philippines Press, 2008.

Iriarte, J. Augstín, and Fabian M. Jaksic. "The Fur Trade in Chile: An Overview of Seventy-Five Years of Export Data (1910–1984)." *Biological Conservation* 38, no. 3 (1986): 243–53.

Iriye, Akira. "Internationalizing International History." In *Rethinking American History in a Global Age*, edited by Thomas Bender, 47–62. Berkeley: University of California Press, 2002.

Jacobs, Margaret D. *A Generation Removed: The Fostering and Adoption of Indigenous Children in the Postwar World.* Lincoln: University of Nebraska Press, 2014.

Jacobs, Margaret D. *White Mother to a Dark Race: Settler Colonialism, Maternalism, and the Removal of Indigenous Children in the American West and Australia, 1880–1940.* Lincoln: University of Nebraska Press, 2009.

Jacobson, Matthew Frye. *Barbarian Virtues. The United States Encounters Foreign Peoples at Home and Abroad.* New York: Hill and Wang, 2000.

James, Winston. *The Struggles of John Brown Russwurm: The Life and Writings of a Pan-Africanist Pioneer, 1799–1851.* New York: New York University Press, 2010.

Jensen, Joan M. *Passage from India: Asian Indian Immigrants in North America.* New Haven, CT: Yale University Press, 1988.

John, Richard R. *Network Nation: Inventing American Telecommunications.* Cambridge, MA: Belknap Press of Harvard University Press, 2010.

Johnson, Sara E. *The Fear of French Negroes: Transcolonial Collaboration in the Revolutionary Americas.* Berkeley: University of California Press, 2012.

Johnson, Walter. *River of Dark Dreams: Slavery and Empire in the Cotton Kingdom.* Cambridge, MA: Harvard University Press, 2013.

Johnston, Hugh. *The Voyage of the Komagata Maru: The Sikh Challenge to Canada's Colour Bar.* Delhi: Oxford University Press, 1979.

Jones, A. G. E. "The British Southern Whale and Seal Fisheries." *Great Circle* 3, no. 1 (1981): 20–29.

Jones, Dorothy Miriam. *A Century of Servitude: Pribilof Aleuts under U.S. Rule.* Lanham, MD: University Press of America, 1980.

Jones, Peter D'A. "Henry George and British Socialism." *American Journal of Economics and Sociology* 47, no. 4 (1988): 473–91.

Jones, Richard M. "Sealing and Stonington: A Short-Lived Bonanza." *Log of Mystic Seaport* 28 (1977): 119–26.

Jones, Ryan Tucker. *Empire of Extinction: Russians and the North Pacific's Strange Beasts of the Sea, 1741–1867.* New York: Oxford University Press, 2014.

José, Ricardo T. "War and Violence, History and Memory: The Philippine Experience of the Second World War." *Asian Journal of Social Science* 29, no. 3 (2001): 457–70.

Joseph, Gilbert M. "Close Encounters: Toward a New Cultural History of U.S.–Latin American Relations." In *Close Encounters of Empire: Writing the Cultural History of U.S.–Latin American Relations,* edited by Gilbert M. Joseph, Catherine C. Legrand, and Ricardo D. Salvatore, 3–46. Durham, NC: Duke University Press, 1998.

Jung, Moon-Ho. *Coolies and Cane: Race, Labor, and Sugar in the Age of Emancipation.* Baltimore, MD: Johns Hopkins University Press, 2006.

Jung, Moon-Ho, ed. *The Rising Tide of Color: Race, State Violence, and Radical Movements Across the Pacific.* Seattle: University of Washington Press, 2014.

Kagan, Kimberly, ed. *The Imperial Moment.* Cambridge, MA: Harvard University Press, 2010.

Kamissek, Christoph, and Jonas Kreienbaum. "An Imperial Cloud? Conceptualising Interimperial Connections and Transimperial Knowledge." *Journal of Modern European History* 14, no. 2 (2016): 164–82.

Kaplan, Amy. *The Anarchy of Empire in the Making of U.S. Culture.* Cambridge, MA: Harvard University Press, 2002.

Kark, Ruth. *American Consuls in the Holy Land, 1832–1914.* Detroit, MI: Wayne State University Press, 1994.

Karl, Rebecca E. *Staging the World: Chinese Nationalism at the Turn of the Twentieth Century.* Durham, NC: Duke University Press, 2002.

Kass, Amalie M., and Edward H. Kass. *Perfecting the World: The Life and Times of Dr. Thomas Hodgkin, 1798–1866*. Boston: Harcourt Brace Jovanovich, 1988.

Kasson, Joy S. *Buffalo Bill's Wild West: Celebrity, Memory, and Popular History*. New York: Hill and Wang, 2000.

Kaur, Amarjit. "Indian Labour, Labour Standards, and Workers' Health in Burma and Malaya, 1900–1940." *Modern Asian Studies* 40, no. 2 (2006): 425–75.

Kelley, Lawrence C. *The Assault on Assimilation: John Collier and the Origins of Indian Policy Reform*. Albuquerque: University of New Mexico Press, 1983.

Kemble, John Haskell. *The Panama Route, 1848–1869*. Berkeley: University of California Press, 1943.

Kennedy, Charles Stuart. *The American Consul: A History of the United States Consular Service, 1776–1924*. 2nd ed. Washington, DC: New Academia, 2015.

Kent, Christopher A. "Smith, Goldwin (1823–1910)." In *Oxford Dictionary of National Biography*, edited by H. C. G. Matthew and Brian Harrison. Oxford: Oxford University Press, 2004. https://doi.org/10.1093/ref:odnb/36142.

Kerkvliet, Benedict J. *The Huk Rebellion: A Study of Peasant Revolt in the Philippines*. Lanham, MD: Rowman and Littlefield, 2002.

Kim, Ju Yon. *The Racial Mundane: Asian American Performance and the Embodied Everyday*. New York: New York University Press, 2015.

Kinloch Tijerino, Frances. *Nicaragua: Identidad y Cultura Política (1821–1858)*. Managua: Banco Central de Nicaragua, 1999.

Kinzer, Stephen. *The True Flag: Theodore Roosevelt, Mark Twain, and the Birth of American Empire*. New York: Henry Holt, 2017.

Kirkwood, Patrick M. "'Lord Cromer's Shadow': Political Anglo-Saxonism and the Egyptian Protectorate as a Model in the American Philippines." *Journal of World History* 27, no. 1 (2016): 1–26.

Klubock, Thomas Miller. *La Frontera: Forests and Ecological Conflict in Chile's Frontier Territory*. Durham, NC: Duke University Press, 2014.

Knapman, Gareth. *Race and British Colonialism in South-East Asia, 1770–1870*. New York: Routledge, 2016.

Knowles, Richard D. "Transport Shaping Space: Differential Collapse in Time-Space." *Journal of Transport Geography* 14, no. 2 (2006): 407–25.

Kousser, J. Morgan. *The Shaping of Southern Politics: Suffrage Restriction and the Establishment of the One-Party South, 1880–1910*. New Haven, CT: Yale University Press, 1974.

Kramer, Paul A. *The Blood of Government: Race, Empire, the United States, and the Philippines*. Chapel Hill: University of North Carolina Press, 2006.

Kramer, Paul A. "Embedding Capital: Political-Economic History, the United States, and the World." *Journal of the Gilded Age and Progressive Era* 15, no. 3 (2016): 331–62.

Kramer, Paul A. "Empires, Exceptions and Anglo-Saxons: Race and Rule between the British and United States Empires, 1880–1910." *Journal of American History* 88, no. 4 (2002): 1315–53.

Kramer, Paul A. "Imperial Openings: Civilization, Exemption, and the Geopolitics of Mobility in the History of Chinese Exclusion, 1868–1910." *Journal of the Gilded Age and Progressive Era* 14, no. 3 (2015): 317–47.

Kramer, Paul A. "Power and Connection: Imperial Histories of the United States in the World." *American Historical Review* 116, no. 5 (2011): 1348–91.

Kramer, Paul. "Reflex Actions: Colonialism, Corruption and the Politics of Technocracy in the Early Twentieth Century United States." In *Challenging US Foreign Policy: America and the World in the Long Twentieth Century*, edited by Bevan Sewall and Scott Lucas, 14–35. London: Palgrave Macmillan, 2011.

Kuiper, Koos. "Du Nouveau sur la mystérieuse mission de Batavia à Saigon en 1890." *Archipel* 77 (2009): 27–44.

Kumar, Krishan. "Empires and Nations: Convergence or Divergence?" In *Sociology and Empire: The Imperial Entanglements of a Discipline*, edited by George Steinmetz, 279–99. Durham, NC: Duke University Press, 2013.

LaDow, Beth. *The Medicine Line: Life and Death on a North American Borderland*. New York: Routledge, 2001.

LaFeber, Walter. *The Cambridge History of American Foreign Relations*. Vol. 2: *The American Search for Opportunity, 1865–1913*. Cambridge, U.K.: Cambridge University Press, 1993.

LaFeber, Walter. *The New Empire: An Interpretation of American Expansion, 1860–1898*. Ithaca, NY: Cornell University Press, 1963.

LaFollette, Robert, Jr. "The Adoption of the Australian Ballot in Indiana." *Indiana Magazine of History* 24, no. 2 (1928): 105–20.

Laidlaw, Zoë. "Breaking Britannia's Bounds? Law, Settlers, and Space in Britain's Imperial Historiography." *Historical Journal* 55, no. 3 (2012): 807–30.

Laidlaw, Zoë. "Heathens, Slaves and Aborigines: Thomas Hodgkin's Critique of Missions and Anti-slavery." *History Workshop Journal* 64, no. 1 (2007): 133–61.

Laidlaw, Zoë. "Indigenous Interlocutors: Networks of Imperial Protest and Humanitarianism in the Mid-Nineteenth Century." In *Indigenous Networks: Mobility, Connections and Exchange*, edited by Jane Carey and Jane Lydon, 114–39. New York: Routledge, 2014.

Laidlaw, Zoë. "'Justice to India—Prosperity to England—Freedom to the Slave!' Humanitarian and Moral Reform Campaigns on India, Aborigines and American Slavery." *Journal of the Royal Asiatic Society* 22, no. 2 (2012): 299–324.

Laidlaw, Zoë. "Slavery, Settlers and Indigenous Dispossession: Britain's Empire through the Lens of Liberia." *Journal of Colonialism and Colonial History* 13, no. 1 (2012). https://muse.jhu.edu/.

Lake, Marilyn, and Henry Reynolds. *Drawing the Global Colour Line: White Men's Countries and the International Challenge of Racial Equality*. New York: Cambridge University Press, 2008.

Lambert, David, and Alan Lester, eds. *Colonial Lives across the British Empire: Imperial Careering in the Long Nineteenth Century*. Cambridge, U.K.: Cambridge University Press, 2006.

Lamoreaux, Naomi R. *Great Merger Movement in American Business*. Cambridge, U.K.: Cambridge University Press, 1985.

Lanzona, Vina A. *Amazons of the Huk Rebellion: Gender, Sex, and Revolution in the Philippines*. Madison: University of Wisconsin Press, 2009.

Lasch, Christopher. "The Anti-Imperialists, the Philippines, and the Inequality of Man." *Journal of Southern History* 24, no. 3 (1958): 319–31.

Lasso, Marixa. *Erased: The Untold Story of the Panama Canal*. Cambridge, MA: Harvard University Press, 2018.

Lawrence, Elwood P. *Henry George in the British Isles*. East Lansing: Michigan State University Press, 1957.

Learned, Henry Barrett. "William Learned Marcy." In *The American Secretaries of State and Their Diplomacy*, edited by Samuel Flagg Bemis, 6:145–294. New York: Cooper Square, 1963.

Lefebvre, Henri. *Critique of Everyday Life*. Vol. 2. London: Verso, 1991.

Legarda, Benito Justo. *Occupation: The Later Years*. Quezon City, Philippines: De La Salle University–Manila, 2007.

Lester, Alan, and Fae Dussart. *Colonization and the Origins of Humanitarian Governance: Protecting Aborigines across the Nineteenth-Century British Empire*. Cambridge, U.K.: Cambridge University Press, 2014.

Levine, Robert S. "Fifth of July: Nathaniel Paul and the Construction of Black Nationalism." In *Genius in Bondage: Literature of the Early Black Atlantic*, edited by Vincent Carretta and Philip Gould, 242–60. Lexington: University Press of Kentucky, 2001.

Linder, Marc. *Projecting Capitalism: A History of the Internationalization of the Construction Industry*. Westport, CT: Greenwood Press, 1994.

Lord, Carnes. *Proconsuls: Delegated Political-Military Leadership from Rome to America Today*. Cambridge, U.K.: Cambridge University Press, 2012.

Love, Eric T. *Race over Empire: Racism and U.S. Imperialism, 1865–1900*. Chapel Hill: University of North Carolina Press, 2004.

Luis-Brown, David. *Waves of Decolonization: Discourses of Race and Hemispheric Citizenship in Cuba, Mexico, and the United States*. Durham, NC: Duke University Press, 2008.

Lumba, Allan E. S. "Imperial Standards: Colonial Currencies, Racial Capacities, and Economic Knowledge during the Philippine-American War." *Diplomatic History* 39, no. 4 (2015): 603–28.

Mabalon, Dawn Bohulano. "As American as Jackrabbit Adobo: Cooking, Eating, and Becoming Filipina/o American before World War II." In *Eating Asian America: A Food Studies Reader*, edited by Robert Ji-Song Ku, Martin F. Manalansan IV, and Anita Mannur, 147–76. New York: New York University Press, 2013.

MacDonagh, Oliver. "The Anti-Imperialism of Free Trade." *Economic History Review* 14, no. 3 (1962): 489–501.

Maceda, Teresita Gimenez. *Bride of War: My Mother's World War II Memories*. Mandaluyong City, Philippines: Anvil, 2011.

Magee, Gary B., and Andrew S. Thompson. *Empire and Globalisation: Networks of People, Goods and Capital in the British World, c. 1850–1914*. Cambridge, U.K.: Cambridge University Press, 2010.

Maier, Charles S. *Among Empires: American Ascendancy and Its Predecessors*. Cambridge, MA: Harvard University Press, 2006.

Makemson, Harlen Eugene. "Images of Scandal: Political Cartooning in the 1884 Presidential Campaign." PhD diss., University of North Carolina at Chapel Hill, 2002.

Mallon, Florencia. *Courage Tastes of Blood: The Mapuche Community of Nicolás Ailío and the Chilean State, 1906–2001*. Durham, NC: Duke University Press, 2005.

Manela, Erez. *The Wilsonian Moment: Self-Determination and the International Origins of Anticolonial Nationalism*. New York: Oxford University Press, 2007.

Markowitz, Gerald E., ed. *American Anti-Imperialism 1895–1901*. New York: Garland Library of War and Peace, 1976.

Martínez, Julia, and Claire Lowrie. "Transcolonial Influences of Everyday American Imperialism: The Politics of Chinese Domestic Servants in the Philippines." *Pacific Historical Review* 81, no. 4 (2012): 511–36.

Martinic, Mateo. "Actividad Lobera y Ballenera en Litorales y Aguas de Magallanes y Antartica, 1866–1916." *Revista de Estudios del Pacífico* 7 (1973): 7–26.

Martinic, Mateo. "Navegantes norteamericanos en aguas de Magallanes durante primer mitad del siglo XIX." *Anales del Instituto de la Patagonia*, Serie Ciencias Sociales 17 (1987): 11–17.

Mason, John Edwin. *Social Death and Resurrection: Slavery and Emancipation in South Africa*. Charlottesville: University of Virginia Press, 2003.

Matthiessen, Sven. *Japanese Pan-Asianism and the Philippines from the Late Nineteenth Century to the End of World War II: Going to the Philippines Is Like Coming Home?* Leiden, Netherlands: Brill, 2015.

May, Robert E. "Culture Wars: The U.S. Art Lobby and Congressional Tariff Legislation during the Gilded Age and Progressive Era." *Journal of the Gilded Age and Progressive Era* 9, no. 1 (2010): 37–91.

May, Robert E. *Manifest Destiny's Underworld: Filibustering in Antebellum America*. Chapel Hill: University of North Carolina Press, 2002.

May, Robert E. *Slavery, Race, and Conquest in the Tropics: Lincoln, Douglas, and the Future of Latin America*. Cambridge, U.K.: Cambridge University Press, 2013.

May, Robert E. *The Southern Dream of a Caribbean Empire, 1854–1861*. Baton Rouge: Louisiana State University Press, 1973.

Mayorga Z., Marcelo. "Antecedentes históricos referidos a la caza de Lobos Marinos y su interacción con el medio geográfico y humano en el extremo Austral Americano: El caso del lobero escocés William Low." *Magallania* 44, no. 2 (2016): 37–64.

McCormick, Thomas J. *China Market: America's Quest for Informal Empire, 1893–1901*. Chicago: Ivan R. Dee, 1967.

McCoy, Alfred W. *Policing America's Empire: The United States, the Philippines and the Rise of the Surveillance State*. Madison: University of Wisconsin Press, 2009.

McCoy, Alfred W., and Francisco Scarano, eds. *Colonial Crucible: Empire in the Making of the Modern American State*. Madison: University of Wisconsin Press, 2009.

McDaniel, W. Caleb. *The Problem of Democracy in the Age of Slavery: Garrisonian Abolitionists and Transatlantic Reform*. Baton Rouge: Louisiana State University Press, 2013.

McGuinness, Aims. *Path of Empire: Panama and the California Gold Rush*. Ithaca, NY: Cornell University Press, 2008.

McKee, Thomas Hudson, ed. *Protection Echoes from the Capitol*. Washington, DC: McKee, 1888.

McKenna, Mark. *Building 'a Closet of Prayer' in the New World: The Story of the Australian Ballot*. London: Menzies Centre for Australian Studies, 2002.

McKenna, Thomas M. *Muslim Rulers and Rebels: Everyday Politics and Armed Separatism in the Southern Philippines.* Berkeley: University of California Press, 1998.

McManus, Sheila. *The Line Which Separates: Race, Gender, and the Making of the Alberta-Montana Borderlands.* Lincoln: University of Nebraska Press, 2005.

Medak-Saltzman, Danika. "Transnational Indigenous Exchange: Rethinking Global Interactions of Indigenous Peoples at the 1904 St. Louis Exposition." *American Quarterly* 62, no. 3 (2010): 591–615.

Meeks, Eric W. *Border Citizens: The Making of Indians, Mexicans, and Anglos in Arizona.* Austin: University of Texas Press, 2007.

Merleaux, April. *Sugar and Civilization: American Empire and the Cultural Politics of Sweetness.* Chapel Hill: University of North Carolina Press, 2015.

Metcalf, Thomas R. *Imperial Connections: India in the Indian Ocean Arena, 1860–1920.* Berkeley: University of California Press, 2007.

Middleton, Alex. "French Algeria in British Imperial Thought, 1830–70." *Journal of Colonialism and Colonial History* 16, no. 1 (2015). doi:10.1353/cch.2015.0012.

Millar, Sue. "Middle Class Women and Public Politics in the Late Nineteenth and Early Twentieth Centuries: A Study of the Cobden Sisters." MA thesis, University of Sussex, 1985.

Miller, J. R. *Shingwauk's Vision: A History of Native Residential Schools.* Toronto: University of Toronto Press, 1996.

Milloy, John S. *A National Crime: The Canadian Government and the Residential School System, 1879 to 1986.* Winnipeg: University of Manitoba Press, 1999.

Mitchell, Nancy. *The Danger of Dreams: German and American Imperialism in Latin America.* Chapel Hill: University of North Carolina Press, 1999.

Mojares, Resil B. "The Formation of Filipino Nationality under US Colonial Rule." *Philippine Quarterly of Culture and Society* 34, no. 1 (2006): 11–32.

Monnais-Rousselot, Laurence. "La médicalisation de la mère et de son enfant: L'exemple du Vietnam sous domination française, 1860–1939." *Canadian Bulletin of Medical History* 19, no. 1 (2002): 113–37.

Monroe, Alexander G. "Commander Silas Duncan and the Falkland Islands Affair." *Log of Mystic Seaport* 25 (1973): 76–77.

Montemayor, Michael Schuck. *Captain Herman Leopold Schuck: The Saga of a German Sea Captain in 19th-Century Sulu-Sulawesi Seas.* Honolulu: University of Hawai'i Press, 2006.

Moore, Brian L., and Michele A. Johnson. *Neither Led nor Driven: Contesting British Cultural Imperialism in Jamaica, 1865–1920.* Mona, Jamaica: University of West Indies Press, 2004.

Mrazek, Rudolf. *Engineers of Happy Land: Technology and Nationalism in a Colony.* Princeton, NJ: Princeton University Press, 2009.

Mukherjee, Tapan K. *Taraknath Das: Life and Letters of a Revolutionary in Exile.* Calcutta: National Council of Education, Jadavpur University, 1998.

Murphy, Erin Leigh. "Anti-imperialism during the Philippine-American War: Protesting 'Criminal Aggression' and 'Benevolent Assimilation.'" PhD diss., University of Illinois at Urbana-Champaign, 2009.

Murphy, Erin Leigh. "Women's Anti-imperialism: 'The White Man's Burden,' and the Philippine-American War: Theorizing Masculinist Ambivalence in Protest." *Gender and Society* 23, no. 2 (2009): 244–70.

Murray, Robert. *The Making of Australia: A Concise History*. Kenthurst, Australia: Rosenberg, 2014.

Nagel, Daniel. *Von republikanischen Deutschen zu deutsch-amerikanischen Republikanern: Ein Beitrag zum Identitätswandel der deutschen Achtundvierziger in den Vereinigten Staaten 1850–1861*. St. Ingbert, Germany: Röhrig Universitätsverlag, 2012.

National Audubon Society. *Guide to Marine Mammals of the World*. New York: Knopf, 2002.

Neale, R. S. "H. S. Chapman and the 'Victorian' Ballot." *Historical Studies: Australia and New Zealand* 12, no. 48 (1967): 506–21.

Neill, Deborah. *Networks in Tropical Medicine: Internationalism, Colonialism, and the Rise of a Medical Specialty, 1890–1930*. Stanford, CA: Stanford University Press, 2012.

Neptune, Harvey R. *Caliban and the Yankees: Trinidad and the United States Occupation*. Chapel Hill: University of North Carolina Press, 2007.

Nevins, Allan. *Grover Cleveland: A Study in Courage*. New York: Dodd, Mead, 1933.

Newbury, Colin. "Historical Aspects of Manpower and Migration." In *Colonialism in Africa, 1870–1960*, edited by L. H. Gann and Peter Duigan, 4:523–45. Cambridge, U.K.: Cambridge University Press, 1975.

Newton, Bernard. "The Impact of Henry George on British Economists I: The First Phase of Response, 1879–82. Leslie, Wicksteed and Hobson." *American Journal of Economics and Sociology* 30, no. 2 (1971): 179–86.

Newton, Bernard. "The Impact of Henry George on British Economists II: The Second Phase of Response, 1883–84. Marshall, Toynbee and Rae." *American Journal of Economics and Sociology* 30, no. 3 (1971): 317–27.

Newton, Bernard. "The Impact of Henry George on British Economists III: The Third Phase of Response, 1885–1901. Rogers, Symes and McDonnell." *American Journal of Economics and Sociology* 31, no. 1 (1972): 87–102.

Nicholls, David. "Richard Cobden and the International Peace Congress Movement, 1848–1853." *Journal of British Studies* 30, no. 4 (1991): 351–76.

Nickles, David Paull. *Under the Wire: How the Telegraph Changed Diplomacy*. Cambridge, MA: Harvard University Press, 2003.

Non, Domingo M. "Moro Piracy during the Spanish Period and Its Impact." *Southeast Asian Studies* 30, no. 4 (1993): 401–19.

Nowak, Ronald W. *Walker's Marine Mammals of the World*. Baltimore: Johns Hopkins University Press, 2003.

O'Gorman, Frank. "The Secret Ballot in Nineteenth-Century Britain." In *The Hidden History of the Secret Ballot*, edited by Romain Bertrand, Jean Louis Briquet, and Peter Pels, 16–42. Bloomington: Indiana University Press, 2006.

Oliver, Roland. *Sir Harry Johnston and the Scramble for Africa*. London: Chatto and Windus, 1957.

O'Neill, Sally, and Thérèse Radic. "Lyster, William Saurin (1828–1880)." In *Australian Dictionary of Biography*, edited by Douglas Pike, vol. 5. Melbourne: Melbourne University Press, 1974. http://www.adb.online.anu.edu.au/biogs/A050136b.htm.

Onuf, Peter. *Jefferson's Empire: The Language of American Nationhood.* Charlottesville: University of Virginia Press, 2000.

Orquera, Luis Abel. "The Late-Nineteenth-Century Crisis in the Survival of the Magellan-Fuegian Littoral Natives." In *Archaeological and Anthropological Perspectives on the Native Peoples of Pampa, Patagonia, and Tierra del Fuego to the Nineteenth Century,* edited by Claudia Briones and José Luís Lanata, 145–58. Westport, CT: Greenwood Press, 2002.

Orquera, Luis Abel, and Ernesto Luis Piana. *La Vida Material y Social de Los Yámana.* Buenos Aires: Editorial de la Universidad de Buenos Aires, 1999.

Orquiza, René Alexander, Jr. "Lechon with Heinz, Lea & Perrins with Adobo: The American Relationship with Filipino Food, 1898–1946." In *Eating Asian America: A Food Studies Reader,* edited by Robert Ji-Song Ku, Martin F. Manalansan IV, and Anita Mannur, 177–85. New York: New York University Press, 2013.

Osborne, Thomas J. *Annexation Hawaii.* Waimanalo, HI: Island Style Press, 1998.

Palen, Marc-William. "Adam Smith as Advocate of Empire, c. 1870–1932." *Historical Journal* 57, no. 1 (2014): 179–98.

Palen, Marc-William. "British Free Trade and the International Feminist Vision for Peace, c. 1846–1946." In *Imagining Britain's Economic Future, c. 1800–1975: Trade, Consumerism and Global Markets,* edited by David Thackeray, Richard Toye, and Andrew Thompson, 115–31. London: Palgrave Macmillan, 2018.

Palen, Marc-William. "The Civil War's Forgotten Transatlantic Tariff Debate and the Confederacy's Free Trade Diplomacy." *Journal of the Civil War Era* 3, no. 1 (2013): 35–61.

Palen, Marc-William. *The "Conspiracy" of Free Trade: The Anglo-American Struggle over Empire and Economic Globalisation, 1846–1896.* Cambridge, U.K.: Cambridge University Press, 2016.

Palen, Marc-William. "Empire by Imitation? U.S. Economic Imperialism in a British World System." In *Oxford History of the Ends of Empire,* edited by Martin Thomas and Andrew Thompson, 195–211. Oxford: Oxford University Press, 2018.

Palen, Marc-William. "Foreign Relations in the Gilded Age: A British Free-Trade Conspiracy?" *Diplomatic History* 37, no. 2 (2013): 217–47.

Palen, Marc-William. "Free-Trade Ideology and Transatlantic Abolitionism: A Historiography." *Journal of the History of Economic Thought* 37, no. 2 (2015): 291–304.

Palen, Marc-William. "The Imperialism of Economic Nationalism, 1890–1913." *Diplomatic History* 39, no. 1 (2015): 157–85.

Parker, Matthew. *Panama Fever: The Epic Story of the Building of the Panama Canal.* New York: Anchor Books, 2007.

Parrini, Carl P., and Martin J. Sklar. "New Thinking about the Market, 1896–1904: Some American Economists on Investment and the Theory of Surplus Capital." *Journal of Economic History* 43, no. 3 (1983): 559–78.

Patterson, David. *Toward a Warless World: The Travail of the American Peace Movement, 1887–1914.* Bloomington: Indiana University Press, 1976.

Peckham, Robert. "Hygienic Nature: Afforestation and the Greening of Hong Kong." *Modern Asian Studies* 49, no. 4 (2015): 1177–209.

Peckham, Robert. "Infective Economies: Empire, Panic and the Business of Disease." *Journal of Imperial and Commonwealth History* 41, no. 2 (2013): 211–37.

Peckham, Robert, and David M. Pomfret, eds. *Imperial Contagions: Medicine, Hygiene, and Cultures of Planning in Asia*. Hong Kong: Hong Kong University Press, 2013.

Pérez, Louis A., Jr. *Cuba: Between Reform and Revolution*. New York: Oxford University Press, 1988.

Pérez, Louis A., Jr. *The War of 1898: The United States and Cuba in History and Historiography*. Chapel Hill: University of North Carolina Press, 1998.

Pérez, Louis A., Jr. "We Are the World: Internationalizing the National, Nationalizing the International." *Journal of American History* 89, no. 2 (2002): 558–66.

Perrin, William F., Bernd Würsig, and J. G. M. Thewissen, eds. *Encyclopedia of Marine Mammals*. New York: Academic Press, 2002.

Phelps, Nicole M. *U.S.-Habsburg Relations from 1815 to the Paris Peace Conference: Sovereignty Transformed*. New York: Cambridge University Press, 2013.

Phillips, Paul T. *The Controversialist: An Intellectual Life of Goldwin Smith*. London: Praeger, 2002.

Philp, Kenneth R. *John Collier's Crusade for Indian Reform, 1920–1954*. Tucson: University of Arizona Press, 1977.

Phoenix, Karen. "A Social Gospel for India." *Journal of the History of the Gilded Age and Progressive Era* 13, no. 2 (2014): 200–222.

Pickering, Paul A. "A Wider Field in a New Country: Chartism in Colonial Australia." In *Elections: Full, Free and Fair*, edited by Marian Sawer, 28–44. Sydney: Federation Press, 2001.

Pietsch, Tamson. *Empire of Scholars: Universities, Networks and the British Academic World, 1850–1939*. Manchester, U.K.: Manchester University Press, 2013.

Pitts, Jennifer. *A Turn to Empire: The Rise of Imperial Liberalism in Britain and France*. Princeton, NJ: Princeton University Press, 2005.

Platt, D. C. M. *The Cinderella Service: British Consuls since 1825*. London: Longman, 1971.

Plesur, Milton. *America's Outward Thrust: Approaches to Foreign Affairs, 1865–1890*. DeKalb: Northern Illinois University Press, 1971.

Pletcher, David M. *The Diplomacy of Trade and Investment: American Economic Expansion in the Hemisphere, 1865–1900*. Columbia: University of Missouri Press, 1998.

Pletcher, David M. "Rhetoric and Results: A Pragmatic View of American Economic Expansionism, 1865–98." *Diplomatic History* 5, no. 2 (1981): 93–106.

Pomfret, David M. *Youth and Empire: Trans-colonial Childhoods in British and French Asia*. Stanford, CA: Stanford University Press, 2016.

Porter, Bernard. *Critics of Empire: British Radicals and the Imperial Challenge*. London: I. B. Tauris, 2007.

Porter, Roy. *The Greatest Benefit to Mankind: A Medical History of Humanity*. New York: Norton, 1997.

Post, Louis F. *The Prophet of San Francisco: Personal Memories and Interpretations of Henry George*. New York: Vanguard Press, 1930.

Potter, Simon J., and Jonathan Saha. "Global History, Imperial History and Connected Histories of Empire." *Journal of Colonialism and Colonial History* 16, no. 1 (2015). doi:10.1353/cch.2015.0009.

Priest, Andrew. "Imperial Exchange: American Views of the British Empire during the Civil War and Reconstruction." *Journal of Colonialism and Colonial History* 16, no. 1 (2015). doi:10.1353/cch.2015.0015.

Priest, Andrew. "Thinking about Empire: The Administration of Ulysses S. Grant, Spanish Colonialism and the Ten Years' War with Cuba." *Journal of American Studies* 48, no. 2 (2014): 541–58.

Putnam, Lara. "The Making and Unmaking of the Circum-Caribbean Migratory Sphere: Mobility, Sex across Boundaries, and Collective Destinies, 1840–1940." In *Migrants and Migration in Modern North America: Cross-Border Lives, Labor Markets, and Politics*, edited by Dirk Hoerder and Nora Faires, 99–126. Durham, NC: Duke University Press, 2011.

Putnam, Lara. *Radical Moves: Caribbean Migrants and the Politics of Race in the Jazz Age.* Chapel Hill: University of North Carolina Press, 2013.

Quartly, Marian, Shurlee Swain, and Denise Cuthbert. *The Market in Babies: Stories of Australian Adoption.* Clayton, Victoria, Australia: Monash University Press, 2013.

Quintera Toro, Camilo. *Birds of Empire, Birds of Nation: A History of Science, Economy and Conservation in United States–Colombia Relations.* Bogotá: Universidad de los Andes, 2012.

Rafael, Vicente L. "Anticipating Nationhood: Collaboration and Rumor in the Japanese Occupation of Manila." *Diaspora: A Journal of Transnational Studies* 1, no. 1 (1991): 67–82.

Raffety, Matthew T. *The Republic Afloat: Law, Honor, and Citizenship in Maritime America.* Chicago: University of Chicago Press, 2013.

Redfern, Martin. "Wiring up the 'Victorian Internet.'" *BBC News*, November 29, 2005. http://news.bbc.co.uk/2/hi/science/nature/4475394.stm.

Reeves-Ellington, Barbara, Kathryn Kish Sklar, and Connie A. Shemo, eds. *Competing Kingdoms: Women, Mission, Nation, and the American Protestant Empire, 1812–1960.* Durham, NC: Duke University Press, 2010.

Reuter, William C. "The Anatomy of Political Anglophobia in the United States, 1865–1900." *Mid-America* 61 (April–July 1979): 117–32.

Reyes, Raquel A. G. "Modernizing the Manileña: Technologies of Conspicuous Consumption for the Well-to-Do Woman, circa 1880s–1930s." *Modern Asian Studies* 46, no. 1 (2012): 193–220.

Richardson, Bonham C. "Depression Riots and the Calling of the 1897 West India Royal Commission." *New West Indian Guide* 66, nos. 3–4 (1992): 169–91.

Richardson, Bonham C. "The Migration Experience." In *General History of the Caribbean.* Vol. 5: *The Caribbean in the Twentieth Century*, edited by Bridget Brereton, 434–64. New York: UNESCO and Macmillan, 2004.

Richardson, Bonham C. *Panama Money in Barbados, 1900–1920.* Knoxville: University of Tennessee Press, 2004.

Richardson, Sarah. "'You Know Your Father's Heart': The Cobden Sisterhood and the Legacy of Richard Cobden." In *Rethinking Nineteenth-Century Liberalism: Richard Cobden Bicentenary Essays*, edited by Anthony Howe and Simon Morgan, 229–46. Aldershot, U.K.: Ashgate, 2006.

Ring, Natalie J. *The Problem South: Region, Empire, and the New Liberal State, 1880–1930.* Athens: University of Georgia Press, 2012.

Rodgers, Daniel T. *Atlantic Crossings: Social Politics in a Progressive Age.* Cambridge, MA: Belknap Press of Harvard University Press, 1998.

Roediger, David, and Elizabeth D. Esch. *The Production of Difference: Race and the Management of Labor in U.S. History.* New York: Oxford University Press, 2012.

Rosenberg, Emily S. *Financial Missionaries to the World: The Politics and Culture of Dollar Diplomacy, 1900–1930.* Cambridge, MA: Harvard University Press, 1999.

Rosenberg, Emily S. "Transnational Currents in a Shrinking World." In *A World Connecting, 1870–1945,* edited by Emily S. Rosenberg, 815–996. Cambridge, MA: Harvard University Press, 2012.

Rothman, E. Natalie. *Brokering Empire: Trans-Imperial Subjects between Venice and Istanbul.* Ithaca, NY: Cornell University Press, 2012.

Rouleau, Brian. *With Sails Whitening Every Sea: Mariners and the Making of an American Maritime Empire.* Ithaca, NY: Cornell University Press, 2014.

Rozwadowski, Helen M. "The Promise of Ocean History for Environmental History." *Journal of American History* 100, no. 1 (2013): 136–39.

Rupp, Leila J. *Worlds of Women: The Making of an International Women's Movement.* Princeton, NJ: Princeton University Press, 1997.

Rush, James R. *Opium to Java: Revenue Farming and Chinese Enterprise in Colonial Indonesia, 1860–1910.* Ithaca, NY: Cornell University Press, 1990.

Rydell, Robert W. *All the World's a Fair: Visions of Empire at American International Expositions, 1876–1916.* Chicago: University of Chicago Press, 1984.

Santa Maria, Felice Prudente. *The Governor-General's Kitchen: Philippine Culinary Vignettes and Period Recipes: 1521–1935.* Pasig City, Philippines: Anvil, 2006.

Saunier, Pierre-Yves. *Transnational History.* New York: Palgrave Macmillan, 2013.

Schiedt, Hans-Ulrich. *Die Welt neu erfinden: Karl Bürkli (1823–1901) und seine Schriften.* Zurich: Chronos Verlag, 2002.

Schirmer, Daniel. *Republic or Empire: American Resistance to the Philippine War.* Cambridge, MA: Schenkman, 1972.

Schoonover, Thomas. "Misconstrued Mission: Expansionism and Black Colonization in Mexico and Central America during the Civil War." *Pacific Historical Review* 49, no. 4 (1980): 607–20.

Schottelius, Herbert. *Mittelamerika als Schauplatz deutscher Kolonisationsversuche, 1840–1865.* Hamburg, Germany: Christians Druckerei, 1939.

Schult, Volker. "Sulu and Germany in the Late Nineteenth Century." *Philippine Studies* 48, no. 1 (2000): 80–108.

Schumacher, Frank. "The American Way of Empire: National Tradition and Transatlantic Adaptation in America's Search for Imperial Identity, 1898–1910." *German Historical Institute Bulletin* 31 (2002): 35–50.

Schumacher, Frank. "The United States: Empire as a Way of Life?" In *The Age of Empires,* edited by Robert Aldrich, 278–303. London: Thames and Hudson, 2007.

Scott, Ernest. "The History of the Victorian Ballot." *Victorian Historical Magazine* 8, no. 1 (1920): 1–14.

Scott, James C. *Seeing Like a State: How Certain Schemes to Improve the Human Condition Have Failed*. New Haven, CT: Yale University Press, 1999.

Semmel, Bernard. *The Liberal Ideal and the Demons of Empire*. Baltimore: Johns Hopkins University Press, 1993.

Sexton, Jay. "Anglophobia in Nineteenth-Century Elections, Politics, and Diplomacy." In *America at the Ballot Box: Elections and Political History*, edited by Gareth Davies and Julian E. Zelizer, 98–117. Philadelphia: University of Pennsylvania Press, 2015.

Seymour, Richard. *American Insurgents: A Brief History of American Anti-Imperialism*. Chicago: Haymarket Books, 2012.

Shah, Nayan. *Stranger Intimacy: Contesting Race, Sexuality, and the Law in the North American West*. Berkeley: University of California Press, 2011.

Shreve, Bradley. *Red Power Rising: The National Indian Youth Council and the Origins of Native Activism*. Norman: University of Oklahoma Press, 2011.

Shulman, Peter A. *Coal and Empire: The Birth of Energy Security in Industrial America*. Baltimore: Johns Hopkins University Press, 2015.

Sim, David. *A Union Forever: The Irish Question and U.S. Foreign Relations in the Victorian Age*. Ithaca, NY: Cornell University Press, 2014.

Sinn, Elizabeth. *Pacific Crossing: California Gold, Chinese Migration, and the Making of Hong Kong*. Hong Kong: Hong Kong University Press, 2013.

Slap, Andrew L. *The Doom of Reconstruction: The Liberal Republicans in the Civil War Era*. New York: Fordham University Press, 2006.

Slate, Nico. *Colored Cosmopolitanism: The Shared Struggle for Freedom in the United States and India*. Cambridge, MA: Harvard University Press, 2012.

Smallwood, Stephanie E. *Saltwater Slavery: A Middle Passage from Africa to American Diaspora*. Cambridge, MA: Harvard University Press, 2007.

Smith, Paul Chaat, and Robert Allen Warrior. *Like a Hurricane: The Indian Movement from Alcatraz to Wounded Knee*. New York: New Press, 1996.

Smith, Stacey L. *Freedom's Frontier: California and the Struggle over Unfree Labor, Emancipation, and Reconstruction*. Chapel Hill: University of North Carolina Press, 2013.

Smith, Walter Burges. *America's Diplomats and Consuls of 1776–1865: A Geographic and Biographic Directory of the Foreign Service from the Declaration of Independence to the End of the Civil War*. Arlington, VA: Center for the Study of Foreign Affairs, 1986.

Sneider, Allison L. *Suffragists in an Imperial Age: U.S. Expansion and the Woman Question, 1870–1929*. New York: Oxford University Press, 2008.

Sohi, Seema. *Echoes of Mutiny: Race, Surveillance and Indian Anticolonialism in North America*. New York: Oxford University Press, 2014.

Spall, Richard Francis. "Free Trade, Foreign Relations, and the Anti-Corn-Law League." *International History Review* 10, no. 3 (1988): 405–32.

Speck, Mary. "Closed-Door Imperialism: The Politics of Cuban-U.S. Trade, 1902–1933." *Hispanic American Historical Review* 85, no. 3 (2005): 449–83.

Stackpole, Edouard A. *The Sea-Hunters: The New England Whalemen during Two Centuries, 1635–1835*. Philadelphia: J. B. Lippincott, 1953.

Stasiulis, Daiva, and Nira Yuval-Davis, eds. *Unsettling Settler Societies: Articulations of Gender, Race, Ethnicity and Class*. London: Sage, 1995.

Stehberg, Rubén. *Arqueología Histórica Antártica: Aborígenes Sudamericanos en Los Mares Subantárticos en el Siglo XIX*. Santiago, Chile: DIBAM, 2003.

Stephens, Michelle Ann. *Black Empire: The Masculine Global Imaginary of Caribbean Intellectuals in the United States, 1914–1962*. Durham, NC: Duke University Press, 2005.

Stigler, George J. "Alfred Marshall's Lectures on Progress and Poverty." *Journal of Law and Economics* 12, no. 1 (1969): 181–226.

Stoler, Ann Laura. "Considerations on Imperial Comparisons." In *Empire Speaks Out: Languages of Rationalization and Self-Description in the Russian Empire*, edited by Ilya Gerasimov, Jan Kusber, and Alexander Semyonov, 33–55. Boston: Brill, 2009.

Stoler, Ann Laura. "Imperial Debris: Reflections on Ruins and Ruination." *Cultural Anthropology* 23, no. 2 (2008): 191–219.

Stoler, Ann Laura. "Tense and Tender Ties: The Politics of Comparison in North American History and (Post) Colonial Studies." *Journal of American History* 88, no. 3 (2001): 829–65.

Stoler, Ann Laura, and Carole McGranahan. "Introduction: Refiguring Imperial Terrains." In *Imperial Formations*, edited by Ann Laura Stoler, Carole McGranahan, and Peter C. Perdue, 3–42. Santa Fe, NM: School For Advanced Research Press, 2007.

Sweeney, Stuart. *Financing India's Imperial Railways, 1875–1914*. London: Pickering and Chatto, 2011.

Tagliacozzo, Eric. *Secret Trades, Porous Borders: Smuggling and States along a Southeast Asian Frontier, 1865–1915*. New Haven, CT: Yale University Press, 2005.

Tan, Samuel K. *Sulu under American Military Rule, 1899–1913*. Quezon City: University of the Philippines Press, 1968.

Tarling, Nicholas. "Further Notes on the Historiography of British Borneo." *Borneo Research Bulletin* 36 (2005): 213–28.

Taylor, Antony. "Richard Cobden, J. E. Thorold Rogers and Henry George." In *The Land Question in Britain, 1750–1950*, edited by M. Cragoe and P. Readman, 146–66. London: Palgrave Macmillan, 2010.

Taylor, Nikki M. *Frontiers of Freedom: Cincinnati's Black Community, 1802–1868*. Athens: Ohio University Press, 2005.

Teisch, Jessica. *Engineering Nature: Water, Development and the Global Spread of American Environmental Expertise*. Chapel Hill: University of North Carolina Press, 2011.

Terami-Wada, Motoe. "The Japanese Propaganda Corps in the Philippines." *Philippine Studies* 38, no. 3 (1990): 279–300.

Terrill, Tom. *The Tariff, Politics, and American Foreign Policy, 1874–1901*. Westport, CT: Greenwood Press, 1973.

Thistlethwaite, Frank. *The Anglo-American Connection in the Early Nineteenth Century*. Philadelphia: University of Pennsylvania Press, 1959.

Thomas, John L. *Alternative America: Henry George, Edward Bellamy, Henry Demarest Lloyd and the Adversary Tradition*. Cambridge, MA: Harvard University Press, 1983.

Thomas, Martin, and Andrew Thompson. "Empire and Globalisation: from 'High Imperialism' to Decolonisation." *International History Review* 36, no. 1 (2014): 142–70.

Thomson, Janice. *Mercenaries, Pirates, and Sovereigns: State-Building and Extraterritorial Violence in Early Modern Europe*. Princeton, NJ: Princeton University Press, 1994.

Thomson, Rosemarie Garland, ed. *Freakery: Cultural Spectacles of the Extraordinary Body.* New York: New York University Press, 1996.

Tomich, Dale, and Michael Zeuske. "Introduction: The Second Slavery. Mass Slavery, World-Economy, and Comparative Microhistories." *Review (Fernand Braudel Center)* 31, no. 2 (2008): 91–100.

Tompkins, E. Berkeley. *Anti-imperialism in the United States: The Great Debate, 1890–1920.* Philadelphia: University of Pennsylvania Press, 1970.

Tompkins, E. Berkeley. "The Old Guard: A Study of the Anti-imperialist Leadership." *Historian* 30, no. 3 (1968): 366–88.

Tone, John Lawrence. *War and Genocide in Cuba, 1895–1898.* Chapel Hill: University of North Carolina Press, 2006.

Topik, Steven C., and Allen Wells. "Commodity Chains in a Global Economy." In *A World Connecting, 1870–1945,* edited by Emily S. Rosenberg, 593–812. Cambridge, MA: Belknap Press of Harvard University Press, 2012.

"Trans-Imperial Cooperation and Transfers in the Age of Colonial Globalization: Towards a Triangular History of Colonialism?" Gotha Research Centre and Erfurt University Conference, Gotha, Germany, March 23–24, 2018. https://www.forum-global -condition.de/veranstaltung/trans-imperial-cooperation-and-transfers-in-the-age-of -colonial-globalization/.

Trocki, Carl A. *Opium and Empire: Chinese Society in Colonial Singapore, 1800–1910.* Ithaca, NY: Cornell University Press, 1990.

Trocki, Carl A. *Opium, Empire and the Global Political Economy: A Study of the Asian Opium Trade, 1750–1950.* London: Routledge, 1999.

Truett, Samuel. *Fugitive Landscapes: The Forgotten History of the U.S.-Mexico Borderlands.* New Haven, CT: Yale University Press, 2006.

Tuffnell, Stephen. "Engineering Inter-Imperialism: American Miners and the Transformation of Global Mining." *Journal of Global History* 10, no. 1 (2015): 53–76.

Tuffnell, Stephen. "'Uncle Sam Is to Be Sacrificed': Anglophobia in Late Nineteenth-Century Politics and Culture." *American Nineteenth Century History* 12, no. 1 (2011): 77–99.

Tully, John. "A Victorian Ecological Disaster: Imperialism, the Telegraph, and Gutta-Percha." *Journal of World History* 20, no. 4 (2009): 559–79.

Tyrrell, Ian. *Crisis of the Wasteful Nation: Empire and Conservation in Theodore Roosevelt's America.* Chicago: University of Chicago Press, 2015.

Tyrrell, Ian. "Empire of Denial: American Empire, Past, Present and Future." *Ian Tyrrell* (blog), October 8, 2008. https://iantyrrell.wordpress.com/empire-of-denial-american -empire-past-present-and-future/.

Tyrrell, Ian. *Reforming the World: The Creation of America's Moral Empire.* Princeton, NJ: Princeton University Press, 2010.

Tyrrell, Ian. "The Regulation of Alcohol and Other Drugs in a Colonial Context: United States Policy towards the Philippines, c. 1898–1910." *Contemporary Drug Problems* 35, no. 4 (2008): 539–69.

Tyrrell, Ian. *Transnational Nation: United States History in Global Perspective since 1789.* New York: Palgrave Macmillan, 2007.

Tyrrell, Ian. *Woman's World, Woman's Empire: The Woman's Christian Temperance Union in International Perspective, 1880–1930*. Chapel Hill: University of North Carolina Press, 1991.

Tyrrell, Ian, and Jay Sexton. Introduction to *Empire's Twin: U.S. Anti-Imperialism from the Founding Era to the Age of Terrorism*, edited by Ian Tyrrell and Jay Sexton, 1–18. Ithaca, NY: Cornell University Press, 2015.

Ulbert, Jörg, and Lukian Prijac, eds. *Consuls et Services Consulaires Au XIXe Siecle = Die Welt Der Konsulate Im 19. Jahrhundert = Consulship in the 19th Century*. Hamburg, Germany: DOBU, 2010.

Unger, Steven. "The Indian Child Welfare Act of 1978: A Case Study." PhD diss., University of Southern California, 2004.

Unterman, Katherine. "Boodle over the Border: Embezzlement and the Crisis of International Mobility, 1880–1890." *Journal of the Gilded Age and Progressive Era* 11, no. 2 (2012): 151–89.

Veeser, Cyrus. *A World Safe for Capitalism: Dollar Diplomacy and America's Rise to Global Power*. New York: Columbia University Press, 2002.

Veracini, Lorenzo. *Settler Colonialism: A Theoretical Overview*. Houndmills, U.K.: Palgrave Macmillan, 2010.

Von Eschen, Penny M. *Race against Empire: Black Americans and Anticolonialism, 1937–1957*. Ithaca, NY: Cornell University Press, 1997.

Von Houwald, Götz. "¿Quién fue Maximiliano von Sonnenstern realmente?" In *Maximiliano von Sonnenstern y el primer mapa oficial de la República de Nicaragua*, edited by Orient Bolívar Juárez, 1–5. Managua: INETER, 1995.

Walther, Karine V. *Sacred Interests: The United States and the Islamic World, 1821–1921*. Chapel Hill: University of North Carolina Press, 2015.

Ware, Alan. "Anti-Partism and Party Control of Political Reform in the United States: The Case of the Australian Ballot." *British Journal of Political Science* 30, no. 1 (2000): 1–29.

Warren, James Francis. *Pirates, Prostitutes, and Pullers: Explorations in the Ethno- and Social History of Southeast Asia*. Crawley: University of Western Australia Press, 2008.

Warren, James Francis. *The Sulu Zone: The Dynamics of External Trade, Slavery, and Ethnicity in the Transformation of a Southeast-Asian Maritime State*. Singapore: National University of Singapore Press, 2007.

Warren, James Francis. "The Sulu Zone, the World Capitalist Economy and the Historical Imagination: Problematizing Global-Local Interconnections and Interdependencies." *Southeast Asian Studies* 35, no. 2 (1997): 177–222.

Weber, Torsten. *Embracing "Asia" in China and Japan: Asianism Discourse and the Contest for Hegemony, 1912–1933*. New York: Palgrave Macmillan, 2018.

Weeks, William Earl. *The New Cambridge History of American Foreign Relations*. Vol. 1: *Dimensions of the Early American Empire, 1754–1865*. New York: Cambridge University Press, 2013.

Weitz, Eric D. "From the Vienna to the Paris System: International Politics and the Entangled Histories of Human Rights, Forced Deportations, and Civilizing Missions." *American Historical Review* 113, no. 5 (2008): 1313–43.

Welch, Richard E., Jr. "American Atrocities in the Philippines: The Indictment and the Response." *Pacific Historical Review* 43, no. 2 (1974): 233–53.

Welch, Richard E., Jr. *Response to Imperialism: The United States and the Philippine-American War, 1899–1902.* Chapel Hill: University of North Carolina Press, 1979.

Whelan, Bernadette. *American Government in Ireland, 1790–1913: A History of the US Consular Service.* Manchester, U.K.: Manchester University Press, 2010.

Wigen, Karen. "AHR Forum: Oceans of History: Introduction." *American Historical Review* 111, no. 3 (2006): 717–21.

Wilkinson, Charles. *Blood Struggle: The Rise of Modern Indian Nations.* New York: Norton, 2005.

Williams, William Appleman. *Roots of the Modern American Empire: A Study of the Growth and Shaping of Social Consciousness in a Marketplace Society.* New York: Vintage Books, 1969.

Winseck, Dwayne R., and Robert M. Pike. *Communication and Empire: Media, Markets, and Globalization, 1860–1930.* Durham, NC: Duke University Press, 2007.

Wolfe, Patrick. "Land, Labor, and Difference: Elementary Structures of Race." *American Historical Review* 106, no. 3 (2001): 866–905.

Wolman, Paul. *Most Favored Nation: The Republican Revisionists and U.S. Tariff Policy, 1897–1912.* Chapel Hill: University of North Carolina Press, 1992.

Wong, David C. "A Theory of Petty Trading: The Jamaican Higgler." *Economic Journal* 106, no. 435 (1996): 507–18.

Wood, John D. "Transatlantic Land Reform: America and the Crofters' Revolt 1878–1888." *Scottish Historical Review* 63, no. 175 (1984): 79–104.

Woolford, Andrew. *This Benevolent Experiment: Indigenous Boarding Schools, Genocide, and Redress in Canada and the United States.* Lincoln: University of Nebraska Press, 2015.

Wray, William. *Mitsubishi and the N.Y.K., 1870–1914: Business Strategy in the Japanese Shipping Industry.* Cambridge, MA: Harvard University Press, 1984.

Wright, Ashley. *Opium and Empire in Southeast Asia: Regulating Consumption in British Burma.* Basingstoke, U.K.: Palgrave Macmillan, 2014.

"Yakama Nation History." *Yakama Nation.* http://www.yakamanation-nsn.gov/history3.php.

Yamaguchi, Kiyoko. "The New 'American' Houses in the Colonial Philippines and the Rise of the Urban Filipino Elite." *Philippine Studies* 54, no. 3 (2006): 412–51.

Yeoh, Brenda S. A. "Urban Sanitation, Health and Water Supply in Late Nineteenth and Early Twentieth-Century Colonial Singapore." *South East Asia Research* 1, no. 2 (1993): 143–72.

Zimmerman, Andrew. *Alabama in Africa: Booker T. Washington, the German Empire, and the Globalization of the New South.* Princeton, NJ: Princeton University Press, 2010.

Zimmerman, James A. "Who Were the Anti-Imperialists and the Expansionists of 1898 and 1899? A Chicago Perspective." *Pacific Historical Review* 46, no. 4 (1977): 589–601.

Zurita, Rafael. "Ecos de Europa: La Representación Parlamentaria en el Chile Liberal del Siglo XIX." *Journal of Iberian and Latin American Research* 20, no. 1 (2014): 98–110.

Zwick, Jim. "The Anti-Imperialist League and the Origins of the Filipino-American Oppositional Solidarity." *Amerasia Journal* 24, no. 2 (1998): 64–85.

Contributors

IKUKO ASAKA is an associate professor of history at the University of Illinois. She researches imperial aspects of women, gender, and sexuality in the nineteenth century. She is the author of *Tropical Freedom: Climate, Settler Colonialism, and Black Exclusion in the Age of Emancipation* (2017).

OLIVER CHARBONNEAU is lecturer in American history at the University of Glasgow. His book, *Civilizational Imperatives: Americans, Moros, and the Colonial World* (2020), explores four decades of U.S. imperial rule in the Islamic Philippines. Essays from this project have appeared in *Diplomatic History* and the *Journal of the Gilded Age and Progressive Era*.

GENEVIEVE CLUTARIO is the Andrew W. Mellon assistant professor of American Studies at Wellesley College. She is currently finishing her first book, on beauty regimes and the gendered labor of appearance in the Philippines (Duke University Press, forthcoming), and is the author of "Pageant Politics: Tensions of Power, Empire, and Nationalism in Manila Carnival Queen Contests," published in *Gendering the Transpacific World: Diaspora, Empire and Race* (2017).

ANNE L. FOSTER is an associate professor of history at Indiana State University and coeditor of *Diplomatic History*. She is the author of *Projections of Power: The United States and Europe in Colonial Southeast Asia, 1919–1941* (Duke University Press, 2010). She also coedited and contributed to *The American Colonial State in the Philippines: Global Perspectives* (Duke University Press, 2003).

JULIAN GO is a professor of sociology at Boston University. His books include *American Empire and the Politics of Meaning: Elite Political Cultures in the Philippines and Puerto Rico during U.S. Colonialism* (Duke University Press, 2008), *Patterns of Empire: The British and American Empires, 1688 to the Present* (2011) and *Postcolonial Thought and Social Theory* (2016).

MICHEL GOBAT is a professor of history at the University of Pittsburgh. He is the author of *Confronting the American Dream: Nicaragua under U.S. Imperial Rule* (Duke University

Press, 2005) and *Empire by Invitation: William Walker and Manifest Destiny in Central America* (2018).

JULIE GREENE is a professor of history and the director of the Center for Global Migration Studies at the University of Maryland at College Park. She is the author of *The Canal Builders: Making America's Empire at the Panama Canal* (2009) and coeditor, with Leon Fink, of a special issue of the journal *Labor: Studies in Working-Class History* devoted to labor and empire (December 2016).

KRISTIN L. HOGANSON is the Stanley S. Stroup Professor of U.S. History at the University of Illinois, Urbana-Champaign. Her publications include *Fighting for American Manhood: How Gender Politics Provoked the Spanish-American and Philippine-American Wars* (1998), *Consumers' Imperium: The Global Production of American Domesticity, 1865–1920* (2007), *American Empire at the Turn of the Twentieth Century: A Brief History with Documents* (2016), and *The Heartland: An American History* (2019).

MARGARET D. JACOBS is the Chancellor's Professor of History at the University of Nebraska–Lincoln (UNL), where she has been based since 2004. She received an Andrew Carnegie Fellowship for 2018–20 for her project "Does the United States Need a Truth and Reconciliation Commission?" She is also the codirector of the Genoa Indian School Digital Reconciliation Project at UNL. From 2015 to 2016 she served as the Pitt Professor of American History and Institutions at Cambridge University. She has published thirty-five articles and three books, including *White Mother to a Dark Race: Settler Colonialism, Maternalism, and the Removal of Indigenous Children in the American West and Australia, 1880–1940* (2009), which won the 2010 Bancroft Prize from Columbia University.

MOON-HO JUNG is the Dio Richardson Professor of History at the University of Washington. He is the author of *Coolies and Cane: Race, Labor, and Sugar in the Age of Emancipation* (2006) and the editor of *The Rising Tide of Color: Race, State Violence, and Radical Movements across the Pacific* (2014).

MARC-WILLIAM PALEN is senior lecturer in history at the University of Exeter. He is the author of *The "Conspiracy" of Free Trade: The Anglo-American Struggle over Empire and Economic Globalisation, 1846–1896* (2016).

NICOLE M. PHELPS is an associate professor of history at the University of Vermont. She is the author of *U.S.-Habsburg Relations from 1815 to the Paris Peace Conference: Sovereignty Transformed* (2013). The dissertation on which the book is based received the Austrian Cultural Forum Dissertation Prize and an honorable mention for the Betty Unterberger Dissertation Prize from the Society for Historians of American Foreign Relations.

JAY SEXTON is the Kinder Institute Chair of Constitutional Democracy at the University of Missouri. He writes about nineteenth-century international history. His publications include *Debtor Diplomacy: Finance and American Foreign Relations in the Civil War Era,*

1837–1873 (2005), *The Monroe Doctrine: Nation and Empire in Nineteenth-Century America* (2011), and, most recently, *A Nation Forged by Crisis: A New American History* (2018).

JOHN SOLURI is an associate professor and the director of Global Studies in the History Department at Carnegie Mellon University. He recently edited, with Claudia Leal and José Augusto Pádua, *A Living Past: Environmental Histories of Modern Latin America* (2018). His book *Banana Cultures: Agriculture, Consumption, and Environmental Change in Honduras and the United States* (2006) won the George Perkins Marsh Award for best book in environmental history.

STEPHEN TUFFNELL is an associate professor of modern U.S. history at the University of Oxford. He is the coeditor of *A Global History of Gold Rushes* (2018) with Benjamin Mountford. He is currently completing a manuscript titled "Emigrant Foreign Relations: Independence and Interdependence in the Nineteenth-Century Atlantic."

Index

Note: Page numbers in *italics* indicate figures and tables.

Preston, John W., 276–77
Preuss, Oscar, 189
Pribilof Islands, 30–33
Pribylov, Gavriil, 30
Prichard, James Cowles, 215
Progress and Poverty (George), 171–72
Project Ku-nak-we-shaw, 285, 288, 292. *See also* Robbins, Maxine
protectionism, 161–72, 174–75
Protection or Free Trade (George), 165, 174
Public (Georgist publication), 172, 174
Puerto Rico, 103, 169
Punta Arenas. *See* Chile

Quinan, William Russell, 47
quinine, 116, 129n20, 231

racism: adoption and, 290–91; Australian Constitution and, 283; in the Carribbean, 229–30; climatic essentialism and, 205–18; European radicals and, 86; filibusters and, 83; Indian labor and, 56–58; Panama Canal and, 235–36; registration laws and, 208; secret ballot system and, 101–2; whites-only settler societies and, 210. *See also* African Americans; slavery
railways: in Burma, 47; Ugandan, 50–58, 52, 54, 56–57, 60; U.S. engineering firms and, 46
Raousset-Boulbon, Gaston de, 73
Reily, Charles H., 269–70
Rendel, Alexander M., 51
Researches into the Physical History of Mankind (Prichard), 215
Rethinking American History in a Global Age (Bender), 2
Rhodes, Cecil, 47
Ricardo, David, 162
Richards, John Altyman, 229
Richardson, Bonham, 227
Rizal, José, 9, 183
Robbins, Maxine, 281–88, 292–96
Rodgers Act (1924), 153, 155
Room for One More (Dyer), 295
Roosevelt, Theodore, 122, 168, 234
Root, Elihu, 122
Rosenberg, Emily, 189
Russia: Alaska, sale of, 30–31, 40; fur sealing and, 30–31; manifest destiny and, 78

Russian American Company (RAC), 30
Russwurm, John, 209–10

Sadler, Sir James Hayes, 55
Saluda incident, 217
Samoa, 167–68
Sampaio, Francisco, 36
Saunier, Pierre-Yves, 185
Schuck family, 192–93
Schurman, Jacob Gould, 195
Schurz, Carl, 167
Schwartz, Adolph, 84–85
Scott, Hugh, 195
secret ballot system: in Australia, 97–99; class and, 97; innovation of, 95–97; modern democracy and, 107–8; Philippines and, 93–94, 102–7; spread of, 94, 96; support for, 96–97; United States and, 99–102; voter disenfranchisement and, 100–102; voter turnout and, 100, 102. *See also* democracy
settler colonialism: American Colonization Society and, 205–6, 209–13, 216–17; American contractors and, 46; British humanitarian attitudes toward, 207, 213; climatic essentialism and, 205–18; empires and, 4–5, 282–83; indigenous child removal and, 282–83, 294; in Liberia, 206–7; logic of elimination and, 282; William Walker and, 70, 72–74, 80–81, 83–85; whites-only settler societies and, 210–11. *See also* colonialism
Sexton, Jay, 159
Shanghai Opium Commission (1909), 125–26
Shin Seiki (magazine), 249
Shuster, W. Morgan, 189
Sierra Leone, 207, 210–11
Singh, Bhagwan, 273–77. *See also* Dayal, Har
Singh, Rajah, 267
single tax ideology, 171–75
Slacum, George, 26
slavery: American Cobdenites and, 162–63; annexation of Nicaragua and, 79; black convention movement and, 205; British Empire and, 82; British Foreign Anti-Slavery society, 50; in Central America, 73; Civil War and, 163; Liberian colonization and, 213; Portugal and, 144, 156n15; William Walker and, 70, 72, 75, 81–82. *See also* African Americans; racism; Wilberforce colony

United States (cont.)
    by non-Indian families, 285–86; purchase
    of Alaska, 30–31, 40; removal of indigenous
    children and, 281, 284, 286; Republican
    Party, 161–68, 170, 172; Samoa and, 167–68;
    secret ballot system and, 99–102; shift in
    federal Indian policy, 284; Spanish-American
    War and, 168; surveillance/intelligence
    program of, 262–63, 265–66, 268, 274–76;
    telegraph technology and, 3–4; U.S. Foreign
    Service, 135; World War II, role in, 244–46.
    See also Dayal, Har; Panama Canal; Singh,
    Bhagwan; U.S. imperialism
Upper Canada. *See* Canada
U.S. Civil War, 4, 151, 163
U.S. Consular Service (USCS): 1789 to 1856,
    140–43; 1856 to 1906, 143–45; 1872 to
    1906, 145–52; 1906 to 1924, 152–55; British
    Empire and, 138–39, 144–45; British subjects
    serving in, 157n18; Canada, location of U.S.
    Consular posts in, 146–47; Civil War and,
    143–44; civil war veteran pensions and, 151;
    consuls general at large (CGALS), 153–54;
    corruption and, 143; day-to-day activities
    of, 145, 148; extraterritorial system and, 137,
    142–43; gender and, 156n5; immigration
    and, 150, 154; informal empire and, 137–38,
    145; language deficiencies and, 142–43;
    length of service in, 156n14; Portuguese
    Empire and, 144; reform of, 139, 152–55;
    reporting by, 151; Rodgers Act (1924), 153,
    155; role of, 135, 137, 139; salaries within,
    141–43, 156n11; size of, *138*; trade promotion
    activities of, 151–52; U.S.-Canadian trade
    relationship, 149, 152; World War I and, 154.
    See also consular system
U.S. Department of Agriculture, 151
U.S. Foreign Service, 153, 155
U.S. imperialism: British empire and, 49; col-
    laboration in the Philippines and, 185–91,
    195–96; free trade and, 160–61, 169–70;
    immigration and, 265; obscuring of, 5,
    183; Panama Canal and, 167; preexisting
    networks in the Philippines and, 191–95;
    rule of the Philippines and, 183–85, 195–97,
    241–54; scholarship on, 6–7, 13–14; William
    Walker and, 86–87. *See also* United States
USS *Lexington*, 26

U.S. Steel Corporation, 58–59
U.S. Supreme Court: *Downes v. Bidwell* case,
    169; immigration law and, 266–67; im-
    pounding of fur sealing ships and, 27

vaccines, 114
Valle, José María, 75, 77, 83
Vanderbilt, Cornelius, 73, 79–80
Vernet, Louis, 26–27
viaducts. *See* engineering
Victoria Sealing Company, 38
violence: filibusterism and, 70; fur sealing and,
    36; Panama Canal and, 235–36; Philippines
    and, 189, 195; settler colonial, 213–14;
    William Walker and, 77
voting. *See* secret ballot system

Walker, William: annexation of Nicaragua and,
    79; democracy and, 83–84; *El Nicaraguense*
    and, 75, 77–79, 82; European colonization
    projects and, 74; European Forty-Eighters
    and, 83–86; evangelicalism and, 81; filibus-
    ter army and, 80; inspiration and, 71, 73,
    82; liberal imperialism and, 69–70, 72–74;
    public health and, 80–81; regime of, 75–77;
    settler colonialism and, 80; slavery and, 70,
    75, 81–82; support for, 73, 75, 87; U.S. gov-
    ernment support and, 82. *See also* Nicaragua
Wallace, Arthur, 99–100
Wallace, John, 228
Walrond, Eric, 232, 236
Wealth of Nations, The (Smith), 162
Wells, David Ames, 164–65
Wernher, Beit & Co., 47
White, Edward Douglass, 266
Whitehouse, Sir George, 53, 57
Wilberforce, William, 208
Wilberforce colony, 205–17
Wilkeson, Samuel, 217
Williams, William Appleman, 160
Wilson, William B., 266
Wilson, Woodrow, 105, 170, 266
Winslow, Erving, 169
Wolfe, Patrick, 282
Woman's Peace Party, 169–70
women: Caribbean labor migration and, 227;
    colonial intimacies and, 193; Filipino women
    and World War II, 241–54; imperial patrio-

tism and, 237; indigenous activism and, 281–96; opium use and, 115, 124

Wood, Leonard, 188, 191, 195–96

Wood, R. E., 227

World Anti-Slavery Convention, 216–18

World War I, 154, 264, 276

World War II, 244–54

Wright, Hamilton, 126

Yakama Nation. *See* indigenous peoples